FEMINIST TRANSFORMATIONS AND DOMESTIC VIOLENCE IN DIVIDED BERLIN

A British Academy Monograph

The British Academy has a scheme for the selective publication of monographs arising from its British Academy Postdoctoral Fellowships, British Academy Newton International Fellowships and British Academy / Wolfson Fellowships. Its purpose is to assist individual scholars by providing a prestigious publishing opportunity to showcase works of excellence.

Jane Freeland is a Lecturer in History and Fellow at the Institute for the Humanities and Social Sciences at Queen Mary University of London. Her research examines the history of feminism in Germany and Europe in the twentieth century, with a particular focus on feminist activism against domestic violence and feminism and the media.

FEMINIST TRANSFORMATIONS AND DOMESTIC VIOLENCE IN DIVIDED BERLIN

1968–2002

Jane Freeland

Published for THE BRITISH ACADEMY
by OXFORD UNIVERSITY PRESS

Oxford University Press, Great Clarendon Street, Oxford OX2 6DP

First edition published 2022
Reprinted 2023

British Library Cataloguing in Publication Data
Data available

Library of Congress Cataloging in Publication Data
Data available

Typeset by Newgen Publishing UK
Printed in Great Britain by
TJ Books Ltd, Padstow, Cornwall

ISBN 978-0-19-726711-0

Contents

List of Figures and Table   *vi*
Acknowledgements   *vii*

Introduction   1

1   The Origins of the Women's Shelter Movement   27

2   The Cost of Political Support   56

3   Race, Class and Everyday Life in the Shelter   88

4   Domestic Violence and Women's Lives Under Socialism   110

5   Feminism and Domestic Violence Activism in the GDR   137

6   The Possibilities of Feminism After Reunification   162

    Conclusion   192

    Bibliography   *202*
    Index   *233*

List of Figures and Table

Figures

1.1   The *Statement of Accounts* of the Frankfurt *Weiberrat*, 1968.   37

2.1   *KICKED, BEATEN, HUMILIATED. WOMEN are abused by men! Where can they find help? We need a WOMEN'S SHELTER!*, 1976.   69

6.1   Founding UFV members sitting on stage at the Berlin *Volksbühne* on 3 December 1989. From left to right: Petra Wunderlich (foreground), Christina Schenk, Brigitta Kasse, Katrin Bastian, Gabi Zekina and Christiane Schindler.   164

6.2   Actress Walfriede Schmitt takes the Berlin *Volksbühne* stage at the formation of the UFV, 3 December 1989.   165

Table

4.1   Percentage of divorce cases alleging domestic violence heard at the Berlin Municipal Court, between 1970 and 1988.   113

Acknowledgements

Completing this book has been a long journey. From its conception out of a brief research trip to the University of Massachusetts Amherst in 2009, through comprehensive exams at Carleton University, many research trips to Berlin, a cross-Atlantic move, various universities and academic institutions and a global pandemic, the road has been long. But it has not been lonely. Along the way, I have gained immensely from the time, expertise and work of a good many friends, colleagues, archivists, librarians and family members.

In particular, I have benefited from the supervision and mentorship of three of the most generous scholars: Jennifer Evans, Josie McLellan and Paul Betts. Jen has been a source of support since day one. She helped (and continues to help) me navigate both the Ph.D. and my career. She leads by example and has been a true role model for feminist scholarship and academic practice. Working with her has meant so much for me personally and professionally. After moving to the UK, I was lucky to work with Josie and then Paul. Josie's guidance fundamentally changed how I write as an historian and Paul's mentorship helped take me from a handful of chapters to a full manuscript. I would not be the scholar I am without them.

Over the course of writing this book, I have also gained from the knowledge and expertise of my colleagues and friends at Carleton University, University of Bristol, University of Sheffield, Queen Mary University of London and the German Historical Institute London. Particular thanks go to: Angela Davies, James Ellison, Erica Fagen, Johanna Gehmacher, Christina von Hodenberg, Meghan Lundrigan, Jessica Plummer, Alexandria Ruble, Charlotta Salmi, Falko Schnicke, Joe van der Voort, Christine Whitehouse and the participants of the International Standing Working Group in Medialization and Empowerment. Thank you all for your feedback, encouragement and for generally making academia a nicer place to work. I would particularly like to thank Jennifer Rodgers and Charmian Mansell for their detailed comments and support of my writing.

This book has also gained from the work of countless archivists, librarians and administrators. The team at the British Academy monograph series, in particular Portia Taylor, Mary McCormick and Jeanne Brady, have been vital to getting this project off the ground and I thank them for all of their support and patience.

I would also like to thank the archivists at the Berlin Landesarchiv, the FFBIZ and the Robert Havemann Archiv where I spent most of my time researching. Thanks must also go to the interviewees who allowed me to record the stories of their important work tackling violence against women.

I would also like to acknowledge the organisations that have provided financial support for my research, enabling me to spend considerable time in German and American archives. I would like to thank the Government of Ontario, the Council for European Studies, the German Historical Institute in Washington, DC, the German Academic Exchange Service, the Centre for Contemporary History in Potsdam, the Central European History Society and the Canadian Research Institute for the Advancement of Women. In the UK, I benefited from the support of a Newton International Fellowship and from funding from the German Federal Ministry of Education and Research under the grant number U1UG1903.

Much of this book was conceived of and written on the traditional unceded territory of the Algonquin Anishnaabeg Nation. I myself was born on the lands of the Turrbal and Jagera peoples and grew up on the lands of the Kaurna people. I thank these First Nations peoples and pay my respect to the Elders past and present for their stewardship and care of the lands that I have been so privileged to live on.

The final word of thanks goes to my family. Thank you for making me laugh, letting me vent, putting up with my absence as I've travelled between Australia, Canada, Germany and the UK and for always being there when I needed. An extra thank you goes to Lesley and Richard, who have kept me on task and to Frank and Nancy, who have always been so supportive of my work and who I consider my #1 fans. Lastly, to Brendan. Thank you. With all my heart, thank you.

While every effort has been made to contact the copyright holders of the images contained within this book, if anyone has been inadvertently overlooked, the British Academy will be pleased to make the necessary arrangements at the first opportunity.

Introduction

This is a book about feminism in Germany after 1968 – about the changes it has created and about how it has changed in turn. It asks what happened to the hopes of 1968 and the visions of transforming society to be more equal, democratic, free and less authoritarian, violent and individualistic? What happened as the New Women's Movement embarked on the 'Long March' through the institutions? How did feminists wedge a space for women's rights in divided and then reunified Berlin and to what extent did their activism (successfully) spur social and political change? But also, how did this process tangibly shape feminism and what are the boundaries or preconditions of feminist social change?

To answer these questions, this book analyses the history of feminist activism against domestic violence in divided Berlin from the late 1960s to the introduction of the *Gewaltschutzgesetz* (Protection from Violence Act) in 2002. This is uncharted territory: the role of feminism in shaping responses to gender inequalities is largely unexplored in the scholarship on divided Germany. Yet, feminism and feminist practices have fundamentally shaped understandings of and responses to domestic violence, both internationally and in Germany.[1] Starting

---

[1] Katharina Karcher, *Sisters in Arms. Militant Feminisms in the Federal Republic of Germany since 1968* (Oxford: Berghahn, 2017); Patricia Melzer, *Death in the Shape of a Young Girl: Women's Political Violence in the Red Army Faction* (New York: New York University Press, 2015); Clare Bielby, *Violent Women in Print: Representations in the West German Print Media of the 1960s and 1970s* (Rochester: Camden House, 2012); Ilse Lenz, ed, *Die Neue Frauenbewegung in Deutschland: Abschied vom kleinen Unterschied. Eine Quellensammlung*, 2nd ed. (Wiesbaden: VS Verlag für Sozialwissenschaften, 2010); Myra Marx Ferree, *Varieties of Feminism. German Gender Politics in Global Perspective* (Stanford: Stanford University Press, 2012); Jane Freeland, 'Women's Bodies and Feminist Subjectivity in West Germany' in *The Politics of Authenticity: Countercultures and Radical Movements across the Iron Curtain, 1968-1989*, edited by Joachim Häberlen, Mark Keck-Szajbel and Kate Mahoney (New York: Berghahn, 2019): pp. 131–150; Christopher Neumaier, *Familie im 20. Jahrhundert: Konflikte um Ideale, Politiken und Praktiken* (Berlin: De Gruyter, 2019). On the history of domestic violence in Germany, see Eva Brücker, '"Und ich bin heil da rausgekommen": Gewalt und Sexualität in einer Berliner Arbeiternachbarschaft zwischen 1916/17 und 1958' in *Physische Gewalt: Studien zur Geschichte der Neuzeit*, edited by Thomas Lindenberger and Alf Lüdtke (Frankfurt am Main: Suhrkamp Verlag, 1995), pp. 337–365; Martin Soder, *Hausarbeit und Stammtischsozialismus: Arbeiterfamilie und Alltag im Deutschen Kaiserreich*

in the 1970s, feminists in West Berlin took what was a taboo subject and propelled it to public and political attention. They exposed domestic violence as a fundamental issue of women's inequality and challenged the heteropatriarchal structures that made women vulnerable to male violence. Most importantly, they worked to open a women's shelter in the divided city, so that women and children could find safe harbour away from their abusers. Despite its grassroots origins, this shelter project found wide political and media support, enabling the group to open the first women's refuge in either German state in 1976.

From this starting point, sustained feminist activism has led to an entire network of support services for women experiencing violence in the home. Each year, approximately 34,000 women and children seek out one of the almost 400 women's shelters and emergency housing services in Germany. It is no wonder that in 2012 the Federal Ministry for Family, Seniors, Women and Youth concluded that there was now a 'dense and diverse network of support services … abused women can find regular and immediate protection from violence, alongside counselling and support in professional organisations'.[2]

Of course, thinking about the successes of feminism is not necessarily something we are accustomed to doing.[3] A cursory glance at the statistics of violence against women might prompt us to question the extent to which feminist activism has been effective. It is currently estimated that every third woman in Germany will experience physical and/or sexual violence and one in four women will experience physical and/or sexual abuse at the hands of a current or former intimate partner.[4] These statistics are certainly not unique to Germany. Reporting from the European Union (EU) indicates similar rates of gender-based violence across Member States, with one in three women experiencing some form of physical or sexual assault from the age of 15 and 22 per cent of women experiencing

(Giessen: Focus Verlag, 1980); Vandana Joshi, 'The "Private" became "Public": Wives as Denouncers in the Third Reich', *Journal of Contemporary History*, Vol. 37, No. 3 (2002): pp. 419–435. On the global movement, see Margaretta Jolly, *Sisterhood and After: An Oral History of the UK Women's Liberation Movement, 1968–Present* (Oxford: Oxford University Press, 2019); Zsófia Lóránd, 'Feminism and Violence against Women in Yugoslavia during State Socialism' in *Women, Global Protest Movement and Political Agency: Rethinking the Legacy of 1968*, edited by Sarah Colvin and Katharina Karcher (London: Routledge, 2019): pp. 84–97; Alana Piper and Ana Stevenson, eds, *Gender Violence in Australia: Historical Perspectives* (Melbourne: Monash University Press, 2019); Janet Elise Johnson, *Gender Violence in Russia: The Politics of Feminist Intervention* (Bloomington: Indiana University Press, 2009).

[2] Bundesministerium für Familie, Senioren, Frauen und Jugend, *Bericht der Bundesregierung zur Situation der Frauenhäuser, Fachberatungsstellen und anderer Unterstützungsangebote für gewaltbetroffene Frauen und deren Kinder* (Berlin: Bundesministerium für Familie, Senioren, Frauen und Jugend, 2013), p. 22.

[3] Clare Hemmings, *Why Stories Matter: The Political Grammar of Feminist Theory* (Durham: Duke University Press, 2011).

[4] Bundesministerium für Familie, Senioren, Frauen und Jugend, 'Formen der Gewalt erkennen', 22 December 2021. Accessed on 3 August 2022: https://www.bmfsfj.de/bmfsfj/themen/gleichstellung/frauen-vor-gewalt-schuetzen/haeusliche-gewalt/formen-der-gewalt-erkennen-80642

physical and/or sexual abuse by a male intimate partner.[5] Globally, the World Health Organization estimates that around 30 per cent of all women over the age of 15 worldwide have been subjected to physical and/or sexual intimate-partner violence or to sexual violence from someone who is not an intimate partner.[6]

These statistics represent more than just numbers. They reveal a world in which women's lives are shaped by the fear of potential and actual male violence. Whether it is walking the long way home from the bus stop to avoid a dark alley, ensuring that no drink is left unattended, or being cautious about inviting male acquaintances for dinner or drinks, the omnipresence of violence in the lives of women influences how they interact with the physical world and with men.[7] They also signal a world in which women's voices and their stories of male violence, are neither heard nor taken seriously: only 14 per cent of women report the 'most serious' incidents of intimate-partner violence to the police across the EU. Indeed, as the EU Agency for Fundamental Rights argues, male violence against women represents a 'violation of women's fundamental rights with respect to dignity, equality and access to justice'.[8]

In the face of such sustained and unfathomable violence, calling the feminist campaign against domestic violence a success might seem unjustified. And yet, one of the foundational arguments of this book is that domestic violence has been one of the issues most effectively addressed by the women's movement in Germany. But how can it be called a success when so many women are still experiencing abuse at the hands of the men they love and trust? Of course, to call it a success is not to say that the work against domestic violence is done. Rather, it is to acknowledge what feminists have achieved and how much they have accomplished in the protection of women's rights. It is also to propose a different reading of the history of feminism and women's rights activism in Germany, one that challenges and complicates what feminism in Germany is and what it has done.

The history of feminism in divided Berlin after 1968 is part of a longer story of women's rights activism in Germany. Although marked by ruptures of war, defeat, revolution, economic and political instability, Nazism and communism, the evolutions and transformations of feminism in the past crucially shaped the work of the activists discussed in this book. As such, it is worth mapping out the longer trajectory of feminism in Germany.

---

[5] European Union Agency for Fundamental Rights, *Violence Against Women: An EU-Wide Survey* (Luxembourg: Publications Office of the European Union, 2014).

[6] World Health Organization, on behalf of the United Nations Inter-Agency Working Group on Violence Against Women Estimation and Data (VAW-IAWGED), *Violence Against Women Prevalence Estimates, 2018: Global, Regional and National Prevalence Estimates for Intimate Partner Violence Against Women and Global and Regional Prevalence Estimates for Non-Partner Sexual Violence Against Women* (Geneva: World Health Organization, 2021), p. 33.

[7] Ann Cahill, *Rethinking Rape* (Ithaca: Cornell University Press, 2001).

[8] European Union Agency for Fundamental Rights, *Violence Against Women*, p. 7.

Histories of women's rights activism in Germany typically begin in the 19th century.[9] Buoyed by the revolutions of 1848 and 1849, women throughout the German Confederation started to campaign for women's political rights, education and their economic security. However, the conservative backlash against the liberal aims of the revolutions meant that for the second half of the 19th century, women in some German states – including Prussia, the largest in the Confederation – were barred from taking part in political organisations or attending political gatherings.[10]

While not totally wiping out women's political organisation, the reassertion of conservative politics across Germany after 1848 certainly entrenched women as outsiders for much of the 19th and early 20th centuries.[11] This was further underpinned socially by the widespread ideal of the bourgeois, Christian family. Reflecting notions of men's and women's 'natural' differences, lawmakers, social elites and both the Catholic and Protestant churches valorised women for their reproductive and maternal roles and positioned them primarily within the private sphere.[12] These ideals were not only socially and politically accepted, but they were also embedded in the patriarchal order enacted in the Civil Code of the newly unified German Empire in 1900. Drawing from a long-standing legal tradition, women's roles were circumscribed both politically, as only adult male citizens had the right to vote and privately, as the Civil Code ensured male authority over the household and limited women's rights to earn money, inherit property and make financial decisions. The codification of a patriarchal family unit at this time and its widespread political acceptance has led historians to argue that liberal development in Germany went hand-in-hand with the entrenchment of a deeply conservative sexual-moral backlash that sought to maintain heteropatriarchal gender norms and bourgeois family ideals.[13] This sexual-moral order haunted developments in women's rights throughout the 20th century.

At the same time, the socialist movement, which was gaining momentum in Germany over the course of the 19th century, played an important role in shaping

---

[9] See, for example, Ferree, *Varieties of Feminism*; Ann Taylor Allen, *Feminism and Motherhood in Germany* (New Brunswick: Rutgers University Press, 1991); Angelika Schaser, Sylvia Schraut and Petra Steymans-Kurs, eds, *Erinnern, vergessen, umdeuten? Europäische Frauenbewegungen im 19. und 20. Jahrhundert* (Frankfurt am Main: Campus, 2019).

[10] See, for example, Preußisches Vereinsgesetz von 1850, §8. This law governed women's political organisation in Prussia until 1908.

[11] Ferree, *Varieties of Feminism*.

[12] See the discussion of the emergence of bourgeois family ideals in Neumaier, *Familie im 20. Jahrhundert*.

[13] See Lynn Abrams and Elizabeth Harvey, eds, *Gender Relations in German History: Power, Agency and Experience from the Sixteenth to the Twentieth Century* (Durham: Duke University Press, 1996); Ute Gerhard, *Verhältnisse und Verhinderungen: Frauenarbeit, Familie und Rechte der Frauen im 19. Jahrhundert mit Dokumenten* (Frankfurt am Main: Suhrkamp Verlag, 1978); Robert G. Moeller, *Protecting Motherhood: Women and the Family in the Politics of Postwar West Germany* (Berkeley: University of California Press, 1993); Neumaier, *Familie im 20. Jahrhundert*.

the history of feminism.[14] Founding socialist figures like Karl Marx, Friedrich Engels and August Bebel, questioned bourgeois visions of the family and, in so doing, the role of women in society. For Engels, bourgeois norms left wives in the role of 'head servant', with marriage merely a form of 'open or veiled domestic slavery' for women.[15] But it was Bebel, a leading figure in the emerging social democratic movement in Germany, who penned one of the most well-known socialist critiques of gender roles. *Woman and Socialism*, first published in 1879 and reprinted 50 times by 1909, argued that women's oppression arose from their economic dependence on men, in a similar way to the oppression of workers by capitalism.[16] Women's liberation was intimately tied with the class struggle for Bebel and could only be realised through socialism.

It was in this context of class division, liberalism and nation building that a women's movement, bubbling just below the surface since 1848, came to prominence in Germany and the early 20th century saw a boom in women's activism. As in other European countries, the German women's movement focused on issues of suffrage alongside education, maternal care, reproductive choice and work. But what particularly marked German feminism from other women's movements at this time was its division along class lines.[17] As Jean Quataert writes, ideas of equal pay and women's right to work and education resonated differently among women across the class divide that split German society in the 19th century. At the same time, the introduction of Chancellor Otto von Bismarck's Anti-Socialist Laws in 1878 created a climate of distrust and exacerbated class tensions in a way that reverberated across feminist activism.[18] Liberal feminist organisations such as the *Bund Deutscher Frauenvereine* (Federation of German Women's Organisations), formed in 1894, focused on the issues of the middle and upper classes and banned socialist women's groups from joining their ranks, even after the Reichstag refused to renew the Anti-Socialist Laws for a fifth time in 1890. Meanwhile, feminists associated with socialist politics or involved with the newly formed Social Democratic Party (SPD), including Clara Zetkin, were intensely critical of so-called '*Frauenrechtlerinnen*' (women's righters), namely those women who advocated a

---

[14] Jean H. Quataert, *Reluctant Feminists in German Social Democracy, 1885–1917* (Princeton: Princeton University Press, 1979); Marilyn J. Boxer and Jean H. Quataert, eds, *Socialist Women. European Socialist Feminism in the Nineteenth and Early Twentieth Centuries* (New York: Elsevier, 1978)

[15] Friedrich Engels, *Ursprung der Familie*, quoted in Neumaier, *Familie im 20. Jahrhundert*, p. 49.

[16] Rida Vaquas, 'Radical Books: August Bebel's Women and Socialism', *History Workshop Journal Online*. Accessed on 20 March 2022: https://www.historyworkshop.org.uk/radical-books-august-bebels-women-and-socialism/

[17] Quataert, *Reluctant Feminists*; Jean H. Quataert, 'Unequal Partners in an Uneasy Alliance: Women and the Working Class in Imperial Germany' in Boxer and Quataert, *Socialist Women*, pp. 112–145; Ferree, *Varieties of Feminism*; Richard J. Evans, *The Feminist Movement in Germany, 1894–1933* (London: Sage Publications, 1976).

[18] Quataert, 'Unequal Partners'.

liberal or bourgeois feminist platform. For Zetkin and her SPD comrades, such an approach undercut the more important class struggle. However, despite the antipathy and tension between the two movements, their division should not be overstated. Although they may have advocated different solutions or focused on different groups of women, bourgeois and socialist feminists overlapped on certain issues such as political equality, educational opportunities and improving the rights and lives of working women and mothers.[19]

To be sure, the meaning of feminism at that time was very different from how it is understood and practiced today. Feminists often relied on class-based and racialised ideas of women's innate goodness and natural or spiritual motherhood – the very ideas used to limit women's roles to the home – to legitimise their advocacy for women's rights.[20] And even across political lines, the sexual-moral order and norm of the male breadwinner/female housewife family were either not challenged by feminists or, in the case of socialist feminists, accepted in the name of toeing the party line.[21]

By the start of the First World War, women's involvement in socialist party politics had blossomed and Germany had one of the strongest socialist women's movements in Europe.[22] In the five years following the 1908 relaxation of laws banning women's political activity, the number of women members of the SPD

---

[19] Barbara Greven-Aschoff, *Die bürgerliche Frauenbewegung in Deutschland, 1894–1933* (Göttingen: Vandenhoek and Ruprecht, 1981). Also note that Angelika Schaser argues that the separation of bourgeois and socialist feminism in the historiography of Germany in part resulted from the dismissal and erasure of socialist and working women's feminism produced by the historicisation project of Helene Lange and Gertrud Bäumer, who purposefully obscured radical feminism from their publications on women's activism. See: Angelika Schaser, 'Helene Lange und Gertrud Bäumer als Historiographinnen der Frauenbewegung' in Schaser, Schraut and Steymans-Kurs, *Erinnern, vergessen, umdeuten?*, pp. 170–197.

[20] Note that while Richard Evans has understood the inflection of gender ideals in 19th-century German feminism as evidence of the weakness of feminist claims, others have argued that gender norms provided feminists with an important path from which they could legitimise their claims to women's rights. See: Evans, *The Feminist Movement in Germany*; Greven-Aschoff, *Die bürgerliche Frauenbewegung*; Catherine L. Dollard, *The Surplus Woman: Unmarried in Imperial Germany, 1871–1918* (New York: Berghahn, 2009); Allen, *Feminism and Motherhood in Germany*. Also see Lora Wildenthal for an examination of how women used German imperialism, gender norms and racial hierarchies to carve more independence for white, German women. Lora Wildenthal, *German Women for Empire, 1884–1945* (Durham: Duke University Press, 2001).

[21] Neumaier, *Familie im 20. Jahrhundert*; Ferree, *Varieties of Feminism*; Quataert, *Reluctant Feminists*. Given the legal restrictions on women's membership to political organisations, women activists belonging to the socialist movement initially organised separately from the SPD. As Karen Honeycutt argues, during this time socialist feminists developed independent gender-oriented critiques. However, once women could join the SPD in 1908, the SPD co-opted socialist women's politics, orienting them towards issues of class and away from gender. This meant that even the most critical of socialist feminists, including Clara Zetkin, ended up supporting an increase in men's wages in the name of strengthening the Party, but at the expense of women's ability to earn an independent income. See: Karen Honeycutt, 'Socialism and Feminism in Imperial Germany', *Signs*, Vol. 5, No. 1 (1979): pp. 30–41. Also see, Quataert, *Reluctant Feminists*.

[22] Honeycutt, 'Socialism and Feminism'.

had increased from 30,000 in 1908 to 175,000 in 1914.[23] The bourgeois movement, meanwhile, had pluralised and straddled a spectrum of conservative and more radical feminist demands in what Barbara Greven-Aschoff calls a 'fragile unity'.[24] Throughout the early 20th century, groups such as the *Bund für Mutterschutz* (League for the Protection of Mothers) and the *Bund Deutscher Frauenvereine* were the site of intense debate among middle-class feminists on the nature of women's emancipation, including issues of women's access to education and career paths (at least before marriage), contesting the patriarchal family order and promoting ideas of women's sexual self-determination.[25]

The outbreak of war did little to dampen this activism. Although the *Burgfrieden*, a truce agreed by political parties and trade unions to support the war effort, temporarily limited socialist agitation, women's political engagement grew throughout the war. Severe food shortages, unequal and class-based distribution policies and the death of children, husbands and fathers either in battle or from starvation on the home front brought women into the political sphere as never before. It was these hardships that motivated women, especially those from the working and lower classes, to make political demands and claim the rights of citizenship at a time when women were not accorded them.[26] As Belinda Davis has argued, these demands were not simply economic in nature, but rather women's wartime protest formed a constitutive part of a broader political transformation of German society throughout the war and one that anticipated the foundation of democracy in the Weimar Republic.[27]

The overthrow of the monarchy in 1918 and the introduction of democracy led many feminists to hope for the future.[28] Certainly, there was reason to believe in change. Women's political status improved under the new electoral law of 1918, granting women citizens the right to vote and stand for Parliament in the first democratic elections of 1919. But women never managed to break into politics as hoped. Only 41 women (out of a total of 423 delegates) were elected to the National Assembly in 1919, a feat that would not be beaten in any subsequent

---

[23] Ibid; Quataert, *Reluctant Feminists*. As Honeycut discusses, the SPD actively sought to recruit women to the Party in a marked difference to other political parties at the time.

[24] Greven-Aschoff, *Die bürgerliche Frauenbewegung*, p. 192.

[25] Allen, *Feminism and Motherhood in Germany*; Greven-Aschoff, *Die bürgerliche Frauenbewegung*; Elizabeth Harvey, 'The Failure of Feminism? Young Women and the Bourgeois Feminist Movement in Weimar Germany 1918–1933', *Central European History*, Vol. 28, No. 1 (1995): pp. 1–28; Evans, *The Feminist Movement*.

[26] Belinda J. Davis, *Home Fires Burning: Food, Politics, and Everyday Life in World War I Berlin* (Chapel Hill: University of North Carolina Press, 2000). For more on working-class women in the First World War, see: Ute Daniel, *Arbeiterfrauen in der Kriegsgesellschaft. Beruf, Familien und Politik im Ersten Welt Krieg* (Göttingen: Vandenhoeck and Ruprecht, 1989).

[27] Davis, *Home Fires Burning*.

[28] Harvey, 'The Failure of Feminism?'; Helen Boak, *Women in the Weimar Republic* (Manchester: Manchester University Press, 2013).

election in the Weimar Republic.[29] Moreover, the new Constitution left in place restrictions on women's civil rights in marriage and the home and only provided an ambiguous guarantee of women's legal equality to men. Article 109 of the 1919 Weimar Constitution stated that 'Men and women have, in principle, the same rights and duties as citizens', with the inclusion of the modifier 'in principle' leaving room for women's equality to be challenged. This was actively protested by Social Democratic women, but ultimately, they were unable to enact reform.[30]

Abortion became a particular flashpoint for debates over women's rights in the Weimar Republic. While groups like the *Bund für Mutterschutz* had been calling for the decriminalisation of abortion since the early 20th century, their campaign intensified in the interwar era. Although they saw abortion as an issue of women's self-determination, Atina Grossmann has warned historians to view the movement for sex reform critically. Although a broad coalition of feminists, communists, reformers and medical professionals called for the decriminalisation of abortion, as Grossmann highlights this unlikely coalition was not reflective of a widespread commitment to women's rights. Instead, the movement was built on a 'motherhood-eugenics consensus' that saw motherhood as 'a natural and desirable instinct in all women, only needing to be properly encouraged, released and regulated, and which understood the bearing of healthy offspring as a crucial social task'.[31]

Like many attempts at social reform in the Weimar Republic, however, feminism suffered from the social cleavages already present within the women's movement and intensifying throughout German politics more broadly.[32] Despite the strength of the movement, the political divisions within the Reichstag meant that an abortion reform bill never got off the ground. At the same time, the rifts within the women's movement deepened. The *Bund Deutscher Frauenvereine* was fractured by tensions between the group's liberal leadership and some of the more conservative member organisations; the socialist women's movement was divided into socialist and communist camps, reflecting the schisms that had divided the Left since the First World War and resulted in the separation of the Communist Party of Germany (KPD) from the SPD. Furthermore, young women no longer seemed interested in mobilising along gender lines. The onset of the Great Depression in 1929 further weakened feminism, as mass unemployment, intensifying political polarisation, the crumbling of democratic institutions and a renewed turn towards authoritarianism resulted in what Elizabeth Harvey

---

[29] Ibid.
[30] Kathleen Canning, *History in Practice: Historical Perspectives on Bodies, Class and Citizenship* (Ithaca: Cornell University Press, 2006).
[31] Atina Grossmann, *Reforming Sex: The German Movement for Birth Control and Abortion Reform, 1920–1950* (New York: Oxford University Press, 1995), p. 15.
[32] Harvey, 'The Failure of Feminism?'; Canning, *History in Practice.*

has called a 'powerful antifeminist reaction' in the years leading up to the Nazi seizure of power.[33]

Certainly, the National Socialist regime undid much of what feminists in Germany had achieved. The *Bund Deutscher Frauenvereine* was disbanded in 1933 and the outlawing of the KPD in March 1933 and subsequent persecution of both communists and socialists over the course of the Nazi regime brought a swift end to working-class women's activism. But it is too easy to define Nazism as simply antifeminist, when the Nazis co-opted much of the language of natural and spiritual motherhood and of the rationalisation of reproduction that had also been used by the women's movement.

Reflecting this, historians have highlighted the complicated nature of Nazism for women and women's rights in Germany.[34] Women were officially barred from working in senior positions within the civil service in 1937 and myriad policies encouraged 'racially fit' women to procreate and take on the role of mother and homemaker. Reproduction was firmly tied to the regime's racist aims and extensive measures were introduced to ensure the 'strength' of the *Volksgemeinschaft*. As early as 1933, the Law for the Prevention of Genetically Diseased Offspring mandated the sterilisation of men and women with disabilities deemed as inheritable. In 1936, the Reich Central Office for the Combatting of Homosexuality and Abortion was established. But whereas 'racially fit' women were subject to pronatalist policies and were severely punished (even with the death penalty in 1943, as wartime fortunes deteriorated) for obtaining an abortion, this was not the case for women from racialised groups or those with physical and mental disabilities. From 1938, Jewish women in Germany could legally obtain an abortion. Gender also tangibly shaped the fates of men and women in the Holocaust, with Jewish women exterminated at much higher rates than Jewish men in the concentration camp system.[35]

---

[33] Harvey, 'The Failure of Feminism?', p. 18.

[34] On women under Nazism see: Zoë Waxman, *Women in the Holocaust: A Feminist History* (Oxford: Oxford University Press, 2017); Annette Timm, 'Mothers, Whores or Sentimental Dupes? Emotion and Race in Historiographical Debates about Women in the Third Reich' in *Beyond the Racial State: Rethinking Nazi Germany*, edited by Devin O. Pendas, Mark Roseman and Richard F. Wetzell (Cambridge: Cambridge University Press, 2017): pp. 335–361; Anna Hájková, 'Sexual Barter in Times of Genocide: Negotiating the Sexual Economy of the Theresienstadt Ghetto', *Signs*, Vol. 38, No. 3 (2013): pp. 503–533; Dagmar Herzog, *Sex After Fascism: Memory and Morality in Twentieth-Century Germany* (Princeton: Princeton University Press, 2005); Anna Hájková, Elissa Mailänder, Atina Grossmann, Doris Bergen and Patrick Farges, 'Holocaust and the History of Gender and Sexuality', *German History*, Vol. 36, No. 1 (2018): pp. 78–100; Wendy Lower, *Hitler's Furies: Women in the Nazi Killing Fields* (London: Chatto and Windus, 2013); Renate Bridenthal, Atina Grossmann and Marion Kaplan, eds, *When Biology Became Destiny: Women in Weimar and Nazi Germany* (New York: Monthly Review Press, 1984).

[35] Marion Kaplan, *Beyond Dignity and Despair: Jewish Life in Nazi Germany* (Oxford: Oxford University Press, 1996). Also see: Waxman, *Women in the Holocaust*.

However, Nazism also opened new avenues for those women it deemed racially fit, as their 'biology' gave them access to social and economic advancements. German women could take up opportunities as settlers in the conquered Eastern territories or as guards in concentration camps.[36] Women were also increasingly called upon to take part in the labour effort as the war progressed. Unsurprisingly, these tensions and contradictions in the Nazi treatment of women have caused considerable discussion among historians. The *Historikerinnenstreit* or 'female historian's debate' famously tackled this issue in the late 1980s and early 1990s, as Claudia Koonz critiqued Gisela Bock's emphasis on the persecution of women under Nazism, instead highlighting the opportunities the Nazi racial regime afforded certain women.[37] While this debate has subsided in the intervening years, one thing remains clear: women's roles and lives in the Third Reich were contingent on their perceived biology, their political ideals and the progress of the war.

The Nazi defeat in 1945 also brought significant consequences for women in Germany. Given wartime mobilisation and losses, women now made up the majority of the population in the occupied country. They had borne the brunt of aerial warfare, material deprivation and the street battles that marked the end of the war. They were responsible for much of the early physical reconstruction efforts, taking to the streets to collect bricks and rebuild bombed-out cities. They also faced the wrath of occupying soldiers in the form of mass rape and sexual violence.[38] Whether during the Soviet advance across what is now Poland and the Czech Republic or the occupation of Germany, the rape of civilian women by Soviet soldiers was particularly high.[39] It is estimated that Red Army soldiers

---

[36] Elissa Mailänder, *Gewalt im Dienstalltag: Die SS-Aufseherinnen des Konzentrations-und Vernichtungslagers Majdanek 1942–1944* (Hamburg: Hamburger Edition, 2009); Nicole Kramer, *Volksgenossinnen an der Heimatfront. Mobilisierung, Verhalten, Erinnerung* (Göttingen: Vandenhoek and Ruprecht, 2011); Elizabeth Harvey, *Women and the Nazi East: Agents and Witnesses of Germanization* (New Haven: Yale University Press, 2003).

[37] See Claudia Koonz, *Mothers in the Fatherland: Women, the Family and Nazi Politics* (New York: St Martin's Press, 1987) and Gisela Bock's response 'Die Frauen und der Nationalsozialismus: Bemerkungen zu einem Buch von Claudia Koonz', *Geschichte und Gesellschaft*, Vol. 15, No. 4 (1989): pp. 563–579; Atina Grossmann, 'Feminist Debates about Women and National Socialism', *Gender and History*, Vol. 3, No. 3 (1991): pp. 350–358. For a recent reflection on the debate, see Timm, 'Mothers, Whores or Sentimental Dupes?'.

[38] On the memory of women in the immediate post-war era, see Elizabeth Heineman, 'The Hour of the Woman: Memories of Germany's "Crisis Years" and West German National Identity', *American Historical Review*, Vol. 101, No. 2 (1996): pp. 354–395; Leonie Treber, *Mythos Trümmerfrauen: Von der Trümmerbeseitigung in der Kriegs- und Nachkriegszeit und der Entstehung eines deutschen Erinnerungsortes* (Essen: Klartext Verlag, 2014).

[39] Norman Naimark, *The Russians in Germany: A History of the Soviet Zone of Occupation, 1945–1949.* (Cambridge: Belknap Press, 1995); Atina Grossmann, 'A Question of Silence. The Rape of German Women by Occupation Soldiers', *October*, Vol. 72 (1995): pp. 42–63; Atina Grossmann, *Jews, Germans and Allies: Close Encounters in Occupied Germany* (Princeton: Princeton University Press, 2007). For more on sexual violence against women during and after the Second World War, see Special issue of *Journal of the History of Sexuality* on 'Transgressive Sex, Love and Violence in World War II Germany and Britain', Vol. 26, No. 3 (2017); Mary Louise Roberts, *What Soldiers Do: Sex and the American GI in World War II France* (Chicago: University of Chicago Press, 2013); Birgit Beck, 'The Military Trials of Sexual Crimes Committed by Soldiers in the Wehrmacht,

raped anywhere between 20,000 and 1 million women in Berlin, many within the first week of Soviet occupation.[40] This was a pivotal experience that would mark women's lives into the post-war era. As Regina Mühlhäuser has shown, women experienced the rapes as 'an attack on their innermost being ... their physical and psychological integrity was damaged for the rest of their lives.'[41]

Against this turbulent backdrop, the issue of women's rights soon reappeared, as gender roles became a key source of forging political legitimacy and social stability under Allied occupation and later in the divided German states. Women activists – many of whom had campaigned in the Weimar Republic – resumed their work and politicians like Elisabeth Selbert and Marie-Elisabeth Lüders worked to ensure women's issues and voices were heard during political reconstruction in the West. Despite safeguarding women's constitutional equality in the Basic Law of 1949, post-war reconstruction and the search for stability in the aftermath of defeat and occupation took on distinctly gendered, if not patriarchal, tones in the new Federal Republic. The Wilhelmine sexual-moral order re-emerged, as the conservative Christian Democratic government of Konrad Adenauer officially encouraged women to return to the home. The issue of patriarchal authority in the family was again revisited in political debate, as politicians weighed women's constitutional equality against the protection of the family unit.[42] Although patriarchal authority was ultimately not enacted in West German family law, historians such as Robert Moeller, Frank Biess and Uta Poiger have understood the post-war years as a time of 'remasculinisation', where the male breadwinner/female homemaker family model was promoted as a source of social stability. Moreover, as Cold War borders calcified, it stood as a bulwark to the politicisation of the family and women's roles under Nazism and in the Communist East.[43]

1939–1944' in *Homefront: The Military, War and Gender in Twentieth-Century Germany*, edited by Karen Hagemann and Stefanie Schüler-Springorum (New York: Berg, 2002): pp. 255–274; Catherine Merridale, *Ivan's War: Life and Death in the Red Army, 1939–1945* (New York: Henry Holt and Company, 2006); Regina Mühlhäuser, *Eroberungen. Sexuelle Gewalttaten und intime Beziehungen deutscher Soldaten in der Sowjetunion, 1941–1945* (Hamburg: Hamburger Edition, 2010).

[40] See discussion of statistics in Grossmann, 'A Question of Silence?'

[41] Regina Mühlhäuser, 'Vergewaltigung in Deutschland 1945: Nationaler Opferdiskurs und individuelles Erinnern betroffener Frauen' in *Nachkrieg in Deutschland*, edited by Klaus Naumann (Hamburg: Hamburg Institut für Sozialforschung, 2001): pp. 384–408.

[42] Moeller, *Protecting Motherhood*.

[43] Moeller, *Protecting Motherhood*; Frank Biess, *Homecomings: Returning POWs and the Legacies of Defeat in Postwar Germany* (Princeton: Princeton University Press, 2006); Uta G. Poiger, 'Krise der Männlichkeit. Remaskulinisierung in beiden deutschen Nachkriegsgesellschaften' in Naumann, *Nachkrieg in Deutschland*, pp. 227–266; Elizabeth Heineman, 'Complete Families, Half Families, No Families at All: Female-Headed Households and the Reconstruction of the Family in the Early Federal Republic', *Central European History*, Vol. 29, No. 1 (1996): pp. 19–60; Elizabeth Heineman, *What Difference Does a Husband Make? Women and Marital Status in Nazi and Postwar Germany* (Berkeley: University of California Press, 1999); Maria Höhn, *GIs and Fräuleins: The German-American Encounter in 1950s West Germany* (Chapel Hill: University of North Carolina Press, 2002); Robert G. Moeller, 'The "Remasculinization" of Germany in the 1950s: Introduction' *Signs*, Vol. 24, No. 1 (1998): pp. 101–106; Susan Jeffords, 'The "Remasculinization" of Germany in the 1950s: Discussion' *Signs*, Vol. 24, No. 1 (1998): pp. 163–169.

In East Germany, however, the socialist ideological project, alongside the demographic realities, meant that women's equality and women's rights took on different political meanings. Women's equality to men was – at least rhetorically – a key part of constructing and legitimising socialist rule in the shadow of the Cold War. With a largely female population, the ruling Socialist Unity Party (SED) tentatively encouraged women to join the workforce and participate in socialist world-making and politics, a task complicated by experiences of rape and sexual violence at the hands of the Red Army. Women's bodies, according to Jennifer Evans, 'became the site of this struggle between the fascist past and the communist future', as the SED grappled with engaging women, while also separating German socialist rule from the violence of the Soviet occupation.[44] Much like in the West, the SED resolved this issue by drawing on long-standing and familiar gender norms from the Weimar and Nazi eras.[45]

Over time, the SED more actively engaged with women and throughout the 1950s and 1960s, the private sphere and women's roles became a Cold War battleground for the Party.[46] Whether through competition over home furnishings and consumer goods or in the promotion of shared household duties between husband and wife, the notion of having more modern, loving and egalitarian homes was used by the SED to legitimise socialist rule in the face of what increasingly appeared to be an abiding German division. Central to this programme was women's equality, which provided political capital to East Germany in its attempt to gain the moral high ground over the West, where officials and the general public still debated issues of female employment

[44] Jennifer V. Evans, 'Constructing Borders: Image and Identity in "Die Frau von Heute," 1945–1949' in *Conquering Women: Women and War in the German Cultural Imagination*, edited by Hilary Collier Sy-Quia and Susanne Baackmann (Berkeley: University of California, 2000): pp. 40–60, p. 41.

[45] See, for example, Donna Harsch, *Revenge of the Domestic: Women, the Family, and Communism in the German Democratic Republic* (Princeton: Princeton University Press, 2007); Josie McLellan, *Love in the Time of Communism: Intimacy and Sexuality in the GDR* (Cambridge: Cambridge University Press, 2011); Josie McLellan, 'State Socialist Bodies: East German Nudism from Ban to Boom', *Journal of Modern History*, Vol. 79, No. 1 (2007): pp. 48–79; Herzog, *Sex After Fascism*; Jane Freeland, 'Creating Good Socialist Women: Continuities, Desire and Degeneration in Slatan Dudow's "The Destinies of Women"', *Journal of Women's History*, Vol. 29, No. 1 (2017): pp. 87–110.

[46] On this shift away from Stalinism see: Konrad H. Jarausch, 'Care and Coercion: The GDR as Welfare Dictatorship' in *Dictatorship as Experience: Towards a Socio-Cultural History of the GDR*, edited by Konrad H. Jarausch (New York: Berghahn Books, 1999), pp. 47–69. On the private sphere as a site of Cold War conflict see: Eli Rubin, *Synthetic Socialism. Plastics and Dictatorship in the German Democratic Republic* (Chapel Hill: University of North Carolina Press, 2008); Greg Castillo, *Cold War on the Home Front: The Soft Power of Mid Century Design* (Minneapolis: University of Minnesota Press, 2010); Susan E. Reid, 'Cold War in the Kitchen: Gender and the De-Stalinization of Consumer Taste in the Soviet Union under Khrushchev', *Slavic Review*, Vol. 61, No. 2 (2002): pp. 211–252; Christine Varga-Harris, 'Homemaking and the Aesthetic and Moral Perimeters of the Soviet Home during the Khrushchev Era', *Journal of Social History*, Vol. 41, No. 3 (2008): pp. 561–589.

and women's roles in the family.[47] But this is not to say that the SED fundamentally challenged patriarchal gender norms. Leader Walter Ulbricht maintained a conservative agenda and those advancing the sexually liberal politics of the Weimar KPD were actively purged from the Party. Consequently, much like in the West, up until the 1970s, pro-natalist policies encouraged women to bear children for socialism and women's caring responsibilities remained unchanged.

This is the point at which this book begins. The late 1960s and early 1970s were a critical time of transformation for women's rights and roles in the divided German states. In the West, a New Women's Movement emerged out of the student activism of 1968. Seeking to create a more democratic, less authoritarian world, women activists were confronted with the gendered double-standards prevalent within the student movement. Despite advocating equality, male activists belittled and objectified their female comrades. Chafing against this treatment and the gender norms that limited their lifeworlds, by the early 1970s women were organising in outwardly feminist groups throughout the Federal Republic and politicising issues of motherhood, reproductive rights and violence against women. During the 1970s and 1980s, a diverse and dynamic movement for women's rights emerged across West Germany.[48]

The situation in the German Democratic Republic (GDR) in the 1970s was markedly different for women. Not only did the new Family Law Code of 1965 provide greater protection for women's rights, but gender policy became an important issue following the leadership transition to Erich Honecker in 1971.[49] Throughout the 1970s, the SED introduced various policies aimed at reconciling women's paid employment with their familial responsibilities. Childcare expanded, working hours were reduced for mothers with two or more children under age 17, maternity leave was increased and women were even granted a so-called '*Babyjahr*' or 'Baby Year' of 12 months' paid maternity leave for their second child in 1976.[50] Women in the GDR also had access to unrestricted first trimester abortions from 1972. Although many of the rights feminists fought for in the West were already protected in the East, a small women's movement nevertheless developed in the

---

[47] Jennifer V. Evans, 'The Moral State: Men, Mining, and Masculinity in the Early GDR', *German History*, Vol. 23, No. 3 (2005): pp. 355–370.
[48] Karcher, *Sisters in Arms*; Melzer, *Death in the Shape of a Young Girl*; Bielby, *Violent Women in Print*; Lenz, *Die Neue Frauenbewegung*; Dagmar Herzog, *Unlearning Eugenics: Sexuality, Reproduction, and Disability in Post-Nazi Europe* (Madison: University of Wisconsin, 2018); Tiffany N. Florvil, *Mobilizing Black Germany: Afro-German Women and the Making of a Transnational Movement* (Champaign: University of Illinois Press, 2020).
[49] On the comparative development of family law in divided Germany, see the forthcoming monograph by Alexandria Ruble, *Protecting Families, Dividing States: The Struggle to Reform Family Law in East and West Germany, 1945–1976*.
[50] See discussion in Harsch, *Revenge of the Domestic*.

GDR in the 1980s, as East German women actively organised for women's rights and the rights of East German citizens more broadly.[51]

This book owes much to and builds upon this longer history (and historiography) of feminism and women's activism in modern Germany. Like this scholarship, it reveals a diverse, and at times divided, movement that advocated for women's rights and fought to make gender inequality into a fundamental political issue. It shows the enduring ways in which feminists in Germany marshalled ideas of rights, politics, citizenship, race, motherhood and gender roles, often in terms that would strike a contemporary observer as profoundly un-feminist.

But unlike these previous women's movements, violence, in particular violence against women, was a central issue for the emerging women's movements in East and especially West Germany. Throughout the 1970s, violence came to signify a host of forms of gender oppression and discrimination, and feminists used the concept of violence as a way of understanding and protesting women's inequality. Work against domestic violence was a crucial part of this activism, yet historians of Germany have only recently begun to study violence against women in the home.[52] Moreover, most of this scholarship has focused on West Germany as the locus of women's activism against violence.

This book not only forges a space for the study of domestic violence in the history of feminism in Germany, but it further challenges the historiography in two key ways. Firstly, by detailing and complicating the successes of feminism, and secondly, by decentring the inherent connection between feminism and liberalism through an examination of women's activism under socialism.

A History of Feminist Success

The stories we tell about the past matter; they are a way of challenging normative assumptions and of addressing the politics of the present through a recasting of the past.[53] Histories of women activists of colour, of Black and postcolonial

---

[51] For an overview of the diversity of women's groups in the GDR, see: Samirah Kenawi, *Frauengruppen in der DDR der 80er Jahre. Eine Dokumentation* (Berlin: GrauZone, 1995). For an example of recent historiographical research, see: Maria Bühner, 'The Rise of a New Consciousness: Lesbian Activism in East Germany in the 1980s' in Häberlen, Keck-Szajbel and Mahoney, *The Politics of Authenticity*, pp. 151–173.

[52] See, for example, Karcher, *Sisters in Arms*; Melzer, *Death in the Shape of a Young Girl*; Freeland, 'Women's Bodies and Feminist Subjectivity in West Germany'; Neumaier, *Familie im 20. Jahrhundert*; Bernhard Gotto, *Enttäuschung in der Demokratie. Erfahrung und Deutung von politischem Engagement in der Bundesrepublik Deutschland während der 1970er und 1980er Jahre* (Berlin: De Gruyter, 2018).

[53] Antoinette Burton, 'Thinking Beyond the Boundaries: Empire, Feminism and the Domain of History', *Social History*, Vol. 26, No. 1 (2001): pp. 60–71; Elizabeth Grosz, 'Histories of a Feminist Future', *Signs*, Vol. 25, No. 4 (2000): pp. 1017–1021.

feminism, of coalition building between queer and heterosexual women, between migrant women workers and trade unions, have all helped to complicate the histories of women's rights activism and move it away from a story of white, western, middle-class women.[54] At a time when feminism holds a tenuous position in society, when women's rights and feminism are pitted against other rights-based movements and forms of oppression in ways that uphold a privileged few while undercutting the rights of others, the stories we tell about feminism have never been more important.[55]

But what is the story of German feminism? On the one hand, among the many survey volumes of 20th-century German history, women's rights and the feminist movement are hailed – albeit cursorily – as one of the many successes of democratisation after 1945.[56] On the other, as Clare Hemmings has argued, one of the most common tropes in the history of western feminism is loss.[57] We are accustomed to thinking about feminism as something that has not worked, that has tried to create meaningful change, but come up short. Stalled attempts to decriminalise abortion, half-hearted efforts of creating equality between men and women, anxieties over working mothers and the struggle to build coalitions between women have all featured prominently in the scholarship on Germany, often as a corrective to overly positive narratives of liberalisation.[58] I myself have argued that by centring gender inequality in the history of post-1945 Germany,

---

[54] See, for example, Florvil, *Mobilizing Black Germany*; Karcher, *Sisters in Arms*; Jennifer Miller, 'Her Fight is Your Fight: "Guest Worker" Labor Activism in the Early 1970s West Germany', *International Labor and Working-Class History*, Vol. 84 (2013), pp. 226–247.

[55] Hemmings, *Why Stories Matter*; Angela McRobbie, *Feminism and Youth Culture* (Basingstoke: Macmillan, 2000); Angela McRobbie, *The Aftermath of Feminism: Gender, Culture and Social Change* (London: Sage, 2008); Uma Narayan, *Dislocating Cultures: Identities, Traditions and Third-World Feminism* (New York: Routledge, 1997); Rosalind Gill, *Gender and the Media* (Cambridge: Polity, 2007); Inderpal Grewal and Caren Kaplan, *Scattered Hegemonies: Postmodernity and Transnational Feminist Practices* (Minneapolis: University of Minnesota Press, 1994); Susan Gal and Gail Kligman, *The Politics of Gender after Socialism* (Princeton: Princeton University Press, 2000); Biljana Kašić, 'Feminist Cross-Mainstreaming within "East-West" Mapping', *European Journal of Women's Studies*, Vol. 11, No. 4 (2004): pp. 473–485; Almira Ousmanova, 'On the Ruins of Orthodox Marxism: Gender and Cultural Studies in Eastern Europe', *Studies in Eastern European Thought*, Vol. 55, No. 1 (2003): pp. 37–50; Gloria Wekker, 'Still Crazy after All These Years…Feminism for the New Millenium', *European Journal of Women's Studies*, Vol. 11, No. 4 (2004): pp. 487–500; Chandra Mohanty, ' "Under Western Eyes" Revisited: Feminist Solidarity through Anticapitalist Struggles', *Signs*, Vol. 28, No. 2 (2002): pp. 499–535; Chandra Mohanty, *Feminism without Borders: Decolonizing Theory, Practicing Solidarity* (Durham: Duke University Press, 2003).

[56] For examples of these survey volumes, see: Hans-Ulrich Wehler, *Deutsche Gesellschaftsgeschichte, Bd. 5: Bundesrepublik und DDR, 1949–1990* (Munich: C.H. Beck, 2008); Ulrich Herbert, *Geschichte Deutschlands im 20. Jahrhundert* (Munich: C.H. Beck, 2014); Heinrich August Winkler, *Der lange Weg nach Westen, Bd. 2: Deutsche Geschichte vom Dritten Reich bis zur Wiedervereinigung* (Munich: C. H. Beck, 2000). See also: Christina von Hodenberg, 'Writing Women's Agency into the History of the Federal Republic: "1968," Historians, and Gender', *Central European History*, Vol. 52, No.1 (2019): pp. 87–106.

[57] Hemmings, *Why Stories Matter*.

[58] See, for example, Grossmann, *Reforming Sex*; Moeller, *Protecting Motherhood*; Heineman, *What Difference Does a Husband Make?*

the history of feminism shows that assertions of the success of West German liberalisation are deeply flawed.[59]

In contrast, this book examines both the hard-won successes of feminism and enduring gender inequality as integral parts of the history of post-war Germany. This does not mean tracing a linear trajectory from feminist awakening to liberation, or of the democratisation and liberalisation of German politics and society in the wake of fascism. Such teleological narratives of liberal progress typically work to marginalise the voices and experiences of women, workers, the LGBTQ community and people of colour. But it is also to step away from an emphasis on feminist failure that does not take into account how, or to what extent, social and political change has occurred. Instead, to write the history of feminism from the standpoint of success is to question how, what and why success was made possible. How did feminists steer domestic violence onto the popular and political agenda? And what were the costs of doing so? By using domestic violence activism as its lens, this book reveals how feminism has both transformed German society and in the process been transformed itself, not always for the better.

In doing so, I contextualise the interventions of sociologists and queer theorists who have examined the reception of radical, rights-based movements in mainstream western politics.[60] Despite originating out of grassroots, anti-authoritarian and autonomous women's movements, scholars have shown that feminist principles have now been co-opted into the (neo)liberal political agenda, with complicated effects. While the institutionalisation of certain feminist principles has ensured a level of popular political support for women's rights and gender equality (especially in Global North), it has also meant that feminist politics have been shaped to fit pre-existing structures built on gendered and heteropatriarchal ideals and perpetuated by a global market that relies on the labour of women and girls in the developing world.[61] Rather than challenge these structures, activists have often been required to work within them. As Angela McRobbie has argued, this has meant that 'gender retrenchment is secured, paradoxically, through the wide dissemination of discourses of female freedom and (putative) equality.'[62]

Creating this 'feminist common-sense' as McRobbie refers to the co-optation of feminist ideals has not only led to the subtle deradicalisation of feminist politics, but has also worked to privilege certain women and certain women's rights.

---

[59] Jane Freeland, 'Gendering Value Change: Domestic Violence and Feminism in 1970s West Berlin', *German History* Vol. 38, No. 4 (2020): pp. 638–655.
[60] Kristin Bumiller, *In An Abusive State: How Neoliberalism Appropriated the Feminist Movement Against Sexual Violence* (Durham: Duke University Press, 2008); Jasbir Puar, *Terrorist Assemblages: Homonationalism in Queer Times* (Durham: Duke University Press, 2007); Angela McRobbie, 'Top Girls? Young Women and the Post-Feminist Sexual Contract', *Cultural Studies* Vol. 21, Nos. 4–5 (2007): pp. 718–737; Mohanty, ' "Under West Eyes" Revisited'.
[61] Judith Butler, *Gender Trouble: Feminism and the Subversion of Identity* (London: Routledge, 1990); Mohanty, " 'Under Western Eyes" Revisited'.
[62] McRobbie, 'Top Girls?', p. 720.

Indeed, the popularisation of feminism has allowed women's equality to be pressed into the service of political agendas and a global world order that prioritise white, middle-class and heterosexual women at the expense of the rights of racialised and marginalised communities and women in the developing world.[63] By no means have feminists been innocent bystanders in this process of appropriation either. In an analysis of sexual violence activism in the United States, Kristin Bumiller has shown that feminists have often colluded in these hegemonic agendas to serve their political goals. She argues that the 'feminist movement became a partner in the unforeseen growth of a criminalised society, a phenomenon with negative consequences not only for minority and immigrant groups of men but also for those women who are subject to scrutiny within the welfare state.'[64]

While much of this work examines the impact of mainstreaming feminism, how it has happened historically is less clear. This book uses the history of domestic violence activism in divided Berlin to trace these processes of co-optation. Embedding violence against women into the popular political field was an important part of popularising women's rights and feminism in Germany. Unlike the debate surrounding abortion and reproductive rights, which faced considerable controversy, activism against domestic violence – and violence against women more generally – quickly found political support. In 1976, after two years of intense campaigning, the West Berlin women's shelter project was approved by the Federal Ministry of Youth, Family and Health as a pilot scheme for addressing domestic violence. Jointly funded by the federal government and the Berlin Senate, the West Berlin group opened the first women's shelter in Germany in November 1976. Despite popular anxieties surrounding the feminist approach adopted within this shelter, it soon received cross-partisan support in West Berlin, as the women's shelter movement worked together with the federal government and West Berlin Senate. Following reunification, this support transferred to the former East, as new shelter projects there were quickly granted funding.

And yet, at the same time, this popular success also changed the nature of feminism itself. As this book argues, official support for domestic violence activism was predicated on the dilution of the feminist ideals and practices that had initially guided the shelter movement. In order to make the feminist orientation of domestic violence activism palatable for a political elite and public that were wary of radical politics, activists were encouraged by their supporters to dissociate the shelter from feminism. Activists, alongside the media and politicians, distanced domestic violence from radical critiques of patriarchy and instead relied on gendered imagery of women as helpless victims in need of protection from violent – and often foreign – men. This also meant that political support for campaigns

---

[63] Mohanty, '"Under West Eyes" Revisted'.
[64] Bumiller, *In An Abusive State*, p. XII.

condemning violence against women was often built on traditional ideas of women as vulnerable and in need of protection, not on the basis that women have a fundamental right to physical autonomy. Ultimately then, conservative ideas of what it means to be a woman have been solidified in domestic violence activism in modern Germany.

In examining these processes of co-optation and transformation, I focus particularly on the interactions and discussions among feminists, politicians and the general public, with the media as a key interlocutor between these three groups. The mass media has emerged as an important site for thinking about processes of liberalisation and democratisation in Europe.[65] Throughout the post-war era, the media landscape in West and to a lesser extent East, Germany transformed.[66] In West Germany, while popular printed media, like *Stern*, *Bild* and *Hör Zu!*, maintained high circulations, technological advances, alongside increased purchasing power resulting from the rapid economic growth of the 1950s *Wirtschaftswunder* (Economic Miracle), resulted in the dominance of television in the mass media.[67] However, for much of the 1950s, popular media content – whether in the printed press or on television – primarily featured socially conservative, apolitical and family-oriented reporting.[68] This started to change in the late 1950s, as critical political content increasingly became the norm across television and print media. Accelerating across the 1960s, by the 1970s the mass media was an important site of political critique and commentary. Illustrated news magazines, especially *Stern* and *Der Spiegel*, grew in prominence precisely due to their political focus. The 1970s also saw the creation of feminist counter-media spaces. Major feminist publishing houses and magazines like *EMMA* and *Courage* enabled women from West Germany to engage with one another and with feminism.

[65] Axel Schildt, 'Das Jahrhundert der Massenmedien. Ansichten zu einer künftigen Geschichte der Öffentlichkeit', *Geschichte und Gesellschaft*, Vol. 27, No. 2 (2001): pp. 177–206; Ronald Inglehart, *The Silent Revolution. Changing Values and Political Styles among Western Publics* (Princeton: Princeton University Press, 1977); Christina von Hodenberg, *Television's Moment: Sitcom Audiences and the Sixties Cultural Revolution* (New York: Berghahn, 2015); Thomas Raithel, Andreas Roedder and Andreas Wirsching, *Auf dem Weg in eine neue Moderne?: Die Bundesrepublik Deutschland in den siebziger und achtziger Jahren* (Munich: Oldenbourg, 2009); Andreas Rödder and Wolfgang Elz, *Alte Werte - Neue Werte: Schlaglichter des Wertewandels* (Göttingen: Vandenhoeck & Ruprecht, 2008).
[66] Schildt, 'Das Jahrhundert der Massenmedien'; Hodenberg, *Television's Moment*; Christina von Hodenberg, 'Mass Media and the Generation of Conflict: West Germany's Long-Sixties and the Formation of a Critical Public Sphere', *Contemporary European History*, Vol. 15, No. 3 (2006): pp. 367–395.
[67] Christina von Hodenberg, 'Square-Eyed Farmers and Gloomy Ethnographers: The Advent of Television in the West German Village', *Journal of Contemporary History*, Vol. 51 (2016): pp. 839–865. See also John Ellis, *Seeing Things: Television in the Age of Uncertainty* (London: I.B. Tauris, 2000).
[68] Hodenberg, 'Mass Media and the Generation of Conflict'. For a comparison with cinema see: Heide Fehrenbach, *Cinema in Democratizing Germany: Reconstructing National Identity after Hitler* (Chapel Hill: University of North Carolina Press, 1995). The major exception to this was *Der Spiegel*, which maintained a political focus. However, it was only in the early 1960s that the market share of *Der Spiegel* grew significantly.

Certainly, the spread and growth of the mass media throughout the second half of the 20th century has been understood as pivotal to processes of social change by theorists and historians alike.[69] What has been less clear is the way in which the mass media, as an historical actor, actually enabled or produced this liberalisation. Christina von Hodenberg has gone the furthest in tracing the impact of popular media on value change. Examining audience responses to the sitcom *All in the Family* (*Ein Herz und eine Seele* in German), she argues that the popular media enabled liberal change by reaching mass publics and presenting them with depictions of changing social norms and mores. Moreover, it was new ideas about gender and women's roles arising out of feminist movements that particularly resonated with viewers, but only after television producers had watered them down and made them palatable for a mass audience.[70]

The present study bears these findings out: the media was essential to the success of domestic violence activism. By giving feminists a forum in which to discuss the gender norms that endangered women, as well as portray the widespread experiences of domestic abuse, both the feminist and popular press created social change. Feminists shaped their protests to capture media attention and worked alongside journalists from both the mainstream and feminist press to draw attention to women's issues. Indeed, it was in part due to media pressure that the first women's shelter in Germany opened.

But this book also asks what this meant for feminism. Although largely supportive of domestic violence activism, by translating feminist politics for the masses, the popular media, in particular the printed press, enabled and perpetuated the deradicalisation of feminist principles. Reporting on domestic violence decontextualised and depoliticised women's activism and, in doing so, provided a way for the public to support women's rights as the same time as leaving the status quo intact. While this may have solidified domestic violence activism, it marginalised broader issues of structural gender inequality.

Feminist domestic violence activism was not only transformed through the media. This book also acknowledges the important role that interactions with so-called 'battered women' played in processes of feminist social change. This interaction – between feminist activists and the 'ordinary' women subjects of their politics – is a largely overlooked dynamic in the history of feminism, and yet, as I show, a key element in understanding the institutionalisation of feminist politics. The principles of the women's shelter movement were not only negotiated externally through the media, but were also transformed from within as the class and racial biases of the women's movement were challenged by the predominantly working-class and migrant women who sought out the shelter. Uninterested in

---

[69] Schildt, 'Das Jahrhundert der Massenmedien'; Hodenberg, *Television's Moment*; Raithel, Roedder and Wirsching, *Auf dem Weg in eine neue Moderne?*; Rödder and Elz, *Alte Werte - Neue Werte*.
[70] Hodenberg, *Television's Moment*.

feminist politics, these residents confronted the idealistic goals of early shelter workers who saw women's refuges as venues for raising feminist consciousness. Shelters eventually turned away from these ideological goals to more concretely meet the needs of residents. By unravelling the ways in which activism against domestic violence was both an agent and subject of change, this book traces how the success of women's activism was predicated on the twin processes of the dilution of feminist politics and the reassertion of patriarchal gender norms.

A History of Feminism in Divided Berlin

With all this attention on feminism and (neo)liberal state-making in the scholarship, where does the history of East Germany fit? Although socialism was central to the development of feminism in the 19th and early 20th centuries in Germany, historians have tied the struggle for women's rights after 1945 to liberalism and liberalisation. While West German feminism is touted (even if cursorily) as a key example of the social movements that helped to propel liberalisation and social change in the Federal Republic (or FRG), the meaning and practice of feminism under socialism in East Germany is still largely absent in the scholarship.[71] When it is discussed, it is mostly with a view to the role of women in the collapse of socialism and German reunification in 1989 and 1990, as though a feminist consciousness only emerged in the months prior to the fall of the Berlin Wall.[72] The absence of East Germany in the history of feminism is particularly striking at a time when global, transnational and postcolonial histories have revealed the instability of supposedly universal categories of liberalism, democracy and feminism, and queried the centrality of national boundaries.[73] Why then have historians been so reluctant to study the history of East German feminism?

The history of divided Germany is one marked by contradictions. On the one hand, the two states experienced growing asymmetries throughout division.

---

[71] One important recent text addressing this lacuna is Jessica Bock, *Frauenbewegung in Ostdeutschland. Aufbruch, Revolte und Transformation in Leipzig 1980–2000* (Halle: Mitteldeutscher Verlag, 2020).

[72] Eva Maleck-Lewy and Bernhard Maleck, 'The Women's Movement in East and West Germany' in *1968. The World Transformed*, edited by Carole Fink, Philipp Gassert and Detlef Junker (Cambridge: Cambridge University Press, 1998): pp. 373–396.

[73] On global, entangled and transnational history see: Richard Drayton and David Motadel, 'Discussion: The Futures of Global History', *Journal of Global History*, Vol. 13, No. 1 (2018): pp. 1–21; Sebastian Conrad and Shalini Randeria, eds, *Jenseits des Eurozentrismus: Postkoloniale Perspektiven in den Geschichts- und Kulturwissenschaften* (Frankfurt am Main: Campus, 2002); Michael Werner and Bénédicte Zimmermann, 'Beyond Comparison: Histoire Croisée and the Challenge of Reflexivity', *History and Theory*, Vol. 45 (2006): pp. 30–50; Frederick Cooper and Ann Laura Stoler, eds, *Tensions in Empire: Colonial Cultures in a Bourgeois World* (Berkeley: University of California Press, 1997); C.A. Bayly, Sven Beckert, Matthew Connelly, Isabel Hofmeyr, Wendy Kozol and Patricia Seed, 'AHR Conversation: On Transnational History', *American Historical Review*, Vol. 111, No. 5 (2006): pp. 1441–1464.

While the social and economic significance of West Germany intensified for the East as the socialist economy declined throughout the 1970s and 1980s, the West increasingly turned away from East Germany, looking instead towards its western allies. On the other hand, there is not only a shared history after 1990, but there are discernible similarities and entanglements and even, as Josie McLellan has shown 'comparable social experiences' across the Berlin Wall.[74] For example, in the 1960s and 1970s, both states saw growing media consumption, expanding welfare systems, increasing levels of education attainment and the liberalisation of gender and sexual norms.

These contradictions undoubtedly complicate the task of bringing the histories of East and West Germany together. Indeed, clear comparisons between East and West are confounded by the fact that – despite similarities – change often occurred at different times, in different manners and in different places. This was certainly the case for domestic violence activism and feminism. Although women living with a violent partner had similar experiences, the nature, timing and path of feminist activism diverged.[75] Whereas in West Germany, there was a vocal women's movement that politicised violence against women throughout the 1970s, women's activism in East Germany did not start until the 1980s and even then, violence was not a central theme. Moreover, while West Berlin was a central hub of feminist domestic violence activism, feminist networks in the GDR were smaller and more diffuse, with important groups in Berlin, but also in Leipzig and Weimar.

Yet, as this book argues, including the GDR in the history of feminism in Germany and decentring the focus on the Federal Republic is essential to understanding gender inequality and feminist practice after 1990.[76] As such, it adopts a broadly chronological approach and traces the path of domestic violence activism within the divided city. It does not seek to draw direct comparisons, nor contrast parallel histories and while focused on the history of Berlin as an important centre of feminism in Germany, at times it looks at developments outside of the city. In doing so, it draws on methods developed by global historians.

---

[74] McLellan, *Love in the Time of Communism*, p. 4; Frank Bösch, ed, *Geteilte Geschichte: Ost- und Westdeutschland 1970–2000* (Göttingen: Vandenhoek and Ruprecht, 2015).

[75] On similar experiences see Jane Freeland, 'Domestic Abuse, Women's Lives and Citizenship: East and West Policies during the 1960s and 1970s' in *Gendering Post 1945 German History: Entanglements*, edited by Friederike Brühöfener, Karen Hagemann and Donna Harsch (New York: Berghahn, 2019): pp. 253–273.

[76] For examples of other entangled histories of East and West Germany, see Bösch, *Geteilte Geschichte*; Brühöfener, Hagemann and Harsch, *Gendering Post-1945 German History*; Anna von der Goltz, 'Attraction and Aversion in Germany's 1968: Encountering the Western Revolution in East Berlin', *Journal of Contemporary History* Vol. 50, No. 3 (2015): pp. 536–559; Edith Scheffer, *Burned Bridge: How East and West Germans Made the Iron Curtain* (Oxford: Oxford University Press, 2011); Phil Leask, *Friendship Without Borders: Women's Stories of Power, Politics, and Everyday Life Across East and West Germany* (New York: Berghahn Books, 2020).

As Isabel Hofmeyr argued in the 2006 forum on transnational history in the *American Historical Review*, the 'claim of transnational methods is not simply that historical processes are made in different places but that they are constructed in the movement between places, sites, and regions.'[77] And that is what this book does: it examines the flow of feminist ideas and practices, whether that is between activists globally, the public and the media in West Germany, across the Cold War divide, or among dissident circles under socialism in the GDR.

To this end, it contests a history of a unidirectional flow of ideas and activist politics across the Berlin Wall from West to East. Instead, this book shows that although feminist ideas certainly moved from West to East Germany, they were not simply adopted wholesale. Feminist critiques were translated and adapted by East Germans to fit the exigencies of life under socialism in a way that made domestic violence activism in the GDR distinct from feminist practices in the Federal Republic. Moreover, these East German approaches to domestic violence did not disappear with reunification, but continued to shape practices in Germany after 1990.

Examining East German perspectives also complicates historical (and his-toriographical) understandings of feminism in Germany. As Lucy Delap asserts, feminism is a deeply ambivalent term. Since its emergence in the 18th century, its meaning has changed and evolved to suit the political context of the time. It has also been practiced in different ways globally and has resonated differently for women across political and social divisions. For some women, feminism has meant liberation, for others it has 'been rejected as too divisive, too Euro-American, too white, too middle-class'.[78] To this end, Delap uses the metaphor of a mosaic to capture both the ever-changing plurality of feminisms and their fractures, as feminists have often struggled to address differences of sexuality, class, race and ability in their advocacy for women's rights.[79]

Unsurprisingly then, existing definitions of feminism are rather broad. Myra Marx Ferree defines feminism as 'activism for the purpose of challenging and changing women's subordination to men'.[80] Delap has similarly argued that 'Feminism seeks an alliance that spans more than half of humanity ... All share the insight that being a woman means disadvantage vis-à-vis men and that this can be addressed through struggle.'[81] At the same time, while Delap emphasises the importance of activists' own self-definition as determinative for defining

---

[77] Bayly, Beckert, Connelly, Hofmeyr, Kozol and Seed, 'AHR Conversation', p. 1444.
[78] Lucy Delap, *Feminisms: A Global History* (London: Penguin Books, 2020) p. 5.
[79] Ibid.
[80] Myra Marx Ferree, 'Globalization and Feminism. Opportunities and Obstacles for Activism in the Global Arena' in *Global Feminism. Transnational Women's Activism Organizing and Human Rights*, edited by Myra Marx Ferree and Aili Mari Tripp (New York: New York University Press, 2006): pp. 3–23, p. 6.
[81] Delap, *Feminisms*, p. 5.

feminism, other scholars have instead used the label more flexibly to encompass a range of activisms for women's rights.[82]

The example of East Germany underscores these very issues and this book reveals East German feminism as an ambivalent, limited and fluid concept and practice. Feminism was viewed with official scepticism under socialism. Drawing on the pattern established in the 19th-century German socialist movement, feminism was considered a bourgeois ideology by the SED. It not only undercut socialism's main goal of liberating the proletariat, but was also simply unnecessary, given the purported realisation of gender equality in the GDR. Reflecting this, while some women took up the label of feminist, others resisted this designation, despite coalescing around gender and advocating for women's rights. These tensions were also evident when feminists from across the Cold War divide encountered one another after the fall of the Berlin Wall. What was feminist in East Germany did not necessarily translate to the West and women struggled to recognise each other's politics. Consequently, this book does not draw on a rigid definition of feminism and nor does it seek to develop one. Feminism in Germany was by no means a homogenous movement; it evolved over time and was expressed differently across and within the two German states. Instead, I use feminism as a lens into understanding the shared campaign against domestic violence and for women's rights across the Berlin Wall.

Studying German feminism in this way also reveals the limitations of global feminist sisterhood. Unhelpful periodisations of 'waves' have long dominated the history of feminism.[83] In this rendering, a first 'wave' of feminism emerged in the 19th century, as women coalesced around suffrage and civil rights, and was followed in the 1960s and 1970s by the so-called 'second wave', with its focus on women's bodies, work and self-determination. Feminists of colour and from the Global South have critiqued these narratives, seeing them as evidence of a 'hegemonic feminism' that prioritises the histories and activism of white, middle-class American and European women and their efforts to attain equality with men.[84] In doing so, the wave metaphor obscures – if not erases – the lives and work of women of colour, while also presenting a homogenised and univocal history of feminist activism based on a supposedly universal, liberal emancipatory politics.

---

[82] Ibid.
[83] See discussion on the wave metaphor in Nancy Hewitt, ed, *No Permanent Waves: Recasting Histories of U.S. Feminism* (New Brunswick: Rutgers University Press, 2010). Also: Chiara Bonfiglioli, 'Communisms, Generations and Waves. The Cases of Italy, Yugoslavia and Cuba' in *Gender, Generations and Communism in Central and Eastern Europe and Beyond*, edited by Anna Artwińska and Agnieszka Mrozik (New York: Routledge, 2020): pp. 66–81.
[84] Chela Sandoval, *Methodology of the Oppressed* (Minneapolis: University of Minnesota Press, 2000); Becky Thompson, 'Multiracial Feminisms: Recasting the Chronology of Second-Wave Feminism', *Feminist Studies*, Vol 28, No. 2 (2002): pp. 336–360; Kumari Jayawardena, *Feminism and Nationalism in the Third World* (London: Zed, 1986); Narayan, *Dislocating Cultures*; Grewal and Kaplan, *Scattered Hegemonies*.

A similar pattern can also be observed in the historiography of feminism in Germany, with its focus on the West and liberalism. The two most well-developed periodisations of German feminism, from Ilse Lenz and Ferree, pay only cursory attention to East German women's activism before the fall of the Berlin Wall. Consciously or not, such a narrative emphasises the very issues highlighted by postcolonial feminists and feminists of colour.[85] Feminism appears as a Western export, built around the experiences of white, middle-class West German women, to the exclusion of both East Germans and women of colour. This not only does a disservice to the activism of Black and migrant feminists in West Germany, but also ignores the vibrant feminist activism and thought that existed under socialism before 1989.

This book challenges this narrative and complicates notions of a monolithic and hegemonic feminism. It pays attention to the role of working-class and migrant women in transforming domestic violence activism in the West. It reveals the translation of feminist ideas across the Berlin Wall and the development of feminist practices and politics that spoke to the context of state socialism. It highlights the confrontations and collaborations between feminists across reunification as they campaigned for women's rights. But most importantly, it showcases the role of East Germans in shaping the development of feminist domestic violence activism before and after reunification.

Organisation

This book begins by tracing the evolution of feminism in West Germany out of the student activism of 1968. Although the late 1960s are commonly thought of as a time of sexual liberation, experimentation, anti-authoritarianism and protest, for many women involved in the student movement in West Germany, it was the moment when the gender hierarchies they lived under became manifestly clear. Ignored by their male comrades and unable to pursue careers or political activism because of childcare responsibilities, women started to question the structures and norms that perpetuated their inequality in the Federal Republic. It was these questions that led to action and resulted in the creation of what is often termed the 'New Women's Movement' in the early 1970s.

The first chapter focuses particularly on the movement to decriminalise abortion. This was the first major test for the New Women's Movement: would they be able to decriminalise abortion and protect the reproductive rights of

---

[85] For work on feminism in postsocialism see: Gal and Kligman, *The Politics of Gender after Socialism*; Kašić, 'Feminist Cross-Mainstreaming'; Ousmanova, 'On the Ruins of Orthodox Marxism'; Nora Jung, 'Eastern European Women with Western Eyes' in *Stirring It: Challenges for Feminism*, edited by Gabriele Griffin, Marianne Hester and Shrin Rai (London: Taylor and Francis, 1994): pp. 195–211.

women? Despite successfully mobilising a mass movement that engaged women, men, medical professionals, members of the clergy and even the media, the change that resulted from the campaign was not what feminists originally envisioned. Although the law was briefly liberalised to allow abortion for any reason in the first trimester, it was quickly struck down by the Constitutional Court.

As Chapter 1 argues, this defeat – and indeed the entire campaign – was a formative experience for both feminist activists and, crucially, politicians. In particular, feminists learned how vital building a base of support was for creating change. This meant not only getting women on side, but also harnessing the power of the media to reach a mass audience. However, the abortion campaign also underscored the fact that there were still many prejudices and anxieties about feminism that made politicians cautious when supporting feminist causes.

This lesson was borne out in the path of domestic violence activism and in the project of opening the first women's shelter in Germany in 1976. Chapter 2 looks at the historical development of responses to domestic violence and highlights how feminists in West Berlin challenged the passive acceptance of violence against women and made it into a social issue. It also discusses the way feminists created a movement against domestic violence and successfully pitched their project to the federal government and Berlin Senate. While they may have received funding as a pilot project, in the election year of 1976, the governing SPD moved cautiously. They not only sought to distance the project from its radical grassroots approach, but also introduced mechanisms of oversight aimed at making feminism palatable to a wary public. The chapter further argues that the media were complicit in this deradicalisation as they emphasised gendered stories of women's victimhood and suffering.

But it was not only the media and the government that sought to transform feminist domestic violence activism. As Chapter 3 shows, women themselves – as activists or even as residents of the Berlin shelter – brought about significant changes to feminist domestic violence activism. Women arriving at the Berlin shelter (and at shelters throughout the Federal Republic) eschewed feminist politics and consciousness raising in favour of getting practical and professional support. This pushed activists to change their approach to addressing domestic violence and transition away from grassroots autonomous support into an institutionalised social service. Similarly, women of colour challenged the politics of race in the shelter – and the feminist movement more broadly – so that by the 1980s, increasingly specialised services for women experiencing abuse were opened throughout Berlin.

Chapter 4 moves the story to East Berlin. While domestic violence is typically thought of as a taboo subject under socialism, the chapter uncovers the ways it was discussed in the family and criminal courts and in the media. Despite official proclamations about women's equality under socialism, the apple fell far from the tree. Women experiencing domestic violence under socialism faced a legal system that simply did not prioritise their safety. Instead, as the chapter argues, men's socialist comportment and pro-natalist goals of maintaining families often meant women's divorce applications were denied on the basis that their marriage still held meaning for socialist society.

In making this argument, this chapter sheds light on much of the recent scholarship that has cast the 1970s in East Germany as a time of liberalisation. Although women often remained tied to abusive husbands, critical change was evident in the cultural arena. By the mid-1970s, film-makers and authors were increasingly thematising both women's inequality to men and even violence in the home. But these cultural changes were not the extent of feminist awakening in East Germany. Chapter 5 explores the meaning and practice of feminism under socialism in the years before and after German reunification. It reveals the unique approaches taken to domestic violence in the GDR and the commonalities with feminist practice in the West and in doing so contests scholarly claims that there was no women's movement under socialism in East Germany.

The final chapter returns to the issue of abortion. While the fall of the Berlin Wall saw a revitalisation of intervention strategies and activism against violence towards women, including the introduction of the *Gewaltschutzgesetz*, the first piece of legislation targeted at addressing domestic violence, the same cannot be said for reproductive rights. Abortion became a flashpoint for East German women activists campaigning to have their voices heard across the reunification process and once again the political resolution resulted in a limitation of women's rights. This chapter asks why domestic violence activism continued to find success when the renewed abortion campaign failed, and what, in turn, this tells us about the co-optation of feminism in the Federal Republic.

The history unravelled in this book is a difficult one. It is maddening, uncomfortable, hopeful and inspiring, all at once. Some of the stories of abuse contained within may be triggering and upsetting. And some of the actions of feminist activists might seem problematic from a contemporary perspective. But it is all too easy to criticise and dismiss feminists from the 1970s. What is much more difficult is to assess what they have achieved, while also acknowledging the normative structures they worked within and even at times, upheld. That is exactly what this book does. It traces the path of domestic violence activism from the grassroots to the mainstream, from East to West, and from divided to reunified Germany. In doing so, it assesses how feminism has transformed Germany and how Germany has transformed feminism.

1

The Origins of the Women's Shelter Movement

It started with tomatoes. On 13 September 1968, at the 23rd National Assembly of the *Sozialistischer Deutscher Studentenbund* (German Socialist Student Association or SDS), the new West German women's movement was born after activist Helke Sander gave a lecture on women in the SDS and the New Left. A founding member of the Berlin *Aktionsrat zur Befreiung der Frauen* (Action Council for the Liberation of Women), Sander took the SDS to task for failing to engage with women's issues. 'We will no longer be satisfied that women are occasionally permitted to say a few words, that you, because you are good anti-authoritarians, listen to, only to then return to the agenda', Sander began. In particular, she criticised the SDS for maintaining the long-standing distinction between the public sphere of politics and the supposedly 'apolitical' private sphere in their work. In doing so, she argued that 'the specific relationship of exploit-ation, under which women live, is suppressed, ensuring that men need not give up their old identity granted through patriarchy'. Although the SDS, as one of the major organisations of the West German student movement, saw itself as a radical alternative to the traditional vestiges of political power, Sander stated forthrightly that by upholding such patriarchal norms and failing to see the private sphere as a site of politics, the SDS was both a 'mirror for broader social relations' and 'no different from the unions and political parties'.[1] Moreover, she concluded by saying that if the SDS failed to address her claims, they would reveal themselves to be 'nothing more than a puffed-up, counter-revolutionary ball of dough'.[2]

When Sander's speech ended, the meeting moved on to other matters – just as she had predicted. The SDS' blatant failure to examine their own politics and take

---

[1] 'Die Rede von Helke Sander für den Aktionsrat zur Befreiung der Frauen auf der 23. Delegiertenkonferenz des SDS (1968)' in *Die Neue Frauenbewegung in Deutschland: Abschied vom kleinen Unterschied. Eine Quellensammlung*, edited by Ilse Lenz, 2nd ed. (Wiesbaden: VS Verlag für Sozialwissenschaften, 2010), p. 58.

[2] Ibid., p. 61.

women's inequality seriously angered fellow Berlin activist Sigrid Rüger. Taking to her feet, she began throwing tomatoes at the stage, yelling 'Comrade Krahl [Hans-Jürgen Krahl, an SDS leader], you are objectively a counter-revolutionary and an agent of the class-enemy to boot!'[3] Sitting at the intersection of socialist, 1968 activism and the formation of a feminist consciousness, the significance of the *Tomatenwurf* (literally 'tomato throw') within the history of West German feminism is contested.[4] Although some scholars see it as the inaugural act of the New Women's Movement in West Germany, others have questioned this teleological interpretation, arguing instead that class oppression was the dominant paradigm at this time.[5] However defined, as SDS member and feminist activist Frigga Haug reflected in 1986, 'by accusing male comrades, friends, brothers, fathers, in short the entire sex, and exposing them as the practical beneficiaries and agents of day-to-day oppression, women gave a new shape and direction to political struggle.'[6] Indeed, by criticising the demarcation of the public from the private, Sander underscored the very message that would dominate the women's movements of the 1960s and 1970s: that the personal is political.

However, these actions and critiques also provoked widespread angst. By revealing fundamental inequalities and power structures, by accusing both men and the state of being complicit in these structures, and by challenging long-standing gender roles, feminism (and feminists) proved to be a destabilising force in West Germany in the late 1960s and early 1970s. These issues struck at the very heart of the post-war West German state, built as it was on the reinscription of patriarchal gender norms and the idealisation of the male breadwinner/female homemaker family. But they also went much deeper. Since the 19th century, patriarchy had been woven into the very foundation of the German state, as a sexual-moral order tied German liberalism to patriarchal gender roles.[7] In this way,

---

[3] Alice Schwarzer, *So fing es an! 10 Jahre Frauenbewegung* (Cologne: Emma-Frauenverlags GmbH, 1981), p. 13.

[4] See discussion in Christina von Hodenberg, 'Writing Women's Agency into the History of the Federal Republic: "1968," Historians, and Gender', *Central European History*, Vol. 52, No.1 (2019): pp. 87–106. Also: Katharina Karcher, *Sisters in Arms. Militant Feminisms in the Federal Republic of German since 1968* (Oxford: Berghahn, 2017); Ingo Cornils, *Writing the Revolution. The Construction of '1968' in Germany* (Rochester: Camden House, 2016).

[5] Lenz, *Die Neue Frauenbewegung*; Myra Marx Ferree, *Varieties of Feminism: German Gender Politics in Global Perspective* (Stanford: Stanford University Press, 2012); Ute Frevert, *Frauen-Geschichte. Zwischen Bürgerlicher Verbesserung und Neuer Weiblichkeit* (Frankfurt am Main: Suhrkamp Verlag, 1986); Kristina Schulz, *Der lange Atem der Provokation: Die Frauenbewegung in der Bundesrepublik und in Frankreich 1968–1976* (Frankfurt am Main: Campus, 2002); Kristina Schulz, 'Remembering 1968: Feminist Perspectives' in *Women, Global Protest Movements, and Political Agency. Rethinking the Legacy of 1968*, edited by Sarah Colvin and Katharina Karcher (Abingdon: Routledge, 2019): pp. 19–32.

[6] Frigga Haug, 'The Women's Movement in West Germany', *New Left Review*, Vol. 155, No.1, 1986, pp. 50–74.

[7] Lynn Abrams and Elizabeth Harvey, eds, *Gender Relations in German History: Power, Agency and Experience from the Sixteenth to the Twentieth Century* (Durham: Duke University Press, 1996); Ute Gerhard, *Verhältnisse und Verhinderungen: Frauenarbeit, Familie und Rechte der Frauen im 19. Jahrhundert mit Dokumenten* (Frankfurt am Main: Suhrkamp Verlag, 1978); Robert G. Moeller, *Protecting Motherhood:*

by contesting patriarchy, feminists also challenged much else, sparking myriad popular anxieties and fears: over the status of the family, the role of women and men and even over the role of the state in the private lives of West Germans.

These anxieties surrounding feminism in the late 1960s indelibly shaped domestic violence activism in Berlin from the mid-1970s onwards. The years following the SDS conference in September 1968 to the start of the women's shelter movement in late 1974 were formative for domestic violence work. This period not only moulded feminist approaches to domestic and gender-based violence, but it solidified an awareness among activists that in order to legitimise the Berlin shelter project, they had to navigate these popular fears of feminism. As such, this chapter examines the formation and politics of the New Women's Movement in West Germany, from its emergence out of 1968 and the student movement, to the rise of feminist domestic violence activism in the mid-1970s. It focuses particularly on the formative example of reproductive rights activism and explores both how feminists sought to provoke and challenge the status quo and how the public, especially the media, responded to their critiques.[8] While there are already several studies examining media responses to women activists that show how they ridiculed, demonised and even pathologised feminism and women's emancipation, this chapter asks what this meant for later feminist projects like the women's shelter campaign. It argues that these anxieties, especially those surrounding the perceived gender transgressions of women activists and the connection between feminism and terrorism, set the stage for the institutionalisation of domestic violence activism.

The New Women's Movement in West Germany emerged both out of and in response to the student movement of the late 1960s. Like many other countries at this time, demographic, political and socio-economic changes throughout the post-war era in West Germany ignited generational rebellion.[9] Against the backdrop of the unprecedented growth of the *Wirtschaftswunder*, the baby boom and a corresponding increase in the number of students in higher education, not to mention successive conservative, Christian Democratic (CDU) governments since 1949, the ground was ripe for change in the 1960s. At this time, a broad coalition

---

Women and the Family in the Politics of Postwar West Germany (Berkeley: University of California Press, 1993); Christopher Neumaier, *Familie im 20. Jahrhundert: Konflikte um Ideale, Politiken und Praktiken* (Berlin: De Gruyter, 2019).
[8] Fahlenbrach has argued that the media were central to 1968 activism, going so far as to say that the media has 'dominated the public understanding of their [1968ers] goals, their motives and even 'their collective identities'. See Kathrin Fahlenbrach, Erling Siversten and Rolf Weremskjold, eds, *Media and Revolt: Strategies and Performances from the 1960s to the Present* (New York: Berghahn, 2014), p. 8–9.
[9] Arthur Marwick, *The Sixties: Cultural Revolution in Britain, France, Italy and the United States* (New York: A & C Black, 1999); Carole Fink, Philipp Gassert and Detlef Junker, eds, *1968. The World Transformed* (Cambridge: Cambridge University Press, 1998); Martin Klimke and Joachim Scharloth, eds, *1968 in Europe. A History of Protest and Activism, 1956–1977* (New York: Palgrave Macmillan, 2008).

of students, activists, trade unionists, liberals and socialists came together to protest against university over-crowding, the failures of de-Nazification and democratisation and the lingering presence of authoritarianism, fascism and imperialism in West Germany as well as globally.[10] They took part in radical protests and demonstrations and generally attempted to enact their anti-authoritarian, collectivist politics in their everyday lives, forming communes and spaces where they could discuss and live out their political ideals.[11]

The SDS was a particularly important organisation within the broader student movement.[12] Formed in 1946, the SDS was originally closely tied to the West German SPD.[13] However, at a time of strong anti-communism, the SDS' increasingly socialist, New Left orientation concerned the Social Democrats. Not only had the Communist Party been banned in West Germany in 1956, but the 1959 Godesberg Program eliminated the SPD's lingering Marxist policies in favour of refashioning itself as a general party for the political left. Wanting to distance itself from the strongly ideological student organisation and with growing tensions between the two groups over West German rearmament, the SPD separated from the SDS in November 1961.

Although popular concerns over the state of West German democracy had been mounting throughout the Adenauer era, it was the formation of the grand coalition between the CDU and SPD in 1966 that brought the SDS to prominence.[14] The CDU had held the Chancellorship since its inception in 1949, mostly in coalition with the smaller Free Democratic Party (FDP). But when the FDP withdrew their support in 1966, CDU-leader Kurt-Georg Kiesinger turned to

[10] On the global dimensions of 1968 in West Germany, see Timothy Scott Brown, *West Germany and the Global Sixties. The Antiauthoritarian Revolt, 1962-1978* (Cambridge: Cambridge University Press, 2013).
[11] Sven Reichardt, *Authentizität und Gemeinschaft. Linksalternatives Leben in den siebziger und frühen achtziger Jahren* (Berlin: Suhrkamp Verlag, 2014); Donatella della Porta, *Social Movements, Political Violence, and the State. A Comparative Analysis of Italy and Germany* (Cambridge: Cambridge University Press, 1995); Klimke and Scharloth, *1968 in Europe.*
[12] Martin Klimke, 'West Germany' in Klimke and Scharloth, *1968 in Europe*: pp. 97–110. Also della Porta, *Social Movements.*
[13] For a detailed history of the SDS, see Tilman Fichter and Siegward Lönnendonker, *Kleine Geschichte des SDS. Der Sozialistische Deutsche Studentenbund von 1946 bis zur Selbstauflösung* (Berlin: Rotbuch Verlag, 1977).
[14] See, for example, the debates around the lingering spectre of Nazism within the West German government and the role of the *éminence grise* in decision making; the 1962 *Spiegel* Affair; and debates around rearmament and reparations, all of which put democracy in the FRG to the test: Robert G. Moeller, *War Stories: The Search for a Usable Past in the Federal Republic of Germany* (Berkeley: University of California Press, 2001); Thomas Reuther, 'In Hitler's Shadow' in *The United States and Germany in the Era of the Cold War, 1945–1990: A Handbook*, edited by Detlef Junker, Phillipp Gassert, Wilfried Mausbach and David M. Morris (Cambridge: Cambridge University Press, 2004): pp. 601–607; Malte Herwig, *Die Flakhelfer: Wie aus Hitleres jüngsten Parteimitgliedern Deutschland führende Demokraten wurden* (Munich: Deutsche Verlags-Anstalt, 2003).

Willy Brandt of the SPD to form a government. As the two largest political parties in the Federal Republic, this grand coalition held 90 per cent of the seats in the Bundestag. This not only rendered the official opposition powerless, but laid the path for the seamless introduction of the *Notstandsgesetze* or Emergency Acts, a controversial piece of legislation that would give the state the ability to act extra-constitutionally and suspend civil liberties in the event of a crisis. Fearing what this meant for democracy, particularly in light of the abuses of emergency powers during the late Weimar and early Nazi eras, various left-wing political groups, including the SDS, formed an *Außerparlamentarische Opposition* (Extra-Parliamentary Opposition or APO), offering a voice to students and the New Left in West Germany. The SDS quickly became a leading organisation within the APO. Drawing heavily on critical theorists and psychoanalysts such as Theodor Adorno, Herbert Marcuse and Wilhelm Reich, the SDS shaped the theoretical foundations of the student movement and coordinated collective action and protest across the country.[15]

From the very beginning, women were actively involved in both the SDS and the student movement more generally. They took part in political debates, protests and militant actions.[16] Women also made up approximately 30 per cent of SDS members, a figure even more significant given that in 1965 only 28 per cent of all students entering higher education in the Federal Republic were women.[17] Despite women's engagement in radical politics and although the student movement espoused equality, liberation and the end of oppression and exploitation, the topographies of the West German student movement were distinctly gendered. This is clearly portrayed in the accounts of women student activists, who frequently highlight their misogynistic treatment within the ostensibly progressive Left.[18] Certainly, whereas men's activism was hailed by the movement as revolutionary and transformative, women were marginalised into supportive roles. As Silvia Bovenschen, a leading activist in Frankfurt, reveals, it was unquestionable that

---

[15] Karcher, *Sisters in Arms*, p. 4.

[16] Karcher, *Sisters in Arms*; Lenz, *Die Neue Frauenbewegung*; Ferree, *Varieties of Feminism*; Morvarid Dehnavi, *Das politisierte Geschlecht. Biographische Wege zum Studentinnenprotest von '1968' und zur Neuen Frauenbewegung* (Bielefeld: Transcript Verlag, 2013); Cornils, *Writing the Revolution*.

[17] For the statistics on the SDS, see Dehnavi, *Das politisierte Geschlecht*. The numbers of female students in higher education in West Germany rose throughout the late 1960s, increasing to 37.9 per cent of all students in 1970 and then remaining stagnant until 1989. In comparison, data for universities showed that by 1980, 43.6 per cent of students were women. See Marianne Kriszio, 'Frauen im Studium' in *Handbuch zur Frauenbildung*, edited by Wiltrud Gieseke (Opladen: Leske und Budrich, 2001): pp. 293–302.

[18] On this see Christina von Hodenberg, *Das andere Achtundsechzig: Gesellschaftsgeschichte eine Revolte* (Munich: C.H. Beck, 2018); Ute Kätzel, *Die 68erinnen. Porträt einer rebellischen Frauengeneration* (Berlin: Rowohlt, 2002); Karcher, *Sisters in Arms*; Dagmar Herzog, *Sex After Fascism: Memory and Morality in Twentieth-Century Germany* (Princeton: Princeton University Press, 2005). Although note that both Susanne Schunter-Kleeman and Helke Sander mention the SDS as being less misogynistic than other Leftist groups in the 1960s. See Kätzel, *Die 68erinnen*, p. 183.

the 'men held the big lectures and the women gave out the flyers.'[19] Even when women attempted to make their voices and opinions heard in discussions and meetings, their male comrades patronised them and treated them with condescension. Activist and writer Inga Buhmann's 'main criticism' of the men associated with the Frankfurt School and the SDS was that they 'used their knowledge as an arrogant instrument of power, above all against women. It was often the case that if I asked a question, I received a sermon in response consisting of a continuous series of quotes from the five books that everyone had to read in order to be "in".'[20]

These attitudes also translated into a broad-ranging objectification of women in the student movement. Annemarie Tröger, an SDS member, remembers that women's identity in the SDS was defined by the 'status of their current comrade … their husband or boyfriend', with women typically dismissed as merely 'her comrade's appendage'.[21] Student activist and wife of famed student leader Rudi Dutschke, Gretchen Dutschke similarly describes men treating women in the movement like 'accessories that could be put away at will'.[22] Summing this up succinctly, Buhmann describes the roles available to women in the student movement:

> Every new woman in the group either had to quickly catch herself an alpha male as a boyfriend or, presenting herself as emancipated, sleep her way through the various beds to find a bit of affection and recognition, or she had to play the strong woman, who could do without such things, that is, adjust as best she could to the men and surpass them in "male virtues of power".[23]

This objectification of women was further amplified by the sexual revolution, where access to women's bodies was politicised as a form of socialist liberation from the bourgeois norms of heterosexual monogamy.[24] A popular anti-authoritarian saying at the time even maintained that 'whoever sleeps with the same woman twice already belongs to the establishment.'[25] Unsurprisingly, as one woman reflected in 1975, 'women were so clearly oppressed in the SDS that the idea [of separating] had been in the air a long time.'[26]

These dismissive attitudes towards women activists also echoed in the mass media at the time.[27] Christina von Hodenberg has argued that in the 1960s women

[19] Tobias Rapp and Claudia Voigt, 'Kinder sind die Falle', *Der Spiegel*, 10 January 2011.
[20] Inga Buhmann, *Ich habe mir eine Geschichte geschrieben* (Frankfurt am Main: Zweitausendeins, 1983), pp. 233–234.
[21] Annemarie Tröger, quoted in Siegward Lönnendonker, ed, *Linksintellektueller Aufbruch zwischen 'Kulturrevolution' und 'kultureller Zerstörung': Der Sozialistische Deutsche Studentenbund (SDS) in der Nachkriegsgeschichte 1946–1969* (Wiesbaden: VS Verlag, 1998), p. 216.
[22] Gretchen Dutschke, *Wir hatten ein barbarisches, schönes Leben. Rudi Dutschke: Eine Biographie* (Cologne: Kiepenheuer and Witsch, 1996), p. 81.
[23] Buhmann, *Ich habe mir*, p. 237.
[24] Herzog, *Sex After Fascism*.
[25] Ibid., p. 231.
[26] *Frauenjahrbuch '75* (Frankfurt am Main: Verlag Roter Stern, 1975), p. 15.
[27] This is also how women 1968ers are still remembered with the narratives and myths of 1968, in particular, focusing heavily on the actions of male student leaders, while obscuring the participation

were typically represented as either 'sex objects' or 'asexual mothers and house-wives' in the West German media and this was reflected in the depictions of women student activists.[28] On the one hand, the media objectified them as 'beau-tiful embellishments', 'ladies in panther-fur', or in the case of communard and model Uschi Obermaier, as the '"pin-up" of the revolution'.[29] On the other, they were mocked for any transgression of typical feminine norms. As *Der Spiegel* flor-idly described, women activists were 'dangerous eyeshadow-accretions in combat boots and slovenly jeans, upper-class girls with floppy hats and pony-tails, nappy-tired young mothers'.[30] Much like their male comrades, the media were more concerned with women activists' looks, bodies and sex lives, than with their ideas or political work.[31]

It was in this context that Sander came to speak at the SDS conference in September 1968. Despite her legendary role in that day's events, her political engagement in women's issues predated the *Tomatenwurf*. Trained as a film-maker and actor, Sander returned to Berlin from Helsinki in 1965 after separ-ating from her husband. Living as a single mother and studying at the Berlin Film and Television Academy, Sander became involved in the SDS and Leftist pol-itical causes.[32] However, Sander – like many other women at this time – faced the problem of combining her political interests with her studies and full-time childcare responsibilities. This led her, along with other SDS women, to form the *Aktionsrat zur Befreiung der Frauen* in late 1967, a group which aimed to address women's isolation and representation within the Left. Much like Sander's speech at the 1968 SDS conference, the *Aktionsrat* highlighted the discrepancy between socialist politics of equality and women's lived experiences. As the group's first flyer proclaimed 'We were jealous, because equality was always harder for us than for our fellow male students, because for us the longing for inspired flights of fancy never quite fits and we were sad because in our individual attempts to com-bine study, love and children, we got bogged down or simply encrusted.'[33]

---

of women. See von Hodenberg, *Das andere Achtundsechzig*; Kätzel, *Die 68erinnen*; Karcher, *Sisters in Arms*.

[28] von Hodenberg, *Das andere Achtundsechzig*, p. 124. Also, Clare Bielby, *Violent Women in Print: Representations in the West German Print Media of the 1960s and 1970s* (Rochester: Camden House, 2012).

[29] Quoted in Kristina Schulz, 'Ohne Frauen keine Revolution', *Bundeszentrale für politische Bildung*. Accessed on 10 November 2020: https://www.bpb.de/geschichte/deutsche-geschichte/68er-bewegung/51859/frauen und 68?p=all. See also: Cornils, *Writing the Revolution*.

[30] 'Die rose Zeiten sind vorbei', *Der Spiegel*, 25 November 1968.

[31] von Hodenberg, *Das andere Achtundsechzig*. On the history of West German feminist critiques of make-up and the objectification of women in the media, see Uta G. Poiger, 'Das Schöne und das Hässliche. Kosmetik, Feminismus und Punk in den siebziger und achtziger Jahren' in *Das Alternative Milieu. Antibürgerlicher Lebensstil und linke Politik in der Bundesrepublik Deutschland und Europa, 1968–1983*, edited by Sven Reichardt and Detlef Siegfried (Göttingen: Wallstein, 2010): pp. 222–243.

[32] Helke Sander, 'Nicht Opfer sein, sonder Macht Haben' in Kätzel, *Die 68erinnen*, pp. 161–180.

[33] Aktionsrat für die Befreiung der Frauen, 'Wir sind neidisch und wir sind traurig gewesen' (1968) in Lenz, *Die Neue Frauenbewegung*, p. 51.

Motherhood was a particular concern for the *Aktionsrat*. Women with children were especially vulnerable to the exigencies of the prevailing gender norms in West Germany. The Adenauer government had strongly promoted patriarchal family structures as a path to reasserting social stability in the wake of Nazi defeat and male breadwinner/female housewife families were still the norm in the late 1960s. This resulted in limited – and typically authoritarian – public childcare options, which meant that having a child signalled the end of many women's careers.[34] For women involved in socialist politics at this time, this was a hard pill to swallow. Their participation in a movement aimed at questioning oppression only made them more aware of their own inequality. At the same time, having children also limited women's ability to engage in revolutionary politics: with their male comrades unwilling to take on care responsibilities and children not allowed at demonstrations, mothers were forced out of the student movement. As the *Aktionsrat* argued, 'Those women who have children realise quicker that the existing working conditions must simply be killed off – whether through the authoritarian state kindergartens, the musty atmosphere of the family, or the nervous haste of single women. We don't need a scientific analysis to see clearly that this society must fundamentally change'.[35]

A single mother herself, Sander understood this frustration first hand. Her handwritten leaflet *first attempt. to find the right question* articulated the experiences of many women in West Germany when it first circulated in February 1968.[36] 'i got married, because i was pregnant and for economic reasons could not afford to remain unmarried', explained Sander, continuing,

> of course, it was natural that i would interrupt my studies, so that my husband could complete his. it was obvious, that the man must study, just as it is natural that the man must support his family, that the man must have an education and that the woman must take care of the children. this is simply how it is.[37]

But this had left Sander feeling resentful, even 'aggressive'. With echoes of Betty Friedan's 'the problem that has no name', Sander believed she was not alone: 'every thinking woman is emotionally fed up with this system, even if she can't articulate it. she's fed up because she senses that this system will never be ready to even slightly fulfil her desires'.[38]

---

[34] Neumaier, *Familie im 20. Jahrhundert*.
[35] Aktionsrat für die Befreiung der Frauen, 'Wir sind neidisch und wir sind traurig gewesen', p. 54.
[36] Lack of capitalisation from the German original. Helke Sander, '1. versuch. die richtigen fragen zu finden' (February 1968) in Lenz, *Die Neue Frauenbewegung*, pp. 53–57.
[37] Ibid.
[38] Ibid. Betty Friedan, *The Feminine Mystique* (New York: W.W. Norton, 2001, originally published 1963). See also Jane Freeland, 'Women's Bodies and Feminist Subjectivity in West Germany' *The Politics of Authenticity: Countercultures and Radical Movements across the Iron Curtain, 1968-1989*, edited by Joachim Häberlen, Mark Keck-Szajbel and Kate Mahoney (New York: Berghahn, 2019), pp. 131–150.

Sander was, in fact, not alone. From its beginnings around a kitchen table in December 1967, the *Aktionsrat* grew in numbers throughout 1968, eventually peaking at 500.[39] Hosting weekly meetings at the West Berlin SDS 'Republican Club', the *Aktionsrat* formed working groups on sexual health, women's financial independence and children's education. What they are most famous for, however, is their work to establish *Kinderläden* (childcare centres opened in empty West Berlin storefronts), which found strong support from women and the student movement. Offering an anti-authoritarian and collective alternative to state-run childcare, the *Kinderläden* not only gave mothers an opportunity to participate in politics and activist work, but also reflected the student movement's broader critiques of the fascist tendencies present within capitalist West German society. As Sander argued, 'the main goal' of the *Kinderläden* was 'to give children the strength to resist by supporting their emancipatory energies, so that they can address their own conflicts with the system by changing the world'.[40] By the time of Sander's speech to the SDS, there were already five such childcare centres in Berlin with others opening up throughout West Germany in the wake of the *Tomatenwurf*.[41]

It was out of her work with the *Aktionsrat* that Sander came to speak at the SDS conference in September 1968. She was there to present the Council's strategies and work in an attempt to build an alliance with the SDS. But more than this, Sander's presentation was about engaging with the SDS and showing them what women could bring to the table. In her own words, Sander wanted to speak at the conference because 'the most intelligently-informed public and arguments that we encountered at the big events on the Vietnam War, on the manipulation of the press, on the Greek Junta, on the Emergency Acts and on many other topics, would never be experienced anywhere else.' At the same time, she also wanted to make it clear to her 'esteemed comrades … that we [women] had the potential to raise new questions of shared interest and as a result also offered new capabilities'.[42]

However, the response of the SDS – to simply move on with the agenda – sent a clear message to women. Reporting on the significance of the *Tomatenwurf* for the radical newspaper *Konkret*, then-journalist Ulrike Meinhof argued that unlike other student protest actions, the *Tomatenwurf* was not symbolic, but rather the final straw. 'These Berlin women in Frankfurt no longer want to play along', argued Meinhof. Moreover, 'the consequence of Frankfurt can only be that more women examine their problems, organise themselves, work through their issues and learn

[39]   Helke Sander, 'Der Seele ist das Gemeinsame eigen, das sich mehrt' in *Wie weit flog die Tomate?: Eine 68erinnen-Gala der Reflexion* (Berlin: Heinrich Böll Stiftung, 1999), pp. 43–56.
[40]   'Die Rede von Helke Sander für den Aktionsrat zur Befreiung der Frauen auf der 23. Delegiertenkonferenz des SDS (1968)' in Lenz, *Die Neue Frauenbewegung*, p. 60–61.
[41]   Ibid., p. 61.
[42]   Sander, 'Der Seele ist das Gemeinsame eigen', p. 48.

to express themselves. And demand nothing more from their men, other than to be left alone in these matters and to wash their own tomato-stained shirts.'[43]

In the aftermath of Sander's speech and Rüger's subsequent protest, women across the West German student movement began to organise. Alongside the *Aktionsrat* in Berlin, women organised *Weiberräte*. Often translated as witches' or hags' council, the name *Weiberrat* plays on an antiquated and pejorative term for woman or wife (*Weib*), combined with *Rat* (council), a word evoking the revolutionary councils formed in the aftermath of the First World War.[44] According to Silvia Bovenschen, much like the *Aktionsrat*, the first *Weiberrat* came together because women 'had had enough of being treated like children by their fellow male students'.[45] By the time of the next SDS meeting in November 1968, there were already eight *Weiberräte* in the Federal Republic. It was at this SDS conference that the Frankfurt *Weiberrat* gained notoriety with their leaflet *Statement of Accounts*. In a short paragraph, the *Weiberrat* criticised the SDS for their treatment of women activists. 'We're not opening our mouths', began the leaflet, 'If we left them open, they'd be crammed with: petit-bourgeois dicks, the socialist pressure to fuck, socialist children, love … platitudes, potent socialist lechery … revolutionary groping … superficial socialist emancipation.'[46] After listing even more examples of misogyny within the socialist left, the leaflet proclaimed: 'Liberate the socialist elites from their bourgeois dicks.' Alongside this statement, the leaflet featured an illustration of a naked witch, reclining on a chaise-longue and holding a battle-axe in her right hand. Above her head, six penis trophies are mounted on the wall, each with a number corresponding to the name of a male SDS leader (see Figure 1.1). This image clearly played upon the concept of the group as a council of witches or crones, as well as evoking the collective power of women and the threat that they posed to men. Indeed, the figure of the witch would become a prominent symbol of women's strength as the women's movement developed in West Germany.

Although the activism of both the Frankfurt *Weiberrat* and the Berlin *Aktionsrat* have clear links to feminism, for most of the late 1960s, women's activism in West Germany was firmly embedded within socialist politics. In a flyer from October 1968, the Berlin *Aktionsrat* specifically defined itself as a 'political group, belonging to the anti-authoritarian camp and working together with the APO'. Moreover, they were definitively not a 'bourgeois emancipation movement … We do not strive for the "emancipation" of women that will give

---

[43] Ulrike Meinhof, 'Die Frauen im SDS', *Konkret*, 7 October 1968.
[44] The term was appropriated by women activists, after male SDS members at the Frankfurt conference had used the term to deride women's groups. See Dehnavi, *Das politisierte Geschlecht*, p. 33.
[45] Rapp and Voigt, 'Kinder sind die Falle'.
[46] 'Rechenschaftsbericht, Flugblatt des Frankfurter Weiberrates', A Rep 400, 17.20 0–4, FFBIZ.

RECHENSCHAFTSBERICHT

des weiberrats der gruppe frankfurt

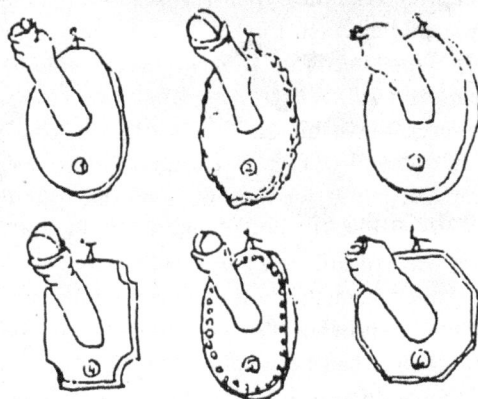

1) schauer

2) gäng

3) kunzelmann

4) krahl

5) rabehl

6) reiche

7) ....

Figure 1.1 The *Statement of Accounts* of the Frankfurt *Weiberrat*, 1968.

Credit: Image courtesy of FrauenMediaTurm, Cologne (FB.04.188a).

us the same opportunities to compete with men socially and economically'. Instead, they wanted to 'overthrow the system of competition between people', something they believed was only possible through the 'transformation of the means of production and the system of power in a socialist society'.[47] Even the texts the *Aktionsrat* and the Frankfurt *Weiberrat* read were a blend of foundational socialist works, including August Bebel's *Woman and Socialism* and Clara Zetkin's *On the History of the Proletarian Women's Movement in Germany*, alongside contemporary feminist writing.[48]

By the 1970s, however, the status quo was starting to change. The Grand Coalition came to an end with the 1969 elections, which brought a Social Democratic government to power for the first time since the creation of the Federal Republic 20 years earlier. The new chancellor Willy Brandt, working in coalition with the FDP, ushered in a new era of politics for West Germany with an expansion of the welfare system, the creation of more universities and the start of rapprochement with the communist East through *Ostpolitik*. At the same time, the student movement, which had been splintering since the Emergency Acts were passed in 1968, was coming to an end. Facing internal divisions and competing ideological approaches, the SDS disbanded in 1970.[49] Similar tensions were also evident in women's organising. The first Frankfurt *Weiberrat* disbanded in 1969, after its numbers grew too large to effectively enable the kind of egalitarian and anti-authoritarian organisation desired by the group.[50] Likewise, the Berlin *Aktionsrat* was split between activists focused on discussing socialist theory and those interested in the *Kinderläden* and project work. It, too, dissolved in 1970.

Yet amid these transformations, a self-consciously feminist movement started to emerge in West Germany. The New Women's Movement, as it was known, owed much to this earlier activism. Despite defining themselves as socialist, groups like the *Aktionsrat* and the *Weiberräte* were formative for the creation of a women's movement and many activists moved seamlessly from the student movement into the New Women's Movement. Indeed, historians have variously labelled this early women's organising as the 'roots' of the later feminist movement and as the 'most important outcome' of 1968, enabling both a change in women's roles and 'society as a whole'.[51] As Katharina Karcher has aptly described, 1960s student activism formed an 'explorative phase in which women on the Left began to organize, think and mobilize independently from their male comrades to work towards new forms of political subjectivity'.[52]

---

[47] Selbstverständnis des Aktionsrats zur Befreiung der Frauen, A Rep 400, 17.20 0–4, FFBIZ.
[48] Karcher, *Sisters in Arms*, p. 25.
[49] Della Porta, *Social Movements*; Klimke and Scharloth, *1968 in Europe*.
[50] *Frauenjahrbuch '75*, p. 18.
[51] Dehnavi, *Das politisierte Geschlecht*, p. 33; Kätzel, *Die 68erinnen*, p. 9.
[52] Karcher, *Sisters in Arms*, p. 23.

The late 1960s were also pivotal to shaping public responses to feminism, as the media's derision of women activists and women's emancipation continued into the 1970s. Feminists used this attention to their advantage, deliberately provoking the media by staging confrontational and even militant protest actions, which were designed to challenge preconceptions of women's roles. While this activism and the media have been vitally important for ushering in the liberalisation of gender norms in the Federal Republic, they also created a new set of challenges.

The New Women's Movement

Although Germany had been a locus for women's activism since the 19th century (what has been called the 'First Wave'), the upheavals of the world wars and Nazism meant that by the 1970s there was little awareness of this earlier women's activism.[53] From Olympe de Gouges to the women's suffrage movement, as Bovenschen declared, 'we didn't know anything about all that when we started at uni in 1968. ... Suffragette was a bad word when I was young. If a man said that to a woman, it meant she was sexually unappetising.'[54]

But more than just lacking an historical role model, women activists were also missing a language to describe the shared experiences that brought them together as women. Compared to women's movements in the United States and Western Europe in the 19th century, the earlier women's movement in Germany was starkly divided along political lines between liberal-bourgeois feminists and socialist feminists. As Myra Marx Ferree has argued, this historical legacy hindered the emergence of gender as a politically unifying category for women in Germany, as political organisation had traditionally been firmly tied to class.[55] This meant

[53] Feminist and women's rights campaigners had in fact been active in West Germany since 1945, as figures like Elisabeth Selbert, Marie-Elisabeth Lüders, Erna Scheffler, Ilse Lederer, Ilse Brandt and Anne-Marie Durand-Wever fought to wedge open a space for women's rights in the emerging Federal Republic. See Moeller, *Protecting Motherhood*; Christina von Oertzen, *Pleasures of a Surplus Income: Part-Time Work, Gender Politics and Social Change in West Germany, 1955–1969* (Oxford: Berghahn, 2007); Ann-Katrin Gembries, Theresia Theuke and Isabel Heineman, eds, *Children by Choice? Changing Values, Reproduction and Family Planning in the 20th Century* (Berlin: De Gruyter, 2018). On memory in 1960s/1970s feminism, see Ilse Lenz, 'Wer sich wo und wie erinnern wollte? Die Neuen Frauenbewegungen und soziale Ungleichheit nach Klasse, "Rasse" und Migration' in *Erinnern, vergessen, umdeuten? Europäische Frauenbewegungen im 19. und 20. Jahrhundert*, edited by Angelika Schaser, Sylvia Schraut and Petra Steymans-Kurs (Frankfurt am Main: Campus, 2019): pp. 255–284.
[54] Rapp and Voigt, 'Kinder sind die Falle'. See also Belinda Davis, 'The Personal is Political: Gender, Politics, and Political Activism in Modern German History' in *Gendering Modern German History. Rewriting Historiography*, edited by Karen Hagemann and Jean H. Quataert (New York: Berghahn, 2007): pp. 107–127.
[55] Ferree, *Varieties of Feminism*.

that when women began organising in the 1970s, they needed to determine what brought them, and would hold them, together as a movement.[56]

To this end, in the early 1970s, women in the Federal Republic formed physical and discursive spaces where they could discuss their shared experiences of womanhood. In Berlin, building on the work of the *Aktionsrat*, Helke Sander formed a new women's group, *Brot und Rosen* (Bread and Roses) in 1971. At the same time, six women from the gay rights group Homosexual Action West Berlin formed their own autonomous women's group.[57] Together, these two groups opened Germany's first Women's Centre in West Berlin's Kreuzberg neighbourhood in March 1973.[58] This centre would be a major meeting point for feminist activism in the city.[59] A Federal Women's Congress also convened for the first time in Frankfurt in 1972, bringing together 400 women from across the country to discuss women's issues and enable feminist networking at a federal level. Later in the 1970s, the development of feminist media also enabled conversations between women, with the first feminist publishing house, *Frauenoffensive*, starting in 1975 followed by the release of the major feminist magazines *Courage* and *EMMA* in 1976 and 1977, respectively. Aside from these developments, women also met around kitchen tables and in church halls; they raised women's issues at their unions and took part in protests and demonstrations.[60] This early activism touched on many key issues of women's inequality: pay discrimination, women's education, gender in the workplace and the international position of women.[61]

But by far the largest, and most unifying, campaign focused on abortion. Starting in the early 1970s, women in West Germany converged around the issue of reproductive rights and the decriminalisation of abortion. This was the first major campaign of the New Women's Movement and was a formative example for domestic violence activism. West German feminists were not alone in their fight either: the 1970s were a hugely active time for reproductive rights activism globally. Although many European states – the United Kingdom and most of Scandinavia

---

[56] See reflection of Helke Sander on the significance of feminism for her self-realisation: 'I learned back then how to take myself seriously ... that meant that I intellectually and emotionally examined my own situation and saw myself as a woman, an artist, a mother, a European, a white person, as a wage slave etc.' Interview with Sander in 'Wer glaubt noch an die Revolution?', *Die Tageszeitung*, 10 February 1981.

[57] See Cristina Perincioli, *Berlin wird feministisch! Das Beste, was von der 68er Bewegung blieb* (Berlin: Querverlag, 2015). This group would later become the *Lesbisches-Aktionszentrums* (Lesbian Action-Centre) in 1975.

[58] '"Frauen gemeinsam sind stark", Flugblatt, 1973', *FrauenMediaTurm*. Accessed on 10 November 2020: https://frauenmediaturm.de/wp-content/uploads/2018/04/73_D6_Rundbrief_gr.jpg.

[59] Karcher, *Sisters in Arms*; Perincioli, *Berlin wird feministisch!*.

[60] Lenz, *Die Neue Frauenbewegung*.

[61] See also the 'Protokoll zum Plenum des Bundesfrauenkongresses am 12. März 1972 in Frankfurt/M', *FrauenMediaTurm*. Accessed on 10 November 2020: https://frauenmediaturm.de/neue-frauenbeweg ung/protokoll-plenum-bundesfrauenkongress/. Also Lenz, *Die Neue Frauenbewegung*.

and Eastern Europe – had decriminalised abortion by this time, across Western Europe, the United States and parts of Australia, obtaining an abortion remained a criminal act.[62] The issues of birth control, reproductive rights and women's ability to make decisions about their own bodies thus became central campaigns for the emerging transnational women's movement.[63]

For much of the 20th century, access to and control of reproductive choice has been one of the most crucial flashpoints for women activists globally.[64] As historians have highlighted, the regulation of family planning and contraception and the concomitant debates about who should bear children and how many they should ideally have, have long been tied to state- and nation-building projects. Indeed, birth control has facilitated the realisation of racial or eugenic ideals and has been used to limit the reproductive decision-making power of women, especially women from racialised or colonised groups and working-class women.[65] Margaret Sanger, a pioneer of birth control, even toyed with calling her movement 'race control' and 'population control'.[66]

---

[62] The GDR lagged behind many other socialist states at this time, only introducing first-trimester abortions in 1972. On abortion in the GDR, see Donna Harsch, 'Society, the State and Abortion in East Germany, 1950–1972', *American Historical Review*, Vol. 102, No. 1 (1997): pp. 53–84.

[63] See, for example, the emerging work of Maud Anne Bracke on the history of reproductive rights in Europe. Maud Anne Bracke, 'Inventing Reproductive Rights: Sex, Population, and Feminism in Europe, 1945–1990'. *Podcasts of the German Historical Institute London*, 15 July 2020.

[64] For global and transnational studies, see Gembries, Theuke and Heineman, *Children by Choice?*.

[65] For further examples on the historical linkages between abortion, birth control, eugenics and nation-building, see Susanne Klausen, *Abortion under Apartheid: Nationalism, Sexuality, and Women's Reproductive Rights in South Africa* (New York: Oxford University Press, 2015); Anna Davin, 'Imperialism and Motherhood', *History Workshop*, No. 5 (1978): pp. 9–65; Ayça Alemdaroğlu, 'Politics of the Body and Eugenic Discourse in Early Republican Turkey', *Body and Society*, Vol. 11, No. 3(2005): pp. 61–76; Erica Millar, '"Too Many": Anxious White Nationalism and the Biopolitics of Abortion', *Australian Feminist Studies*, Vol. 30, No. 83 (2015): pp. 82–98; Kate Fisher and Simon Szreter, '"They Prefer Withdrawal": The Choice of Birth Control in Britain, 1918–1950', *The Journal of Interdisciplinary History*, Vol. 34, No. 2 (2003): pp. 263–291; Lynn M. Thomas, *Politics of the Womb: Women, Reproduction, and the State in Kenya* (Berkeley: University of California Press, 2003); Janet Farrell Brodie, *Contraception and Abortion in Nineteenth-Century America* (Ithaca: Cornell University Press, 1994); Linda Gordon, *Woman's Body, Woman's Right: A Social History of Birth Control in America* (New York: Viking, 1976). Also note that, as various historians have highlighted, feminist abortion rights campaigns have also been complicit in exploiting eugenic ideals and racial, class-based and ableist hierarchies to advocate for the rights of white, middle-class, heterosexual women. See, in particular, the discussion in Susanne Klausen and Alison Bashford, 'Eugenics, Feminism and Fertility Control' in *The Oxford Handbook of the History of Eugenics* (Oxford: Oxford University Press, August 2010), pp. 98–115. Also Ann Taylor Allen, 'Feminism and Eugenics in Germany and Britain, 1900–1940. A Comparative Perspective', *German Studies Review*, Vol. 23, No. 3 (2000): pp. 477–505; Dagmar Herzog, *Unlearning Eugenics: Sexuality, Reproduction, and Disability in Post-Nazi Europe* (Madison: University of Wisconsin, 2018); Bracke, 'Inventing Reproductive Rights.'

[66] Sanger made the following observation on the naming of 'birth control' in her autobiography: 'A new movement was starting and the baby had to have a name. It did not belong to Socialism nor was it in the labour field and it had much more to it than just the prevention of conception … The word control was good, but I did not like limitation – that was too limiting … My idea of control was bigger and freer. I wanted family in it, yet family control did not sound right. We tried population control,

This was certainly the case in Germany, where Paragraph 218, the law criminalising abortion, was first introduced in the Imperial Criminal Code of 1871.[67] From this time – and for much of the 20th century – debate and reform of Paragraph 218 centred on issues of religion, motherhood, declining birth rates, the defence of the German nation, self-determination and the rights of women as citizens, as well as eugenic and racial concerns.[68] This final element found its most radical expression during the Third Reich, as the Nazis bound the politics of reproduction to their racist and ultimately genocidal aims.[69] Under Hitler, punishments for encouraging, performing or receiving an abortion were increased, especially in cases involving women deemed racially fit by the regime. A 1943 Executive Order on the Protection of Marriage, Family and Motherhood even authorised the death penalty for cases where the abortion endangered the 'life blood of the German people'.[70] However, in cases where a foetus was believed to be disabled, or where the parents were Jewish or carriers of a genetic disorder, abortion was permitted. Parallel to this, the Law for the Prevention of Hereditary Diseases introduced in 1933 enabled the forced sterilisation of individuals determined to have certain mental or physical disabilities and conditions. Abortion was briefly permitted in the aftermath of the Second World War in response to the widespread rape of German women by occupying soldiers. However, following division in 1949, West Germany reverted to the pre-1933 formulation of Paragraph 218. In comparison, after 1950, East Germany permitted abortion on medical grounds, or if one of the parents carried a genetic illness and from 1972 women were able to obtain an

---

race control and birth rate control. Then someone suggested, "Drop the rate". Birth rate control was the answer; we knew we had it': Margaret Sanger, *An Autobiography* (London: Victor Gollancz, 1939), p. 105.

[67] Although introduced across the Empire in 1871, the criminalisation of abortion in German-speaking lands reaches further back to the early modern era. For example, Article 133 of the 1532 *Constitutio Criminalis Carolina* made abortion punishable by death (either through drowning, or burial and impalement) in the Holy Roman Empire. Related laws were also enacted in 1572 in the *Kursächsische Constitution*, the Bavarian Criminal Codex of 1751 and the Hapsburg 1769 *Constitutio Criminalis Theresiana*. See Margaret Brannan Lewis, *Infanticide and Abortion in Early Modern Germany* (London: Routledge, 2016); Günter Jerouschek, 'Die juristische Konstruktion des Abtreibungsverbots' in *Frauen in der Geschichte des Rechts: von der frühen Neuzeit bis zur Gegenwart*, edited by Ute Gerhard (Munich: C.H. Beck, 1997): pp. 248–264.

[68] For scholarship on abortion and contraception in modern Germany, see Atina Grossmann, *Reforming Sex: The German Movement for Birth Control and Abortion Reform, 1920–1950* (New York: Oxford University Press, 1995); Cornelie Usborne, *Cultures of Abortion in Weimar Germany* (Oxford: Berghahn, 2007); Ann Taylor Allen, 'Mothers of the New Generation: Adele Schreiber, Helene Stöcker and the Evolution of a German Idea of Motherhood, 1900–1914', *Signs*, Vol. 10, No. 3 (1985): pp. 418–438; Ann Taylor Allen, *Feminism and Motherhood in Germany, 1800–1914* (New Brunswick: Rutgers University Press, 1991); Frevert, *Frauen-Geschichte*; Julia Roos, *Weimar through the Lens of Gender. Prostitution Reform, Woman's Emancipation, and German Democracy, 1919–33* (Ann Arbor: University of Michigan Press, 2010); Annette Timm, *The Politics of Fertility in Twentieth-Century Berlin* (New York: Cambridge University Press, 2010). See also the special issue on 'Abtreibung', *Aus Politik und Zeitgeschichte*, Vol. 20 (2019).

[69] For a detailed exploration of Nazism's link to sexuality, see Herzog, *Sex After Fascism* and the special issue on 'Sexuality and German Fascism' in *Journal of the History of Sexuality*, Vol. 11, No. 1/2 (2002).

[70] Verordnung zum Schutz von Ehe, Familie und Mutterschaft, Reichsgesetzblatt I 1943, S. 140.

abortion for any reason in the first trimester.[71] Despite these reforms, the historical links between abortion, racial and eugenic thinking did not disappear in the two Germanies with Nazi defeat.[72]

At the same time, however, Germany also has a strong history of advocacy for reproductive rights. The German *Bund für Mutterschutz* was one of the first women's organisations in the world to directly address abortion and birth control. As early as 1908, the *Bund Deutscher Frauenvereine* (an umbrella organisation for the growing feminist and women's rights movement in Wilhelmine Germany) debated the removal of Paragraph 218 at their annual conference in Breslau.[73] Although this discussion touched on women's right to sexual and reproductive self-determination, it was enveloped in a broader gendered framework of women's 'natural' maternal instincts and responsibilities.[74] In this way, decriminalising abortion was less about recognising women's autonomy and more about creating better mothers: by enabling women to give birth on their own terms, abortion would improve women's ability to care for their children. Abortion was also a central concern in the Weimar era, as a coalition of feminists, socialists, sex reformers and doctors called for the removal of Paragraph 218. Much like pre-First World War activism, however, abortion in the Weimar Republic was not understood in terms that would be classed as feminist today. At a time when the women's movement was starkly divided along class lines, abortion was primarily framed as an issue of class and economics.[75]

Against this backdrop, the abortion rights activism developing in the early 1970s was markedly different. From the late 1960s, Paragraph 218 came under increasing public and political scrutiny as part of a broad-scale reform of the Criminal Code. Although the criminalisation of abortion was upheld in the amended Code of 1969, with an estimated 300,000 to 1 million illegal abortions yearly in the Federal Republic in the 1960s, it was clear that reform was needed.[76] But this is also what

---

[71] Kirsten Poutrus, 'Von den Massenvergewaltigungen zum Mutterschutzgesetz: Abtreibungspolitik und Abtreibungspraxis in Ostdeutschland, 1945–1950' in *Die Grenzen der Diktatur. Staat und Gesellschaft in der DDR*, edited by Richard Bessel and Ralph Jessen (Göttingen: Vandenhoeck & Ruprecht, 1996): pp. 170–198; Atina Grossmann, 'A Question of Silence. The Rape of German Women by Occupation Soldiers', *October*, Vol. 72 (1995): pp. 42–63; Harsch, 'Society, the State and Abortion in East Germany'.

[72] Grossmann, *Reforming Sex*; Herzog, *Unlearning Eugenics*.

[73] Allen, *Feminism and Motherhood in Germany*.

[74] Ibid.

[75] Grossmann, *Reforming Sex*.

[76] On the reform of the Criminal Code, see Bundesgesetzblatt, Nr. 52, 30.6.1969. Also: Dirk von Behren, 'Kurze Geschichte des Paragrafen 218 Strafgesetzbuch', *Aus Politik und Zeitgeschichte*, Vol. 20 (2019): pp. 12–19. Statistics on the rate of illegal abortion come from journalist Susanne von Paczensky, who estimated that in 1965, 300,000 women had an illegal abortion in the FRG. Later figures from Frauenaktion 70 and Alice Schwarzer placed the numbers higher, at between 500,000 and 1 million. See Susanne von Paczensky, *Gemischte Gefühle: Von Frauen, die ungewollt schwanger sind* (Munich: C.H. Beck, 1987); Frauenaktion 70, 'Argumente und Forderungen' in Lenz, *Die Neue Frauenbewegung*, p. 75; 'Wir haben abgetrieben!', *Stern*, 6 June 1971.

brought women to feminism and bound them together as a political movement: at a time when access to the contraceptive pill was tightly restricted and sexual education primarily focused on abstinence, unwanted pregnancy and illegal abortion was a widely shared experience for women in West Germany.[77] The call to decriminalise abortion resonated strongly with women and throughout the early 1970s, feminist organising against Paragraph 218 grew rapidly. In Frankfurt, there was the *Weiberrat* and *Frauenaktion 70* (Women's Action 70); in Munich, there was the *Rote Frauen* (Red Women) and Berlin had *Brot und Rosen*, not to mention the many other smaller groups and everyday discussions that women engaged in about their reproductive rights. At the federal level, *Aktion-218* (Action-218) acted as an umbrella organisation, bringing together women's groups from across West Germany and coordinating national protest against the continued criminalisation of abortion.[78] While women from only seven cities took part in the first national meeting of *Aktion-218*, at the second meeting, only one month later in July 1971, women from 16 women's groups and 20 different cities took part. The movement only grew from there.

But it was not only the experience of unwanted pregnancy that brought women to abortion rights activism. It was also the broader issues of self-determination and autonomy, which had slipped off the feminist agenda in the 1920s, that so echoed with women. Much like the *Aktionsrat*'s work on motherhood and *Kinderläden*, Paragraph 218 was a tangible example of the systemic ways in which society not only limited women's choices, but also placed them outside of their control.[79] With clear echoes to Sander's earlier writings, the 1972 *Women's Handbook* published by *Brot und Rosen* declared 'We [women] must, through an illegal abortion, become criminals, just so that we can do normal things that are essential for our self-worth, such as finishing our studies, keeping our jobs and avoiding the physical and material damage of having children.'[80]

As Ilse Lenz highlights, in the 1960s and 1970s, although women were typically the ones who maintained a lifelong responsibility for a child, the decision of whether to have a baby in the first place was largely in men's hands. At that time, not only did men have a legal right to have sex with their wife, but the majority

[77] Claudia Roesch, *Wunschkinder: Eine transnationale Geschichte der Familienplanung in der Bundesrepublik Deutschland* (Göttingen: Vandenhoeck & Ruprecht, 2021); Eva-Marie Silies, *Liebe, Lust und Last. Die Pille als weibliche Generationserfahrung in der Bundesrepublik 1960–1980* (Göttingen: Wallstein Verlag, 2010).

[78] *Frauenjahrbuch '75*.

[79] Motherhood continued to bind women to the feminist cause throughout the 1970s and 1980s: Yanara Schmacks, '"Motherhood is Beautiful": Conceptions of Maternalism in the West German New Women's Movement between Eroticization and Ecological Protest', *Central European History*, Vol. 53, No. 4 (2020): pp. 811–834. Lucy Delap similarly describes motherhood as a site of feminist 'gut feeling': Delap, *Feminisms*, p. 242.

[80] Brot und Rosen, *Frauenhandbuch Nr. 1. Abtreibung und Verhütungsmittel* (Berlin: Brot und Rosen Selbstverlag, 1972), p. 21.

of doctors were men, as were the criminal court judges who presided over cases of illegal abortion.[81] In this way, contesting Paragraph 218 was about putting control of women's bodies back into the hands of women.[82] As a 1975 flyer from the Frankfurt Women's Centre argued, 'Paragraph 218 is more than just a paragraph that bans or permits abortion. It reveals all the contempt for women and misogyny that rules in this society.'[83]

Unlike previous women's activism, the campaign to decriminalise abortion was heavily mediatised. Women's groups and feminist activists purposefully engaged in provocative protests that were designed to capture media attention. Moreover, progressive male and feminist journalists used their editorial positions to publicly advocate for women's rights.[84] One of the most prominent figures in the Paragraph 218 campaign in West Germany was feminist activist and journalist Alice Schwarzer. Originally from Wuppertal, Schwarzer spent the 1960s living between Paris and West Germany, and worked as a freelance political journalist between 1970 and 1974.[85] It was in Paris that Schwarzer started her engagement in feminism and women's politics, befriending Simone de Beauvoir and joining the Parisian feminist organisation, *Le Mouvement pour la libération des femmes* (Movement for the Liberation of Women). As a member of this group, Schwarzer was involved in the campaign to decriminalise abortion in France and assisted with the *Manifestes des 343* (Manifesto of the 343).[86] In this manifesto, published in the magazine *Nouvel Observateur* on 5 April 1971, 343 French women admitted to having had an illegal abortion. Although this self-incrimination exposed the signatories to criminal prosecution, it also tangibly demonstrated the failure of the law to prevent abortion.[87]

Not long after its publication, magazines began contacting the two journalists responsible for organising the Manifesto. Wary of what this would mean for the campaign, one of the original journalists, Jean Moreau, asked Schwarzer to run a

---

[81] Lenz cites that in 1970, 80 per cent of doctors and 94 per cent of judges in the Federal Republic were male: Lenz, *Die Neue Frauenbewegung*, p. 70.

[82] Similar critiques, about the way women's bodies were objectified in society were made as early as 1969 in the foundational article, Karin Schrader-Klebert, 'Die kulturelle Revolution der Frau', *Kursbuch* 17 (June 1969), pp. 1–46.

[83] 'Flugblatt zur §218-Demonstration, February 1975' in *Frauenjahrbuch '75*, p. 75.

[84] Note, however, that Christina von Hodenberg argues that the liberalisation of the media throughout the late 1960s and 1970s was not wholly a result of the entrance of young, progressive-minded journalists into the field. Instead, it reflects longer trends in the West German media landscape: Christina von Hodenberg, 'Der Kampf um die Redaktionen. «1968» und der Wandel der westdeutschen Massenmedien', in *Wo '1968' liegt: Reform und Revolte in der Geschichte der Bundesrepublik*, edited by Christina von Hodenberg and Detlef Siegfried (Göttingen: Vandenhoeck and Ruprecht, 2006): pp. 139–163.

[85] Alice Schwarzer, *Lebenslauf* (Cologne: Kiepenheuer and Witsch, 2011).

[86] Ibid.

[87] On abortion rights campaigns in France, see Schulz, *Der lange Atem der Provokation*; Ann Taylor Allen, *Women in Twentieth-Century Europe* (Basingstoke and New York: Palgrave Macmillan, 2007).

similar action in West Germany. Wanting to ensure that it was taken seriously as a form of 'collective, political action' and not simply sensational gossip, she approached the editor of the illustrated weekly newsmagazine *Stern* and promised to find 300 to 400 women, including celebrities, who would publicly admit to having obtained an abortion.[88] This resulted in one of the most infamous pieces of feminist publishing in the Federal Republic: the 'We Had Abortions!' exposé. Published almost a month after the French *Manifestes*, on 6 June 1971, 374 West German women claimed: 'I've had an abortion. I am against Paragraph 218 and for children who are wanted.'[89]

Such provocative protest methods only escalated as debate over abortion reform continued at a federal level. Between 1972 and 1974, the Bundestag deliberated between two alternative solutions to Paragraph 218. On the one hand was the *Indikationsmodell*, or the indication model, which was initially proposed by the federal government in 1972 and was in part supported by the Christian Democrats. Under this reform, women would be able to receive an abortion on the basis of certain 'indicators', which included socio-economic considerations, the health of the mother, whether the pregnancy had been conceived through rape or incest and eugenic concerns. On the other hand, was the *Fristenmodell* or time-limited model. This reform, favoured by feminists and some SPD and FDP members, would allow a woman to obtain an abortion at any point in the first trimester, regardless of the circumstances. While the Bundestag debated these different legal alternatives to Paragraph 218, women from across the Federal Republic took part in mass protests, demonstrations, teach-ins and even started a letter-writing campaign to the Justice Minister Gerhard Jahn.[90]

The third reading of the proposed amendment to Paragraph 218 was set for April 1974. In the lead-up to this vote, feminists throughout West Germany organised confrontational and provocative campaigns in order to persuade sitting members of the SPD and FDP to support the *Fristenmodell*. On 6 February 1974, nearly 2,000 women attended a meeting organised by *Brot und Rosen* at the Technical University in Berlin to coordinate protest efforts.[91] One month later, a group of Berlin-based feminists, including Alice Schwarzer, organised a state-wide demonstration called *Letzter Versuch* or 'Last Try'.[92] As a part of this action, Schwarzer, along with other feminist activists, gathered the support of the medical community.[93] On 9 March, 14 doctors performed a public abortion in a Berlin

---

[88] Schwarzer, *Lebenslauf*, p. 235.
[89] 'Wir haben abgetrieben!', *Stern*.
[90] 'Aktion-218' in Lenz, *Die Neue Frauenbewegung*.
[91] Brot und Rosen. '"Einladung" (1974)', *FrauenMediaTurm*. Accessed on 10 November 2020: https://frauenmediaturm.de/wp-content/uploads/2018/04/74_0a_EinlBrotRosen.jpg.
[92] Initiativgruppe 218 Letzte Versuch, 'Rundbrief', 20 February 1974. *FrauenMediaTurm*. Accessed on 10 November 2020: https://frauenmediaturm.de/wp-content/uploads/2018/06/Rundbrief_Aktion_letzter_Versuch_1974.jpg.
[93] Schwarzer, *Lebenslauf*.

apartment, using the vacuum aspiration method, that was not yet in use in the Federal Republic.[94] Schwarzer even arranged for the procedure to be filmed as part of a special report on abortion for the public news programme, *Panorama*. At the press conference ahead of the procedure, the doctors declared that 'Every day in the Federal Republic, 2,000 to 3,000 illegal abortions are performed. Our action shall end this hypocrisy. We demand equal rights for all, the development of safe contraception and child-friendly living conditions.'[95] Two days later, in an extension of the previous 'We Had Abortions!' campaign, in the 11 March 1974 issue of *Der Spiegel*, 329 doctors not only admitted to having 'without financial advantage, performed abortions or helped women obtain an abortion', but also that they would do so again, despite its illegality.[96]

In many respects, these campaigns were successful. It was estimated that between 70 to 80 per cent of women backed the decriminalisation of abortion.[97] The popular liberal press – *Stern* and *Der Spiegel* – were also largely supportive of decriminalising abortion, even if their attitudes towards women remained problematic in other ways.[98] Despite such widespread support, this activism also provoked consternation, fear and backlash. Soon after the release of the initial 'We Had Abortions!' issue of *Stern*, police in various cities in West Germany led raids and crackdowns on women's groups, using the article as a 'hit-list' to target women who had had illegal abortions and the groups that supported them.[99] Most shockingly, Schwarzer's report on abortion was pulled from screening by the directors-general of the ARD (an organisation of public regional broadcasters) only an hour before it was due to air. The special had gained media attention in the days prior. *Der Spiegel* even needled NDR, the regional broadcaster responsible for producing *Panorama*, saying 'On Monday this week [11 March], if the NDR hasn't yet gotten a stomach ache, the television program "Panorama" will show a documentary made by the French-residing journalist Alice Schwarzer. The film shows an abortion performed using vacuum aspiration.'[100] Unsurprisingly, the

---

[94] Vacuum aspiration is now the most common method of abortion used in Germany.

[95] Quoted in 'Abtreibung: Aufstand der Schwestern', *Der Spiegel*, 11 March 1974. Also quoted in Schwarzer, *Lebenslauf*, p. 273.

[96] '329 Mediziner bezichtigen sich des Verstoßes gegen Paragraph 218 'Hiermit erkläre ich ...'', *Der Spiegel*, 11 March 1974, p. 30.

[97] Brot und Rosen, *Frauenhandbuch Nr. 1*; '329 Mediziner bezichtigen sich'.

[98] The liberalisation of pornography laws in the late 1960s and early 1970s led to a 'porn wave' in the West German media, which feminists actively challenged. See Elizabeth Heineman, *Before Porn Was Legal: The Erotica Empire of Beate Uhse* (Chicago: University of Chicago Press, 2013); Sybille Steinbacher, *Wie der Sex nach Deutschland kam. Der Kampf um Sittlichkeit und Anstand in der frühen Bundesrepublik* (Munich: Siedler, 2011). On the representation of gender in the media more broadly, see Adrian Bingham, *Gender, Modernity, and the Popular Press in Inter-war Britain* (Oxford: Oxford University Press, 2004).

[99] Lenz, *Die Neue Frauenbewegung*.

[100] 'Abtreibung: Aufstand der Schwestern'.

broadcaster received various letters of complaint from the public, including one sent by Cardinal Julius Döpfner, the chair of the German Conference of Bishops, as well as the Archbishop of Munich and Freising.[101] Döpfner's protest, alongside the fact that he pressed for charges for the illegal abortion filmed for the report, was one of the main reasons it was pulled from air. In solidarity with Schwarzer, the other *Panorama* journalists refused to allow their reports to be shown in the episode and for 45 minutes only an empty studio was broadcast.

Despite these responses, the *Letzter Versuch* campaign was successful, albeit short-lived. The *Panorama* scandal provoked a mass media response and resulted in even more protest, catapulting Paragraph 218 into the public eye as never before.[102] At the third reading of the Criminal Code reform, the ruling coalition changed their support for the indication model of abortion and instead backed a time-limited law. In June 1974, the Federal President signed a bill allowing women to obtain an abortion in the first 12 weeks of pregnancy for any reason, so long as it was performed by a doctor and following prior medical consultation. However, the constitutionality of the new law was quickly challenged by the national CDU and its Bavarian counterpart, the Christian Social Union (CSU), as well as the minister presidents of other federal states. In 1975, the Constitutional Court in Karlsruhe struck down the new law on the basis of the constitutional guarantee of the sanctity of life. In place of the new reform then, the *Indikationsmodell* was introduced, allowing women to obtain an abortion only under certain conditions. In 1976 – five years after the publication of the groundbreaking 'We Had Abortions!' statement – this new law came into effect. This was also the same year that the first domestic violence shelter opened in West Berlin.

The legacy of this abortion rights campaign is complicated. The legal defeat resonated throughout the women's movement in West Germany and left its mark on the years to come, including on domestic violence activism.[103] Although the hopes for unrestricted abortion were defeated and the broad-scale coalition for women's rights largely dissolved afterwards, activism against Paragraph 218 brought women in West Germany together as never before. Reproductive rights fomented the feminist movement and opened the door to a broader examination of the ways in which society limited, regulated and controlled women's bodies, choices and lifeworlds simply because of their gender. Paragraph 218 activism

---

[101] Günter Quast, 'Eine Meldung der NDR-Pressestelle', 11 March 1974. *FrauenMediaTurm*. Accessed on 10 November 2020: https://frauenmediaturm.de/neue-frauenbewegung/guenter-quast-meldung-ndr-pressestelle-panorama-1974/; 'NDR sendet Abtreibungsfilm allein', *Frankfurter Neue Presse*, 13 March 1974. *FrauenMediaTurm*. Accessed on 3 May 2022: https://frauenmediaturm.de/wp-content/uploads/2018/04/74_D6_TZ_AliceNDR.jpg); Schwarzer, *Lebenslauf*.

[102] 'NDR sendet Abtreibungsfilm allein'; Karl-Hein Janßen, 'Keine Abtreibung auf dem Bildschirm? Warum und wie eine Panorama-Sendung verhindert wurde' *Die Zeit*, 15 March 1974; 'Sprengsatz für die Moral', *Der Spiegel*, 18 March 1974. Also Schulz, *Der lange Atem der Provokation*, pp. 168–169.

[103] See 'Von hinten gegriffen', *Der Spiegel*, 24 February 1975.

was also a gateway to address related issues of birth control, women's health and sexuality and even violence against women.[104] As Alice Schwarzer has argued, while the failure of the abortion rights campaign was 'a dark hour in the history of women's struggle', it was also 'not a total defeat. The §218 campaign shook women awake. The fight against compulsory motherhood must be thanked for making women realise what §218 has to do with their stunted sexuality and being underpaid in their jobs.'[105]

Abortion activism also underscored important political lessons for activists. Since the late 1960s, women's political organisation had largely taken place without men. Groups like the *Aktionsrat* and the *Weiberrat* excluded men in order to create spaces where, unlike the student movement, women could talk freely and share their ideas. Reflecting on this, Bovenschen argued that 'what was so astonishing for us was that we needed to separate [from men]. We had to separate ourselves and that had no great programmatic foundation, it was just so that we could get to know one another. We kicked men out forcefully, in order to make this happen. We had to separate, in order to initiate the understanding process with one another.'[106] Notwithstanding the coalitions that were built with men, especially male doctors, over the course of the abortion campaign, separatism and autonomy became entrenched as fundamental principles of the New Women's Movement.[107] If anything, the failure of the state and Leftist politics to acknowledge the rights of women to make decisions about their own bodies and define their own life choices, only made feminists more determined to work without men and the state.

The politics of separatism and autonomy not only shaped the way women organised, but also how they approached women's emancipation. In this way, feminism in West Germany became less about being equal with men and more about creating a world in which women could define their own success and not be bound by patriarchal norms and worldviews. As the 1976 *Women's Year Book* argued

> women should break into male-dominated fields. More women in politics! More women in the sciences etc. Men should get involved in the traditionally female fields (the household) ... Women should be able to do what men do. This idea of women's emancipation formally remains, because what men do is not conceptually challenged. The principle of "we want to too" or "we can too" measures emancipation

---

[104] Freeland, 'Women's Bodies and Feminist Subjectivity in West Germany'.

[105] Alice Schwarzer, 'Nach 100 Jahren wieder Frauenklinik', *EMMA* (May 1977): p. 9.

[106] Sylvia Bovenschen, Sigrid Damm-Rüger and Sybille Plogstedt, 'Diskussionsleitung: Halina Bendkowski Antiautoritärer Anspruch und Frauenemanzipation – Die Revolte in der Revolte', 1 June 1988. Accessed on 10 November 2020: http://www.infopartisan.net/archive/1968/index.html

[107] As Ferree notes, there were significant historical legacies marking German feminism as separatist and autonomous: Ferree, *Varieties of Feminism*.

against men, and in doing so defines what we want against men. … The fight against women's [traditional] roles cannot become the fight for men's roles.[108]

This approach to women's rights, with its emphasis on autonomy, separatism and anti-authoritarianism, led to a significant transformation of feminist activism by 1976, which the literature has described as a turning point for feminism. In comparison to the mass mobilisation of the Paragraph 218 campaign, the years spanning from 1976 to 1985 have been labelled by scholars as the 'women's project movement', with activists working to create spaces for the performance of an alternative, feminist womanhood.[109] Women's centres, bookstores and cafes proliferated throughout West Germany during this period, as activists attempted to put the politics of West German feminism into everyday practice. The exclusion of men, non-hierarchical structures and *Parteilichkeit* (solidarity among women), to name a few, were key parts of this practice of living feminism. More fundamentally though, activists designed these sites as an alternative venue for womanhood and its expression outside of the patriarchy of the Left-scene and the state. As the 1976 *Women's Year Book* warned women: 'The idea of entering into and mixing as equals in male institutions will not break the thousand-year-old power of men, will not bring into question their values that hide within every fibre of these institutions.'[110]

But the abortion rights campaign also created challenges for feminism going forward. This was a major defeat for a years-long feminist campaign and women's emancipation was still not universally accepted. Abortion was contested by Christian Democrats at both federal and state levels. Religious leaders, especially Catholics, also opposed abortion. Although the liberal press, including *Der Spiegel* and *Stern*, had supported abortion rights, they nevertheless continued to brazenly objectify women and frequently used gratuitous female nudity to bolster sales.[111] Moreover, the rise of left-wing terrorism, of female terrorists and the confrontational, militant tactics used by feminist activists during the Paragraph 218 campaign created a widespread conflation of female violence and an excess of women's emancipation. As the works of Clare Bielby, Katharina Karcher and Patricia Melzer have shown, in the popular imagination and the media, feminism was linked with violence and fears of violence.[112] This was not only rhetoric or fear-mongering: on 18 December 1975, 12 members of the West German state security searched the rooms of the West Berlin Women's Centre supposedly looking for an anarchist.

---

[108] *Frauenjahrbuch '76* (Munich: Verlag Frauenoffensive, 1976): pp. 77–78.
[109] Ferree, *Varieties of Feminism*; Lenz, *Die Neue Frauenbewegung*.
[110] *Frauenjahrbuch '76*, p. 79.
[111] For a feminist discussion on the use of naked images of women in advertising and the media, see Rosalind Gill, *Gender and the Media* (Cambridge: Polity, 2007).
[112] Bielby, *Violent Women in Print*; Karcher, *Sisters in Arms*; Patricia Melzer, *Death in the Shape of a Young Girl: Women's Political Violence in the Red Army Faction* (New York: New York University Press, 2015).

In the process of the search, however, they also took the names of all the women present at the centre, went through the records of the women who had visited the centre for pregnancy counselling, sketched a floorplan of the centre, made notes of the posters on the walls and finally they took all the women without identification to the station for processing.[113]

In light of the defeat of Paragraph 218 and the turn towards project-based activism, it is not wholly surprising that scholars posit 1976 as a liminal threshold for feminism in West Germany. But while the campaign to decriminalise abortion may have largely come to an end, as domestic violence activists in Berlin would discover, it had left a lasting impression and would continue to shape feminist practices.

Domestic Violence Activism

The movement to tackle domestic violence in the Federal Republic began in the winter of 1974. The initial successes of the Paragraph 218 campaign had already proven tenuous: the new law permitting first-trimester abortions was under judicial review and the Constitutional Court was only months away from declaring the law invalid. And yet, the New Women's Movement, which had coalesced so strongly around the issue of reproductive rights, was blossoming. Despite its limited success, the Paragraph 218 campaign galvanised other women's issues in West Germany and the plethora of issue-based projects and groups emerging in the mid-1970s proved that the women's movement would endure.

One such group emerged at the Berlin Women's Centre in Kreuzberg, which had already been a significant locus of feminist activism against Paragraph 218. Known as '*Projekt Frauenhaus*' (Project Women's Shelter), the group's precise membership in these early days is difficult to ascertain. What we do know is that it initially consisted of five women, of whom most came from the wartime or postwar generation. Importantly, they all worked in the social sciences or social welfare and had, either professionally or through their engagement with the women's movement, experience working with 'battered women'.[114] As such, they were not only well aware of the serious issues women faced in the home, but knew that there was very little effective support available to women living with a violent husband.

The group was determined to change this reality. By creating a shelter and counselling service that would operate as 'part of the women's movement' and not as part of the state or welfare system, they sought to empower women to leave

---

[113] Frauenzentrum Berlin, *Gewalt gegen Frauen in Ehe, Psychiatrie, Gynäkologie, Vergewaltigung, Beruf, Film und was Frauen dagegen tun. Beiträge zum Internationalen Tribunal über Gewalt gegen Frauen, Brüssel März 1976* (Berlin, 1976), A Rep 400 BRD 22 Broschuren, FFBIZ.

[114] Konstanze Pistor, 'Frauenhaus Berlin' in *Gewalt in der Ehe und was Frauen dagegen tun*, edited by Sarah Haffner (Berlin: Verlag Klaus Wagenbach, 1981), pp. 141–150.

abusive relationships.[115] For activists, this program of autonomous, grassroots feminist support stood in stark contrast with the work of institutionalised and state-run social and welfare services, which feminists argued provided women with 'almost no chance of becoming independent and re-integrating into society' and only left them vulnerable to further violence.[116]

At a time when there was very little critical public engagement with gender-based violence, the shelter group's first task was to unmask it. For two years, the group researched, organised, discussed and campaigned against domestic abuse. They worked to get public and political recognition that domestic violence was a serious issue of women's inequality and that support services were urgently needed. They also spent time investigating how to organise and run a shelter, looking at international shelter projects and best practices. By mid-1975, they started a public campaign, hanging posters and giving out pamphlets on violence against women. They created a bank account for donations and slowly started to engage the popular media.[117] They also participated in international feminist events, attending the 1976 International Tribunal on Crimes against Women held in Brussels.[118] The group itself grew larger, reaching 15 members before the opening of the shelter in 1976.

In doing so, these shelter activists also claimed domestic violence as a feminist issue. Just as Paragraph 218 campaigners linked the criminalisation of abortion to the broader ways in which women's lives and bodies were controlled, feminists made domestic violence into an issue of women's rights and their fundamental inequality to men. As the shelter project's proposal to the Berlin Senate began 'The general discrimination of women in all areas of society finds its most brutal expression in the humiliating and life-threatening abuse they experience in their private lives at the hands of men.'[119] The fact that men could beat and kill their wives with impunity, that women were not listened to or helped, that people could hear or know what was happening to their neighbours and friends and do nothing, served as proof that women were not equal and that patriarchal structures and power imbalances served to keep women down. The shelter project was aimed at challenging this patriarchal order, not only by exposing it, but by supporting women to become empowered. As an early piece on the shelter project argued, 'We are of the opinion that women must begin to help, protect and defend themselves.'[120]

Feminists used these radical critiques to challenge and contest the prevailing social order. Since the establishment of the Federal Republic, women's roles were

---

[115] Ibid., p. 141.
[116] Projektantrag zur Einrichtung eines Frauenhauses in Berlin (West) (1976), B Rep 002/12504, LAB.
[117] Pistor, 'Frauenhaus Berlin'.
[118] *Frauen gegen Männergewalt. Berliner Frauenhaus für misshandelte Frauen. Erster Erfahrungsbericht* (Berlin-West: Frauenselbstverlag, 1978).
[119] Projektantrag zur Einrichtung eines Frauenhauses in Berlin (West) (1976), B Rep 002/12504, LAB.
[120] Pistor, 'Frauenhaus Berlin', p. 141.

primarily based in the home, as mothers and as wives. This was not only a corner-stone of the post-war political rehabilitation of West Germany, but also reflected the long-standing political tradition that, since the 19th century, tied liberalism to a patriarchal sexual-moral order in Germany.[121] Despite legislating women's equality in the 1949 Constitution, West German policy and lawmaking had been guided by conservative, Christian patriarchal norms that delimited women's roles to the family.[122] Given this historical legacy, how would the feminist challenge resonate publicly and politically? How would West Germans respond to the creation of spaces where women and children could go to escape their violent husbands and fathers? Would domestic violence be taken seriously as a sign of women's inequality? Moreover, what would be made of the feminist orientation of the shelter project, especially in light of the failure of Paragraph 218 reform?

Conclusion

Projekt Frauenhaus would open its domestic violence shelter on 1 November 1976. The first of its kind in Germany, news of the shelter spread quickly in the West German media. Most news outlets drafted their articles based on the information given to the German Press Agency by the shelter organisers. This included providing the phone number and mailing address of the shelter for any woman in need of help.[123] The tabloid *Bild*, however, took a different approach. Rather than use the information provided by the organisation, *Bild* sent an undercover journalist to the shelter under the pretence of being a battered woman. In the article 'Women's Shelter: I was happy once I was outside', the journalist reported

> women and children who can't laugh … a massive kitchen and – women. One
> stares off into space, a cigarette hanging from the corner of her mouth. Before her
> on the table a cup of coffee. Others are arguing. It's about the cleaning duties for

---

[121] Lynn Abrams, 'Concubinage, Cohabitation and the Law: Class and Gender Relations in Nineteenth Century Germany', Vol. 5, No. 1 (1993), pp. 81–100; Lynn Abrams, 'Martyrs or Matriarchs? Working-Class Women's Experience of Marriage in Germany before the First World War', *Women's History Review*, Vol. 1, No. 3 (1992), pp. 357–376; Abrams and Harvey, *Gender Relations in German History*; Gerhard, *Verhältnisse und Verhinderungen*; Moeller, *Protecting Motherhood*.

[122] Moeller, *Protecting Motherhood*; Herzog, *Sex After Fascism*; Elizabeth Heineman, *What Difference Does a Husband Make?: Women and Marital Status in Nazi and Postwar Germany* (Berkeley: University of California Press, 1999).

[123] 'Tabuthema wird nun endlich öffentlich diskutiert', *Metall*, 14 December 1976; Monika Held, 'Warum schlagen eigentlich so viele Männer ihre Frauen? Von kleinauf heißt's: Du bist nichts und er ist alles', *Metall*, 14 December 1976; Ulrike Pfeil, 'In der Festung des Mannes. Von den Schwierigkeiten, ein "privates" Problem öffentlich anzugehen', *Stuttgarter Zeitung*, 22 May 1978; 'Frauenmißhandlung in der Bundesrepublik. Schrei, wenn du kannst!', *Das da*, February 1977; 'Schrei leise', *Hessische Allgemein*, 25 September 1976; Ilja Weiss 'Warum Männer Frauen schlagen: Strafe häufigstes Motiv – Kaum Folgen für die Täter', *Darmstädter Echo*, 18 December 1976; 'Zuflucht für misshandelte Frauen', *Der Abend*, 1 November 1976.

tomorrow: who is mopping the stairs and whose fault is it that the toilets are always clogged. And in the middle, children. I have hardly seen a smile. ... The bathroom is filthy. The whole house is filthy ... The only way of spending the time: television or books like *Women's Fight in the Soviet Union*, or bickering.[124]

This report clearly plays on gendered and class-based stereotypes of battered women, as broken, working-class individuals, not living up to middle-class ideals of femininity. But it also critiques the feminist orientation of the shelter, presenting it as a hotbed for communism, reminiscent of the earlier mocking depictions of women student activists. To add insult to injury, the article also gave the physical address of the shelter and told women to first contact their local council authorities. In doing so, they put the lives of all the women at the shelter at risk and upheld the power of the very institutions that had left women unprotected for so long. How much then had really changed between 1968 and 1976?

Over the course of the late 1960s, feminist politics spread throughout West Germany. From the *Tomatenwurf* to the formation of groups like the Berlin *Aktionsrat* and *Weiberräte*, women in West Germany were beginning to see how their lives and choices were shaped by their gender. But it was the emergence of a movement to decriminalise Paragraph 218 in the early 1970s that brought the feminist movement in West Germany into the public consciousness. Enmeshed in transnational networks, West German women took up many of the issues feminist movements in the West fought over. Women's health, reproductive rights, motherhood, sexuality and violence against women were all key concerns examined by the New Women's Movement in West Germany. However, at a time when patriarchal gender roles still very much governed society, feminism and women's organising were also incredibly destabilising to this status quo. They upset the gender order and in doing so shook the foundations of the West German state. Indeed, this was the very intention of feminist activism. Actions like 'We Had Abortions' were meant to challenge and critique the existence of gender inequalities.

Echoing this, the mainstream press sent contradictory messages about the nature and consequences of feminism and women's emancipation. Women activists had been mercilessly mocked and objectified in the media in the late 1960s, thereby pacifying their resistance and the challenges they presented to the established gender order. Moreover, as women engaged in militant protest and even terrorism, newspapers conflated female violence with women's emancipation. Although this changed to some extent with the campaign against Paragraph 218, as magazines, such as *Stern* and *Der Spiegel*, and the television programme *Panorama* supported the cause, this is not to say they wholeheartedly supported feminism or women's emancipation. Alongside publicising feminist campaigns,

---

[124] Quotes extracted from Frauengruppe am Institut für Publizistik, 'Frauen starren stumpfsinnig vor sich hin', *Courage* 2 (1977), p. 35 and Alice Schwarzer, 'Ein Tag im Haus für geschlagene Frauen', *EMMA*, 1 March 1977.

the media, in particular the commercial mass press, also perpetuated the object-ification and commodification of women's bodies. For example, despite having published 'We Had Abortions' in 1971, *Stern* continually used highly sexualised and objectifying images of women on their covers. In 1978, this even led Alice Schwarzer, alongside her magazine *EMMA*, to press charges against *Stern* for damaging the honour of women.

When the women's shelter movement emerged in 1974, they had to deal with this complicated inheritance. On the one hand, this process was productive. The years of feminist theorising and practice helped to define the way they approached and understood domestic violence. On the other hand, when they came to approach the government for funding, they also faced a legitimacy problem. Not only did mixed messages abound in the media about women's emancipation, but it was just over a year since the Constitutional Court had determined that the new abortion law was unconstitutional. Although there had been strong public support for the reform of Paragraph 218, there was still significant resistance from the CDU and the Catholic Church, as the *Panorama* scandal had revealed. What's more, the defeat of the new abortion law in 1975 deepened scepticism of the effect-iveness of feminist approaches. This posed a particular problem for the SPD, who had changed their platform at the last minute to support unrestricted abortion. In the lead-up to the 1976 election, the SPD faced a difficult choice. Would they again back feminist activists?

The following two chapters detail the evolution of *Projekt Frauenhaus*. They explore the politics, principles and, most importantly, the transformation of feminist domestic violence activism. From its radical origins, a well-established system of social care emerged in the Federal Republic. Politicians, across party divisions, came to accept the need for shelters and supported feminist domestic violence activism – something that never happened with abortion rights. Part of this transformation was due to the resolution of the challenge feminists and fem-inism posed. But this is not to say that feminist politics of domestic violence were seamlessly taken up. Instead, the evolution of domestic violence activism involved a long-standing process of negotiation, as activists attempted to resolve anxieties and legitimise feminism, which, as the next chapters reveal, ultimately involved the dilution and deradicalisation of feminist politics.

2

The Cost of Political Support

In late August 1976, a Dr Walter Scheuneman wrote to the Governing Mayor of West Berlin regarding the construction of a women's shelter near his home in the leafy suburb of Grunewald.[1] By this time, the Senate Office for Family, Youth and Sport had arranged for the shelter initiative to use a former Red Cross villa for their proposed project. Set outside of the inner city and with three floors of living space and a large garden, the house was ideal for this purpose. Indeed, it had already been used as a refuge for migrants from Poland and the Eastern Bloc arriving in Berlin after 1945. While Scheuneman's original letter is missing from the archive, presumably lost after the mayor's office forwarded it to the senator, it is clear from the response that Scheuneman had several questions about the project. Aside from details about the amount of construction required to the house, the letter centres on the care of the future shelter residents. Scheuneman was informed by the Senate Office that the planned shelter would offer enough space for 'at least 30 women and their children' and that it was intended for 'temporary accommodation'. Furthermore, any women residents with no independent income would be able to apply for welfare and there would be childcare available for working mothers. Ending on a slightly ominous note, however, the letter concluded by stating that 'It cannot be excluded that individual men will attempt to gain access to the shelter in order to get their wives back.'[2]

This clearly did little to allay the concerns of Dr Scheuneman. Only a week after the Senate Office replied to his initial letter, Scheuneman wrote again, but this time to both the Governing Mayor and the Senator for Family, Youth and Sport. In his letter to the mayor, Scheuneman complained about the unsatisfactory response of the Senate Office:

---

[1] Parts of this chapter were first published as: Jane Freeland, 'Gendering Value Change: Domestic Violence and Feminism in 1970s West Berlin', *German History*, Vol. 38, No. 4 (2020): pp. 638–655.
On 3 September 1976, the Mayor's office wrote to Scheuneman regarding his letter from 27 August 1976 saying that they had forwarded his concerns to the Senator for Family, Youth and Sport. Brief an Herrn. Dr.jur. Walter Scheuneman, 3 September 1976, B Rep 002, 12504, LAB.
[2] Brief an Herrn. Dr.jur. Walter Scheuneman, 22 September 1976, B Rep 002, 12504, LAB.

The Senate Office is not addressing the central problem nor the legal position, and still thinks that the luxury villa in Grunewald is particularly suited for this centre ... It is entirely inappropriate to bring up to 30 women into this misadventure ... If it must be so, then only Church institutions, which can be found in all parts of the city, are appropriate for dealing with this issue.

He then ended his letter with a plea for the mayor to 'personally intervene in this project before it is too late'.[3] His letter to the senator was even more alarmist, detailing what he thought were the 'serious considerations' the office had failed to consider. Not only was he wary of the costs of the shelter, but he was fearful of the danger it posed to the entire neighbourhood, with potentially violent men attempting to retrieve their wives and children. He also had much more fundamental concerns about what the shelter meant for the enduring stability of the family and West German society more generally.

Scheuneman's letters reveal palpable anxieties that the traditional structures and vestiges of power in West Germany were under threat. Assisting women fleeing an abusive husband was not in the purview of the Berlin Senate, argued Scheuneman, as 'No sovereign power can disregard a father's right to custody'.[4] Taking this line of argument even further, he claimed that the shelter actually impinged on men's paternal rights by allowing women to take their children away. Throughout the letter, he expresses extensive concern for the children living at the shelter. 'The primary goal of this project should be the care of children!', he declared, 'they've suffered enough from their family's misery. Now you want to lay another burden on their shoulders.' This burden, as he explained, included having to leave their homes in 'Kreuzberg, Tegel, Steglitz or Wannsee', only to have to travel back to these areas each day for school. Doing so, he believed was 'not good for their health or their learning! The children are guaranteed to be held back in work and in their career!' More worryingly for Scheuneman, 'That this congregation of potentially hyper-nervous women and their terrified children, who have to decide between father and mother, will not lead directly to saving the marriage, should be apparent.' Instead, he reiterated, it was the Church – not the state or a women's shelter – that should be responsible for such matters.[5]

Doctor Scheuneman, a jurist by education, continued to write to both the mayor and the senator until March 1977 – four months after the shelter he so vehemently opposed opened its doors.[6] Despite his stated concerns for the welfare of children, his letters reveal much else about his attitudes towards the sanctity

---

[3] Brief an Herrn Regierenden Bürgermeister von Berlin, 29 September 1976, B Rep 002, 12504, LAB.
[4] Brief Senator für Familie, Jugend und Sport, 28 September 1976, B Rep 002, 12504, LAB.
[5] Ibid.
[6] See the collection of Scheuneman's letters in B Rep 002, 12504, LAB. Some of Scheuneman's letters are also published in *Frauen gegen Männergewalt. Berliner Frauenhaus für misshandelte Frauen. Erster Erfahrungsbericht* (Berlin: Frauenselbstverlag Berlin-West, 1978).

of marriage, the family and domestic violence. His letters are couched in gendered and class-oriented rhetoric that frames domestic abuse as a working-class problem and presents battered women as mentally ill, bickering busybodies. It is no coincidence that he lists 'Kreuzberg' first: a traditionally working-class area of Berlin, by the 1970s, it was home to a large migrant population and was vastly different from the wealthy neighbourhood and villas of Grunewald. Women, meanwhile, are dismissed as 'hyper-nervous' and Scheuneman even queries their ability to care for their children: 'How will 30 women prepare breakfast and lunch for their school-aged children at the same time! And when and how will the groceries be taken care of?' Men's roles in the family, meanwhile, remain unchallenged by Scheuneman and not once does he mention domestic violence. Rather, he positions men as the real victims of the shelter. By allowing mothers to remove children from their homes, he presents the shelter as a danger to paternal rights and uses the rhetoric of children's welfare to advocate for the preservation of abusive marriages. His solution – to involve the Church, rather than a specialist women's organisation – belies his real priority: the maintenance of the patriarchal status quo.

Scheuneman was certainly not alone in his complaints.[7] Other neighbours similarly wrote with objections: one even engaged a lawyer to write to the owners of the land and the shelter itself. From the noise made by the children, to the fouling of the neighbourhood and claims that the children were being 'radicalised' in the shelter after one neighbour was called a 'capitalist pig', it is clear that coexistence with the shelter was uneasy.[8] In all these letters, however, what remained undiscussed was domestic violence and the fact that without this shelter these women and children would have nowhere else to turn.

Such sentiments might seem alien today. That someone should raise such extensive and problematic concerns about the shelter, but not once mention the importance of protecting women and children from male violence in the home highlights how far feminist domestic violence activism has come. As Alf Lüdtke and Thomas Lindenberger have argued, violence only becomes a problem when it is deemed illegitimate.[9] This is exactly what feminist activists did: working in West Germany and globally in the 1970s, feminists turned complaints like those in Grunewald on their head by centring domestic violence as the problem. They took it from a taboo, even largely tolerated occurrence, and made it visible and into a key issue of gender inequality.

Changing these preconceived notions was not a seamless process. Although Scheuneman's letters ultimately went unheeded, his complaints reveal the nerve

---

[7] A collection of letters written by neighbours to the shelter are published in *Frauen gegen Männergewalt.*
[8] Letter from Max Wolter in *Frauen gegen Männergewalt*, p. 68.
[9] Thomas Lindenberger and Alf Lüdtke, eds, *Physische Gewalt: Studien zur Geschichte der Neuzeit* (Frankfurt am Main: Suhrkamp Verlag, 1995).

hit by domestic violence activism. In 1976, allowing, even encouraging, women to leave their husbands and flee to a shelter with their children was ground-breaking. The shelter went against the very foundation of the West German state; as Scheuneman highlighted, it encroached on the patriarchal rights of fathers and husbands that had been enshrined in German law since the 19th century. Moreover, it challenged the inviolability of the family as a constitution-ally protected institution.[10] Despite ongoing processes of liberalisation and value change after 1945, there was still widespread popular support for conservative family ideals into the 1970s.[11]

Feminist activists would constantly come up against these beliefs in their work to address domestic violence, in particular as they sought public funding and pol-itical support. Cooperating with the Berlin Senate and the federal government led to a host of changes being made to the shelter project and feminist politics more broadly. Activists were not only required to work around popular concerns and anxieties, but also had to legitimise the feminist approach to domestic vio-lence: an important task given the failure of the abortion reform movement and the mixed messages circulating in the popular media about feminism, discussed in the first chapter.

This chapter explores this process, examining how feminists broke the taboo of domestic violence and created popular and political support for their movement. How did *Projekt Frauenhaus* evolve from a handful of women working at the Berlin Women's Centre in 1974 to a publicly funded three-year pilot project sponsored by the federal government and the Berlin Senate less than two years later? It also asks what this transformation and support meant for feminist politics. How did the requirements of working within the public and political system shape both the organisation and language of feminist approaches to domestic violence? What was the real cost of 'marching through the institutions'? And what did it mean for the feminist project of making the personal political?

The answers to these questions are complicated. Aside from enabling much-needed assistance for women living with violence, working with the state funda-mentally changed public and political attitudes towards violence against women and women's equality. It led to cross-party and popular support for protecting women and children from violence and resulted in wider and more critical public discussions of domestic abuse. It also shed light on other forms of gender-based and interpersonal violence, including sexual violence and child abuse and led to the development of support networks for women and children throughout the Federal Republic.

---

[10] Robert G. Moeller, *Protecting Motherhood: Women and the Family in the Politics of Postwar West Germany* (Berkeley: University of California Press, 1993).
[11] Christopher Neumaier, *Familie im 20. Jahrhundert: Konflikte um Ideale, Politiken und Praktiken* (Berlin: De Gruyter, 2019).

But as the project was taken up politically and popularly, feminist politics were transformed. Before the shelter even opened, the federal government and Berlin Senate required feminists to move away from their grassroots, autonomous organisation to fit into an institutional framework. More problematic, however, was the way politicians and the media reframed the feminist project adopted by the shelter. Critiques of patriarchy all but disappeared from public discussions of domestic abuse and the Berlin shelter's feminist orientation and origins were largely absent in media reporting. Politicians and journalists interpreted feminist politics simplistically, as key concepts and practices such as empowerment, self-help and women-helping-women were reinterpreted and their radical approach to inequality dulled. At the same time, images of women's victimhood, initially used by shelter activists as a way of drawing attention to women's inequality, were wholeheartedly adopted by both politicians and the mainstream media. In this way, popular support for domestic violence activism was partly built on a paternalistic rhetoric of protecting women, rather than out of a concern for women's rights.

Ultimately, this chapter argues that the effect of this transformation and the co-optation of feminist politics was deradicalising. These changes may have helped garner support for the shelter initiative, but by simplifying feminist practices and politics, obscuring critiques of patriarchy and emphasising women's vulnerability, the broader struggle for women's equality was simultaneously undercut. Examining this process of deradicalisation reveals the normative boundaries of the putative 'success story' historians have mapped out for West German democracy after 1945. Far from contesting inequality, fomenting popular support for domestic violence has meant that women in West Germany are protected from abuse not because of a shift in thinking about women's rights as humans or as citizens, but because they are women.

Prior to feminist engagement with gender violence, domestic abuse was rarely a topic of critical public or political interest. For much of the early 20th century, violence against wives was simply understood as a normal – even necessary – part of marriage. Men's violence against women was legitimised on the back of gendered narratives of female hysteria and rationalised as a corrective to perceived wifely transgressions.[12] In Germany, as elsewhere, it was closely associated with the working classes and linked with excessive alcohol consumption, low education, poor living standards and the pressure to provide for

---

[12] As Joanna Bourke has shown into the 1950s and 1960s, marriage advice manuals discussed marital rape as a legitimate way of responding to women's frigidity. See Joanna Bourke, *Rape: A History from 1860 to the Present Day* (London: Virago, 2007).

large families.[13] Women living with an abusive husband were simply 'unlucky' or deemed 'incapable of finding a "normal" husband'.[14] As such, domestic violence was often dismissed as an inevitable outcome of the pressures and realities of working-class life, captured succinctly in the popular refrain '*Pack schlägt sich, Pack verträgt sich*' ('though the proles fight, they soon reunite'). In Weimar Berlin, for example, writer Justus Ehrhardt's depiction of *Prügelfreitag* or 'beating Friday' is telling. According to Ehrhardt, on Fridays – the day when workers would receive their weekly pay and typically return home drunk – the screams of women could be heard 'three courtyards away'.[15]

This also meant there was little recourse for women experiencing family violence. At a time when there was no specific law against domestic violence, women's primary options were to place criminal charges or obtain a divorce. Neither option, however, was ideal. Filing assault charges required that women deal with the police and convince them a criminal act had taken place. This was an extremely difficult task, given the private nature of domestic abuse and popular attitudes towards women and violence in the family. Getting a divorce presented similar issues. Following the introduction of the Civil Code in 1900, divorce in Germany was fault-based.[16] This not only required the court to establish whether the marriage was truly dissolved, but also which party was guilty of ending it. While violence could be used to establish fault, if a woman wanted to divorce her husband on this basis, she had to prove that the abuse had occurred, either by providing evidence or witnesses. Unsurprisingly, the tacit acceptance of violence in the home meant that such evidence was difficult to obtain. Complicating matters further, the determination of fault in divorce proceedings was also used to decide alimony and the division of marital assets. For most of the 20th century, marriage played an important role in women's financial security; men were the primary breadwinners, while women's work was concentrated in unpaid labour in the home, or in part-time and underpaid employment. This meant that establishing fault had important ramifications for women's ongoing financial security after divorce.[17] In spite of

---

[13] Carol Hagemann-White, Barbara Kavemann, Johanna Kootz, Ute Weinmann, Carola Christine Wildt, Roswitha Burgard and Ursula Scheu, *Hilfen für mißhandelte Frauen: Abschlussbericht der wissenschaftlichen Begleitung des Modellprojekts Frauenhaus Berlin* (Stuttgart: Kohlhamer, 1981).

[14] Ibid., p. 20.

[15] Justus Ehrhardt, *Strassen ohne Ende* (Berlin: Agis Verlag, 1931).

[16] See Bürgerliches Gesetzbuch (1900), Paragraphs 1565–1567. Divorce would remain fault-based until 1965 in East Germany and 1977 in West Germany.

[17] As Christina von Oertzen argues, since the 19th century women's employment outside the home in Germany had been 'regarded exclusively as a burden, legitimate only when economic circumstances rendered it all but unavoidable'. See Christina von Oertzen, *Pleasures of a Surplus Income: Part-Time Work, Gender Politics and Social Change in West Germany, 1955–1969* (Oxford: Berghahn, 2007), p. 2.

these limitations, spousal abuse was one of the most common reasons for divorce in the first half of the 20th century.[18]

This situation changed little under Hitler's rule. Although there has been much debate over the extent to which the virulent misogyny of the Nazi regime persecuted or empowered German women, it is now clear that for those women deemed racially and politically fit, the Third Reich opened up a wider opportunity structure.[19] This included more avenues for dealing with abusive husbands, although ultimately there was little change in attitudes towards violence against women in the home. In a fascinating study of women's denunciations in Düsseldorf, historian Vandana Joshi reveals that aside from divorce, women in Nazi Germany could – and did – turn to the Gestapo for assistance with domestic violence. Specifically, women would denounce their violent husbands to the Gestapo, alleging crimes of political sedition as a way of having them removed from the home. In many of these cases, however, and in spite of accusations of subversive behaviour, the Gestapo still typically sided with the husbands. According to Joshi (who herself repeats class-based assumptions of domestic violence), the Gestapo 'judged erring, oppressive or drunk husbands with compassion. Such behaviour might have been typical of working-class men and many of the functionaries who dealt with such cases might have found themselves in the same situation at home.'[20]

Despite the dismantling of the Nazi state following German defeat, there were striking continuities in approaches and attitudes to domestic violence after 1945. In both East and West Germany, women still faced limited options for dealing with a violent husband and on both sides of the Berlin Wall, domestic violence was rarely a matter of protecting women.[21] While the situation in East Germany

---

See also the special issue of *Contemporary European History* on women, work and value in post-war Europe, Vol. 28, No. 4 (2019).

[18] Vandana Joshi, 'The "Private" became "Public": Wives as Denouncers in the Third Reich', *Journal of Contemporary History*, Vol. 37, No. 3 (2002): pp. 419–435. Also, Gabriella Czarnowski, 'The Value of Marriage for the Volksgemeinschaft: Policies towards Women and Marriage under National Socialism' in *Fascist Italy and Nazi Germany: Comparisons and Contrasts*, edited by Richard Bessel (Cambridge: Cambridge University Press, 1996): pp. 94–112.

[19] See, for example, Gisela Bock, 'Racism and Sexism in Nazi Germany' in *When Biology Became Destiny: Women in Weimar and Nazi Germany*, edited by Renate Bridenthal, Atina Grossmann and Marion Kaplan (New York: Monthly Review Press, 1984): pp. 271–296; Claudia Koonz, *Mothers in the Fatherland. Women, the Family and Nazi Politics* (New York: St. Martin's Press, 1987); Annette Timm, 'Mothers, Whores or Sentimental Dupes? Emotion and Race in Historiographical Debates about Women in the Third Reich' in *Beyond the Racial State: Rethinking Nazi Germany*, edited by Devin O. Pendas, Mark Roseman and Richard F. Wetzell (Cambridge: Cambridge University Press, 2017): pp. 335–361; Elizabeth Harvey, *Women and the Nazi East: Agents and Witnesses of Germanization* (New Haven: Yale University Press, 2003).

[20] Joshi, 'The "Private" became "Public"', p. 426.

[21] On the comparison between East and West Germany, see Jane Freeland, 'Domestic Abuse, Women's Lives and Citizenship: East and West Policies during the 1960s and 1970s' in *Gendering Post-1945 German History: Entanglements*, edited by Friederike Brühöfener, Karen Hagemann and Donna Harsch (New York: Berghahn, 2019): pp. 253–273.

is discussed in detail in Chapter 4, in the Federal Republic, the rehabilitation of German men and masculinity was prioritised in the aftermath of defeat. The concomitant consecration of the private sphere further meant that domestic violence was rarely discussed publicly, even though the mental traumas experienced by returning soldiers frequently played out in acts of familial abuse.[22] This contrasted starkly with the mass rape of German women by occupying soldiers, which was initially publicly discussed as a serious social and medical issue and later embedded in the public memory of the Second World War in West Germany.[23] However, as Elizabeth Heineman and Atina Grossmann warn, the adoption of rape as an issue in the post-war public sphere was not a recognition of the harm of sexual violence nor of women's inequality. Instead, it spoke to racialised fears of the conquering Red Army that fed into and legitimised the narratives of victimhood which girded West German identity.[24]

In the rare instances where domestic violence was discussed in the post-war era, it was framed as an issue of child protection, rather than women's safety, echoing earlier fears about the deleterious effect the war and post-war privations had on children.[25] This is most clearly articulated in the discussions surrounding marriage law reform in the late 1960s. At this time, the federal government was considering introducing no-fault divorce, which would allow couples to dissolve their marriage without having to prove guilt. To this end, in 1968, the Marriage Reform Commission planned a survey examining the effect of divorce on youths with a criminal record. In particular, the Commission was interested to learn about the role of violence in the family, connecting a violent home life with later criminal activity.[26] Similar concerns for childhood development were echoed when federal parliamentary representative Martin Hirsch argued for the preservation of fault-based divorce. For Hirsch, ascribing fault in divorce helped prevent children from being exposed to further violence, as custody and parental rights

---

[22] Svenja Goltermann, *The War in their Minds: German Soldiers and their Violent Pasts in West Germany* (Ann Arbor: University of Michigan Press, 2017); Frank Biess, *Homecomings: Returning POWs and the Legacies of Defeat in Postwar Germany* (Princeton: Princeton University Press, 2006).

[23] Atina Grossmann, 'A Question of Silence. The Rape of German Women by Occupation Soldiers', *October*, Vol. 72 (1995): pp. 42–63; Elizabeth Heineman, 'The Hour of the Woman: Memories of Germany's 'Crisis Years' and West German National Identity', *American Historical Review*, Vol. 101, No. 2 (1996): pp. 354–395.

[24] Ibid; Atina Grossmann, *Jews, Germans and Allies: Close Encounters in Occupied Germany* (Princeton: Princeton University Press, 2007); Robert G. Moeller, *War Stories: The Search for a Usable Past in the Federal Republic of Germany* (Berkeley: University of California Press, 2001).

[25] Uta G. Poiger, *Jazz, Rock and Rebels: Cold War Politics and American Culture in a Divided Germany* (Berkeley: University of California Press, 2000); Tara Zahra, *The Lost Children: Reconstructing Europe's Families after World War II* (Cambridge: Harvard University Press, 2011).

[26] Bundesministerium der Justiz. Gesetz zur Änderung des Ehegesetzes – Statistisches Material der Eherechtkommission, 1968–1970, B 141/25140, BArch-K.

would be determined on the basis of fault.[27] The question of women's safety, however, remained undiscussed.

Against this backdrop, there were very few options for women living with an abusive husband. Divorce reform would only be enacted in 1977 and the social welfare system was built around maintaining marriages. Even if social workers or counsellors wanted to help, they had little power to do so.[28] Indeed, women's testimonies collected by the West Berlin shelter project reveal that prior to the opening of the shelter, women experiencing abuse faced multiple significant, and often intersecting, difficulties. These included issues associated with access to resources, misogynistic attitudes towards women and single mothers, drug and alcohol dependencies and legal barriers that prevented women from escaping abuse. Moreover, many of these issues were compounded for women who were already socially vulnerable, whether due to social class, ability, age or residency status.

Take Monika, for example. The 31-year-old seamstress was one of the first residents in the Berlin shelter in 1976. Before this point, however, Monika had already experienced first-hand the frustrations and limitations of a social welfare system that was simply not geared towards helping women. She first attempted to get help following a particularly violent attack by her husband, which had led her to flee the apartment with their three-year-old daughter. When the 'very nice' woman from child services came, Monika told her about her husband's abuse. But after she spoke to Monika's husband, suddenly 'everything changed', and instead of receiving help, Monika was given 'suggestions'. The woman told her to get a restorative tonic prescribed by the doctor and made the husband promise not to hit his family any more. She even suggested that Monika was experiencing the symptoms of perimenopause.[29] Monika later went to child services again; in the interim, her child had been removed from her care and she had spent time in a clinic for mental health and drug addiction issues. While she thought the woman 'understood her better and wanted to help' at this second meeting, the service's overarching goal was the protection and preservation of the family, leaving Monika with very little faith in the system. Still facing abuse at home and having lost her job, Monika's options were severely limited and she ended up moving into a homeless shelter. At least there she said she was safe and 'happy'.[30]

[27] RA Martin Hirsch MdB, Korreferat 7. März 1969: 'Zerrüttung und Verschulden als Grundlage der Ehescheidung und die gesetzlichen Scheidungsgründe', Bundesministerium der Justiz. Gesetz zur Änderung des Ehegesetzes – Referate der Eherechtskommission (Sammlung) 1968–1972, B 141/25143, BArch-K. See also: Dr Gerold Klemm, Referat, 16. Januar 1970: 'Folgeentscheidungen anlässlich der Ehescheidung', Bundesministerium der Justiz. Gesetz zur Änderung des Ehegesetzes – Referate der Eherechtskommission (Sammlung) 1968–1972, B 141/25144, BArch-K.
[28] See, for example, the Berlin Senate's response to the Information Request on violence against women, published in Sarah Haffner, ed, *Gewalt in der Ehe und was Frauen dagegen tun* (Berlin: Verlag Klaus Wagenbach, 1981), p. 60–61. Also discussed in further detail later in this chapter.
[29] Hagemann-White *et al.*, *Hilfen*, p. 109.
[30] Ibid., p. 110.

Regina, another resident of the West Berlin shelter, faced similar issues, revealing the overlapping and compounding difficulties that women experienced when seeking help with domestic abuse. Living with an already violent husband, the situation deteriorated further for the 33-year-old secretary after she got pregnant. Neither Regina nor her husband wanted to have a second child, but because they did not have access to an abortion clinic and travelling to the UK or the Netherlands, where abortion was legal, was out of the question, they decided to proceed with an abortion 'by whatever means necessary'.[31] Soon after the 'miscarriage', Regina's husband brought her some over-the-counter sleeping tablets, to which she quickly became addicted. The tablets, initially intended to help with the pain of the abortion, soon became a way for Regina to cope with her husband's abuse: 'rape or any other non-consensual sexual acts … would lose a bit of their horror under the influence of the tablets.'[32] They were also a way for her husband to control her; as the breadwinner, he would leverage his ability to buy the sleeping tablets in return for sexual access to his wife. Despite attempting to get help from a marriage counsellor and her husband even admitting that he had 'slapped' her occasionally, there was very little that could be done and they remained together. Her husband slowly became more brutal, both towards Regina and their only child. This culminated in Regina attempting suicide and being involuntarily committed to a psychiatric facility. Throughout this entire time, she remained married. Even if she had been able to obtain a fault-based divorce, without a job and with a history of drug addiction and self-harm, the determination would certainly not have worked in her favour. Perhaps this was why, after being released from hospital, she was 'determined' to wait out the two months until the marriage law reform came into effect. In her own words, 'the new divorce law was coming on 1 July 1977, this much I knew.'[33] But even this would prove impossible. Lacking any independent source of income and facing her husband's continued abuse and domination, Regina decided to wait out the two months in the safety of the women's shelter.

For women who had migrated to West Germany, things were even more difficult. In cases where a wife had joined her husband through family migration, the woman's residency permit depended on her continued marital status. For these women, leaving an abusive husband could also mean deportation. This was the situation that Asiye A. faced in 1984. Asiye had come to Berlin from Turkey to be with her husband. However, when she fled to the women's shelter, her residency was put in jeopardy. Shelter activists in Berlin took up Asiye's case and publicly fought for her and two other migrant women facing deportation to stay. Indeed, the very reason we know about Asiye is because her case was discussed as a formative experience for feminists advocating for the rights of women migrants at

---

[31] Hagemann-White *et al.*, *Hilfen*, p. 160.
[32] Ibid., p. 164.
[33] Ibid., p. 167.

the First Conference of German and Foreign Women in March 1984.[34] Despite this campaign and even though her husband was abusive, the Berlin Senate *Ausländerbeauftragte* (Commissioner for Foreigners' Issues) determined that Asiye had not been in the country long enough for an exception to be made. Asiye was required to leave West Germany within six months.[35]

Women experiencing domestic violence, then, were in precarious positions. As the stories of Monika, Regina and Asiye reveal, alongside social stigma, drug addiction and physical and mental health issues, women living with an abusive husband confronted manifold structural and legal barriers that prevented them from escaping abuse. By 1974, when the shelter group came together at the Berlin Women's Centre, it was clear that this needed to change. But in order to create this change, the group had to take domestic violence from a private, taboo subject and bring it into the public eye. They had to tackle the years of silence, when women's screams and cries for help were ignored, and make people see violence against women as an issue of women's equality and convince them of the need for action. Creating this kind of change would involve years of ongoing activist campaigning, support and attention from the media, as well as negotiations with political partners. The first step, however, was to gather the support of women themselves and legitimise violence against women as a key feminist issue.

Building a Base of (Feminist) Support

Starting in the summer of 1975, the Berlin shelter group started raising awareness of domestic violence and building support for their project. They produced posters, collected donations and published their first pamphlet, *Kicked, Beaten, Humiliated*. Much of this early activism was centred in the women's movement and was overtly feminist in its politics. Already at this stage, a feminist playbook for approaching domestic violence was visible. Grounded in the testimony of women, their campaigning called out systemic patriarchy, challenged gender norms and criticised those who failed to help women experiencing abuse. Moreover, they drew on the experiences of feminists worldwide as a foundation for the Berlin shelter and embedded the Berlin project within a growing global feminist movement against domestic violence. These approaches would

---

[34] See the published proceedings of this conference: Neval Gültekin, Brigitte Schulz and Brigitte Sellach, eds, *Ausländische und deutsche Frauen im Gespräch. Sind wir uns denn so fremd?*, 2nd ed. (Berlin: Sub-Rosa-Frauenverlag, 1985).
[35] Traude Ratsch, 'Interview mit Ulrike Palmert und Sadiye Kaygun-Dohmeyer, Mitarbeiterinnen des 2. Berlin Frauenhauses' in Gültekin, Schulz and Sellach, *Ausländische und deutsche Frauen im Gespräch*, pp. 49–53.

decisively mark the future of domestic violence activism and be a lynchpin in the success of the Berlin shelter.

Nowhere is this approach more evident than in *Kicked, Beaten, Humiliated*. Sold by the shelter group for the price of 1.30DM, the pamphlet reveals many of the key feminist narrative strategies against domestic violence. Above all, it publicised the feminist understanding of domestic abuse as a problem resulting from structural patriarchal gender norms that reified women's inequality. 'In the Federal Republic, women face abuse daily', it began, 'Yet the causes and specific conditions of violence against women are hushed-up and practical steps against it are not taken.' As it continued, their feminist critique became clear:

> At the same time women are shut in, beaten, raped and sometimes even murdered, mostly by their husbands. It seems totally normal. Even when women are attacked by men on the street or in a restaurant, no one does anything. Most people think: "that's got to be his wife or girlfriend", as though friendship or marriage gave men the right to be violent to women.[36]

As the shelter project made clear, it was these commonplace ideas about the nature of heterosexual relationships and gender norms that were to blame for the failure to protect women from violence. They allowed people to dismiss violence against women as a normal part of dating or marriage and in doing so endangered women: 'What happens behind closed doors and in the bedrooms of the Federal Republic is totally removed from the public eye. And this always makes women into silent losers.'

But, as *Kicked, Beaten, Humiliated* argued, the problem was not simply that individual people held these views. It was that an entire system built upon these patriarchal norms worked to sustain women's inequality and left them unprotected and unable to escape abuse. Specifically, the pamphlet called out the court system, policing practices and the medical establishment for failing women. Courts were reluctant to grant a divorce on the basis of abuse and police attitudes, it argued, actually 'supported the abuse of women'. According to the pamphlet, the police were the least helpful for addressing violence against women, citing common refrains like 'your husband must have had his reasons' and 'women need it now and again – violence' that were used by the police to dismiss women's allegations of abuse. Doctors were similarly implicated, as they would fail to name domestic violence as the cause of women's injuries, thereby preventing women from having the evidence needed to obtain a divorce. By highlighting this widespread and structural failure to take violence against women seriously, the pamphlet argued that 'women must suffer individually, what is socially conditioned … They are left all alone to deal with the consequences of male abuse. Even though everyday

---

[36] 'Geschlagen—Getreten—Gedemütigt. Frauen werden von Männern misshandelt! Wo finden sie Hilfe? Wir brauchen ein Frauenhaus', E Rep 300–96/ 9, LAB.

violence against women is a social and structural problem, it is women who, in the end, are made responsible for it.'[37]

These were no baseless claims. Drawing on the stories of women themselves, *Kicked, Beaten, Humiliated* revealed the brutality of abuse and how hopeless it was for women to find protection from domestic violence. While Frau Schmidt was knocked unconscious with a suspected skull fracture by her husband, Frau Gerlach's husband threatened to kill her with a long knife if she divorced him and Frau Braun's body was covered in scars from years of abuse by her husband. And yet, each of these women were unable to obtain a divorce on the basis of abuse. In the case of Frau Gerlach, this was because her husband promised the court never to hit her again – a promise that quickly proved illusory.[38]

Stories like these gave empirical proof to feminist claims of the systemic and brutal nature of abuse and the structural patriarchy that prevented women from obtaining effective support. They also served an important political purpose. Using women's testimony was a central tool in feminist activism against domestic violence. It reflected the feminist prioritisation of women's voices and experiences as the foundation of women's rights work. But this was also a way of building support among women. By hearing the experiences of other women, they could come to understand their own oppression better and have their feminist conscience awoken.

However, even at this early stage, a vague tension is palpable between the feminist politics of empowerment and the way women's lives are represented. Despite the important work of *Kicked, Beaten, Humiliated* in promoting feminist renderings of domestic violence, it also leans on a narrative of women's victimhood. Even looking at the pamphlet's cover image (Figure 2.1) we might question the extent to which it builds support on the back of gendered representations of women as victims. The cover features a black-and-white photograph of two young women sitting next to each other, with one woman wearing a wimple and holding a small child between her knees. With somewhat anguished looks on the women's faces, the image is almost reminiscent of Christian charity campaigns. Although the demand emblazoned underneath the photograph – 'Women are abused by men! Where can they find help? We need a WOMEN'S SHELTER' – alongside the inclusion of the Venus symbol positions the pamphlet firmly in the feminist movement, it also draws on this visual rendition of women's suffering to create support.

This is not to say these women were not victims, nor that they had not experienced unfair and brutal treatment at the hands of men who were supposed to love them and a system that did not recognise them as equal. Instead, it is to

[37] Ibid.
[38] Ibid.

Figure 2.1 *KICKED, BEATEN, HUMILIATED. WOMEN are abused by men! Where can they find help? We need a WOMEN'S SHELTER!, 1976.*

Credit: Image courtesy of FrauenMediaTurm, Cologne (PT.047).

ask what it meant to centre feminist politics around experiences of victimhood. Throughout the 1970s, violence and victimhood became a central concern in much feminist activism, both in West Germany and internationally. Indeed, at the same time as *Projekt Frauenhaus* was campaigning for a shelter in Berlin, a global movement against domestic violence was emerging. In 1974, the Women's Liberation Halfway House refuge opened in Melbourne and the Elsie Refuge opened in Sydney, Australia.[39] In the United States, shelters were established in St. Paul, Minnesota in 1974 and in Cambridge, Massachusetts; Lawrence, Kansas; and Minneapolis, Minnesota in 1976.[40] At the same time, the declaration of the International Women's Year in 1975 and the subsequent United Nations Decade for Women from 1976 to 1985, drew public and political attention to issues of women's inequality and violence against women.

Linking the Berlin project to this global movement not only leant feminist credibility to the project, but it also helped to legitimise domestic violence as an urgent issue of women's inequality: other developed, liberal, western countries – and important allies of the Federal Republic – had taken action against gender-based violence and now it was time for West Germany to follow their example. One project, in particular, stood out for the Berlin shelter group. Opened in 1971, Chiswick Women's Aid was one of the world's first modern women's shelters and was brought to international attention through founder Erin Pizzey's groundbreaking book on domestic violence, *Scream Quietly or the Neighbours Will Hear*. Published with Penguin Books in the UK in 1974, the book detailed the everyday life of the London refuge and documented its residents' experiences.[41]

Although the German translation of Pizzey's work would only be published in 1976, *Kicked, Beaten, Humiliated* directly tied the Berlin shelter project to the work of Pizzey and Women's Aid and used it as an example of how supporting feminist activism could create change for women experiencing abuse. As the Berlin shelter argued, the London refuge had transformed the situation for women experiencing abuse in the UK: in its first two-and-a-half years, 5,500 women had sought shelter at Women's Aid. Moreover, it led to the creation of a network of shelters throughout the UK, with 80 further refuges established in the three years after Women's Aid opened.[42] These transnational linkages were even underscored in the

---

[39] For a history of the Australian women's refuge movement, see Adele Murdolo, 'Safe Homes for Immigrant and Refugee Women: Narrating Alternative Histories of the Women's Refuge Movement in Australia', *Frontiers: A Journal of Women's Studies*, Vol.35, No. 3 (2014): pp. 126–153.

[40] Elizabeth B.A. Miller, 'Moving to the Head of the River: The Early Years of the U.S. Battered Women's Movement' (Ph.D. dissertation, University of Kansas, 2010); Alana Piper and Ana Stevenson, eds, *Gender Violence in Australia: Historical Perspectives* (Melbourne: Monash University Press, 2019).

[41] Erin Pizzey, *Scream Quietly or the Neighbours will Hear* (Harmondsworth: Penguin Books, 1974).

[42] 'Geschlagen—Getreten—Gedemütigt. Frauen werden von Männern misshandelt! Wo finden sie Hilfe? Wir brauchen ein Frauenhaus', E Rep 300–96/ 9, LAB.

photograph used on the pamphlet's cover (Figure 2.1), which was actually taken at Chiswick Women's Aid by Berlin feminist and film-maker Cristina Perincioli. Perincioli, one of the founders of the Berlin Women's Centre, travelled to Chiswick in March 1974 – before the shelter group had officially formed in West Berlin – and documented the lives of the women who lived in the refuge. The recordings of women's stories and images taken by Perincioli in London formed a key media resource for Berlin shelter activists, continually underscoring the close connection between the two projects.

But it was not only legitimacy that the Berlin shelter group gained from these transnational connections. They also developed their project within these international feminist networks and spaces. Women's Aid was a formative example for the Berlin shelter group, who modelled their work closely on Chiswick. Another important event was the Brussels Tribunal. Between 4 and 8 March 1976, over 2,000 feminists came together in Brussels to discuss violence against women. The International Tribunal on Crimes Against Women, as it was officially known, drew women from 40 different countries together in a discussion of women's inequality, in service of what Simone de Beauvoir called in her welcome remarks 'a radical decolonization of women'.[43] The idea for a tribunal to address women's oppression, however, first emerged on the small island of Femø, Denmark in August 1974, where women, particularly those associated with the women's movement, have gathered for a yearly summer retreat since 1971.[44] From this seed, a concrete plan emerged only a few months later in November 1974 at the International Feminist Conference held in Frankfurt am Main.[45]

The Tribunal was aimed at exposing women's oppression and 'bring[ing] to light the shameful truths that half of humanity is trying to cover up'.[46] The issues discussed at the conference included reproductive coercion (including lack of information on and availability of contraception and abortion), abusive medical practices (including female genital cutting and forced sterilisation), economic and social discrimination (unequal pay, the double-burden of working mothers, unequal treatment and discrimination of women of colour, women from the developing world and migrant women), oppression of women in the home and in families, the persecution of lesbians and physical violence against women.[47] More generally, though, the Tribunal represented a grassroots feminist response to the 1975 United Nations' International Women's Year. Directed by

---

[43] Simone De Beauvoir, quoted in Diana E.H. Russell, 'Report on the International Trial on Crimes Against Women', *Frontiers: A Journal of Women's Studies*, Vol. 2, No. 1 (1977): pp. 1–6, p. 1.

[44] Russell, 'Report'. On the history of the women's camp on Femø, see https://kvindelejren.dk/womens-camp-frauencamp/history/, accessed 12 May 2022.

[45] Russell, 'Report'. See also 'Statt Blumen', *Der Spiegel*, 25 November 1974, pp. 160–162.

[46] De Beauvoir, quoted in Russell, 'Report', p. 1.

[47] Russell, 'Report'.

international governments and politics, feminists, including de Beauvoir and Tribunal co-organiser Diana Russell, criticised the International Women's Year as too institutional.[48] Rather than question patriarchy, the UN campaign only worked to 'integrate woman into a male society', according to de Beauvoir. In contrast, the women in Brussels were 'gathered to denounce the oppression to which women are subjected in this society'.[49] Even *Der Spiegel* picked up on this discrepancy, contrasting the exuberance and 'vitality' of the International Feminist Conference in Frankfurt with the staid and more 'traditional' events of the Women's Year in Bonn.[50]

Although participants from across the globe attended the Brussels Tribunal, by far the largest contingent (400 delegates) came from West Germany. It was a major event for the West German women's movement, which was increasingly using the concept of violence to signify a 'tool of social control to maintain patri-archal power structures'.[51] More than simply physical abuse or the extreme actions of individual men, as the title of the Berlin Women's Centre publication on the Tribunal highlighted, violence was now a much larger category, encompassing a host of inequalities and forms of discrimination against women. *Violence against Women in Marriage, Psychiatry, Gynaecology, Rape, Film, Work and What Women Can Do about It* not only featured sections on domestic violence and rape, but also on pornography and the objectification of women's bodies in the media, the medicalisation of gender norms in psychiatry and gynaecology, the use of intrusive surgeries to assist women with reproduction and 'frigidity', inequality in the workplace and even the criminalisation of the Berlin Women's Centre, following the police raid in December 1975.

This broader framework of violence allowed feminists to politicise women's inequality as never before and opened up new avenues for women's rights activism. Specifically, by providing a language that encompassed a variety of shared experiences of oppression among women, violence – broadly understood – became an important way of bringing women together en masse.[52] Following the Brussels Tribunal in March 1976, a host of violence-focused, feminist-oriented services and projects opened in West Germany. Women activists organised emergency hotlines, began protest actions against the sexualisation and objectification of women's bodies and in 1977 feminists started the annual *Walpurgisnacht* or Walpurgis Night

---

[48] Ibid. On the co-optation of International Women's Year and the international feminist movement, see Kristen Ghodsee, 'Revisiting the United Nations Decade for Women: Brief Reflections on Feminism, Capitalism and Cold War Politics in the Early Years of the International Women's Movement', *Women's Studies International Forum*, Vol. 33, No. 1 (2010): pp. 3–12.

[49] Russell, 'Report', p. 4.

[50] 'Statt Blumen', *Der Spiegel*.

[51] Patricia Melzer, *Death in the Shape of a Young Girl: Women's Political Violence in the Red Army Faction* (New York: New York University Press, 2015), p. 65.

[52] Ibid.

demonstration. Described by Katharina Karcher as 'the biggest transregional demonstration in the New Women's Movement', *Walpurgisnacht*, a forerunner of the Reclaim the Night movement, brought women from across West Germany to the streets.[53] Dressed as witches and armed with whistles, drums, chants and songs, they challenged the harassment and violence women face in public spaces after dark.

This increased feminist and public attention to the issue of violence buoyed the activism of the Berlin women's shelter project. Although the women's shelter movement in West Germany pre-dated the Tribunal, according to sociologist Carol Hagemann-White, it was nonetheless

> marked by the spirit of the Brussels Tribunal: through the belief that abuse is part of a continuum of oppression and exploitation of women, and the assessment that women's shelters are a part of the fight against this oppression, not some kind of attempted solution for an unwritten social problem.[54]

The Berlin Women's Centre pamphlet, published after the Tribunal, reveals how the shelter project embraced this broader understanding of violence to bolster their work, delegitimising domestic violence and embedding it as a key part of feminism. *Violence against Women in Marriage, Psychiatry, Gynaecology, Rape, Film, Work and What Women Can Do about It* featured a chapter on domestic violence and the Berlin shelter project, which built on the platform developed in *Kicked, Beaten, Humiliated*. It further linked the Berlin project to Chiswick Women's Aid and other international domestic violence projects and argued that

> male violence is so normalised that women resign themselves to silence. Male complicity has till now hindered a public revolt against this widely known issue. Because the neighbour, the cop, the doctor, the judge, the politician is a man – and often an abusive man! … With the emergence of the New Women's Movement, women began to ask themselves how long they have to accept this situation.[55]

Echoing the Brussels Tribunal, the shelter project positioned all men – if not also the state – as at worst, perpetrators, at best, beneficiaries of violence against women. In doing so, it also helped to chip away at the long-standing myths surrounding domestic violence, underscoring that it was not just a working-class problem, but something also perpetrated by social elites. As the pamphlet argued, 'Not only workers are abusive at home, but also men from the "better classes".'[56]

---

[53] Katharina Karcher, *Sisters in Arms. Militant Feminisms in the Federal Republic of German since 1968* (Oxford: Berghahn, 2017), p. 96.
[54] Carol Hagemann-White, 'Die Frauenhausbewegung' in *Der große Unterschied. Die neue Frauenbewegung und die siebziger Jahre*, edited by Kristine von Soden (Berlin (West): Elefanten Press, 1988), pp. 48–52.
[55] Frauenzentrum Berlin, *Gewalt gegen Frauen in Ehe, Psychiatrie, Gynäkologie, Vergewaltigung, Beruf, Film und was Frauen dagegen tun. Beiträge zum Internationalen Tribunal über Gewalt gegen Frauen, Brüssel März 1976* (Berlin, 1976), A Rep 400 BRD 22 Broschuren, FFBIZ.
[56] Ibid.

This new framing of violence also shaped the shelter's vision of support. By discussing their shared experiences of violence, women could become empowered, drawing strength from one another to overcome male violence and patriarchy.[57] These ideas were solidified in the principles of 'self-help' and 'women-helping-women', which went to the heart of West German feminist practice and critique. Reflecting ideals of sisterhood, equality and anti-authoritarianism, 'women-helping-women' and 'self-help' were key parts of the feminist project. Whereas 'women-helping-women' centred on women supporting and learning from one another as a path to empowerment, 'self-help' focused on enabling women to help themselves, becoming empowered through decision making and self-determination. Indeed, as sociologist Myra Marx Ferree has argued, 'the core issue' for the feminist movement 'was self-emancipation: how women acting on their own could help other women realize their autonomy'.[58]

By situating these principles in an international context, the Berlin shelter group was able to legitimise the feminist politics adopted within domestic violence activism. Discussing the work of the UK shelter, *Kicked, Beaten, Humiliated* underscored the therapeutic importance of allowing women to come together in a space without men to share their experiences of abuse. Doing so, they said 'helps women to overcome their situation and develop their self-confidence'. Moreover, they argued that women would be better equipped to help those dealing with domestic abuse 'on the basis of women's own experiences and their shared confrontation [with male violence]'.[59] Following the Brussels Tribunal, the approach of women-helping-women only became more prominent in the shelter movement.[60] 'What can women, in spite of all the difficulties and obstacles, do now to defend themselves or to separate from their husband?', asked *Violence against Women in Marriage, Psychiatry, Gynaecology, Rape, Film, Work and What Women Can Do about It*. Before encouraging women to get their family doctor to attest to the abuse, to search out legal and financial advice or to find a new apartment, the pamphlet instructed women to find another woman with whom they could discuss their situation. First and foremost,

> women who are abused and are in distress should initially find a woman or a public organisation where they can talk over everything in peace and safety. They should – if

---

[57] Myra Marx Ferree, *Varieties of Feminism: German Gender Politics in Global Perspective* (Stanford: Stanford University Press, 2012), p. 84.
[58] Ibid.
[59] 'Geschlagen—Getreten—Gedemütigt. Frauen werden von Männern misshandelt! Wo finden sie Hilfe? Wir brauchen ein Frauenhaus', E Rep 300–96/9, LAB.
[60] Verein zur Förderung des Schutzes misshandelter Frauen (e.V) Projektantrag zur Einrichtung eines Frauenhauses in Berlin (West) (1976) and Konzeption für das zweite Berliner Frauenhaus (1978), B Rep 002/12504, LAB; Hagemann-White, 'Die Frauenhausbewegung'; Sophie von Behr, 'Darum haben Männer im Frauenhaus nichts zu suchen', *EMMA*, 6 (1978), pp. 32–6. See also Ferree, *Varieties of Feminism*.

possible – find a women's centre, a single mothers' association, a mothers' centre or a family counselling centre.[61]

As the following chapter shows, women's self-help was adopted as a key practice within the Berlin women's shelter: it was a woman-only space and shelter residents were encouraged to share their experiences with one another. Positioning these feminist practices in the context of these international examples, shelter activists were able to walk the fine line between cementing their feminist credibility and legitimising activist politics. These were not simply radical practices, but rather tried and tested methods of supporting women experiencing abuse. This legitimacy was even more important as, in the wake of the Brussels Tribunal, the Berlin shelter project increasingly garnered public and political attention.

By 1976, violence against women was a firmly entrenched concept in the feminist politics of West Germany.[62] Through giving women a language to describe a broad range of shared experiences of oppression, discrimination and abuse, violence was bringing women to feminism just as abortion had in the early 1970s. Against this backdrop, the Berlin shelter group forged a solid base of support for their project in the New Women's Movement. Informed by feminist politics and a global movement against domestic violence, the project's early activism not only revealed domestic abuse as a key issue of women's rights, but had also exposed the patriarchal structures and norms that supported the ongoing abuse of women.

At the same time, however, many of these issues were also being taken up in the mass media throughout 1976. Journalists even started to adopt some of the feminist messaging and approaches of the shelter group: they used women's stories of abuse, picked up ideas of women's self-help and empowerment and drew on the international women's movement to bolster the credibility of the West Berlin shelter.

Indeed, international linkages were vital to both solidifying the Berlin shelter's feminist credentials and legitimising the feminist approach to domestic violence. In particular, the Chiswick shelter would be a model for addressing violence against women in the Federal Republic. Yet, in one important way, the Berlin shelter project diverged from the British example. Chiswick Women's Aid was funded through donations, not through public or governmental financing. This was an important lesson for the Berlin shelter project, who did not want women's activism to become an excuse for 'the state to neglect its social responsibilities'.[63] Already in their first pamphlet *Kicked, Beaten, Humiliated*, the Berlin project

[61] Frauenzentrum Berlin, *Gewalt gegen Frauen in Ehe, Psychiatrie, Gynäkologie, Vergewaltigung, Beruf, Film und was Frauen dagegen tun. Beiträge zum Internationalen Tribunal über Gewalt gegen Frauen, Brüssel März 1976* (Berlin, 1976), A Rep 400 BRD 22 Broschuren, FFBIZ.

[62] On the intersection of violence and the West German women's movement, see Clare Bielby, *Violent Women in Print: Representations in the West German Print Media of the 1960s and 1970s* (Rochester: Camden House, 2012); Karcher, *Sisters in Arms*; Melzer, *Death in the Shape of a Young Girl*.

[63] 'Geschlagen—Getreten—Gedemütigt. Frauen werden von Männern misshandelt! Wo finden sie Hilfe? Wir brauchen ein Frauenhaus', E Rep 300–96/9, LAB.

called on the shelter to be financed publicly. Although they were concerned at what taking public funds would mean for the independence of their project and whether it would lead to their 'institutionalisation', as one activist asked 'where else were we going to get the money?'[64] However, before they could even think about approaching the government for funding, they had to build a wider base of support: for the shelter, for women's rights and for domestic violence activism.

Broadening the Agenda

The year 1976 was a major turning point for domestic violence activism in the Federal Republic. It was at this time that the work started by the Berlin shelter initiative in 1974 came to fruition. Domestic abuse was publicly embraced as a serious issue of women's inequality and on 1 November 1976, the first domestic violence shelter in Germany opened in Berlin. This was no small feat and resulted from an intense media campaign increasing the tenor of public support. Throughout 1976, violence against women exploded into the West German media and often in ways that reflected developments in feminism itself.

Somewhat surprisingly, one of the first pieces on domestic violence in West Germany was published in the tabloid *Bild*. In December 1975, under the title 'The Worst Number of the Year: Four Million German Men Beat Their Wives', *Bild* published an exposé on the extent of violence in marriage in the Federal Republic, arguing that 'never before have women in Germany been so often and so quickly beaten by their husbands as in this "Women's Year"'.[65] Only two months later, the newspaper *Die Zeit* published a review of Susan Brownmiller's foundational feminist work on rape, *Against Our Will*.[66] Although primarily focused on rape in the contemporary United States, the review reflected the growing transnational feminist understanding of rape as an assertion of male power and domination over women. It impressed on its readers the widespread prevalence of rape and took apart various rape-myths, instead emphasising that a majority of women are not attacked by strangers, but rather in their own homes. The review is particularly noteworthy as the German translation of Brownmiller's work would not be published until 1978.

Even more tellingly, the illustrated magazine *Stern* published a special feature on marital rape on 14 April 1976. Across seven pages, 'My Husband

---

[64] Konstanze Pistor, 'Frauenhaus Berlin' in Haffner, *Gewalt in der Ehe*, pp. 141–150, pp. 141–142.
[65] 'Die schlimmste Zahl des Jahres: Vier Millionen deutsche Männer schlagen ihre Frauen', *Bild* extracted in Frauenzentrum Berlin, *Gewalt gegen Frauen in Ehe, Psychiatrie, Gynäkologie, Vergewaltigung, Beruf, Film und was Frauen dagegen tun. Beiträge zum Internationalen Tribunal über Gewalt gegen Frauen, Brüssel März 1976* (Berlin, 1976), A Rep 400 BRD 22 Broschuren, FFBIZ.
[66] Rudolf Walter Leonhardt, 'Die Frauen als Opfer der Männer', *Die Zeit*, 27 February 1976.

Raped Me' discussed the results of a survey commissioned by *Stern* on women's so-called 'marital duty'. 'Rape', the article began, 'It was until now a matter of sexual offenders, perverts, criminals. … for the first time it is now revealed that nowhere is rape committed more than in the marital bed.'[67] As the survey highlighted, this equated to one in five marriages, or 2.5 million women in the Federal Republic. The article further showed that in a majority of cases, marital rape was linked to acts of physical violence and, in one third, alcohol abuse.[68] Significantly, the survey showed that a majority of women disagreed with the statement that as a part of marriage, women must be sexually available whenever their husbands want. This was true across all social classes and ages and between Protestants and Catholics, suggesting that violence in marriage, alongside patriarchal gender roles, were increasingly deemed illegitimate by women.[69]

With this groundswell of support emerging, the shelter group started contacting government officials. In January 1976, they wrote to all Berlin land registry offices to enquire whether they had an appropriate building available for use as a shelter. At the same time, they contacted the Berlin senators for Family, Youth and Sport; Work and Social Care; Health; and the Environment, for support with their project. They even sent a proposal to the Federal Ministry for Youth, Family and Health, asking for the Minister's support on the basis that the Berlin shelter could act as a pilot project for the entire Federal Republic.[70]

But it was their collaboration with the Berlin FDP's Working Group on Women's Emancipation, which finally gave the project its political breakthrough. The shelter initiative had been in touch with the group as early as December 1975, but it was not until February 1976 that they created a plan for supporting the project. Alongside helping them to find a house and getting domestic violence onto the FDP's political platform, the working group, together with the shelter initiative, used sitting party members to bring attention to domestic violence in the West Berlin Senate.[71] In March 1976, the FDP's Ulrich Roloff submitted a *Kleine Anfrage* (information request) to the West Berlin Senate, asking for information on the prevalence of domestic violence in the city. The detailed response, returned by the Senate on 5 May 1976 was damning: domestic violence was endemic in the city. In Charlottenburg, of the 360 families supported by social workers, 39 women reported abuse by their husbands or male intimate partners. In Reinickendorf, out of 800 marriage counselling sessions held in 1975, 100 involved instances where the wife requested alternative accommodation for themselves and their children

---

[67] Ulrich Schippke, 'Mein Mann hat mich vergewaltigt', *Stern*, 14 April 1976, pp. 68–73, p. 68.
[68] Ibid., pp. 73–74.
[69] Ibid.
[70] Pistor, 'Frauenhaus Berlin'.
[71] Protokoll der AKE-Sitzung am 10.2.1976, FDP LV Berlin, AK Emanzipation 16844, AdL; Arbeitskreis-Emanzipation, Bibl/Druckschrift D1–592(1978), AdL; Pistor, 'Frauenhaus Berlin'.

in response to abuse at home. In Neukölln, the Health Office reported 114 cases of domestic abuse across a 15-month period. The situation was no better in private welfare organisations, where 8 per cent of family counselling sessions and 5.6 per cent of calls to emergency helplines involved allegations of abuse. Despite these alarming figures, all welfare bodies agreed that these numbers were only the tip of the iceberg, with a large number of domestic violence cases going unreported. Moreover, both public and private counselling services described working with families where violence, including life-threatening acts of abuse, was a regular occurrence and often lasted many years. The conclusion of the response only drove home the urgent need for a domestic violence shelter in the city. Even though counselling services offered various forms of support to women and families, they admitted that it 'was not enough'. Furthermore, they regretted that in acute situations they 'could not offer the necessary concrete support, namely the immediate accommodation of the wife and children'.[72]

While this spurred developments in the Berlin Senate, the Federal Ministry remained unmoved. Despite having written to Katharina Focke, the Federal Minister for Youth, Family and Health, in early 1976, the shelter still had not received a response by the spring. Complicating matters was the federal election scheduled for 3 October that same year. With the failure of the abortion campaign still fresh in their memory and popular anxieties surrounding women's emancipation, offering support to another feminist cause was a contentious issue for the ruling SPD. After all, it was the SPD's support for the abortion campaign that resulted in the ultimately failed reform of Paragraph 218 in 1974. At the same time, as Alice Schwarzer argued in *EMMA*, it was also in large part due to the votes of these 'progressive women voters' that the SPD had been able to retain power at the 1972 elections.[73] Would Focke decide to support the initiative or would she turn her back on one of the key pillars of SPD support?

In this, the role of the media proved decisive to the shelter's success. With mounting public attention, domestic violence was an issue Focke could not ignore. In particular, the television report *Screaming is Useless: Brutality in Marriage*, which aired on ARD on 26 April 1976, spurred the minister to action. This report was the pinnacle of the public engagement work of the shelter project and its resonance cannot be underestimated. Directed by Berlin feminist activist Sarah Haffner, the report detailed the presence of violence in West German homes, highlighted the

---

[72] 'Auszug aus der Antwort des Senats auf die kleine Anfrage Nr. 846 im Berliner Abgeordnetenhaus vom 2. März 1976 über Mißhandlung von Frauen' extracted in Haffner, *Gewalt in der Ehe*, pp. 60–61. Also: Projektantrag zur Einrichtung eines Frauenhauses in Berlin (West), B Rep 002/12504, LAB; Protokoll der AKE-Sitzung am 10.2.1976, FDP LV Berlin, AK Emanzipation 16844, AdL; Arbeitskreis-Emanzipation, Bibl/Druckschrift D1–592(1978), AdL.

[73] Alice Schwarzer, 'Ein Tag im Haus für geschlagene Frauen', *EMMA*, March 1977, p. 9.

lack of assistance for these women in the Federal Republic and juxtaposed this to the system of support for women in Britain, again drawing on the experiences of Chiswick Women's Aid.[74]

Thanks to this report, Haffner quickly became a media figurehead for the Berlin shelter movement: she not only gave a face and a name to the shelter initiative, but presented a relatable and accessible entry-point to domestic violence activism for the West German public.[75] Indeed, her story of 'discovering' domestic violence was featured throughout the West German print media in 1976.[76] Haffner first learned about domestic violence in the early 1970s after a new family moved into her West Berlin apartment building. 'When I heard the screams of my female neighbour for the first time', she recalled, 'I was so terribly paralysed that it never occurred to me to call the police.'[77] But even afterwards, when Haffner did call the police, 'they didn't help' and neither did child protection services, the church or the lawyer she visited.[78] She herself even 'stood in front of their door in the middle of the night', unable to ring the bell out of fear of potential violence and of overstepping the accepted boundaries of a good neighbour.[79] It only became clearer to Haffner 'how hopeless my neighbour's situation was'.[80] As the reports highlight, it was these formative experiences that led Haffner to call for change.

This media attention certainly helped to intensify public attention regarding domestic violence. At the same time, since the report also featured Katharina Focke explaining that from her perspective 'there was no problem' with domestic violence in the Federal Republic, the documentary also resulted in 'laundry baskets

[74] The release of this special report was timed to coincide with the publication of the German translation of Women's Aid founder Erin Pizzey's book *Scream Quietly or the Neighbours will Hear*. Vorlage zur Beschlussfassung über den Modellversuch "Hilfen für misshandelte Frauen" – the report of SenFamJugSport – published by the Abgeordnetenhaus von Berlin on 7.12.79 Drucksache 8/219, B Rep 002, 12504a, LAB.
[75] Given the general reticence of many West German feminists to identify themselves by name, Haffner's prominence in the media is remarkable. Johanna Gehmacher, 'The Productions of Historical Feminisms: Archival Practices and Political Activism'. Paper presented at the conference 'Archiving, Recording and Representing Feminism: The Global History of Women's Emancipation in the 20th Century', German Historical Institute London, 10–12 December 2020.
[76] Ginger Held, 'Gustav, der Knüppel und die Folgen', *Frankfurter Rundschau*, 13 November 1976; Sarah Haffner, 'Gewalt in der Ehe: was können Frauen dagegen tun?—eine Dokumentation', *Der Tagesspiegel*, 14 November 1976; 'Tabuthema wird nun endlich öffentlich diskutiert', *Metall*, 14 December 1976; Monika Held, 'Warum schlagen eigentlich so viele Männer ihre Frauen? Von kleinauf heißt's: Du bist nichts und er ist alles', *Metall*, 14 December 1976; 'Schreien nützt nichts. Brutalität in der Ehe—Bericht von Sarah Haffner', *Frankfurter Rundschau*, 27 April 1976; Ulrike Pfeil, 'In der Festung des Mannes. Von den Schwierigkeiten, ein "privates" Problem öffentlich anzugeben', *Stuttgarter Zeitung*, 22 May 1978; 'Frauenmißhandlung in der Bundesrepublik. Schrei, wenn du kannst!', *Das da*, February 1977.
[77] Haffner, *Gewalt in der Ehe*, p. 6.
[78] Held, 'Gustav'. Also Haffner, *Gewalt in der Ehe*.
[79] Haffner, *Gewalt in der Ehe*.
[80] Haffner, *Gewalt in der Ehe*.

full of letters arriving on Focke's desk'.[81] It is no wonder then that, as one woman connected with the Berlin shelter group wrote, 'we never would have received an answer [to the project proposal], if it hadn't have been for a detailed television report on domestic abuse ... stirring public sentiment, so that even the Family Minister in Bonn felt pressure to offer support quickly and unbureaucratically'.[82]

From this moment, change happened quickly. The shelter was taken up by the Federal Ministry as a pilot project, a house was leased by the German Red Cross and the initiative received 450,000DM to fund their work for the first year. This sum, split between the Family Ministry (80 per cent) and the Berlin Senate (20 per cent), provided enough money for seven paid full-time positions: two social workers, two social researchers/psychologists, two childcare workers and one 'house mother', who was responsible for the shelter's day-to-day organisation.

This was undoubtedly a major win for feminism. Domestic violence was increasingly delegitimised, the shelter had funds and was able to open its doors on 1 November 1976. But success was a double-edged sword. Examining the transformation of feminist politics and principles as they were adopted politically and popularly reveals a considerably more nuanced – and less propitious – picture.

The Cost of Success

Although domestic violence and the Berlin shelter increasingly found political and popular support throughout 1976, this is not to say that feminism found similar traction. Instead, feminist politics and ideas were taken up and popularised within the media and by politicians without the critical feminist scaffolding. As a result, the political content of these feminist approaches was watered down, deradicalised and made 'safe' for consumption by a wary public.

This deradicalisation of feminist domestic violence activism had already begun before the shelter even opened. In June 1976, the Berlin Senate Office for Family, Youth and Sport sent Ilse Haase-Schur, the head of its family policy department, to visit Chiswick Women's Aid for a three-day workshop on the topic of 'Violence in the Family'. This event was aimed at discussing the causes of violence in the family, outlining best practices for supporting women and reflecting on the interaction between Chiswick Women's Aid and other, more established social welfare organisations. As the report on the workshop highlighted, Haase-Schur was the only international attendee at the event and the only representative of the Federal Republic. Significantly, as the senator wrote in her introductory remarks in the report, Haase-Schur was there to learn from the British example, since 'in the

---

[81] Schwarzer, 'Ein Tag im Haus für geschlagene Frauen' p. 9. Also covered in Chantal Louis, 'Ein Blick ins Frauenhaus', *EMMA*, No. 1 (2010): pp. 125–129.

[82] Pistor, 'Frauenhaus Berlin', p. 142.

Federal Republic there have been no studies or experiences to date' that could support the proposed Berlin women's shelter.[83]

Over the three-day event, Haase-Schur attended workshop sessions on domestic abuse. She heard from Women's Aid founder Erin Pizzey, psychiatrist Dr J.J. Gayford, who conducted one of the first studies into 'wife battering', alongside reports from shelter workers and some of the residents themselves.[84] This was a transformative experience and played an important role in the support for the Berlin shelter initiative. Indeed, Haase-Schur's report affirms many of the claims made by Berlin shelter activists. It underscored domestic abuse as a widespread and cross-class problem linked to women's social isolation and their financial dependence on men after marriage. It even highlighted the importance of women's self-help and collective decision making as a form of healing for women who have lived with abuse.

It would seem as though the tactic of linking the Berlin project to Women's Aid had proven effective. The report concluded that a similar refuge was needed in Berlin and would provide 'as yet unavailable help for battered and abused women … and important preventive work for affected children and youths and future generations'.[85] In particular, it underscored six key lessons drawn from Chiswick that should guide the Berlin shelter. Alongside implementing open-door policies, egalitarian decision making and intensive emotional therapy, the conclusions emphasised the importance of continued support for women after leaving the shelter and the need for 'close cooperation' with other social welfare organisations. The final lesson, however, went in a different direction. Despite upholding so many facets of feminist domestic violence work, the Senate's report concluded that 'Presenting the shelter as an organisation of the women's movement should be avoided. Aside from the prejudices and resistance that such a stance would spark, this view of the problem would not do justice to the complexity of the issue.'[86]

This perspective proved prescient. Wariness toward feminism continued to resonate at the federal level and the ministry initiated various control mechanisms to ensure the shelter's legitimacy and constitutionality. Shortly after *Screaming is Useless* was aired, for example, the Federal Ministry wrote to express its interest in the Berlin shelter. However, it said it would only give financial support if the project was affiliated with one of the larger pre-existing public or private welfare organisations. This was 'out of the question' for the initiative. It would not only take the project out of their hands, but endanger their autonomy.[87] After meeting

[83] Ilse Reichel, 'Vorbemerkung' in Ilse Haase-Schur, *Gewalt in Familien: Erfahrungen mit Krisenzentren für mißhandelte Frauen in England* (Berlin: Landespressedienst, 9 July 1976).
[84] Ibid. See also J.J. Gayford, 'Wife Battering: A Preliminary Survey of 100 Cases', *British Medical Journal*, No. 1 (1975): pp. 194–197.
[85] Ibid., p. 10.
[86] Ibid.
[87] Pistor, 'Frauenhaus Berlin', p. 143.

with the Federal Ministry and the Senate Office, the shelter struck a compromise. Firstly, it would need to become a registered association, represented publicly, not by the initiative group, but by a governing body. This body, the *Verein zur Förderung des Schutzes mißhandelter Frauen* or the Association for the Advancement of the Protection of Women from Abuse, would be comprised of six women representing public interests and welfare services, three women from the initiative group, three shelter workers and three (present or former) shelter residents. Secondly, the newly registered organisation was required to clarify and resubmit the proposal and financing schedule for the shelter, and finally, the shelter would be subject to an academic review and evaluation.[88]

When compared to the benefit that a shelter would bring to so many women, this compromise certainly seemed worth making to the activists involved. People were working on all sides to enable a shelter to open, to give it legitimacy and to protect women from violence in the home. One woman involved in the shelter project's early stages remembers being supported by both the Berlin Senate and the Federal Ministry and knew that these decisions and compromises were being made for the advancement of the project and women's rights.[89] However, it is clear that these efforts to legitimise the shelter's standing also meant distancing it from feminist politics and the women's movement, as support for the shelter went hand-in-hand with efforts at regulating activism. According to Karin Kaltenbach, one of the women involved in the shelter initiative, the governing body, in particular the six members representing public interests required by the Federal Ministry, was initially 'tasked with controlling us, the wild bunch of feminists'.[90] Although Kaltenbach says this changed over time, as these representatives started to mentor the shelter organisers, a similar pattern was evident elsewhere. Indeed, the same woman who felt so supported by the government, was also told not to 'write really angry sentences about men and patriarchy' in her public work on the shelter. Instead, she was to 'just let the women [residents] say what they think.'[91]

This distancing between the shelter and feminism fed into and echoed a broader deradicalisation of feminist domestic violence activism within the media. Despite the swathe of articles published throughout 1976 on the topic of domestic violence activism, very few ever connected shelter projects to feminism or the women's movement.[92] Even an article written by Sarah Haffner makes only one reference

---

[88] Brief an den Hauptausschuss, 20.9.1976, B Rep 002/12504, LAB; Brief von Abg. Gisela Fechner an den RBm, 18.10.1979, B Rep 002/12504a, LAB. Also, Pistor, 'Frauenhaus Berlin'.

[89] Interview with 'Dagmar', Osnabrück, 5 August 2013.

[90] Karin Kaltenbach, 'Karin Kaltenbach über die Mentorin des Frauenhauses Barbara von Renthe-Fink', *Feministische Projekte in Berlin, 1974–78*. Accessed on 12 May 2022: https://feministberlin.de/gewalt/frauenhaus/.

[91] Interview with 'Dagmar', Osnabrück, 5 August 2013.

[92] Only two articles mentioned feminism or the women's movement. See Maria Frise, 'Wenn Frauen misshandelt werden', *Frankfurter Allgemeine Zeitung* (1976), A Rep 400 BRD 22.5 (1970–78), FFBIZ and Haffner, 'Gewalt in der Ehe'.

to the women's movement in Germany.[93] This was more than simply overlooking the feminist origins of domestic violence projects. Much like the Senate and the Federal Ministry, the media simultaneously supported shelter activism while also distancing it from feminist politics and critiques of gender inequality.

For example, in an article on domestic violence and the creation of women's shelters from *Der Spiegel* in January 1976, there are no references to feminism beyond one to the American 'women's lib' movement.[94] Instead, the Berlin shelter initiative is described as a 'women's group' and there is no explicit mention of its feminist origins or politics. While the piece critically presents domestic violence, describing it as a 'painful reality' faced by women across all social classes in the Federal Republic, it never links violence against women to broader questions of gender inequality. If anything, the article draws on gendered narratives of women as victims: 'and the oft-asked question why these poor women don't simply leave their brutal husbands … they have no courage, no strength to start a new life and no one to help them.' Discussing statistics gathered from the United Kingdom, the section concludes by saying that although most women leave at some point – many even several times – 'they always go back' to their abuser.[95]

More than simply distancing the shelter from feminism, this article in *Der Spiegel* reveals how feminist approaches were appropriated and reshaped by the media. Like feminist activism, *Der Spiegel* decried the brutal treatment of women and unveiled the years of silence that women had been suffering under. It even linked the West Berlin project to Chiswick Women's Aid and drew its title 'Scream Quietly' from Erin Pizzey's classic text on domestic violence. This narrative was present throughout the media. Almost all of the articles appearing in 1976 emphasised the fact that the Berlin shelter was based on similar projects in the UK and internationally. Most also discussed Pizzey's work and used 'Scream Quietly', or a variation thereof, as a title.[96] The use of women's testimony was also common, with stories of women named Olga, Gudrun and Erika dominating reports of domestic violence.

While such reports reveal how successfully feminists shaped public discourse on domestic violence, it also shows that without feminist scaffolding, the political content of feminist messaging was transformed. Without concomitant critiques of systemic patriarchy and gender roles, women's stories of abuse merely underscored the very norms and ideals feminists were trying to challenge. In stark contrast to feminist literature, women in the mass media were presented as

---

[93] Haffner, 'Gewalt in der Ehe'.

[94] 'Schrei leise', *Der Spiegel*, 18 January 1976, pp. 112–115.

[95] Ibid.

[96] See, for example, 'Schrei leise', *Der Spiegel*; 'Schrei leise', *Hessische Allgemein*, 25 September 1976; Jutta Menschik, 'Schrei Leise. Gewalt gegen Frauen. Erst zögernd beginnen die Betroffenen darueber zu sprechen', *Deutsche Volkszeitung*, 23 September 1976.

the poor, downtrodden victims of men's abuse and as incapable of helping themselves.[97] Moreover, the critique of the gendered private sphere inherent in Pizzey's work *Scream Quietly* simply became a catchy headline.

Even feminist ideas, like self-help and empowerment were interpreted simplistically. One example can be found in Peter Voss's editorial in the women's magazine *Neue Welt*. Picking up on the lack of help for women, Voss asks rhetorically, 'and who helps these women? No one! Neighbours close their doors. Terrible, they think at the most. And: why should we get involved in [others'] marital problems?' Although he 'welcomes' the initiatives of women's groups to create shelters for women and their children, he finishes his editorial by arguing that while shelters 'were a good start', it appears to him that 'it would be better if neighbours were more actively involved. If he wants, neighbour Egon can calm his friend Fritz down and appeal to his conscience better than a psychiatrist or a police officer.'[98] What is so striking about Voss's editorial is that, much like the article in *Der Spiegel*, although it supports feminist activism to address domestic violence, its conclusion undermines the very principles of feminism. While Voss calls on neighbours to be more involved, his solution only privatises responses to domestic violence. For Voss, stopping domestic abuse is about men calming each other down; it is not about making the violence visible to the police or counselling services. He does not even seem to be concerned about women's safety.

Even those politicians closest to the shelter project presented a simplified version of self-help and feminist shelter work to the public. After expressing her support for women's shelters in a 1976 interview, Federal Minister for Youth, Family and Health Katharina Focke stated that ultimately the goal of the shelter should be the maintenance of the family. Moreover, in order to fight the root causes of domestic violence, the state needed to

> make women as a whole more self-sufficient – through better education, better job opportunities, better clarity on their options so that it doesn't even come to the point where women are so dependent on their husbands, that they are even (and sometimes for many years) abused by their husbands.[99]

Similarly, in a 1976 interview, the department head of the Federal Ministry for Youth, Family and Health (and later Hamburg Senator), Helga Elstner, stressed the importance of building up women's independence as a way of tackling domestic violence. Although she acknowledged that women experiencing abuse 'need our

---

[97] For further examples, see Held, 'Gustav'; Peter Voss, 'Meine Meinung: Schläge und Prügel-das haben unsere Frauen nicht verdient', *Neue Welt*, 17 June 1976, p. 2; 'Tabuthema wird neu endlich öffentlich diskutiert'; Haffner, 'Gewalt in der Ehe'; 'Schreien nützt nichts'; 'Soziale Hilfe für geprügelte Frauen', *Die demokratische Gemeinde* (July 1976), pp. 579–580.

[98] Voss, 'Meine Meinung', p. 2.

[99] Parlamentarisch-Politischer Pressedienst, *Das aktuelle PPP-Interview. Brutalität in der Ehe ist ein ernstes Problem*, 6 May 1976, A Rep 400 BRD 22.5 (1970–78), FFBIZ.

help, our solidarity', ultimately she argued that 'effective protection can only be created by the woman herself. She must free herself from the situation.'[100] When it came to the topic of shelters, Elstner further argued that one advantage of refuges is that women can meet other women and together they can support one another.

Similar calls were also made by the FDP and the Christian Democrats in the later 1970s and the 1980s. In a 1978 meeting to discuss the creation of a second domestic violence shelter in Berlin, the FDP's Working Group on Emancipation defined a shelter as 'a group of women who through self-help overcome their problems, wherein the main emphasis lies on the self-initiative of the victim herself'.[101] Hans Geissler, the Christian Democratic Minister for the Family from 1982 to 1985, also drew upon heteropatriarchal tropes when he argued that it was

> the role of the Federal Government and the entire Parliament to stand on the side of those who are weaker physically and socially, and to protect them from the strong ... Women must be made aware that they are not alone with their fates and that they do not need to deal with them alone. That will empower them to search out help and not keep their situation a secret or hushed up.[102]

These ostensibly contradictory messages point to a moderate liberal support for women's rights that had the effect of deradicalising feminist politics and reinforcing patriarchal gender relations. For both Focke and Elstner, the solution to domestic violence (and also to marital breakdown) was fostering women's independence, whether that be through employment and financial independence or by encouraging women to stand up to the violence they experienced. Although this approach appeared to support the work of feminists in empowering women and challenging gender norms, it did so in a way that left the patriarchal status quo largely intact.

Conclusion

Historical scholarship on West Germany – and Western Europe more broadly – has shown that the 1960s and 1970s were marked by a loosening of values and norms as ideas of privacy and intimacy were renegotiated, enabling more personal and sexual autonomy.[103] Historians have typically inscribed these transformations

---

[100] 'Soziale Hilfe für geprügelte Frauen'.
[101] Protokoll der Sitzung vom 20.12.1978, FDP LV Berlin, AK Emanzipation 16850, AdL.
[102] Fachtagung on 'Gewalt gegen Frauen' held by the Bundesminister für Jugend, Familie, Gesundheit, Dr Heiner Geissler, published 13 Jan. 1984 by the Pressedienst der Bundesminister für Jugend, Familie und Gesundheit, B Rep 002/12505, LAB.
[103] On liberalisation and value change, see Konrad H. Jarausch, *After Hitler: Recivilizing Germans, 1945–1995* (Oxford: Oxford University Press, 2006); Ulrich Herbert, ed, *Wandlungsprozesse in Westdeutschland: Belastung, Integration, Liberalisierung, 1945–1980* (Göttingen: Wallstein, 2002); Also see Arthur Marwick, *The Sixties: Cultural Revolution in Britain, France, Italy and the United States* (New York: Bloomsbury, 1999).

in a broader history of the successes of post-war West German democratisation, a process Konrad Jarausch has called 'recivilizing Germans'.[104] This has increasingly been challenged by historians who have shown the conditional nature of liberalisation and the broad-scale failure to examine gender and racial inequality as an integral part of the history of the Federal Republic.[105]

This chapter builds on this historical scholarship, but it also goes further. Examining the transformation of domestic violence work – from its roots in the women's movement to a pilot project with federal funding – it becomes clear that the 'success story' of West German liberalisation was not as successful as previously outlined by historians.[106] Instead, this chapter shows that social change was both limited and functioned within normative boundaries. In fact, the way women's rights were co-opted and popularised indicates that, in some respects, West Germans were not so civilised.

What change did occur was largely contingent on the labour of women and feminists, whose activism challenged the power structures and norms that left women vulnerable to abuse. Throughout the 1970s, feminists successfully delegitimised violence against women. They revealed it as a key issue of women's inequality, highlighted the role patriarchal gender norms played in enabling and perpetuating domestic abuse and they developed a platform for addressing it based on the work of an emerging global shelter movement. Further still, working with the media and politicians, they cemented public and political support for gender violence initiatives and shelters. It was this work that led to the opening of the first domestic violence shelter in Germany in 1976, which the federal government recently called 'a milestone in the development of gender-inclusive policies for the protection of women from violence'.[107] Feminist activists gave women a safe space, where they could access legal, emotional and medical support for dealing with domestic abuse.

---

[104] Jarausch, *After Hitler.*

[105] Christina von Hodenberg, 'Writing Women's Agency into the History of the Federal Republic: "1968," Historians, and Gender', *Central European History*, Vol. 52, No.1 (2019): pp. 87– 106; Frank Biess and Astrid M. Eckert, 'Why Do We Need New Narratives for the History of the Federal Republic?', *Central European History*, Vol. 52, No. 1 (2019): pp. 1–18; Annette Timm, *The Politics of Fertility in Twentieth-Century Berlin* (New York: Cambridge University Press, 2010); Jennifer V. Evans, *Life among the Ruins: Cityscape and Sexuality in Cold War Berlin* (New York: Palgrave, 2011); Dagmar Herzog, *Sex After Fascism: Memory and Morality in Twentieth-Century Germany* (Princeton: Princeton University Press, 2005); Joachim Häberlen, 'Feeling Like a Child: Dreams and Practices of Sexuality in the West-German Alternative Left during the Long 1970s', *Journal of the History of Sexuality*, Vol. 25, No. 2 (2016): pp. 219–245; Lauren Stokes, '"An Invasion of Guest Worker Children": Welfare Reform and the Stigmatisation of Family Migration', *Contemporary European History*, Vol. 28, No. 3 (2019), pp. 1–19; Lauren Stokes, 'The Permanent Refugee Crisis in the Federal Republic, 1949–', *Central European History*, Vol. 52, No. 1 (2019), pp. 19–44; Elizabeth Heineman, *Before Porn Was Legal: The Erotica Empire of Beate Uhse* (Chicago: University of Chicago Press, 2011).

[106] Jarausch, *After Hitler.*

[107] Bundesministerium für Familie, Senioren, Frauen und Jugend. *Bericht der Bundesregierung zur Situation der Frauenhäuser, Fachberatungsstellen und anderer Unterstützungsangebote für gewaltbetroffene Frauen und deren Kinder* (Berlin: Bundesministerium für Familie, Senioren, Frauen und Jugend, 2013) p. 5.

Of course, the media was also a vehicle in driving this change. But it may be best to view their role with circumspect. As Christina von Hodenberg has shown in an analysis of the reception of the sitcom *All in the Family* in the US, West Germany and the UK, writers and producers frequently used changing norms and values emerging out of the women's movement as fodder for plotlines, which they then watered down to appeal to a mass market.[108] This is exactly what happened with domestic violence work. Despite drawing on feminist politics and practice, the media diluted the radical politics underpinning feminist ideas in their reporting on domestic violence. Indeed, the very success of the shelter was, in part, predicated on this deradicalisation and the separation of shelter work from its feminist origins. Politicians supporting the project actively sought to distance the shelter from ideas of patriarchy and the women's movement as a way of legitimising the project. At best this had the effect of depoliticising feminism. At worst, it solidified the very patriarchal gender norms that fed into violence against women in the home.

This further suggests that much of the support for domestic violence activism was built on gendered ideals. In other words, women have been protected from abuse, not out of a commitment to equality, but because they are women. Although this was exacerbated by the media drawing on narratives of women's victimhood, it was also a tension inherent in the feminist activism of the 1970s. While a narrative of vulnerability enabled feminist activists, in particular those seeking to address domestic violence, to advocate for women's issues and gain funding for much-needed women's services, it also worked to codify injury and powerlessness as a part of womanhood.[109] This would haunt women's activism in both West and reunified Germany. As Chapter 6 shows, this gendering of women's rights would have important ramifications in the early 1990s, as the fall of the Berlin Wall and German reunification brought issues of women's rights into the limelight once more.

But the transformation of domestic violence activism did not stop with the media. As the next chapter shows, once activists started engaging with women after the opening of the shelter, feminist principles of self-help, autonomy and empowerment would be put to the test.

---

[108] Christina von Hodenberg, *Television's Moment: Sitcom Audiences and the Sixties Cultural Revolution* (New York: Berghahn, 2015).
[109] Wendy Brown, *States of Injury: Power and Freedom in Late Modernity* (Princeton: Princeton University Press, 1995); Melzer, *Death in the Shape of a Young Girl*; Yanara Schmacks, ' "Motherhood is beautiful": Conceptions of Maternalism in the West German New Women's Movement between Eroticization and Ecological Protest', *Central European History*, Vol. 53, No. 4 (2020): pp. 811– 834.

3

Race, Class and Everyday Life in the Shelter

Four months after the women's shelter opened in West Berlin, Alice Schwarzer published an article on domestic violence work in her recently launched feminist magazine *EMMA*. In what was only its second issue, 'A Day in the House for Battered Women' detailed the stories of the Berlin shelter's first residents.[1] There was Gudrun, 36 years old, housewife and mother of four children, who remarried her abusive husband after he promised to change. Meanwhile, Ilona, 27 years old and mother of three children, had followed a tip about the shelter from a social worker. And Renate, a 48-year-old cashier, who was too afraid of her husband's abuse to apply for a divorce.[2] Along with three other women and two children, they all shared a room in the shelter, living and sleeping together, safely away from their husbands' abuse.

Much like the pamphlets published by the shelter initiative, Schwarzer's article emphasised both the brutality of domestic violence and the structures that prevented women from leaving. Renate's lawyer told her that 'unless she's carrying her head under her arm, there's nothing that can be done and when the police responded to Ilona after her husband had dangled their child out the window, they simply scoffed 'What do you want? The child is still alive.'[3] Over and over, the stories Schwarzer told highlighted the ordinariness of abuse. These women's experiences were not exceptional; they were commonplace. Perpetrated by all social classes, as Schwarzer argued, even the 'most gentle man' could be violent.[4]

But Schwarzer took this further. 'And now it is clear. We are all battered women', she proclaimed. 'Even those of us who are not beaten four times a week must reckon with the possibility of male violence.'[5] According to Schwarzer, the fear of male violence was something all women faced. It fundamentally shaped

---

[1] Alice Schwarzer, 'Ein Tag im Haus für geschlagene Frauen', *EMMA*, March 1977, pp. 6–12.
[2] Ibid., p. 7.
[3] Ibid.
[4] Ibid., p. 9.
[5] Ibid.

women's interactions with the world and other people: 'on the street at night, we speed up our pace as soon as someone starts walking behind us. A drunk swears at us and we don't reply because we're scared of drawing the short straw.'[6] But, as Schwarzer revealed, these experiences could also be productive. Specifically, the recognition that they were shared experiences could open women's eyes to their collective inequality and thereby spur change. Indeed, for Schwarzer, it was precisely because of these experiences that shelter work existed in the first place: 'and when today there is finally this option for the most serious incidents, then that is not thanks to patriarchal society, nor the police, doctors or bureaucrats, but rather it is thanks to women, more precisely feminists … All women, who thanks to their everyday experiences knew: something must change!'[7]

Although such universalising statements might come across as trivialising the experiences of survivors of gender violence, in the 1970s pointing to the ubiquity of violence in women's lives was an important feminist tool to create solidarity among women in West Germany.[8] In the same year that Alice Schwarzer claimed that 'we are all battered women', a feminist group in Marburg went so far as to argue that 'the disavowal of our person, our interests, our thoughts and feelings, that is the violence that is so hard to see and all the more dangerous for it. That is the violence that makes physical abuse possible.' For the Marburg group, violence was something that all women, by virtue of being women, experienced. Whether it was 'being chatted up on the street, a hand suddenly touching your arse … wolf-whistles, suggestive glances and leers … ignoring our thought processes in seminars', violence was a quotidian experience for women. Moreover, these banal acts enabled more extreme forms of violence against women: 'rape and abuse are unthinkable without the general oppression of women as people.'[9]

This feminist understanding of violence against women had important consequences for addressing domestic abuse. It guided both how women activists understood violence in the family and how they sought to address it. Bringing women together to discuss violence was not only a way of creating feminist solidarity, but it was also envisioned as a way of supporting women who were experiencing domestic abuse. This stood at the very heart of the shelter's mission. Built as a site for the realisation of feminist ideals, it was structured on the principles of anti-authoritarianism, equality, separatism and women-helping-women that feminists believed would empower women to unite through their shared victimhood and together cast off the shackles of male oppression.[10]

---

[6] Ibid. See also Ann Cahill, *Rethinking Rape* (Ithaca: Cornell University Press, 2001).
[7] Ibid.
[8] See also Patricia Melzer, *Death in the Shape of a Young Girl: Women's Political Violence in the Red Army Faction* (New York: New York University Press, 2015).
[9] 'Dokumentation der Marburger Gruppe: Gewalt gegen Frauen', A Rep 400 BRD 22 Broschüren gegen Gewalt (1976–2001), FFBIZ.
[10] Projektantrag zur Einrichtung eines Frauenhauses in Berlin (West) (1976), B Rep 002/12504, LAB.

But this did not work as planned. As shelters opened throughout the Federal Republic in the late 1970s and domestic violence activists encountered 'battered women', they realised their expectations would need adjustment. Women arriving at the shelter were not like activists had envisioned; they were simply not interested in feminist politics – instead they wanted help and safe harbour. As it turned out, not all women were battered women and the supposed unity of women was inflected by social disparities and inequalities.

This chapter examines how activists responded to these challenges in ways that irrevocably changed the shelter system. Specifically, it looks at how feminists sought to realise their political aims in the shelter and how women responded to them. Whereas the previous chapter examined the role of the media and politicians in shaping domestic violence activism, here the focus shifts to the transformations brought about by shelter residents and other feminists. In the 1970s, domestic violence activism not only had to 'march through the institutions', but it also had to respond to the very real needs of the women they were trying to help. Everyday interactions within the shelter often served as a reality-check for feminists, as they discovered the objects of their activism had their own ideas and opinions about how best to respond to domestic violence. This was both a productive and transformative experience for shelter activists and workers and led to more responsive and differentiated support for survivors of gender-based violence. However, it also fed into the broader institutionalisation of feminism and feminist politics and, as such, was a disappointment for activists striving to offer autonomous, grassroots support.[11]

Examining this tension, the chapter complicates the history of the deradicalisation of feminist politics. Scholars typically attribute this history to processes of co-optation, whereby the neoliberal state adopts the principles and work of activists and rights-based movements in service of solidifying a broader normative agenda.[12] But the institutionalisation of feminism was not only a result of the co-optation of women's rights activism by the media and the West German state. It also came about out of interactions with shelter residents and other activists who challenged feminist politics and ideals. In particular, this chapter focuses on the role of class and race in the evolution of domestic violence activism.

---

[11] Bernhard Gotto, *Enttäuschung in der Demokratie. Erfahrung und Deutung von politischem Engagement in der Bundesrepublik Deutschland während der 1970er und 1980er Jahre* (Berlin: De Gruyter, 2018).

[12] See, for example, Kristin Bumiller, *In An Abusive State: How Neoliberalism Appropriated the Feminist Movement against Sexual Violence* (Durham: Duke University Press, 2008); Jasbir Puar, *Terrorist Assemblages: Homonationalism in Queer Times* (Durham: Duke University Press, 2007); Wendy Brown, *States of Injury: Power and Freedom in Late Modernity* (Princeton: Princeton University Press, 1995).

After years of campaigning, the shelter initiative – now a registered organisation called *Frauenhaus-Frauen helfen Frauen* or Women's Shelter-Women Helping Women – had achieved its goal. By August 1976, it had met the official requirements laid out by the Federal Ministry for Youth, Family and Health. It had become a publicly registered association, formed a governing body and resubmitted a detailed project proposal to the Ministry and the Berlin Senate. The initiative also agreed to have its work observed and evaluated by an academic research team. In return, the Federal Ministry for Youth, Family and Health and the West Berlin Senate Office for Family, Youth and Sport agreed to support the shelter as pilot project and provide an annual budget of 450,000DM for a three-year trial period.[13] By 1 October, a suitable house had been found on the outskirts of the city and construction was under way to ensure the building was fit for its new purpose. Only 10 days later, and before the official opening, the first woman knocked at the door looking for help.

Although the requirements set by the Ministry were aimed at reining in the shelter group, it is clear that from the very beginning the shelter was a political project. Indeed, the shelter proposal lays out a vision of helping women that is strongly underpinned by feminist politics. First and foremost, the shelter was to be a space for women. No men were allowed in the house, including shelter workers and the older male children of the residents.[14] Not only did the activists in *Frauenhaus-Frauen helfen Frauen* fear the damaging impact that interacting and living with men could have on residents, but they also believed that only other women could understand what it meant to be 'confronted by the position of women in society'. Furthermore, women needed to be free to speak about their experiences, which activists did not believe was possible among men.[15]

Secondly, drawing on grassroots autonomous organising, activists wanted the shelter to offer women an alternative to official welfare services. In comparison to a system that they argued treated women and families like case files, Berlin activists wanted the shelter to be 'unbureaucratic', a place where all women were welcome and treated with respect and dignity.[16] The shelter was to be 'cosy' and

[13] Carol Hagemann-White, Barbara Kavemann, Johanna Kootz, Ute Weinmann, Carola Christine Wildt, Roswitha Burgard and Ursula Scheu, *Hilfen für mißhandelte Frauen: Abschlussbericht der wissenschaftlichen Begleitung des Modellprojekts Frauenhaus Berlin* (Stuttgart: Verlag W. Kohlhammer, 1981).
[14] *Frauen gegen Männergewalt. Berliner Frauenhaus für misshandelte Frauen. Erster Erfahrungsbericht* (Berlin-West: Frauenselbstverlag, 1978).
[15] Verein zur Förderung des Schutzes misshandelter Frauen (e.V) Projektantrag zur Einrichtung eines Frauenhauses in Berlin (West) (1976), B Rep 002/12504, LAB.
[16] Projektantrag zur Einrichtung eines Frauenhauses in Berlin (West) (1976), B Rep 002/12504, LAB; Myra Marx Ferree, *Varieties of Feminism: German Gender Politics in Global Perspective* (Stanford: Stanford University Press, 2012); Myra Marx Ferree, 'Equality and Autonomy: Feminist Politics in the United States and West Germany' in *The Women's Movements of the United States and Western Europe. Consciousness, Political Opportunity, and Public Policy*, edited by Mary Fainsod Katzenstein and Carol McClurg Mueller (Philadelphia: Temple University Press, 1987): pp. 172–195.

not feel like an institution.[17] They believed the shelter should be an equal space, where a 'hierarchical organisation' was 'unthinkable', both between the residents and workers and between the workers themselves. Instead, everyone had to be prepared to do all jobs – there was to be no specialisation according to training.[18] Even the most educated shelter worker had to be ready to get her hands dirty.

By giving women protection from men and from violence, treating them with respect and as equals, activists laid the groundwork for empowering women living with an abusive spouse. This was then reinforced by the organisation of daily life in the shelter, which was ordered around the principle of self-help. 'As far as possible, the women in the shelter should organise their daily life themselves', the shelter proposal declared. Although there was a *Hausmutter* or 'House Mother' who oversaw and coordinated shelter life, it was the residents who were to do the housework and cooking: 'The women arrange the communal life of the house, in which they organise group discussions, whether focused on a topic or improvised, social gatherings and much more themselves.' The goal of this was, firstly, to show residents that they could do things by themselves, giving them self-confidence and independence and secondly, to create solidarity between women.[19]

On 1 November 1976, these ideals became reality, as the first women's shelter in West Germany opened in the wealthy neighbourhood of Grunewald in Berlin's leafy western outskirts. Women flocked to the new shelter from across West Berlin and soon after, similar projects emerged throughout the Federal Republic, with shelters opening in Hamburg, Frankfurt, Cologne and Heidelberg. Unlike these other shelters, however, as a pilot project, part of the Berlin shelter's *raison d'être* was to prove to both the federal and state governments that such services were necessary. As such, it had a significant amount of funding, with almost two-thirds going towards personnel costs. Alongside the 'House Mother', they employed two childcare workers, one administrator, two social researchers/psychologists and two social workers. There was also money to contract freelance consultants in medicine, law and childcare. At the same time, as a pilot project, the Berlin shelter was evaluated by a team of social researchers. The report arising from this investigation, *Help for Abused Women*, not only presented the first raw data on domestic violence in West Germany, but also provided an important glimpse into the lives of women in the shelter.[20]

Help for Abused Women showed that of the 1,000 women surveyed at the shelter, 72.4 per cent were married, 90.1 per cent were between 20 and 50 years

---

[17] Verein zur Förderung des Schutzes misshandelter Frauen (e.V) Projektantrag zur Einrichtung eines Frauenhauses in Berlin (West) (1976), B Rep 002/12504, LAB.
[18] Ibid.
[19] Ibid.
[20] Hagemann-White *et al.*, *Hilfen*; Verein zur Förderung des Schutzes misshandelter Frauen (e.V) Projektantrag zur Einrichtung eines Frauenhauses in Berlin (West) (1976), B Rep 002/12504, LAB.

old and 52 per cent came with one or two children.[21] The women had lived with both physical and emotional abuse for years. While 54 per cent of residents had been living with abuse for between one and three years, as many as 12 per cent had experienced domestic violence for 15 years or more. In terms of the kind of abuse, 83 per cent reported having been physically beaten and abused, 41 per cent said that they were psychologically 'worn out' from mistreatment, 25 per cent were beaten with objects, 29 per cent of women reported being threatened with murder/attempted murder and 50 per cent reported having been forced into non-consensual sex acts.[22]

Having heard about the shelter from family, friends, social workers or even the police, women who arrived at the shelter were greeted with cramped and overcrowded living conditions.[23] Even at 660 square metres and with 15 bedrooms over four floors, the shelter was constantly over capacity. In the first three years, the shelter housed around 2,500 women and just as many children.[24] Designed to house 30 women and around 60 to 70 children at any one time, by autumn 1978 the monthly average was 50 to 60 women with similar numbers of children.[25] Bedrooms were shared by up to 15 people and extra beds were placed in the communal areas as needed. Most residents (around 49 per cent) would only stay one to three days in the shelter, a fact *Help for Abused Women* attributed to the tight living conditions.[26]

The shelter day started at 7 a.m. with the arrival of the first worker. At this time, the employed women and school-aged children left for the day, while the younger children and mothers waited in the living room for the day-care staff to arrive. In these early morning hours, the residents greeted new arrivals and organised the communal childcare, cleaning and groceries. At 9 a.m., the day-care staff arrived to pick up the children. Further shelter workers also arrived at this time and caught up on the newest arrivals before beginning their work assisting the shelter residents. Around 12:30, children began returning from school, group discussions were held with residents and there was a change to the afternoon shift of shelter workers. Twice a week at this same time, there were consultations with lawyers, and once every week, medical and parenting consultants provided advice. Between 2 and 3.30 p.m., school-aged children completed their homework and free time started at 4 p.m. At 7 p.m., the shelter workers left for the day and the women were free to organise their own time until 10 p.m. when it was quiet time.

---

[21] Hagemann-White *et al.*, *Hilfen*, pp. 37–38.
[22] Ibid., p. 83.
[23] Ibid., p. 246.
[24] Ibid., p. 198
[25] Bericht über den Modellversuch 'Hilfen für misshandelte Frauen' (Frauenhaus), B Rep 002/12504a, LAB.
[26] Ibid.; Hagemann-White *et al.*, *Hilfen*, p. 247.

Overnight, residents would manage the shelter hotline, speaking with women needing assistance.[27]

During the pilot phase, 82.4 per cent of the women who came to the shelter were German, coming both from West Berlin and the wider Federal Republic. The remaining 17.6 per cent of women were foreign-born, the largest groups from Turkey and Yugoslavia.[28] Residents came from all over Berlin, with many arriving from the lower socio-economic and working-class areas of Kreuzberg and Neukölln.[29] For the most part, the residents were not financially independent or secure – though 40 per cent of women in the shelter were employed, 21.4 per cent were supported by their husband and 21.6 per cent were on social welfare. Of those with jobs, approximately 11 per cent faced unemployment as a result of absences and other workplace and personal issues resulting from the abuse.[30]

For those women arriving at the shelter, most simply wished for peace and quiet. They wanted help finding an apartment (43 per cent), with getting a job (13 per cent) and legal support (24 per cent). They envisioned finding a safe place for themselves and their children, where they could attain financial and personal stability through employment and skills training. They wanted to heal from the mistreatment from which they had escaped.[31] What few wanted, however, was to live with other women and join women's groups. But this clashed with the expectations that feminists had of battered women; as soon as shelters opened in the Federal Republic, the idealistic principles of feminism were put to the test.

Encountering Battered Women

In 1981, a young woman recounted the story of her first – and only – day volunteering at one of the autonomous women's shelters in Hamburg.[32] She had hoped that shelter work would be a way to achieve her 'vague, idealistic goal' of women's emancipation. But only a few hours in to her first shift, she realised this was impossible.[33] Constantly pestered by residents' trivial matters – whether they could use the house bike or get money for the bus – she soon became critical of the feminist principles she once held, no longer believing that residents could be brought to self-help. Disillusioned, she left shelter work after only a few hours.

---

[27] Hagemann-White *et al.*, *Hilfen*, p. 202–204.
[28] Ibid., p. 36.
[29] Landespressedienst, Berlin, Aus dem Abgeordnetenhaus, 10. Februar 1978, Nr. 30, Kleine Anfrage Nr. 2696 des Abgeordneten Wolfgang Maerz (SPD) vom 17.1. 1978 über Frauenhaus, B Rep 002/12504, LAB.
[30] Hagemann-White *et al.*, *Hilfen*, p. 39.
[31] Ibid., p. 106–107.
[32] 'Unter dem Mantel des Helfenwollens: Fünf Szenen aus dem Frauenhausalltag', *Courage* 11 (1981), p. 16.
[33] Ibid., p. 17.

She was not alone. Her story was one of six former Hamburg shelter workers' accounts published in the West Berlin feminist magazine *Courage*. By the early 1980s, many young feminists had become frustrated with the realities of shelter work and were abandoning domestic violence activism.[34] Although they had begun with lofty goals of liberating women through self-help and creating a network of support outside of the official welfare system, activists were upset when the women they sought to help had different ideas. For one activist in Heidelberg, working in a shelter had only taught her 'to give up the ideals that I still held'.[35] So what exactly had happened to cause such a drastic response?

In the early years of domestic violence work, activists were confronted with the stark realisation that their ideas of self-administration, empowerment, solidarity and equality did not reflect the interests or capabilities of the women they were meant to be helping. Upon working with shelter residents, it became clear that many of the ideals and goals activists had for empowering women would need to be revised. 'Battered women' were not the voiceless, downtrodden victims so often portrayed in the media. Instead, they had their own ideas about what help they wanted and needed and this frequently clashed with feminist politics.

The overarching aim of empowering women to challenge male violence was quickly dashed, as it became clear that women arriving at shelters did not necessarily want to leave their husbands. More than 50 per cent of all the women who stayed at the Berlin shelter during the pilot phase ended up returning to their husbands.[36] Although for some this was the result of financial and familial pressures, for others it was guided by normative expectations of love and idealised visions of family life and marriage. According to the researchers at the shelter, for women it was 'inconceivable to be abused by a man who claims he loves her, especially when she feels affection for him'.[37]

The very norms that feminists were trying to challenge, then, actually contributed to women remaining with and returning to abusive husbands. For example, in response to the question of why they stayed with their abuser, one-quarter of Berlin shelter residents between 1976 and 1979 responded that they believed he would change, one-quarter stayed to keep the family together/for the children and 5 per cent because they loved their husband. Similar findings were also made in an Austrian study of domestic violence conducted by the sociologists Cheryl Benard and Edit Schlaffer. Interviewing women for over five years at Viennese counselling centres, Benard and Schlaffer found that while material

---

[34] 'Wir machen das Haus zu', *Courage* 1 (1981), pp. 4–5; 'Diskussionspapier des Frauenhauses Heidelberg zum Thema Selbstverwaltung, Februar 1981', quoted in Erika Steinert and Ute Straub, *Interaktionsort Frauenhaus. Möglichkeiten und Grenzen einen feministischen Projektes* (Heidelberg: Verlag des Wunderhorn, 1988).

[35] Steinert and Straub, *Interaktionsort*, p. 86.

[36] Hagemann-White *et al.*, *Hilfen*, p. 322.

[37] Ibid., p. 96.

dependence and shared children contributed to women returning to a violent spouse, they were not 'decisive'.[38] Instead what they encountered most often in their interviews with women was 'the fear of losing their partner and not finding a new one'.[39]

Indeed, women arriving at the shelter typically did not want self-help or feminist politicking. Rather they wanted *help* – with finding an apartment, getting a job or a divorce. But shelter residents also needed support with serious problems that activists had not even fully considered. Drug and alcohol dependencies were a particularly common issue for women seeking help from the shelter. In 1978, a Senate enquiry initiated by Social Democratic politician Wolfgang Maerz revealed that the Grunewald shelter had underestimated the addiction problems women faced.[40] The research report from the shelter further revealed that of 51 residents interviewed, 13 either had or previously had drug dependencies.[41] Of particular concern were pill addictions. While doctors would prescribe narcotics to treat the symptoms of abuse (for example, anxiety, depression), for women living with abuse this all too easily became a means of escape.[42] As one Berlin shelter resident recalled: 'somehow with pills and alcohol I blocked it all, I didn't have to think about everything.'[43]

Shelter workers also quickly discovered the impact that domestic abuse could have on children, something feminist approaches had not considered. Soon after the opening of the Grunewald shelter, the childcare workers noticed how distressed some of the children were. Not only did they find that witnessing violence had traumatised the children, but also that some had themselves been beaten and sexually abused.[44] They would not run or play, they were scared of moving around without someone holding their hand, many did not speak or were at a lower developmental stage and they were frightened by loud noises. Also of concern was that it was often the mothers who hit their children.[45]

This was something early domestic violence activists had not reckoned with. A 1987 doctoral dissertation from social scientist Ute Straub underscored the difficulties voluntary shelter workers in Heidelberg faced when they first

---

[38] Cheryl Benard and Edit Schlaffer, *Die ganz gewöhnliche Gewalt in der Ehe. Texte zu einer Soziologie von Macht und Liebe* (Hamburg: Rowohlt Taschenbuch Verlag, 1978), p. 67.
[39] Ibid., p. 68.
[40] Landespressedienst, Berlin, Aus dem Abgeordnetenhaus, 10. Februar 1978, Nr. 30, Kleine Anfrage nr. 2696 des Abgeordneten Wolfgang Maerz (SPD) vom 17.1. 1978 über Frauenhaus, B Rep 002/ 12504, LAB.
[41] Hagemann-White *et al.*, *Hilfen*, p. 151.
[42] Ibid; Sarah Haffner, *Gewalt in der Ehe und was Frauen dagegen tun* (Berlin: Verlag Klaus Wagenbach, 1981).
[43] Hagemann-White *et al.*, *Hilfen*, p. 152.
[44] Interview with 'Dagmar', Osnabrück, 5 August 2013.
[45] Hagemann-White *et al.*, *Hilfen*, p. 175; Ferree, *Varieties of Feminism*.

encountered battered women.[46] For one volunteer Straub interviewed, working in the shelter had

> Proven different than I had theorised. That women would have an interest in joining the women's movement. That they might want to come to group meetings or information sessions. And, in reality, they just want help! … For them the women's shelter really was a support service, and they took that offer seriously and wanted to be taken care of.[47]

Another Heidelberg worker recalled how they would sit around complaining about how difficult it was with the residents, laughing at the havoc the women would wreak in the shelter.[48] Much like the woman in Hamburg, who left after only one day, these workers clearly struggled with the realisation that shelter residents were not ready, willing or perhaps even able to jump into feminist emancipation as activists had initially envisioned.

It seemed then that even though they were all women, the initial ideals of collective sisterhood were proving illusory. Activists attributed these difficulties to class, specifically the difference in social position between themselves and the women arriving at the shelters. While the women who sought help from the shelters were predominantly from working-class backgrounds, domestic violence activists were typically well educated and middle class. Indeed, Straub's analysis shows that the volunteers who started the Heidelberg shelter were drawn to domestic violence activism as a result of being discriminated against during their studies.[49] Similarly, the Berlin shelter organisers were lawyers and social workers.[50] As a result of these differences, feminist discussions of women experiencing domestic violence often point to the inability of working-class women to appreciate self-help, suggesting that they were not 'ready' for feminism and drawing on long-standing bourgeois tropes about the working classes. A 1981 discussion paper from the women's shelter in Heidelberg demonstrates this confrontation with class privilege most precisely:

> Our ideas of self-administration by women assumed structures and capabilities that they, on the basis of their different life experiences, don't have. … A further difficulty is, that the basic principle "women can help women, because we all suffer under the same conditions" has increasingly slipped away from us. The class differences make it hard to find a starting point that reflects both sides.[51]

---

[46] Ute Straub, *Interaktionsort Frauenhaus. Institutionalisierung und Professionalisierung des Frauenhausprojekts* (Ph.D. Diss., Ruprecht-Karls University, 1987).
[47] Ibid., p. 160.
[48] Ibid., p. 159.
[49] Ibid., p. 151.
[50] "Geschlagen—Getreten—Gedemütigt. Frauen werden von Männern misshandelt! Wo finden sie Hilfe? Wir brauchen ein Frauenhaus", E Rep 300–96/ 9, LAB.
[51] 'Diskussionspapier des Frauenhauses Heidelberg zum Thema Selbstverwaltung, Februar 1981', quoted in Steinert and Straub, *Interaktionsort Frauenhaus*, p. 40.

Such comments are particularly striking given the emphasis feminists placed on domestic violence as a cross-class issue. What they had not considered, however, was the fact that although domestic abuse is experienced in both working- and middle-class families, women with greater access to financial resources and more social capital were less likely to need emergency housing. Instead, they could turn to hotels, friends or families and they could seek private legal and medical help. In contrast, the women who sought help from shelters were particularly socially vulnerable, with almost 50 per cent of all residents at the Berlin shelter living on funds from social welfare, unemployment benefits, disability insurance or their husbands.

To contemporary eyes, it might seem peculiar that activists had so misjudged women and that they did not realise that they would want – and expect – help from a women's shelter. It is safe to say that these early activists did not know what issues battered women and their children would have, nor did they fully understand the impact that long-term violence had on women. At the time, research on domestic violence was only in its infancy and mainly emphasised violence in the family as a rare psychological pathology or spoke of it euphemistically.[52] It was only in the 1970s, with the rise of the New Left and the women's movement that academics turned to domestic abuse in a more systematic way.[53] Much of this early academic and activist literature, much of which was in English, focused on showing that abuse in the family existed, that it was a serious issue and resulted from a variety of social factors. In 2005, American feminist Del Martin, who penned *Battered Wives* in 1976, one of the earliest examinations of domestic violence in the US, remarked that her publisher instructed her to 'produce extensive and verifiable statistics on the incidence of violence against women.'[54] It was not until the late 1970s that a more detailed literature reflecting the complexity of domestic abuse emerged, for

[52] Richard J. Gelles, 'Child Abuse as Psychopathology: A Sociological Critique and Reformulation', *American Journal of Orthopsychiatry*, No. 43 (July 1973): pp. 611–621; John J. Spinetta and David Rigler, 'The Child Abusing Parent: A Psychological Review', *Psychological Bulletin* 77 (April) (1972), pp. 296–304; Leroy G. Schultz, 'The Wife Assaulter', *Journal of Social Therapy*, Vol. 6, No. 2 (1960), pp. 103–111; John Snell, Richard J. Rosenwald and Ames Robey, 'The Wifebeater's Wife: A Study of Family Interaction', *Archives of General Psychiatry*, Vol. 11, No. 2 (1964), pp. 107–112. In German see Theodor Bovet, *Die Ehe – ihre Krise und Neuwerdung* (Tübingen: Katzmann Verlag, 1951); Carl Heinrich Huter, *Wie Ehen glücklich werden* (Stuttgart: Annelies Huter Verlag, 1953); Joachim Bodamer, *Schule der Ehe* (Freiburg: Herder-Bücherei, 1960). Also see Julia Spohr, '"Ein bißchen Gewalt dürfen Sie schon anwenden." Zum Umgang mit Gewalt in Paarbeziehungen in deutschen Ehe- und Partnerschaftsratgebern (1950er – 1990er Jahre)'. Paper presented at the conference Revolution der Paarbeziehungen? Der Wandel des Beziehungslebens in Bundesrepublik und DDR, Centre for Contemporary History, Potsdam [online], 12 March 2020.

[53] Richard J. Gelles, 'Violence in the Family: A Review of Research in the Seventies', *Journal of Marriage and Family*, Vol. 42, No. 4 (1980), pp. 873–885; Karrin Hanshew, *Terror and Democracy in West Germany* (Cambridge: Cambridge University Press, 2012).

[54] Del Martin, 'Reflection' in *Violence Against Women: Classic Papers*, edited by Raquel Kennedy Bergen, Jeffrey L. Edleson and Claire M. Renzetti (Boston: Pearson, 2005), pp. 166–167.

example, in the major academic studies of Rebecca and Russell Dobash or Cheryl Benard and Edit Schlaffer.[55]

To fill the lacunae in this literature, activists theorised and drew from feminist evaluations of violence and gender in crafting their approach to domestic abuse. Not yet aware of the complexity of domestic violence, they came up with a political solution for what they saw as a political issue. Although the Berlin shelter, like many other shelters in West Germany and Europe, modelled themselves on London's Chiswick Women's Aid, much of the preliminary organisation and discussion of abuse took place among feminists. Indeed, as the previous chapter showed, the transnational feminist movement was vital to shaping feminist understandings of abuse and domestic violence activism in West Germany. In practice, however, it appears as if working within the feminist milieu created a set of expectations of what working in a shelter would be like. From examining activists' reflections, it becomes clear that they expected shelter residents to be like them: self-reliant, interested in feminist politics and wanting empowerment and solidarity.

This is particularly the case for volunteers in the shelter, who were the most frustrated at the failure of feminist ideals. The Heidelberg women's refuge, for example, was initiated and first run by volunteers, before they left disillusioned by shelter work and were replaced by social workers. Volunteers from the Hamburg shelter were so disappointed with their activism that they published their stories in *Courage*.[56] While the West Berlin shelter was better prepared for working with women, having the advantage of being run by professionals and supported by a research team active and knowledgeable in the field of violence against women, a division grew between the founding organisation – *Frauenhaus-Frauen helfen Frauen* – and the public representatives who sat on the shelter's governing board. Whereas the activists came from a more 'ideological position' and were connected with the broader women's movement, the public representatives were responsible for the shelter's formal organisation. This conflict was discussed in response to a parliamentary enquiry from SPD politician Wolfgang Maerz, when the senator responsible for the shelter, Ilse Reichel, revealed that around six months after the Grunewald shelter opened, 'intense debate' began between these two groups over the 'conceptual foundation' of the house.[57] While she provided no further detail on this conflict, it does suggest a disagreement over the realisation of feminist ideals in the shelter.

---

[55] Emerson Dobash and Russell Dobash, *Violence Against Wives: A Case Against the Patriarchy* (New York: Free Press, 1979); Benard and Schlaffer, *Die ganz gewöhnliche Gewalt in der Ehe*.
[56] 'Unter dem Mantel des Helfenwollens'.
[57] See, for example, Marbach, 'Frauenhaus – der Bedarf ist gross'; Kleine Anfrage Nr. 2696 des Abgeordneten Wolfgang März (SPD) vom 17. Januar 1978, B Rep 002/12504, LAB.

In the shelter's early years then, activists were confronted by the inadequacy of their principles and the class-based assumptions that pervaded them. Encountering women revealed that violence in the family has a wide-reaching impact and responding to it is complex. Self-help and empowerment were not enough, and in response, shelters began to professionalise. At the Heidelberg shelter, for example, the founders of the project – who left in frustration at the failure of their ideals – were slowly replaced by professional social workers, therapists and carers. The initial principle of self-help slipped away, as shelters increasingly turned into a welfare service. Similarly, the attempt to forge equality between workers and residents fell away. Instead, shelter workers increasingly focused on the needs of women, rather than on feminist politics.[58]

This slow institutionalisation of shelter work did not pass activists by. As the young women from the Hamburg shelter wrote in *Courage*, they felt 'torn between the demands of the authorities and the expectations of the residents'.[59] Their goal of creating an egalitarian, grassroots space was dashed as they took on the role of a 'buffer' between residents and the authorities and worked increasingly as the 'long-arm of bureaucracy', rather than as radical activists.[60] As Chapter 6 shows, these nascent critiques and the disappointment at the possibilities of feminist politics would continue to echo into the late 1970s and 1980s when questions of shelter funding and the bureaucratisation of domestic violence work reached a new tenor.

But it was not only 'battered women' that drove the transformation of domestic violence activism. In the 1980s, activists from migrant backgrounds began to speak out against the way their lives and experiences had been used by white, German feminists in service of their cause.

Migrant Women Talk Back

In 1978, *Courage* ran an article outlining the difficult situation facing women migrants:

> In Spain, Greece and Turkey an employed woman is uncommon. ... There it is expected that men provide for the necessary maintenance of the family. ... But, when they migrate to Germany, they [the women] find themselves equal to their husbands. They work just like men, more actually because they are still responsible for the house. So why do they continue to accept the autocratic Pasha at home?[61]

---

[58] Steinert and Straub, *Interaktionsort Frauenhaus*.
[59] 'Unter dem Mantel des Helfenwollens'.
[60] Ibid.
[61] Cornelia Mansfeld, 'Ausländerinnen im Frauenhaus', *Courage* 4 (1978), p. 18.

The article went on to argue that this loss of power in the family and men's con-frontation with women's equality in West Germany not only led male migrants to engage in gambling and other 'semi-legal' activities, but also resulted in violence against women, as these foreign men attempted to keep their wives 'in check' with their fists.[62] After describing the issues facing migrant women within the shelter system, the article finished by providing the banking information for the autono-mous women's shelter in West Berlin where Germans could make donations 'for foreign women'.[63]

As Ilse Lenz, Tiffany Florvil and Jennifer Miller have all highlighted, the women's movement in West Germany was not homogenous: women of colour and migrant women actively took part in feminist politics.[64] However, their involvement in feminism and indeed the intersections of gender and race within feminism have not always been acknowledged, either historically, or within the historiography. And yet, whether through the activism of migrant women and women of colour, or the uncomfortable and sometimes problematic ways feminists marshalled the stories of Turkish migrants, race was central to the evolution of domestic violence work in Germany.[65]

During the model phase of the Grunewald shelter between 1976 and 1979, only 17.6 per cent of residents were from outside of Germany. The largest group of foreign-born residents was from Turkey, likely coming to West Germany as a part of the guest-worker migration programme which recruited men and women from southern Europe and the Mediterranean into the West German labour force from the mid-1950s. Only one-quarter of these women were married to German men. In spite of these relatively low numbers, Turkish women – and foreign women in general – were a focal point of women's activism against domestic violence.[66]

While discussing class was a way to highlight the inadequacy of protection for women in West Germany, talking about race had the opposite effect. Relying on racialised stereotypes that underscored the 'backwardness' of other countries' attitudes towards women, activists emphasised Germany's responsibility for women migrants. For example, *Help for Abused Women* recounts the story of

---

[62] Ibid.

[63] Ibid.

[64] Ilse Lenz, 'Wer sich wo und wie erinnern wollte? Die Neuen Frauenbewegungen und soziale Ungleichheit nach Klasse, "Rasse" und Migration' in *Erinnern, vergessen, umdeuten? Europäische Frauenbewegungen im 19. und 20. Jahrhundert*, edited by Angelika Schaser, Sylvia Schraut and Petra Steymans-Kurs (Frankfurt am Main: Campus, 2019): pp. 255–284; Tiffany N. Florvil, *Mobilizing Black Germany: Afro-German Women and the Making of a Transnational Movement* (Champaign: University of Illinois Press, 2020); Jennifer Miller, 'Her Fight is Your Fight: "Guest Worker" Labor Activism in the Early 1970s West Germany', *International Labor and Working-Class History*, 84 (2013), pp. 226–247.

[65] For a parallel example, see the discussion of dowry murder in India and domestic violence in the US in Uma Narayan, *Dislocating Cultures: Identities, Traditions and Third-World Feminism* (New York: Routledge, 1997).

[66] Hagemann-White *et al.*, *Hilfen*, p. 36.

Fatima, an early resident of the refuge.[67] Fatima emigrated from Turkey, leaving behind her husband and three sons, who joined her later. Already in Turkey, her husband, a man she married at the age of 15, was abusive. Once in West Berlin, she began working at a metal plant, sending money home to her family. She felt 'at ease' in her new life, although she missed her husband and children.[68] On visits to Germany, her husband continued to be violent and would hit her, usually regarding money. This situation escalated after her family fully immigrated to West Berlin, having obtained the necessary residency permits. Following this, Fatima's husband raped and beat her, at one point almost breaking her jawbone. She often sought refuge in the West Berlin shelter and pressed criminal charges for assault and attempted murder against her husband at least five or six times, of which only a few came to trial. According to *Help for Abused Women*, however, her story has a somewhat happy ending:

> Today, she no longer believes that the husband has all the power and is allowed to do what he wants. Since she has had the support of the women's shelter, she is determined to report every new incident to the police, to see through his sentence and to use her last penny to get a divorce and custody of the children.[69]

Stories like Fatima's were presented by activists as 'typical' of the experience of migrant women in Germany. The report presented Fatima as caught between 'two cultures, with all the insecurity that insufficient language skills, little education or knowledge of the Foreign Nationals Act brings with it'.[70] Fatima, like other Turkish and migrant women, symbolised women's supreme vulnerability to violence. She was at once a victim of what was presented as a backward and extremely patriarchal culture (married at 15, beaten and raped by her husband), yet also blithely unaware that this treatment was unacceptable – at least until the end of her story. Yet it is difficult to know what Fatima herself actually thought or felt about her situation: of the three biographies published in *Help for Abused Women*, only Fatima's is written in third person. While there may have been practical reasons of translation that rendered this necessary, it remains striking that the two other, German, women profiled for the book are allowed to speak for themselves.

For feminists, stories like Fatima's highlighted the important role women's shelters played in creating more emancipated, more democratic women. In doing so, they underscored the duty of the Federal Republic, as a developed liberal state with constitutional guarantees of gender equality, to support domestic violence activism. But West German feminist activists were keen to differentiate between the patriarchy that existed in these 'other' cultures and that which

---

[67] Ibid.
[68] Ibid., p. 171.
[69] Ibid., p. 174.
[70] Ibid., p. 170.

existed in Germany. A 1985 women's street-fest in West Berlin spoke directly to 'Turkish women':

> We see you in Kreuzberg [then a predominantly Turkish and working-class area of Berlin], where you slave away in the stores of "your" men, or when you come home from work, as you walk behind your husbands on the streets … Sometimes the screams and cries from your apartment can be heard in the evenings and at night … We feel connected with you, since the men who control your lives and beat and rape you as they please, are the same men who harass, hit and rape us on the streets. Just because we are alone on the street, they think they have the right to call us whores and treat us like dirt.[71]

By emphasising these shared experiences of harassment and abuse by foreign men, the street-fest organisers tried to forge solidarity between German and migrant women. But in doing so, they leant into a discourse that demonised racialised men by pitting them against the virtues of West German liberalism. Specifically, it made the figure of the foreign man – most often the Turkish man – into a symbol of the worst form of male power over women and the basic incompatibility of 'foreign' masculinity with German culture. This position was also echoed in the wider media. In one case from Baden-Württemberg in 1977, a Turkish guest worker was given a three-month prison sentence for assaulting his wife and failing to support her financially. As the *Schwäbische Zeitung* underscored, this was an important lesson that 'even the wives of foreigners in Germany enjoy protection, although other values may rule in their homelands'.[72] In a particularly painful case from 1975, a Turkish woman from outside of Bonn who threw herself and her children off a bridge was charged with murder after one of her children died. She argued that it was ongoing domestic abuse that resulted in her suicide attempt. In reporting on this case, the *Bonner Rundschau* stated that the judge presiding over the matter had to come to terms with the different cultural expressions of family and gender roles in West Germany and Turkey, captured in the pithy refrain 'other countries, other values'.[73]

Although they leant on racialised discourses to create support, shelter activists also spoke out about issues migrant women faced and brought attention to the systemic racism that made migrant lives precarious. Of particular concern was West German migration law, which meant that any woman who entered and lived in Germany on the basis of her marriage to a man who held a residency permit, had to stay married for four years before she could obtain her own permit. During this time, she was not allowed to work, which only made her more dependent on

---

[71] 'Gegen die alltägliche Gewalt der Männer an uns Frauen setzen wir Frauen unsere gemeinsame Stärke, Freude und unserer Interesse aneinander!! Frauen!!! Kommst zur Frauenstrassefest!' (1985), A Rep 400 21.22.6–21.22a (DFB), FFBIZ.
[72] 'Aber scheiden lassen will er sich nicht', *Schwäbische Zeitung*, 10 May 1977.
[73] 'Frau lebte wie Sklavin', *Bonner Rundschau*, 24 April 1975.

her husband and socially isolated. Shelter workers frequently criticised this law. A statement signed by 35 women's shelters in 1989 outlined how migration law made it 'impossible' for women to separate from their husbands. 'In order to stay in the FRG', they argued, a woman 'has to let herself be abused, until she has been here long enough to get her own residency permit'.[74] Indeed, in one case where a woman did dissolve her marriage, her abusive husband was brought before a migration hearing and asked if he would take her back. When he responded negatively, her residency was voided and she was deported.[75] As activists emphasised, returning to their home country could pose a danger for women, as they often faced ostracism and threats and had little possibility of employment.[76]

Despite advocating for migrant women, the West Berlin shelter participated in a system of power where the lives of certain migrants, in particular those from racialised groups in Germany for the purposes of temporary labour migration, were regulated, monitored and marginalised.[77] From the very beginning of the shelter's trial period, the West Berlin Senate was keen to collect data on the kinds of women seeking refuge. In the years following its opening, West Berlin Senate committees and parliamentary members consistently enquired into the situation of the migrant women in the shelter. In 1978, at a meeting of the Committee for Family and Youth of the Berlin Senate examining the first two years of the Grunewald shelter, CDU member Joachim Palm enquired about the percentage of foreign residents.[78] At a similar meeting in 1980 to discuss the continued funding of Berlin shelters, SPD member Rainer Klebba asked what the women's shelter could do to assist foreign families in assimilating and how much of a burden it was to assist Turkish women.[79] Again in 1980, Klebba submitted a parliamentary enquiry to determine what alternative support services migrant women could access if turning to a shelter put them at risk of deportation.[80] This level of attention was particularly significant, given how few migrant women lived in the shelter at this stage.[81]

---

[74] 'Stellungnahme autonomer Frauenhäuser zum Bericht der Bundesregierung über die Lage der Frauenhäuser für misshandelte Frauen und Kinder (1.9.1988)', File 5631, GG.

[75] Traude Ratsch, 'Interview mit Ulrike Palmert und Sadiye Kaygun-Dohmeyer, Mitarbeiterinnen des 2. Berlin Frauenhauses' in *Ausländische und deutsche Frauen im Gespräch. Sind wir uns denn so fremd?* (2nd ed.), edited by Neval Gültekin, Brigitte Schulz and Brigitte Sellach (Berlin: Subrosa Frauenverlag, 1985), pp. 49–53.

[76] 'Stellungnahme autonomer Frauenhäuser zum Bericht der Bundesregierung über die Lage der Frauenhäuser für misshandelte Frauen und Kinder (1.9.1988)', File 5631, GG.

[77] Cornelia Mansfeld, 'Gewalt gegen Frauen zwischen den Kulturen' in Gültekin, Schulz and Sellach *Ausländische und deutsche Frauen im Gespräch*, pp. 226–230; 'Stellungnahme autonomer Frauenhäuser zum Bericht der Bundesregierung über die Lage der Frauenhäuser für misshandelte Frauen und Kinder (1.9.1988)', File 5631, GG.

[78] Besprechung gemäss §21 Abs. 5 GO Abgeordnetenhaus über Situation im Krisenzentrum für misshandelte Frauen (auf antrag der CDU). Ausschuss für Familie und Jugend, B Rep 002/12504, LAB.

[79] 8. Sitzung, Ausschuss für Familie und Jugend, 6. März 1980. B Rep 002/12504a, LAB.

[80] Kleine Anfrage Nr 1719 der Abgeorneten Rainder Klebba (SPD) vom 16. Dezember 1980, B Rep 002/12505, LAB.

[81] 'Zwischenbericht der wissenschaftlichen Begleitung', B Rep 002/12504a, LAB.

While these enquiries demonstrate the success of the women's movement in highlighting the issues faced by migrant women, it also fed into broader attempts to regulate the entry and lives of foreigners in West Germany. As historian Lauren Stokes has argued, from the early 1970s, discussions of family migration to West Germany centred on the perceived problem of 'welfare' migration, whereby migrants from lower-income, racialised countries supposedly brought their families into the country solely to take advantage of benefit schemes. In the wake of the 1970s oil crisis and the demise of the *Wirtschaftswunder*, family migration was perceived as a threat to the Federal Republic's national security and economy.[82]

It was within this context that shelters advocated for migration reform. And yet, despite this activism, they were still working within a system that regulated and controlled migrant life. Even when the West Berlin Senate attempted to address the concerns presented by the shelters, they did so with a view to restricting immigration, upholding popular suspicions of foreigners and family migration. This came to the fore in 1983 when the West Berlin Senate's Committee on Foreigner's Issues discussed the possibility of giving women who held temporary residency status and were experiencing domestic abuse the ability to stay in the Federal Republic before they had been granted their own residency permit. One of the major concerns with this proposed reform was that such a ruling would 'open the floodgates' of migration. For one committee member, to create such an exception for women would

> privilege them over all other foreigners and would open the gate for further arrivals, which is not in German interests with respect to welfare support ... and the Federal position on the relief and safeguarding of the integration through the limitation of further migration.[83]

For others, it opened up the possibility of the spread of marriages of convenience, or *Scheinfamilienzusammenführung*, where people would marry in order to migrate to West Germany, only to separate upon arrival.[84] Although this position was disputed, the state continued to uphold restrictions on residency permits until migration reform in 1999, which reduced the time a couple needed to remain married to two years and widened the scope of the 'hardship clause' to include domestic violence.[85]

---

[82] Lauren Stokes, '"An Invasion of Guest Worker Children": Welfare Reform and the Stigmatisation of Family Migration', *Contemporary European History*, Vol. 28, No. 3 (2019): pp. 372–389.
[83] Inhalts-Protokoll. Ausschuss für Ausländerfragen, 24. Sitzung 4. März 1983. B Rep 002/12505, LAB.
[84] 'Abhängig von der Gunst des Mannes. Initiative für Ausländerinnen', *Die Tageszeitung*, 18 January 1983.
[85] Bundesministerium für Familie, Senioren, Frauen und Jugend. *Aktionsplan der Bundesregierung zur Bekämpfung von Gewalt gegen Frauen. December 1999* (Berlin: Bundesministerium für Familie, Senioren, Frauen und Jugend, 1999).

While emphasising migrant women's vulnerability helped raise awareness of their predicament and potentially encouraged funding for the shelters, from the 1980s feminists from migrant backgrounds increasingly criticised how their lives had been instrumentalised. Specifically, they took issue with the way West German activists had appropriated their stories and failed to address the distinctive needs of migrants.[86] This came to a head at the 1984 First Conference of German and Foreign Women, organised as a way to recognise how migrant women's issues were marginalised in feminist circles.[87] Between 23 and 25 March, over a thousand women gathered in West Berlin to discuss issues facing migrant women and the relationship between German and migrant women activists. This was a landmark event for race relations in the New Women's Movement and migrant women seized the opportunity to confront the way women's activism exploited their voices.[88] For one migrant woman, this Congress represented a radical reversal of the long-standing power relationship between German feminists and migrant women: 'I was always being talked about, I always had to expose myself – now I want the German women to finally get naked as well.'[89] According to Turkish-German feminist journalist Ayse Tekin, such words were difficult to hear, as West German feminists were 'shocked' to discover that 'their students' confronted them with reproach, dismissing 'their well-meaning work as social work, which not only furthered, but even strengthened racist structures'.[90] These migrant activists claimed that by tokenising and speaking for migrant women, feminism and the shelter system had both taken advantage of their vulnerability and fed into a power structure in which the lives of migrants were 'othered', monitored and controlled.

In response to the way women's groups and West German feminism deployed their experiences, second- and third-generation migrant activists started forming separate services aimed at addressing the specific issues faced by migrant women and girls. As one shelter activist phrased it, 'overall it became clear that "being a woman" [*Frau- Sein*] did not suffice as a category for defining systemic power relationships.'[91] It was not until 2001, however, that a major shelter project

---

[86] Gültekin, Schulz and Sellach, *Ausländische und deutsche Frauen im Gespräch*; Ayse Tekin, 'Unterschiede wahren, Zusammenarbeit möglich machen' in *Beiträge zur feministischen Theorie und Praxis* 17 (1994), p. 103–110; Ferree, *Varieties of Feminism*.

[87] Tekin, 'Unterschiede'.

[88] See the report of this event in: Gültekin, Schulz and Sellach, *Ausländische und deutsche Frauen im Gespräch*. See also Pia Marzell, 'Sind wir uns denn so fremd? Aufbrüche in der Rassismusdebatte der Frauenbewegung', in *History|Sexuality|Law*, 8 March 2021. Accessed on 10 June 2021: https://hsl.hyp otheses.org/1608.

[89] Quoted in Tekin, 'Unterschiede', p. 104.

[90] Tekin, 'Unterschiede', pp. 104–105; Ferree, *Varieties of Feminism*.

[91] Nadja Lehmann, 'Migrantinnen im Frauenhaus = Interkulturelles Frauenhaus', 3. Mai 2002, Vortrag gehalten in Münster, A Rep 400 Berlin 21.21.22a-21.22.5 +21.22.15, FFBIZ.

aimed at assisting migrant women opened in Berlin. The *Interkulturelle Initiative* (Intercultural Initiative) was started by Nadja Lehmann, a social worker who had worked in the First Autonomous Women's Shelter in West Berlin. By this time, almost 50 to 60 per cent of shelter residents were from a migrant background, and yet, according to Lehmann, the shelters and the state were not paying enough attention to the unique issues faced by these women.[92] Despite the changes to the Foreign Nationals Act that allowed migrant women to claim residency on the basis of the hardship clause, in order to claim this provision, migrant women needed to appear 'clearly worse-off' than German women in the same position, leaving many women scared of 'running the risk' of applying for the exception and remaining with their husbands.[93]

To address these shortcomings, the *Interkulturelle Initiative*, funded by the Senate Office for the Economy, Employment and Women, opened a shelter with space for 50 individuals, offering services tailored to migrant women. Since most migrant women living in shelters faced considerable legal issues with respect to their residency status, traditional shelters tended to focus on these concerns, rather than tackling the emotional and physical harm experienced by migrant women. Further still, the 'self-help' paradigm was also not appropriate for women who may not have the language skills to fully contribute to shelter life.[94] Consequently, the Initiative offers a broad array of support services for migrant women and their children, including crisis intervention and counselling in various languages, legal support on questions of asylum and residency and German language classes for residents. In addition, they only employ women with 'intercultural' competences, including foreign language skills, anti-racism training and/or knowledge of migration law.

Conclusion

From the moment the Berlin shelter opened its doors on 1 November 1976, domestic violence activism started to transform. Against a backdrop of the broad-scale co-optation and deradicalisation of feminist domestic violence activism, shelter work professionalised in response to the needs of women. As time went on, gender violence work became more specialised, addressing the different needs of women experiencing violence. In 1983, *Wildwasser*, a service aimed at supporting

[92] Nadja Lehmann, 'Projektvorstellung 'Interkulturelles Frauenhaus'', *Berlin Forum Gewaltprävention*, BFG 1 (2002): pp. 116–123. A Rep 400 Berlin 21.21.22a- 21.22.5 + 21.22.15, FFBIZ.
[93] Ibid., p. 118.
[94] Nadja Lehmann, 'Migrantinnen im Frauenhaus = Interkulturelles Frauenhaus', 3. Mai 2002, Vortrag gehalten in Münster, A Rep 400 Berlin 21.21.22a-21.22.5 +21.22.15, FFBIZ.

girls who survived sexual violence, started seeing women in West Berlin and, in 1986, *Frauenzimmer e.V.* began offering emergency shelter for women experiencing violence in the home.[95] Activists also began to address the particular issues facing migrant women in Germany and in the 1980s, two Zuffs shelters opened in Kreuzberg/Neukölln and Tempelhof. They offered refuge to both German and migrant women and of their five-person team, one came from Korea, one from Thailand and one was from Turkey, with another Turkish speaker of German descent.[96] Opened in 1986, Papatya, meanwhile, specifically offered protection and help for girls and young women from migrant families, who 'on the basis of cultural and familial conflict ran away from home and are being threatened by their family'.[97] In this respect, the institutionalisation of domestic violence activism cannot only be attributed to the workings of the media or the requirements of state funding, but also as the productive result of responding to the needs of women, who in many cases, simply had too many other priorities to worry about feminism.

But this transformation also says a lot about the nature of the women's movement in West Germany and the privileges it was built upon. That West German feminists struggled to acknowledge class and racial differences among women is not unusual. Feminist movements across the West have had – and continue to have – difficulties finding and maintaining unity. Whether it is class, race, sexuality or gender identity, white middle-class feminists have been faced with their own prejudices, often not out of choice.[98] To borrow from sociologist

---

[95] Other smaller services opened during the 1980s include: Emergency housing through Brunhilde e.V., Zuffs Kreuzberg/Neukölln and Zuffs Tempelhof. See A Rep 400 Berlin 1.20–1.23 ohne 1.26.8b.6, FFBIZ; Linda Jent and Regula Wyss, *Selbstverteidigung für Frauen* (Basel: Mond Buch, 1984).

[96] A Rep 400 Berlin 1.20–1.23 ohne 1.26.8b.6, FFBIZ. Furthermore, Berlin, alongside Hamburg and Bremen were the only shelters where there was a quota requiring a certain number of migrant women to be employed within shelters.

[97] 'Über uns', *Papatya: anonyme Kriseneinrichtung für Mädchen und junge Frauen mit Migrationshintergrund*. Accessed on 30 August 2015: http://www.papatya.org/ueber-uns.html.

[98] Feminists are currently debating the inclusion of transwomen in women's rights activism, a debate which is largely taking place online. See www.theterfs.com; www.genderidentitywatch.com; Kelsie Brynn Jones, 'Trans-Exclusionary Radical Feminism: What exactly is it and why does it hurt?', *The Huffington Post Blog* http://www.huffingtonpost.com/kelsie-brynn-jones/transexclusionary-radical-terf_b_5632332.html; Penny White, 'Why I No Longer Hate TERFs', *The Feminist Current*, http://www.feministcurrent.com/2015/11/10/why-i-no-longer-hate-terfs/, all accessed on 12 May 2022. On the inclusion of race/class/sexuality see Natalie Thomlinson, *Race, Ethnicity and the Women's Movement in England, 1968–1993* (Basingstoke: Palgrave Macmillan, 2006); Francisca de Haan, Margaret Allen, June Purvis and Krassimira Daskalova, eds, *Women's Activism. Global Perspectives from the 1890s to the Present* (New York: Routledge, 2013); Winifred Breines, *The Trouble Between Us: An Uneasy History of White and Black Women in the Feminist Movement* (Oxford: Oxford University Press, 2006); Barbara Ryan, 'Ideological Purity and Feminism: The US Women's Movement from 1966–1975', *Gender and Society*, Vol. 3, No. 2 (1989), pp. 239–257; Anne Enke, 'Smuggling Sex through the Gates: Race, Sexuality, and the Politics of Space in Second Wave Feminism', *American Quarterly*, Vol. 55, No. 4 (2003), pp. 635–667; Adele Murdolo, 'Safe Homes for Immigrant and Refugee Women: Narrating Alternative Histories of the Women's Refuge Movement in Australia', *Frontiers: A Journal of Women's Studies*, Vol. 35, No. 3 (2014): pp. 126–153; Tikka Jan Wilson, 'Feminism and Institutionalised Racism: Inclusion and Exclusion at an Australian Feminist Refuge', *Feminist Review*, Vol. 52, No. 1 (1996): pp. 1–26.

Winifred Breines, feminists have had to learn that 'in order to be inclusive, they had to lose some of their ideals, to construct relationships based on who they were and not who they wanted to be or wanted others to be.'[99] In other words, they have had to recognise that not all women are battered women, nor are they all white, middle-class and heterosexual.

However, as the West German case makes clear, the short-sightedness of feminist activists when it came to their interactions with working-class, racialised and migrant women is more complex than just racism or classism. Certainly, feminists misjudged battered women, condescendingly seeing their lack of interest in self-help and feminism as an issue of class, not understanding that shelter residents wanted help. They played into racial and racist stereotypes and appropriated migrant women's voices, while letting white women speak for themselves. All in the name of advocating for the rights of women.

That said, feminists wanting to open shelters in Germany were not only working with little information on the impact and consequences of domestic violence, but they also had to fight to get people to believe that domestic violence was a serious issue and not just a private, family matter. In order to build this popular support for their projects, domestic violence activists drew on well-established narratives of gender, racial and class difference. More worryingly, shelter activists were also required to operate within racialised and racist structures that surveilled and regulated the lives of certain migrants in West Germany. While racial and class privilege impacted how activists understood 'battered women' and advocated for women's rights, their advocacy was also fundamentally shaped by the requirements of working within a structure of power built upon and in the service of, white, heteropatriarchal norms.

Without the work of these early activists, there would not be the network of support for women that currently exists in Germany, nor would there be the research on the impact and complexity of abuse that came out of the Grunewald shelter. Encounters with battered women and the work of Turkish and migrant feminists in West Germany, while challenging the shelter movement's political ambitions and ideals, helped to transform feminist responses to domestic violence and improve services for women. However, what attention to this process of professionalisation and institutionalisation of domestic violence work makes clear is that 'well-meaning', white, West German feminist work fed into racial and class-based hierarchies at the same time as they attempted to challenge them. In the context of the deradicalisation of feminist politics, this only served to support normative structures.

---

[99] Breines, *The Trouble Between Us*, p. 4.

4

Domestic Violence and Women's Lives
Under Socialism

A 1978 article in the East German newspaper *Berliner Zeitung* challenged the spread of women's shelters in the Federal Republic. How could such houses help women escape abuse, asked author Susanna Statkowa, when the cause of domestic violence lay in the fundamental organisation of capitalism? Men, she argued, are the 'flotsam and jetsam of capitalist society'. They abuse their wives and children because 'profit', not equality or love, 'is the be all and end all' in capitalism. In stark contrast, under socialism 'the exploitation of people by people has been cast aside and the conditions for a humane existence are provided.' Domestic violence shelters were therefore unnecessary, as 'women and mothers, as men's equals, have law, justice and the welfare of the entire society at their side.'[1]

Three years later, journalist Birgit Walter, toed a similar line. Examining the second women's refuge in West Berlin, she argued that furthering women's equality was the only way to truly combat domestic violence. But, she predicted, such a transformation was unlikely in the West. Instead, the global recession of the early 1980s and the reforms of leaders like Margaret Thatcher had created 'growing unemployment, reduced wages, increased rents'. For Walter, this 'destruction' of the welfare state would only weaken women's rights under capitalism, as the family came under greater economic strain.[2] Although the article did not draw a direct comparison to East Germany, with an expansive title like 'Ways of Living under Capitalism. Women's Shelters as the Last Refuge: Increasing Brutality in Everyday Married Life in Western European Countries', the contrast to women's lives under socialism was evident.

By suggesting that men hit their wives because of the pressures of the capitalist system, both articles denied the existence of domestic violence in the GDR.

---

[1] Susanne Statkowa, 'Zuflucht ohne Recht', *Berliner Zeitung*, 5 August 1978.
[2] Birgit Walter, 'Lebensweise im Kapitalismus: Frauenhäuser als letzte Zuflucht. Zunehmende Brutalität im Ehealltag in westeuropäischen Ländern', *Berliner Zeitung*, 21 November 1981, p. 4.

According to the two authors, women's shelters merely treated the symptom, not the cause of domestic abuse. Under socialism, however, where equality between men and women was officially mandated and where families were supported by the state, men had no need to be violent. Women's shelters, so the argument went, were unnecessary. A version of this message can still be heard to this day in Germany. One of the most common refrains when researching domestic abuse in East Germany is that violence in the family was not talked about under socialism; it was strictly taboo.[3]

Certainly, there was little critical public debate on domestic violence in the GDR, especially when compared with West Germany. Women under socialism were not encouraged to talk about their experiences of abuse in the same way as women were in the West. According to one former East German social worker, women living with abusive husbands were 'totally forced into isolation'. Moreover, 'violence in the family didn't exist and when something doesn't exist, you can't talk about it.'[4] Even academic research on the topic was strictly controlled and social researchers themselves refused to conduct studies on domestic abuse for fear of being held back in their careers.[5]

But that is not to say there was total silence on the topic. Domestic violence *was* discussed in East Germany and women did speak out about it, albeit in very specific ways and locations and often in a shared coded language. There was even official recognition that violence in the family was an issue. Anxieties about rapidly rising divorce rates throughout the 1970s led to a host of studies into the causes of marital breakdown, which provide a glimpse into the extent of domestic abuse in the GDR. In 1978, *Tätlichkeit* (assault) was first listed as a cause for divorce in official statistics and throughout the 1970s and 1980s, between 6 and 36 per cent of divorces in the GDR involved allegations of abuse.[6] A 1974 study from the district court in Halle stated that 22 per cent of divorces in the region were due to abuse.[7] Similarly, a 1984 study on divorce, completed by the Central Institute for Youth Research in Leipzig showed that 36 per cent of the cases they studied listed violence and alcoholism as a cause of divorce.[8] Meanwhile, a 1989

---

[3] Monika Schröttle, *Politik und Gewalt im Geschlechterverhältnis: eine empirische Untersuchung über Ausmaß, Ursache und Hintergründe von Gewalt gegen Frauen in ostdeutschen Paarbeziehungen vor und nach der deutsch-deutschen Vereinigung* (Bielefeld: Kleine Verlag, 1999); Gabriela Eßbach and Vera Fünfstück, *Frauen mit Gewalterfahrung in der ehemaligen DDR: Wahrnehmungszugänge und Bewältigungsstratgien. Eine Untersuchung aus dem Blickwinkel autonomer Frauenhausarbeit in Sachsen* (Diplomarbeit, Evangelischen Fachhochschule für Sozialarbeit Dresden, 1997).

[4] Schröttle, *Politik und Gewalt*, p. 102.

[5] Ibid., p. 97.

[6] Anja Schröter, *Ostdeutsche Ehen vor Gericht. Scheidungspraxis im Umbruch 1980–2000* (Berlin: Christoph Links Verlag, 2018); Lothar Mertens, *Wider die sozialistische Familiennorm. Ehescheidung in der DDR 1950–1989* (Opladen: Westdeutscher Verlag, 1998).

[7] 'Informationsbericht über Probleme des Familienrechts unter Beachtung des Schwerpunktes Ehescheidungen. Bezirksgericht Halle, 22. März 1974', DP 2/2329, BArch.

[8] Dr Sc. A. Pinther; Prof. Dr Habil. W. Friedrich, 'Eine Analyse auf der Grundlage von gerichtlichen Scheidungsakten' (1984), DC 4/518, BArch.

study from the East German Academy of Sciences found that in 1970, 9.9 per cent of divorces were brought about because of abuse, a figure which had dropped to 6.6 per cent in 1985.[9] Historian and social scientist Lothar Mertens also carried out a survey into the causes of divorce in the GDR. He calculated that in 1978, 7.7 per cent of divorces came as the result of violence perpetrated by the husband.[10] From my own review of cases filed at the East Berlin Municipal Court, between 1970 and 1988 between 3.4 and 18.9 per cent of applications alleged physical spousal violence as a reason for seeking a divorce (see Table 4.1).[11] Further, in reports from the East German Ministry of Health in 1976 and 1977, domestic violence is cited as one of the most common reasons to visit a family and marital counselling centre.[12]

Although these statistics give a very unclear picture of exactly how prevalent domestic violence was in East Germany, they are nonetheless instructive. Indeed, statistics on domestic abuse are notoriously unreliable. Not only does under-reporting significantly skew data, but the way researchers understand and define domestic violence can lead to cases being excluded from analysis.[13] What is most significant about these various East German studies is that they exist. They clearly show that domestic violence was at least tacitly acknowledged at the governmental level, it was recorded and tracked, women talked about it and it was not invisible.

This chapter explores the discussions behind these statistics, looking at the way the courts, the criminal justice system and the media addressed domestic violence in East Berlin and, in turn, what this meant for women living with an abusive husband. In doing so, it reveals important information about the changing nature of SED authority and the meaning of gender, sexuality, marriage and the family under socialist rule. This has been a long-standing issue for historians: ever since German reunification, the historiography on East Germany has centred on assessing the extent of state control and surveillance.[14] Most recently, historians

---

[9] Jutta Gysi, Jürgen Dorbritz and Ursula Hespel, *Protokolle und Informationen. Informationen über Ehescheidungen in der DDR*, 1/89 (Berlin: Wissenschaftlicher Rat für Sozialpolitik und Demografie, 1989).

[10] Mertens, *Wider die sozialistische Familiennorm*, p. 59; Lothar Mertens, 'Ungelöstes gesellschaftliches Problem: Ehescheidungen in der DDR' in *Soziale Ungleichheit in der DDR. Zu einem tabuisierten Strukturmerkmal der SED-Diktatur*, edited by Lothar Mertens (Berlin: Duncker und Humblot, 2002), pp. 9–55.

[11] These statistics are drawn from a study of 1,577 divorce cases from the Berlin Municipal Court between 1963 and 1988, LAB.

[12] C Rep 111/499, LAB. See also: Donna Harsch, *Revenge of the Domestic: Women, the Family, and Communism in the German Democratic Republic* (Princeton: Princeton University Press, 2007).

[13] Eve Buzawa and Carl Buzawa, *Domestic Violence: The Criminal Justice Response* (3rd ed.) (Thousand Oaks: Sage Publications, 2003); Ileana Arias and Steven R.H. Beach, 'Validity of Self-Reports of Marital Violence', *Journal of Family Violence* Vol. 2, No. 2 (1987): pp. 139–149; Russell P. Dobash, R. Emerson Dobash, Margo Wilson and Martin Daly, 'The Myth of Sexual Symmetry in Marital Violence', *Social Problems* Vol. 39, No. 1 (1992): pp. 71–91.

[14] Compare for example the findings in Mary Fulbrook, ed, *Power and Society in the GDR, 1961–1979* (New York: Berghahn, 2009); Mary Fulbrook, *The People's State: East German Society from Hitler to*

	Total number of divorce cases appealed at the Berlin Municipal Court	Number of cases alleging abuse	Percentage of cases alleging abuse
1970	62	9	14.5%
1972	165	30	18.2%
1974	159	17	10.7%
1975	169	14	8.3%
1985	183	10	5.5%
1986	172	7	4.1%
1987	180	11	6.1%
1988	205	7	3.4%

Table 4.1 Percentage of divorce cases alleging domestic violence heard at the Berlin Municipal Court, between 1970 and 1988.[15]

have looked to the private lifeworlds of GDR citizens as a way of mapping the evolving terrain of life under socialism. Looking at the family, gender roles, sexuality – even interior design – much of this work has attempted to find a balance between the home as a space of socialist regulation and intervention and the home as a space of self-expression and autonomy.[16]

The 1970s in particular have emerged as a critical turning point in this scholarship on the GDR and the Eastern Bloc more generally.[17] Under the new leadership of Erich Honecker, who manoeuvred into power in 1971, the SED shifted away from the conservative and more hard-lined approach of Walter Ulbricht to a politics of 'real-existing socialism'. Rather than construct socialism on promises of a better tomorrow, Honecker focused on socialism as it actually was in the everyday life of the GDR. Consequently, the 1970s heralded a greater emphasis on the individual wants and needs of citizens, especially within the

---

Honecker (New Haven: Yale University Press, 2005); Katherine Pence and Paul Betts, eds, *Socialist Modern: East German Everyday Culture and Politics* (Ann Arbor: University of Michigan Press, 2008); Eli Rubin, *Synthetic Socialism: Plastics and Dictatorship in the German Democratic Republic* (Chapel Hill: University of North Carolina Press, 2008) to the results of the Enquete Commission, the official German state inquiry into the history of the GDR: *Schlußbericht der Enquete-Kommission 'Überwindung der Folgen der SED-Diktatur im Prozeß der deutschn Einheit'*, Deutscher Bundestag, 13. Wahlperiode, Drucksache 13/11000, 10 June 1998.

[15] These statistics remain incomplete. At the time of research, many of these case files were uncatalogued. It is also unclear how complete the files are. It is possible some cases were not kept, or were simply lost over the years or during reunification. The statistics here represent the cases reviewed by the author in 2014.

[16] Paul Betts, *Within Walls: Private Life in the German Democratic Republic* (New York: Oxford University Press, 2010); Josie McLellan, *Love in the Time of Communism: Intimacy and Sexuality in the GDR* (Cambridge: Cambridge University Press, 2011); Pence and Betts, *Socialist Modern*; Rubin, *Synthetic Socialism*; Fulbrook, *The People's State*.

[17] Betts, *Within Walls*; McLellan, *Love in the Time of Communism*; Fulbrook, *Power and Society in the GDR*; Jeannette Madarasz, *Conflict and Compromise in East Germany, 1971–1989* (New York: Palgrave

private sphere. As Paul Betts has argued, under Honecker, the home became a 'cherished locus of individuality, alternative identity-formation and/or dissent and resistance'.[18]

The history of domestic violence both complements and complicates this historiography. On the one hand, this chapter reveals the ways in which legal and social reform in the 1960s and 1970s changed the landscape for women living with a violent husband. Women could more easily obtain a divorce; indeed, women were far more likely to apply for a divorce than men.[19] It further shows that a critical attitude to official narratives of gender-based violence even developed among artists and activists in the late 1970s and into the 1980s. On the other hand, examining domestic violence cases, it argues that the liberalisation of the 1970s had distinctly gendered limits. Domestic violence was not just a private matter for the ruling SED, but rather presented an opportunity for the Party to intervene in relationships between husband and wife and shape their commitment to socialism. For women experiencing domestic violence this meant they were not able to simply leave an abusive spouse, but rather had to navigate around a system built on political expediency, socialist world-making and heteropatriarchal mores. Despite an improved legal framework, women's divorce applications were still denied by the courts, as patriarchal gender ideals guided legal pronouncements and police approaches to domestic abuse. Official discussions of domestic violence consistently prioritised male socialist self-improvement at the expense of women's safety and autonomy. Even the material conditions of life under socialism constrained women's ability to leave an abusive home, whether that meant having to ask a neighbour to call the police, or having to live with a violent ex-partner after divorce due to the shortage in housing.

Ultimately, then, what this chapter shows are the very real stakes at play in the SED's control over the private sphere, even into the supposedly liberalising 1970s. For women living with an abusive husband, this could mean the difference between life and death.

Discussions of domestic violence in East Germany first emerged in the late 1950s. This was a 'rocky era' for the SED: Cold War tensions were running high and – unlike its West German counterpart – the country was still recovering

---

MacMillan, 2003); Juliane Fürst and Josie McLellan, eds, *Dropping Out of Socialism: The Creation of Alternative Spheres in the Soviet Bloc* (Lanham: Lexington Books, 2017); Joachim Häberlen, Mark Keck-Szajbel and Kate Mahoney, eds, *The Politics of Authentic Subjectivity: Countercultures and Radical Movements across the Iron Curtain, 1968–1989* (New York: Berghahn, 2018).

[18] Betts, *Within Walls*, p. 238.

[19] In 1958, women submitted 53.4 per cent of all applications for divorce in the GDR. This rate steadily increased over the next 31 years, peaking in 1989, with women submitting 69 per cent of all divorce applications. See Mertens, *Wider die sozialistische Familiennorm*, pp. 36–37. Also: Schröter, *Ostdeutsche Ehen*.

from the air raids, street battles and destruction that marked the end of the Second World War. In the midst of this continued tumult, the SED were trying to build a socialist state.[20] Infrastructure, industry, agriculture, education, the legal system and, importantly, the people, had to be rebuilt for the socialist cause. In this context, responding to family matters – such as domestic abuse – was about much more than just dealing with marital discord. Instead, it was a way of dealing with the economic, political and social issues arising out of war and division. Addressing marital violence presented an opportunity to build socialism from the ground up, as judges, co-workers, party functionaries and union officials intervened in citizens' private lives to ensure adherence to socialist principles. Indeed, most of the earliest discussions of domestic violence in the GDR can be found within the legal realm. This was, very simply, because family matters constituted a bulk of the cases heard by the courts and judges were required to make pronouncements on domestic abuse and the harm it caused. But it also tapped into a broader movement within the Ministry of Justice to define the role of the family and of husbands, wives and children, under socialism.

This is clear from one of the first public discussions of domestic violence in the GDR, found on the pages of the legal journal *Neue Justiz*. In 1959, a saleswoman and mother of three young children applied for divorce. The woman had been repeatedly beaten by her husband, at one point even spending a week in hospital due to the severity of her injuries. This culminated in her fleeing their apartment one cold November night. After moving back in with her parents, she initiated a divorce at the Berlin-Lichtenberg Municipal Court in December.[21] Although the judge was concerned the woman might be in danger of further violence, a court appearance could not be arranged prior to the Christmas holidays. The judge, however, was able to refer the case to the husband's workplace collective.

Communal jurisprudence like this was typical of early attempts to create a socialist legal system directed by the morals and values of the working class. Starting in 1953, an entire system of social courts, which included workplace dispute commissions and local arbitration commissions was built up to help address civil and minor criminal matters, including cases of family and marital problems.[22] These bodies, alongside workplace collective intervention, were one of the earliest

---

[20] Harsch, *Revenge of the Domestic*, p. 61.
[21] Horst Glowacz, 'Neue Formen der gerichtlichen Tätigkeit in Zivil- und Familiensachen', *Neue Justiz*, No. 15 (1960): p. 493.
[22] Ministerium der Justiz und Bundesvorstand des FDGB, eds, *Gesellschaftliche Gerichte: Konfliktkommission, Schiedskommission* (Berlin: Verlag Tribüne, 1989); Sabine Langer, Felix Posorski and Rudolph Winkler, *Die Konfliktkommission hat eingeladen … Über die Tätigkeit der Konflikt- und Schiedskommissionen* (Berlin: Staatsverlag der Deutschen Demokratischen Republik, 1984).

sites where the SED attempted to intervene in the shaping of socialist marriages and families, as commissions relied on lay jurists to preside over cases involving their peers and co-workers.[23] As in this case, family matters would reach these courts either by referral from a local judge, who might direct divorcing couples to go to their collective for counselling first, or alternatively, cases could be referred by the local police or criminal courts.[24]

In front of representatives from the SED, the husband's union leaders and some of his co-workers, the couple met to discuss their marriage. But the collective was not as concerned about the violence as they were about the husband's poor conduct at work. Instead, they used the hearing as an opportunity to talk about the fact that he frequently missed shifts because he was drunk, that he got into a fight at a factory event and that he had even been struck off as a candidate for SED membership. It was only through this process of discussing the man's work ethic that the collective eventually came to the subject of the domestic abuse. This was something they clearly struggled with. While his co-workers knew he did not have a good family life, 'no one had ever considered that he was also prone to violence at home.'[25]

But this was a topic the collective could not avoid. Not only was the wife in attendance – a constant reminder of the task at hand – but as the author at *Neue Justiz* was sure to highlight, the collective 'knew that the socialist principles, in particular the duties and rights that each spouse owes to their children and society, are not the sole responsibility of the married couple'. Once the collective had overcome their 'initial amazement' at having to discuss their colleague's private life, they reprimanded the husband and he was forced to listen to the 'tough words' of his co-workers.[26] The article ends by saying only that as a result of this workplace meeting, the couple reconciled. Interestingly, however, the initial divorce application was not rejected. Instead it was delayed for six months, in which time the husband was told to improve his commitment to home and work. What happened at this next hearing, or if there even was one, is unknown.

This case reflects many of the hallmarks of the SED's attempts to shape socialist commitment in the first decade of its rule. Above all else, it shows that in a state

---

[23] Langer, Posorski and Winkler, *Die Konfliktkommission hat eingeladen*; Ministerium der Justiz und Bundesvorstand des FDGB, *Gesellschaftliche Gerichte*; Gerhard Heinze, *Die Tätigkeit der Konfliktkommissionen im VEB Transformatorenwerk 'Karl Liebknecht' Berlin-Oberschöneweide bei der Erziehung aller Werktätigen des Betriebes zur Unterstützung des Produktionsaufgebotes im Kampf um eine hohe Qualität der Arbeit* (Diplomarbeit, Hochschule der Deutschen Gewerkschaften 'Fritz Heckert', 1962).
[24] Glowacz, 'Neue Formen der gerichtlichen Tätigkeit', p. 493; VEB Transformatorenwerk, 'Karl-Liebknecht', 4.11.1970, Konfliktkommission Beschluss, 4.11.1970, C Rep 411/1358, LAB; Case 102d BSR 17.64, 31.3.1964, Stadtgericht Berlin, C Rep 301/3217, LAB; Tord Riemann, *Recht und Gesetz im Sozialismus. Eine Information über die Rechtspflege in der Deutschen Demokratischen Republik* (Berlin: Panorama DDR, 1976).
[25] Glowacz, 'Neue Formen der gerichtlichen Tätigkeit', p. 493.
[26] *Ibid.*

built on the centrality of the worker, yet also plagued by labour shortages and industrial unrest, being a good socialist meant bolstering commitment to the workforce and improving work ethic at every opportunity. But, equally important, is what it reveals about the significance of the family to socialism. According to the 1949 East German Constitution, marriage and the family formed the 'foundation of communal life' in the Democratic Republic.[27] And yet, what precisely this foundation looked like was unclear: as Donna Harsch has highlighted, the SED came to power without a family policy.[28] As such, the role of the family under socialism remained subject to debate for much of the 1950s and 1960s. There were some things on which the SED agreed: the end of the bourgeois patriarchal family, the equalisation of decision making between husbands and wives and the urgent need to enable and support women's work outside of the home.

At the same time, however, the SED wanted stable, reproductive family units. Despite encouraging equality between husband and wife, the SED's vision of family life remained rather conservative. As the 1958 'Ten Commandments of Socialist Morality and Ethics' ordered, 'you should live cleanly and decently and respect your family.'[29] Women were also targeted by pronatalist efforts and increasing the birth rate was a key political issue for the SED. This was central to the reputation of socialism in the GDR and internationally. Throughout the late 1950s, the superpowers increasingly used the private sphere as a Cold War battleground, imbuing marriage and the family with renewed importance.[30] In particular, the notion of having better sex, love and marriages, where men and women could marry out of genuine affection and not economic necessity, was used by the SED to legitimise socialist rule in the

---

[27] Verfassung der Deutschen Demokratischen Republik (1949), Art. 30 (1).

[28] Harsch, *Revenge of the Domestic*.

[29] 'Zehn Gebote für den neuen sozialistischen Menschen' in *DDR-Geschichte in Dokumenten. Beschlüsse, Berichte, interne Materialien und Alltagszeugnisse*, edited by Matthias Judt (Berlin: Christoph. Links Verlag, 1997), p. 54.

[30] On this shift away from Stalinism see Konrad H. Jarausch, 'Care and Coercion: The GDR as Welfare Dictatorship' in *Dictatorship as Experience: Towards a Socio-Cultural History of the GDR*, edited by Konrad H. Jarausch (New York: Berghahn Books, 1999), pp. 47–69. On the private sphere as a site of Cold War conflict see Rubin, *Synthetic Socialism*; Greg Castillo, *Cold War on the Home Front: The Soft Power of Mid Century Design* (Minneapolis: University of Minnesota Press, 2010); Phil Leask, Sara Ann Sewell and Heléna Tóth, 'Families' in *Ruptures in the Everyday. Views of Modern Germany from the Ground*, edited by Andrew Stuart Bergerson and Leonard Schmieding (New York: Berghahn Books, 2017); Susan E. Reid, 'Cold War in the Kitchen: Gender and the De-Stalinization of Consumer Taste in the Soviet Union under Khrushchev', *Slavic Review*, Vol. 61, No. 2 (2002): pp. 211–252; Christine Varga-Harris, 'Homemaking and the Aesthetic and Moral Perimeters of the Soviet Home during the Khrushchev Era', *Journal of Social History*, Vol. 41, No. 3 (2008): pp. 561–589; Susan E. Reid and David Crowley, eds, *Style and Socialism: Modernity and Material Culture in Post- War Eastern Europe* (Oxford: Berg, 2000); Steven E. Harris, *Communism on Tomorrow Street: Mass Housing and Everyday Life after Stalin* (Baltimore: Johns Hopkins University Press, 2013); Deborah A. Field, 'Irreconcilable Differences: Divorce and Conceptions of Private Life in the Khrushchev Era', *Russian Review*, Vol. 57, No. 4 (1998): pp. 599–613.

face of German division.[31] What this also meant was that indications of marital discord – divorce, adultery, separation, domestic violence – were increasingly taken seriously as a barometer of the success of socialism.

As the saleswoman's case reveals, these principles tangibly shaped the way family matters were addressed in East Germany. Decision-making bodies, whether courts or collectives, had to negotiate between competing priorities of improving work output, supporting women's employment and equality in the home, increasing the birth rate and the maintenance of the nuclear family. In this specific case, while the court clearly believed the husband was at fault – after all, the matter was heard by his workplace collective – the abuse was only one issue on a much longer list where he was found wanting. Despite purportedly hearing a divorce application, the collective instead used the opportunity to intervene in the man's life more generally, in an effort to improve his socialist commitment. His lacklustre work performance was the top priority and the issue of his abuse was left until last. When the collective finally turned to the marriage, although they emphasised the family as a site of 'shared responsibility' and equality between husband and wife and even chided the husband for beating his wife, they still encouraged the couple to reconcile. In doing so, the collective was able to uphold the principles of equality between husband and wife (at least rhetorically), while also promoting participation in the workplace and keeping the family together. The woman's safety, however, was not addressed.

Legal scholar Inga Markovits has argued that 'the socialist process of concili-ation, where plaintiff and defendant together are charged with the restoration of social harmony, also subjects both to the state's definition of what harmony should look like.'[32] More often than not, this definition of marital harmony worked in men's favour, as women were subjected to conservative, heteropatriarchal visions of their role in marriage and the family. In another case reported in *Neue Justiz*, in 1963, a woman in an unnamed town in East Germany applied for divorce on the basis of various incidents of physical violence and, what today would be called, emotional abuse.[33] Her husband hurled insults at her for oversleeping following the birth of their son, threw objects at her in a rage and beat her around the head so badly that she missed work for several days. In spite of this, the court rejected her application for divorce on the basis that the 'bond between the couple remained intact'. Evidencing this, the court claimed that the 'marriage,

---

[31] McLellan, *Love in the Time of* Communism; Harsch, *Revenge of the Domestic*; Annette Timm, *The Politics of Fertility in Twentieth-Century Berlin* (New York: Cambridge University Press, 2010).

[32] Inga Markovits, quoted in Peter W. Sperlich, *The East German Social Courts: Law and Justice in a Marxist-Leninist Society* (Westport: Praeger, 2007), p. 8. See also the discussion of married har-mony in: Margarete Wolfram, 'Die Grundung von Ehe und Familie erfordert hohe gesellschaftliche Verantwortung', *Der Schöffe*, 22 (1975): pp. ix–xiv. On the pedagogical role of the courts, see Schröter, *Ostdeutsche Ehen*.

[33] 'Rechtsprechung. Familienrecht', *Neue Justiz* (1963), p. 697.

with certain limitations, had run smoothly' until 1962. Even though the woman had moved back to her mother's home in 1959, the court prioritised the fact that she had 'kept the marital home in order, along with taking care of her husband and had marital relations with him'. Consequently, the court rejected the woman's application, claiming that she had not met the burden of proof.

Although this decision was reversed on appeal to the Supreme Court of East Germany, it reveals how the valorisation of reproductive heterosexual families precipitated serious issues for women living with violence. Primarily, it showed that abuse, in itself, was not always sufficient grounds for a divorce. In this instance, the court weighed their visions of marriage, informed by patriarchal values and pronatalist concerns, against the woman's claims of abuse. By upholding the marriage, the court sent a clear message about the expectations of men and women in the socialist family. Namely, that women's roles – as sexual partner and caregiver – were more important than protecting them from their husband's abuse.

These decisions may not seem particularly remarkable in the context of global approaches to domestic violence in the 1950s and early 1960s. Women in West Germany were similarly denied divorces and were also subject to harmful gender norms that meant their claims of abuse were ignored and denied. In many ways, the vision of the happy, reproductive, nuclear family promoted by the SED was not so different to the ideal of family life in the West. The Adenauer government also attempted to mould the family in the service of state-making. What is particularly striking about the East German case is the way these legal decisions and conservative visions of the family coexisted with a strong rhetoric of equality between men and women at work and in the home, and that condemned domestic abuse as belonging in the 'middle ages'.[34] In a remarkable 1962 article from the official SED newspaper, *Neues Deutschland*, the hypocrisy of preaching about women as 'equal partners in the construction of socialism', while they were still being subjected to abuse behind closed doors was directly challenged. 'Whoever Beats his Wife, Beats the Collective' told the story of an Agricultural Production Cooperative in Damsdorf, Brandenburg, where the former Party sec-retary was known to beat his wife. Despite calling out this man and challenging his co-workers' claims that he was a 'good comrade', the article saw this as a confirm-ation of the need for further socialist transformation. Only by continuing with the socialist project would such double-standards be set aside:

> building socialism in the village … means liberating people from all oppressive bonds. That also means breaking habits that encroach on the rights of others – and when needs must, with the whole strength of the new society. That is also true for

---

[34] Ursula Rebetsky and Arthur Boeck, 'Wer seine Frau schlägt, schlägt die Genossenschaft. Mittelalter und Neuzeit in Damsdorf. Nur eine Familienangelegenheit?', *Neues Deutschland*, 9 February 1962.

the violent husband. Whoever works so well for the collective, must also learn how a socialist lives: cleanly and decently.[35]

But what difference did this rhetoric of socialist equality really make when the end results were often the same? In the West, it was only with the upheavals of the late 1960s and the rise of the New Women's Movement that the landscape for women living with domestic violence changed. While there may not have been a comparable feminist movement in East Germany, historians have clearly shown that the GDR experienced similar liberalising processes during the 1970s. Détente brought a more stable economy, greater participation in higher education, a sexual revolution with a corresponding loosening of social mores and important legal reforms that further enshrined women's equality. Despite these transformations, responses to domestic violence in the GDR were continually marked by the tension between pronatalist goals, patriarchal norms and politicised visions of the ideal family and the ideological (if not also political) aim of gender equality. As the following section shows, it often resulted in very uneven approaches to abuse; while some women could easily obtain a divorce, many others were required to remain married.[36] No matter the result, however, discussing and responding to domestic violence was an opportunity to craft socialism by intervening in the private sphere.

Liberalising 1970s?

Historians have typically thought of late socialism – the era from Khrushchev's renunciation of Stalinism in 1956 until the early 1980s – as a time of social change in the Communist Bloc.[37] Certainly in the GDR, following Honecker's rise to power in 1971, there was a swathe of reforms aimed at shaping the family and reconciling women's roles in the home and in paid employment. New policies pushed for greater equality between husband and wife and offered more support to working mothers. Divorce became much more straightforward and rates soared throughout the 1970s, increasing from 14 divorces per 100 marriages in the early 1960s to 38 per 100 at the end of the 1980s.[38] At the same time, common-law partnerships and co-habitation were normalised.[39] The SED also liberalised laws

---

[35] Ibid.

[36] For a more positive rendering of domestic violence in divorce proceedings, see Betts, *Within Walls*.

[37] See, for example, Reid, 'Cold War in the Kitchen'; Varga-Harris, 'Homemaking and the Aesthetic and Moral Perimeters'; Reid and Crowley, *Style and Socialism*; Harris, *Communism on Tomorrow Street*; Field, 'Irreconcilable Differences'; Neringa Klumbyte and Gulnaz Sharafutdinova, eds, *Soviet Society in the Era of Late Socialism, 1964–1985* (Lanham: Lexington Books, 2013).

[38] Mertens, *Wider die sozialistische Familiennorm*; Andrew Port, 'Love, Lust and Lies under Communism: Family Values and Adulterous Liaisons in Early East Germany', *Central European History*, Vol. 44 No. 3 (2011): pp. 474–505; McLellan, *Love in the Time of Communism*.

[39] On common-law partnerships in the GDR, see Eva Schäffler, *Paarbeziehungen in Ostdeutschland. Auf dem Weg vom Real- zum Postsozialismus* (Wiesbaden: Harrassowitz Verlag, 2017).

and policies governing sexuality in the 1970s: access to the oral contraceptive pill increased and, in 1972, on-demand first-trimester abortion was legalised. Even sex between adult men was decriminalised in 1968.

However, as historian Donna Harsch has shown, many of the reforms liberalising heterosexual relationships had their origins in the introduction of the 1965 Family Law Code. This Code established the role of the family – and its importance – to socialism as never before. According to the new law, the family was the 'smallest cell of society' and everyone was expected to 'protect and serve' its maintenance and development. It also brought in an array of reforms aimed at tying the family to socialism: legislating equality between men and women in the home and ending discrimination against unmarried mothers. Significantly, the Code also reformed divorce law.

Although the East German Ministry of Justice encouraged judges to move towards the principle of 'irreconcilable differences' in divorce cases as early as 1949, no-fault divorce was only finalised in the Family Law Code.[40] While the SED heralded the Code as a liberating reform, historian Andrew Port has shown that it was much more complicated.[41] According to the new divorce law, rather than apportioning blame for the breakdown of the marriage, courts had to ascertain whether the marriage had lost its meaning 'for the couple, the children and also for society' before granting a divorce.[42] But this was a rather subjective task. When analysing judicial decision making, it is clear that even following the introduction of no-fault divorce, judges continued to base their decisions on a vision of marriage that was informed both by heteropatriarchal ideals and socialist visions of family life. Judges, co-workers, witnesses and lawyers would delve into the personal lives of a couple in search for evidence of ongoing intimacy. They would look at how frequently and recently the couple had had sex, whether they had children, if they shared in household and parental duties or if they were good workers, all in an effort to prove whether the marriage could be saved.

For women living with an abusive spouse, the results of this reform were unsurprisingly mixed. On the one hand, the Family Code, with its emphasis on equality, gave women a legal and rhetorical strategy for protesting domestic violence. It was a clear sign of their inequality to their husband. On the other hand, they still had to prove that the marriage had lost its meaning for society and this required them to open their private lives to the court's scrutiny. In doing so, they faced the possibility of a lengthy legal process, losing custody of their children or even having their application for divorce denied. In 1971, for example, a woman

---

[40] Harsch, *Revenge of the Domestic*, p. 216; Schröter, *Ostdeutsche Ehen*.
[41] Port, 'Love, Lust and Lies'.
[42] Familiengesetzbuch 1965 (GDR), §2 and §24(1). This also repeats language used in a 1955 Marriage Decree. See Port, 'Love, Lust and Lies', p. 487 and Schröter, *Ostdeutsche Ehen*.

appealed her rejected divorce application at the Berlin Municipal Court. She had married 'for love' in 1962 and had lived harmoniously with her husband until 1970.[43] They shared their household duties, including caring for their child and had 'lived in good social standing'. Although she cited ongoing sexual differences as a problem at the initial divorce hearing, because the couple had had sex only two months before, the Prenzlauer Berg judge dismissed these claims out of hand. The main basis of her application, however, was that her husband had beaten her after she had told him she was in love with another man. In a state of 'physical frustration', he had hit her around the arms and back. In spite of this, the court rejected her application for divorce, with the judge emphasising that such violent behaviour was out of character for the husband. Instead, because the husband still loved his wife and because a divorce would negatively impact their child, the judge expected the relationship to 'get back to normal'.

On appeal, the wife went even further in her allegations. She claimed that her husband had beaten her around the face and body until she fell to the ground. He then kicked her and stopped her from fleeing the apartment. Another time, after closing all the doors and windows, he turned on the gas in the apartment. He had even been violent after the initial divorce hearing, grabbing her by the hair, pushing her to the ground and kicking her. In this instance, however, she did not press criminal charges, since her husband's work collective wanted to address the issue together. Meanwhile, in his counter-claim, the husband blamed the marital breakdown on his wife, saying it was her affair with another man that caused him to lose control. He denied the allegations of further abuse and asked the court for custody of the child.

The appeal court's decision emphasised how the marriage had initially fulfilled the ideals of the socialist family. It particularly highlighted how the couple had been able to grow together, developing their careers and how they had shared their financial and parental duties. At the same time, in their discussion of the couple's break-up, the court treated the actions of the husband and wife very unequally. Although by this time, the court no longer needed to apportion blame, they clearly saw the woman's behaviour as the cause of the break-up. It was her relationship with another man that had damaged the marriage and it was her claim to love this man that had brought about serious marital differences. By comparison, the husband's violence is treated as a mere aberration and the court refers to it as 'inappropriate' and a 'mistake' that was 'out of character'. The husband claimed to have seen the error of his ways, telling the court he had apologised to his wife and was determined to learn from his mistake. In comparison, the wife had shown no willingness to reconcile following her rejected divorce application and had instead moved out of the marital home.

[43]   Case 3BF 156.70, 1.2.1971, C Rep 301 3746 (1970), LAB.

Although the divorce was granted on appeal, the court paid more attention to what the man had to say than to the woman's claims of abuse. Certainly, the husband's claims dovetailed with socialist ideals. He had shown himself to be a good socialist: he was a committed worker, took part in household duties, he had demonstrated a capacity for growth and self-reflection and, above all, he wanted to stay with his wife. The fact that she did not want to say with him, however, was seemingly less of a concern. It is particularly striking that her claims of sexual dissatisfaction – evidenced through her affair and reference to ongoing sexual differences – are outweighed by the fact that she had had sex with her husband in the two months prior to the initial hearing.

The court's response to her affair also suggests a deep-seated inability to countenance female sexual desire. For East German socialists in the post-war era, the suggestion of sexual pleasure not only recalled memories of the politicisation of sexuality and desire in the Third Reich, but also spurred anxieties about the depravity of western capitalism.[44] Women's sexuality was a particular sticking point, as women's claims to desire and sexual fulfilment came up against these political and moral anxieties and gendered ideals of women as sexually passive and maternal. Throughout the 1950s, a wave of educative films targeted women on the proper channelling of their desires: whether it was fashion or the choice of sexual partner, personal desires always played second fiddle to the advancement of socialism.[45]

In this instance, the court's gendered vision of marriage and family not only shaped how they evaluated the couple's characters, but also ultimately their decision making. The woman's sexuality and her claim to want more from the relationship was used as a tool against her. Her initial application for divorce was denied on the basis that she had sex with her husband only two months before the hearing, and in the end, she lost custody of her child. In the appeal court's opinion, the extramarital affair – and therefore her sexual desires – had caused her to act irresponsibly and to withdraw from her parental duties. She had come home late,

---

[44] McLellan, *Love in the Time of Communism*; Josie McLellan, 'State Socialist Bodies: East German Nudism from Ban to Boom', *Journal of Modern History*, Vol. 79, No. 1 (2007): pp. 48–79; Dagmar Herzog, *Sex After Fascism: Memory and Morality in Twentieth-Century Germany* (Princeton: Princeton University Press, 2005); Jane Freeland, 'Creating Good Socialist Women: Continuities, Desire and Degeneration in Slatan Dudow's "The Destinies of Women"', *Journal of Women's History*, Vol. 29, No. 1 (2017): pp. 87–110.

[45] Freeland, 'Creating Good Socialist Women'; Joshua Feinstein, *The Triumph of the Ordinary: Depictions of Daily Life in the East German Cinema, 1949-1989* (Chapel Hill: University of North Carolina Press, 2002); Andrea Rinke, *Images of Women in East German Cinema, 1972-1982: Socialist Models, Private Dreamers and Rebels* (Lewiston: Edwin Mellen Press, 2006); Jennifer Kapczynski, *The German Patient: Crisis and Recovery in Postwar Culture* (Ann Arbor: University of Michigan Press, 2008); Jennifer Kapczynski, 'Postwar Ghosts: "Heimatfilm" and the Specter of Male Violence', *German Studies Review*, Vol. 33, No. 2 (2010): pp. 305–330; Mila Ganeva, 'Fashion Amidst the Ruins: Revisiting the Early Rubble Films "And the Heavens Above" (1947) and "The Murderers Are Among Us" (1946)', *German Studies Review*, Vol. 37, No. 1 (2014): pp. 61–85.

and often drunk. In spite of the negative effects of the husband's violence, the court still saw him as a better option, citing his ongoing responsibility for the child, even during the divorce proceedings.

Seemingly then, very little had changed since the introduction of the new divorce law. In the decade following its introduction, cases like this were common. After having the minutiae of their family and intimate lives examined by the court, women could not only be sent back to live with a violent husband, but in rare cases they could even lose custody of their children. In a similar case from 1974, a woman appealed the decision to award her ex-husband custody. She claimed he was unbalanced and an alcoholic with violent tendencies. He had even gone to jail for two years following a violent incident in the home. However, in an attempt to escape the abuse, the woman had fled their home, taking her child to stay somewhere with 'confined living conditions'.[46] The court showed very little understanding for what a woman might need to do to escape domestic violence. Instead, they saw it as a sign that she had not properly fulfilled her duties as a mother. Although she eventually won back custody, the court also told her to speak to child services to learn how to take care of her child.

It was particularly common for lower-level courts to reject divorce applications in favour of marital reconciliation. Following the introduction of the Family Code, a person seeking divorce would initially apply to their local district court. If this first application was rejected or one of the parties had an issue with custody or the allocation of housing, they could appeal the decision to the municipal court. Although rejected divorce applications would typically be overturned on appeal to the municipal court, this additional legal stumbling block suggests a delay tactic used by the courts to keep families together and, in the process, build up socialism.[47] Certainly, rising divorce rates were a serious source of concern for the SED; they were an affront to the importance of the family in socialism and flew in the face of the Party's attempts to transform society.[48] Divorce also presented serious practical issues for the SED, not least a severe shortage in housing and an ever-declining birth rate.[49] Even into the 1970s, the SED were encouraging

---

[46]   Case 109 BFB 114.74, 12.8.1974, Stadtgericht Berlin, C Rep 301/3757, 100–149/74, LAB.

[47]   For a detailed discussion of divorce law, see Schröter, *Ostdeutsche Ehen.*

[48]   Betts, *Within Walls*; Harsch, *Revenge of the Domestic*; McLellan, *Love in the Time of Communism.*

[49]   On the politics of housing under socialism in East Germany and the Communist Bloc more generally, see Eli Rubin, *Amnesiopolis. Modernity, Space and Memory in East Germany* (New York: Oxford University Press, 2016); Harris, *Communism on Tomorrow Street*; Lynne Attwood, *Gender and Housing in Soviet Russia: Private Life in a Public Space* (Manchester: Manchester University Press, 2010); Kimberly Elman Zarecor, *Manufacturing a Socialist Modernity: Housing in Czechoslovakia, 1945–1960* (Pittsburgh: University of Pittsburgh Press, 2011); Katherine Lebow, *Unfinished Utopia: Nowa Huta, Stalinism and Polish Society, 1949–56* (Ithaca: Cornell University Press, 2013); Virag Molnar, *Building the State: Architecture, Politics and State Formation in Postwar Central Europe* (New York: Routledge, 2013); Mark Smith, *Property of Communists: The Urban Housing Program from Stalin to Khrushchev* (DeKalb: Northern Illinois University Press, 2010).

divorce courts to use their decisions to keep families together. As law professor Tord Riemann argued in a 1976 booklet aimed at informing foreign countries about the GDR's justice system, the socialist family court was responsible for both determining the causes of marital conflict and evaluating whether there was a possibility of reconciliation. In particular, Riemann revealed, courts were to discourage divorce where they believed the couple had rushed into separation.[50]

Some judges, however, did take a stand against domestic violence. Paul Betts, for example, cites one divorce case where a judge complained that 'It is still quite common among the male citizens of our state to beat their wives. It shows that this bourgeois lord-of-the-house mentality has not yet been overcome ideologically and in the heat of the moment the path of least resistance is taken.'[51] In another case from East Berlin in 1972, a woman, married for the second time, applied for divorce on the basis of ongoing abuse.[52] Her husband was an alcoholic, who would physically and verbally abuse her and even threaten her life. Afraid of further violence, she fled the marital home and moved back in with her parents. The court in this instance granted the divorce on the first hearing of the case. Even when the ex-husband appealed the division of legal costs, the appellate court upheld the decision, stating that such violence 'stands in stark contrast to the moral principles of a marriage'.

On the surface, these contrasting views of domestic violence appear inconsistent. While some divorce applications would be rejected out of hand, others would be successful. Sometimes they would only be successful on appeal. In other instances, judges would chastise men for beating their wives, proclaiming such behaviour as inconsistent with the values of socialism and at other times, they would hold women responsible for the violence inflicted upon them. But there is an underlying logic. What made the difference in these cases is the extent to which the couple lived up to socialist expectations and whether the court, by examining the couple's relationship and sex life, believed the marriage still had meaning. In the case from 1972, for example, although the woman fled to her parents, she did not have any children and there was no evidence of an affair or a continuing sexual relationship with her husband. There was less reason then for the court to hope that the marriage could be saved. There may also have been a darker reason for such varied rulings. As Kerstin Brückweh argues in her study of housing in the GDR, inconsistent application of the law purposefully created legal insecurity, thereby giving the courts, and by extension the SED, greater opportunity for intervention and surveillance in the private sphere.[53]

---

[50] Riemann, *Recht und Gesetz im Sozialismus*, p. 31
[51] Betts, *Within Walls*, p. 111.
[52] Case 109 BFB 28.72, 15.5.1972, C Rep 301/3762, LAB.
[53] Kerstin Brückweh, Clemens Villinger and Kathrin Zöller, eds, *Die lange Geschichte der 'Wende': Geschichtswissenschaft im Dialog* (Berlin: Christoph Links Verlag, 2020). See also Kerstin Brückweh and Mirjam Brusius, 'Home Sweet Home: A "Schriftgespräch" on Doing the Long History of 1989', *German Historical Institute London Bulletin*, Vol. XLIII, No. 1 (2021): pp. 66–86.

Over time, no-fault divorce law was implemented more fully. Throughout the mid- to late 1970s, judges – even at lower levels of decision making – ceased to find reasons to save marriages. Indeed, as Table 4.1 shows, the number of cases involving domestic violence that were appealed to the Berlin Municipal Court had reduced to only 3.4 per cent of all family court appeals by 1988, suggesting that divorces involving domestic violence were increasingly being granted following the initial application. But while this legal change may have streamlined the process of divorce, a concomitant change in attitudes towards women and the family still restricted women's ability to leave an abusive relationship. In particular, women's reliance on help from the police, neighbours or medical practitioners meant that they were often at the mercy of a system and society that did not take women's voices seriously. This, in turn, impacted women's ability to apply for divorce.

This is laid bare in the testimony of Frau A., recorded in the dissertation of two Leipzig activists in 1997.[54] Frau A. first experienced her husband's violence only a few years after getting married in 1984. 'He looked like he wanted to smash all the furnishings, the kitchen and bedroom. And yeah, he beat me up, threw me down the stairs', she remembered in an interview.[55] Yet she did not leave. The next day 'everything was better.' Her husband had cleaned up and promised it would never happen again, and for the next three months, things were fine. But then, whenever he had been drinking, he would become violent. He would 'go off like an atomic bomb', threatening to kill Frau A. and destroying their apartment. One night, she tried to get a neighbour to call the police. Even though her neighbour knew what was happening and was 'otherwise socially engaged and attentive', he refused to help, making her use the phone booth on the street. In this he was not alone. According to Frau A., 'everyone here in the building had clearly closed their ears and eyes' to what was happening in her apartment.

When the three police officers finally arrived, they were less than helpful. Although one officer told her husband that he should not hit his wife, Frau A. 'had the feeling that, at least as far as the other two police officers were concerned, that whatever took place within a marriage, so long as it didn't disturb the peace in the building or anything, wasn't such a big deal.'[56] The very next day, she went to file a charge of assault against her husband. Rather than taking a statement, the police told her to 'think it over' and return in two weeks, because in their experience most women retracted their claims. Indeed, Frau A. withdrew her allegation.

Following this incident everything was 'good' again, but Frau A. could not forget what her husband had done. 'His violence, it had broken so much in me that I couldn't easily forget, I couldn't undo it. A subliminal fear was always there', she recalled. The next time her husband was violent, she was determined to do

---

[54] Eßbach and Fünfstück, *Frauen mit Gewalterfahrung in der ehemaligen DDR*.
[55] Ibid., p. I.
[56] Ibid., p. III.

something about it. Again, however, the police tried to talk her out of pressing charges. She pushed ahead anyway and even applied for a divorce. To strengthen her application, she tried to get a medical certificate that testified her injuries were the result of abuse. Although suffering from a dislocated jaw, the doctor refused to support her, arguing that her injuries could have been caused by falling down the stairs. Consequently, her divorce was rejected by the court and she was instead required to attend two reconciliation sessions with her husband. The police also dropped the charges against the husband due to lack of evidence. This was in 1986. Frau A. then lived with her parents until she was finally able to get a divorce in 1988.

Frau A's story reveals key issues with respect to domestic violence in East Germany. It firstly highlights the significant role alcohol played in abuse. A majority of the cases examined at the Berlin Municipal Court cited alcohol consumption as a contributing factor in instances of abuse. While this was not unique to East Germany, alcoholism was endemic in the GDR and East Germans had the highest rates of alcohol consumption for beer and spirits in the world.[57] A 1988 report from the Central Institute for Youth Research in Leipzig showed that rates of alcohol consumption increased over the 1970s and 1980s. In 1970, the report showed, East Germans were drinking 6.1 litres of pure alcohol per year. This had risen to 10.5 litres by 1986, or as historian Josie McLellan has shown, approximately 23 bottles of spirits each year.[58] This had a clear impact on marriage, with Betts citing alcohol as a cause of almost three-quarters of all divorces in Berlin.[59] Indeed, as a 1970 study on divorce by the College of Lawyers showed, 23 per cent of survey respondents listed alcohol as the reason for separation, compared with 0.2 per cent who listed abuse.[60]

This close connection between alcohol and abuse, as well as alcohol and divorce, also suggests that excessive alcohol consumption was a euphemism for domestic violence. As Frau A's story demonstrates, having to prove that abuse had taken place was not easy in a system that did not listen to women's voices. Alcoholism, by comparison, was less taboo and could be proven in various ways. This connection is also supported by sociologist Monika Schröttle. Examining statistics on divorce in the GDR, Schröttle argued that researchers investigating marital breakdown typically categorised domestic abuse that took place under the

---

[57] On the contemporary links between alcohol and gender-based violence, see Institute for Alcohol Studies, *Alcohol, Domestic Abuse and Sexual Assault* (London: Institute for Alcohol Studies, 2014).

[58] Dr. W. Brück, 'Alkoholkosnum, Alkoholmissbrauch und Kriminalität', Leipzig, Februar 1988. DC/4 738b, BArch; McLellan, *Love in the Time of Communism*; Thomas Kochan, *Blauer Würger: So trank die DDR* (Berlin: Aufbau Verlag, 2011); Richard Millington, '"Crime has no chance": The Discourse of Everyday Criminality in the East German Press, 1961–1989', *Central European History*, Vol. 50, No. 1 (2017): pp. 59–85.

[59] Betts, *Within Walls*, p. 100.

[60] 'Analyse über die Ursachen von Ehekonflikten und die Wirksamkeit der gerichtlichen Tätigkeit in Ehesachen', 1970, Kollegium der Rechtsanwalte, DY 64/52, BArch.

influence of alcohol as 'alcohol abuse', not 'violence'. Similarly, sexual violence was categorised as 'sexual incompatibility'.[61] Given how closely alcohol and abuse were connected, it is likely that many violent relationships were obscured from official data on the causes of divorce.

Frau A's story also reveals the failure of the police and criminal justice system to address domestic violence. Although women in East Germany could use Paragraphs 115, 116 and 249 of the 1968 Criminal Code to charge husbands with assault or with endangering public order through asocial behaviour, often the police did not take the matter seriously. Following interviews with former East German police officers, Schröttle argues that in the case of violence against women and intimate-partner violence, the police 'initiated no consistent intervention nor pressed charges'.[62] Indeed, the East German police intervened in matters of domestic violence even less than their West German colleagues. Only the most extreme cases reached the criminal courts and when they did the court was often still more concerned with family stability than with protecting women.

For example, one February evening in 1973, a married couple were on their way home from a meeting at their sailing club.[63] They began to argue, possibly because the wife had recently filed for divorce. Once home, the wife wanted to go to sleep, while her husband wanted to talk. He followed her into the bedroom, trying to talk things over. At this point, she spat on him, causing him to fly into a rage, hitting her. When she tried to leave, he ripped her pyjamas and locked her in, beating her until she fell down. She even tried to yell for help from a window, but he pulled her away and pressed a cloth soaked in acetone to her mouth. Eventually, she was able to flee the apartment in her stockings. The police charged the man with assault.

Initially sentenced to six months' imprisonment, the man appealed the decision on the basis that the punishment was too severe. In its decision, the Berlin Municipal Court emphasised that the husband had been trying to reconcile with his wife when he lost control. He still loved her and wanted her to take back the divorce application. At the same time, the court determined that the wife had provoked the attack by spitting and scratching at him. Perhaps not surprisingly, the appeal court lowered the sentence to two years of probation with no jail time. Even in criminal decisions, the court was more inclined to see evidence of a marriage that could be saved than to listen to the woman's claims of serious violence. Furthermore, the court actually tacitly condoned the abuse by blaming the wife for provoking the attack.

---

[61] Schröttle, *Politik und Gewalt*, p. 160.
[62] Ibid., p. 122.
[63] C Rep 301/3436 (1974) Case 105 BSB 190.74, 19 and 23.9.1974, LAB.

Alongside legal stumbling blocks, women experiencing domestic abuse also faced structural issues. Even if they were able to get a divorce, this did not necessarily mean they could leave home. Due to the housing shortage in the GDR, divorced couples would often have to keep sharing their home until an alternative could be found. It was often in these cases that women were exposed to further violence. This is certainly what happened to one Berlin woman in 1976.[64] Married in 1972, she divorced her violent husband after only a few years. Following the divorce, they continued to share their flat, but for protection, she had a lock fitted to her bedroom door. One night at the end of August 1975, her ex-husband came home very drunk. Instead of going to his room, he attempted to get into his ex-wife's bedroom. To prevent him from breaking the lock, the woman opened her bedroom door. Still in her nightdress, she shared a cigarette with her ex-husband. Before long, he started to feel up her clothing. When she pushed him away, he became enraged, violently pulling at her nightdress. Eventually, he got up to close the hallway door. At this point, she grabbed a bottle and hit him over the head with it, because as the court pointed out 'she was afraid that he would assault her.' But the bottle did not have the intended effect and the man grabbed it away from the woman and slapped her across the face. Throwing her on to the bed, he continued to slap her. Even more horrifically, he then raped his ex-wife with a broomstick. When she pled with him to stop, he showed no remorse, then raping her anally.

The next day, the woman went to the police. They informed her that even though her divorce had been granted, it was not yet legally in force. Given that marital rape would not be criminalised in Germany until 1997, the woman discovered she would not be able to press charges until her divorce was finalised. She instead filed a temporary injunction against her ex-husband. In the meantime, she left for a holiday. Upon return, she discovered that he was still living in their apartment. Afraid of further violence, she slept with him two or three more times, until he moved out.

The first court sentenced the man to three years' probation, with the penalty of one year's imprisonment if he breached the court's conditions. The appeal court, however, reduced the sentence to two years' probation, during which time he could not change workplaces. In their opinion, the first court had not considered two key factors. Firstly, the court determined that the woman was, in part, responsible for the attack. Although they proclaimed that the man had a 'negative attitude towards the honour and dignity of women', they ultimately concluded that the woman aggravated the situation, specifically she had led him on. She had opened the bedroom door in her nightdress and shared a cigarette with him, only to later spurn his advances and fuel his anger by hitting him with a bottle. The court also cited evidence that the woman had no injuries from the broom and that, after this

---

[64] Case 105 BSB 15.75, 16.2.1976, Stadtgericht Berlin, C Rep 301/3468, 9–59/76, LAB.

incident, the man had not been violent. By using the woman's actions as mitigating circumstances, the court upheld male primacy over women's bodies and within the private sphere. Additionally, because they were legally still married, her husband had a right to access her body at any time he wanted.

Secondly, the appellate court argued that probation itself was a form of rehabilitation. Requiring that the man remain in his job for two years was a way of enacting the redemptive power of work and, in doing so, give meaning to socialism. But this was also about shoring up socialist masculinity. This is made clear in a similar case reported in the widely circulated GDR newspaper, the *Wochenpost*, in 1973.[65] 'The Angry Young Man', Detlef, was 23 years old and described as unquestionably handsome, with a high forehead, a small moustache and a tendency towards alcoholism and cruelty. He had been married to Katrin. But his violence, tyranny and alcoholism led her to divorce. In the proceedings, she was awarded the apartment and sole custody of the children. A court order was also handed down to prevent Detlef from entering the apartment. At the same time, Detlef was also no 'workingman's hero'. Instead, Detlef 'changed jobs like he changed his shirts' and was often unemployed.

Despite the injunction, Detlef had kept a key to the apartment and would come to the house looking to take back his belongings. One time, he broke through the door – even though Katrin had added another bolt – and beat Katrin until she fell down. Although she had bruising on her frontal bone and a contusion on her right shoulder, the newspaper still questioned her claim that Detlef had punched her ten times in the face. After a second break-in, Katrin pressed charges. This time he had stolen a sheet set, one or two table cloths and a pillow. The court gave Detlef a 250 Mark fine and two years' probation, during which time he had to remain employed at the same workplace. If he broke these conditions and 'resumed his slovenly life', he would face a 10-month prison sentence.

The article concluded that this sentence was 'good for Detlef and very good for his children'. Not only because continued employment would mean that Detlef could make his child support payments, but because by making him stay in a job, 'society is forcing Detlef to behave [in an] orderly [way]. But [that] this threat is in no way unlawful, totally the opposite, it is a stroke of luck for Detlef.'[66] More than this though, by emphasising Detlef's good looks, his attention to clothing, poor work ethic and general lack of self-control throughout the article, the *Wochenpost* evoked long-standing visions of a subversive, effeminate and ultimately bourgeois masculinity.[67] The sentence then is all the more important: through hard work, Detlef can not only find redemption and be a

---

[65] Rudolf Hirsch, *Eros and Ehe vor Gericht: Gerichtsberichte* (Berlin: Verlag das Neue Berlin, 1980), p. 67.
[66] Ibid., p. 70.
[67] Freeland, 'Creating Good Socialist Women'.

better socialist, but he can become a better man. Of course, this focus on Detlef obscured the question of Katrin's safety.[68]

In the GDR, addressing domestic violence was put in service of constructing socialism. Whether it was punishing men with sentences that tied them to a particular workplace, encouraging married couples to reconcile or using women's actions as mitigating circumstances in sentencing or custody decisions, it is clear that solidifying socialism, through building up masculinity and socialist manhood, came at the expense of women's safety. What makes this so remarkable is that these invasive processes of constructing socialism continued well into the 1970s and 1980s, an era typically thought of as offering greater freedom in the private sphere. But despite liberalising attitudes towards gender roles and sexuality, women still could not trust the system when it came to addressing domestic violence. Instead, state visions of family life continued to endanger women living with violent partners. They faced the possibilities of losing their children and their home and of further abuse. Although Betts argues that GDR courts took aim at 'patriarchal attitudes and sexism for eradication as part of the larger effort to build a modern form of socialism at home', more concentrated attention on domestic violence in East Germany shows that legal attempts to challenge patriarchy were mixed at best. Even when divorce became more straightforward, the attitudes of the police and the criminal courts, alongside the housing shortage meant that women were still at risk.

But there were some signs of change during late socialism. Even before the rise of the grassroots protest movement of the mid-1980s (discussed in the next chapter), a critical discourse on everyday life under socialism had developed among GDR artists. This included an open discussion of violence in the socialist family.

Signs of Change?

The liberalisation of the private sphere in the 1970s also resonated in the cultural productions of the GDR. Although the public sphere was tightly restricted, the arts remained one of the few venues where taboo topics could be addressed. This was certainly the case following Honecker's rise to power, as the SED backed away from the previous stringent requirement that films and novels present audiences with an idealised socialist worldview. In this new political context, artists were able to explore contemporary social issues and everyday life under socialism became a central theme across the arts after 1971. In cinema, the 1970s even gave rise to a new genre of film, known as the *Alltagsfilm* or 'film of everyday life'. What

---

[68] See Stadtgericht Berlin, C Rep 301/3225, LAB; Stadtgericht Berlin, C Rep 301 3357, LAB; Stadtgericht Berlin, C Rep 301 3434, LAB.

marked these films apart from earlier GDR productions was their concern for the ordinary, even the banal, and for issues of love, life and death.[69]

Stories of women's lives, in particular, came to the fore in this period, as artists used the focus on everyday life to consider questions of gender, sexuality and the home. Portrayals of women shifted from the 'successful model heroine, who opti-mistically pointed the way forward, to the more ordinary protagonist going about her daily life, struggling, making compromises and often failing'.[70] Importantly, female characters also came to represent broader dissatisfaction and disillusion-ment with socialism. Trusting that the censors' patriarchal values meant that they would take little notice of the critical opinions of female characters, directors and writers used female protagonists to highlight the discrepancies between the promise of socialism and the reality of life in East Germany.[71] Many of these new productions explored the omnipresence of violence against women in the GDR. Sexual harass-ment, intimate-partner violence, sexual assault and even rape were portrayed in films such as *Solo Sunny* (directed by Konrad Wolf, 1980), *The Bicycle* (directed by Evelyn Schmidt, 1982) and the novel and film adaptation of Brigitte Reimann's *Franziska Linkerhand* (1974, released in film as *Our Short Life*, directed by Lothar Warneke in 1981). Even Heiner Carow's hugely popular 1973 film *The Legend of Paul and Paula* strongly suggests instances of abuse between Paul and his wife Ines.

In each of these films, violence was used as a vehicle to explore the limits of socialist change within the private sphere and the workforce. At the most basic level, the portrayal of gender-based violence challenged the SED rhetoric of equality between men and women. More fundamentally though, it also drew the viewer's attention to the system's inability to countenance personal happiness and desire. In myriad ways, women's choices in the films were limited, whether by vio-lence, patriarchal attitudes, economic status or the system itself. In the context of 'real-existing socialism', this message resonated all the more critically, especially given Honecker's pronouncement at the 1971 Eighth Party Congress that the SED only knew 'one goal ... to do everything possible for the welfare of the people, for the happiness of the nation, for the interests of the working class and all working people. That is the meaning of socialism. That is what we work and fight for.'[72]

Perhaps the most compelling example of domestic violence on screen is Heiner Carow's 1979 film, *Until Death Do Us Part*. It tells the story of Sonja (Katrin Sass) and Jens (Martin Seifert), a seemingly ideal socialist couple. Young and in love, they marry and quickly have a child. But problems arise when Sonja's maternity leave

[69] Feinstein, *The Triumph of the Ordinary*; Rinke, *Images of Women*.
[70] Rinke, *Images of Women*, p. 8.
[71] Ibid.
[72] 'Aus dem Bericht des Zentralkomitees der Sozialistischen Einheitspartei Deutschlands an den VIII. Parteitag der SED. Berichterstatter: Genosse Erich Honecker, 15.-19. Juni 1971' in *Dokumente zur Geschichte der SED, 1971–1986*, 3rd ed., edited by Günter Benser and Gerhard Naumann (Berlin: Dietz Verlag, 1986), p. 7.

ends and she wants to return to work. Although he cannot financially support the family by himself, Jens wants Sonja to remain a stay-at-home mother, stubbornly refusing her wishes. Sonja chafes against Jens' attempts to control her and secretly studies for a management exam, which she subsequently passes. However, when she shares this good news with Jens, he is incensed at her deception and becomes violent. Despite making up with one another, Jens' abuse – sexual, physical and emotional – worsens. Sonja meanwhile continues to 'deceive' Jens: she not only returns to work part-time, but also has an abortion without telling him. As each lie is uncovered, Jens' brutality and reliance on alcohol increases. The relationship deteriorates, until one evening Jens comes home drunk and Sonja watches silently as he drinks bleach from an unmarked water bottle that she had been using for cleaning. Jens survives, but is left with permanent scarring in his throat. In spite of all this, Sonja and Jens remain together.

The film's portrayal of violence in a socialist home was clearly a sticking point for East German reviewers. Horst Knietzsch, the pre-eminent critic for *Neues Deutschland*, does not even directly mention violence in his review of the film.[73] Instead, he describes how the film-makers 'drastically confront audiences with the conflicts of two young people', dismissing the ongoing abuse between Sonja and Jens as an 'individual case'. Knietzsch is, however, very critical of Jens' character, at different points describing him as a 'slave master', 'intellectually immature' and a 'psychopath'. Although he sees Sonja as a 'child of the socialist society', she also comes under fire for reacting too 'emotionally' to Jens' violence. Ultimately, Knietzsch brushes off the film as 'cheap sensationalism'.

While a direct engagement with domestic abuse is notably absent, what stands out in discussions of the film is a focus on what the story of Sonja and Jens signified about socialism. In this reading, Jens' violence acts as a yardstick between the promises of socialist transformation and the realities of marriage in the GDR. Much like the East German courts and media, *Until Death Do Us Part* presented violence against women as arising from the failings of an individual man. But the film also challenges this official narrative; there is no redemption for Jens and socialism does not save him. In the most extensive review of the film, dramaturge Dieter Wolf particularly draws attention to the film's 'interplay of change and tradition'.[74] Although Sonja embodies many of the promises that socialism held for women – employment, career advancement, sexual autonomy, maternity benefits – Jens' patriarchal vision of family life is seemingly out-modish in the new socialist world. It is this clash between Jens' bourgeois ideals of family life and Sonja's socialist emancipation that drives the marital conflict. However,

---

[73] Horst Knietzsch, 'Aufgefordert, über den anderen nachzudenken „Bis dass der Tod euch scheidet", ein DEFA-Film', *Neues Deutschland*, 29 May 1979.
[74] Dieter Wolf, 'Die Kunst miteinander zu reden: "Bis daß der Tod euch scheidet" im Gespräch', *Film und Fernsehen* 7 (1979): 8–11, p. 10.

despite her ideological credentials, Sonja stays with Jens. The two remain stuck in an unhappy marriage, unable to find a way out as their friends, family and co-workers encourage them to work things through.

Notwithstanding its poor official reception, this message clearly resonated with audiences and Wolf's review details a mass audience engagement with *Until Death Do Us Part*. Whether in the 'big city, in relatively small club meetings with Dynamo-athletes and technical-school students in Luckenwalde or with a few invited guests at the village premiere at a cooperative in Memleben', screenings of the film stirred audiences to debate and discuss the issues presented onscreen.[75] But it was not artistic matters that occupied them. Instead it was 'life, reality, their own impressions of marriage, family, happiness, pleasure and pain, winning and losing'. Moreover, the film 'mobilised viewers to talk about their own experiences and lives'.[76]

While Wolf, like Knietzsch, does not directly tackle domestic violence, these comments certainly suggest that the cultural sphere, especially films, helped to drive a critical discussion of violence and gender inequality in the GDR. Audiences were increasingly engaging with the topics they saw onscreen and their reaction to the portrayal of marriage in *Until Death Do Us Part* hints that a change was under way as East Germans were becoming increasingly bold in their criticisms of the state. The rhetoric of equality between men and women was a particular touchstone for this discontent and as the next chapter shows, would later harness the energies of a growing women's movement.

Conclusion

In 1986, a Potsdam woman applied to leave the GDR with her children.[77] She based her application on claims that her ex-husband, who refused to move out of their home, was violent and threatening to her and the children. The Stasi file even notes that physical traces of abuse were visible on the woman. The only way she could see out of this situation was to move to the Federal Republic; a separation within the GDR would only anger the man further. In support of her application, she wrote to the Ministry of Internal Affairs in 1987, arguing that 'ruining people through mental and physical pressure is not in the spirit of our socialist state.' She even wrote to SED leader Erich Honecker, pleading with him for help: 'my desperation is so great that I must speak to you personally. I don't see any other way out. This letter is a *cry for help!*' [emphasis in the original].

But she also wrote a similar letter to Bavarian Minister President Franz-Josef Strauß, which she asked a contact in West Berlin to send on her behalf. When this

---

[75] Ibid., p. 9.
[76] Ibid.
[77] BV Pdm Abt II 244, BStU.

was discovered by the Stasi, they investigated her for violating Paragraph 219 of the Criminal Code. This provision criminalised contact between East Germans and those people or organisations that stood against the principles and values of the GDR. In spite of this, the woman was never charged. Not only did she prove to be of good socialist character, with excellent references from her previous employers, but they determined that her letter did not pose 'serious danger for the security of the GDR'. In 1988, her application to leave was finally denied, at which point the Stasi recruited her as an informal collaborator, using the promise of emigration to secure her assistance. Despite working for the Stasi, it was only after the Berlin Wall fell in 1989 that the woman was able to leave the GDR.

This case typifies the extreme ways in which women living with an abusive partner were at the mercy of the system in East Germany. The abuse made the woman desperate and vulnerable to exploitation by the state. But this is also a case that fits awkwardly with much of the recent work on private lives in the GDR under late socialism. This scholarship emphasises the 1970s as a key turning point in sexual liberation under socialism. During this time, East Germans had greater opportunities for self-expression and freedom in the pursuit of love and intimacy. While this work has been an essential corrective to totalitarian narratives of life in the GDR that emphasise social control and surveillance, understandings of socialist liberalisation must be put in conversation with stories like those of this woman from Potsdam. Indeed, the history of domestic abuse reveals the importance of examining late socialism as a time when change and continuity, liberalisation and stagnation coexisted. Legal reform went hand-in-hand with ongoing attempts to keep families together. Domestic violence was lambasted as antithetical to socialist ideals, while women were simultaneously blamed for inciting men to hit them.

While women had diverse experiences of dealing with domestic violence, for the most part there was a clear prioritisation of male engagement with the socialist world. Violence in the home signified a man's failed socialist education and the legal system sought to rectify this. Abusive men were given second chances to improve their work ethic and their commitment to family and socialism. For their wives and partners, it meant being sent back to live with their abuser and the issue of their safety was never a real topic of concern. Even up to the late 1980s, official attempts to address domestic violence in East Germany were still being used to construct socialism and maintain families. The courts judged couples on their reflection of socialist traits, receiving preferential treatment if they were good workers and ideologically committed. Even if their divorce application was successful, the ongoing housing shortage meant that divorce did not necessarily mean separation. In so many cases, speaking out about domestic violence only led to women's endangerment.

But certainly, there were some signs of change. The reform of divorce law made it increasingly easier for women to leave abusive husbands and the number of cases involving domestic violence that were appealed to the Berlin District Court steadily reduced over the 1970s and 1980s. While this did not change police attitudes nor fix the housing shortage, it did make divorce much more straightforward. Also, by the mid-1980s there was an official attempt to address domestic violence under socialism. The GDR had long been a leader in the internationalisation of women's rights: it had sat as a member of the Commission for the Status of Women and was one of the earliest Member States to sign and ratify the Convention on the Elimination of all Forms of Discrimination Against Women.[78] This meant that when the 1985 World Conference to Review and Appraise the Achievements of the United Nations Decade for Women listed violence against women as an issue of 'special concern' (a topic which was initially broached at the 1980 Copenhagen conference), the Supreme Court of East Germany responded with requests for a report on the topic of 'Violence in the Family'.[79] What became of this report is unknown; there are no further traces of it in the German archives.

More significant than these institutional transformations, however, was the growing scepticism of the SED rhetoric of gender equality. Women, in particular, were increasingly confident in pointing out the ways in which their experiences of inequality, harassment and violence did not fit with the socialist ideal.[80] This was not only indicative of the wider societal transformations of the 1970s, but would also fuel the anti-violence activism of men and women in the years prior to the fall of the Berlin Wall and German reunification. Their work, the focus of the next chapter, fed into a growing delegitimisation of socialism and helped transform West German feminist organising following reunification.

---

[78] Celia Donert, 'Whose Utopia? Gender, Ideology, and Human Rights at the 1975 World Congress of Women in East Berlin' in *The Breakthrough: Human Rights in the 1970s*, edited by Jan Eckel and Samuel Moyn (Philadelphia: University of Pennsylvania Press, 2014): pp. 68–87; Celia Donert, 'Women's Rights in Cold War Europe: Disentangling Feminist Histories', *Past and Present*, Supplement 8 (2013): pp. 178–202; Ned Richardson-Little, *The Human Rights Dictatorship: Socialism, Global Solidarity and Revolution in East Germany* (Cambridge: Cambridge University Press, 2020).

[79] United Nations, World Conference to review and appraise the achievements of the United Nations Decade for Women: Equality, Development and Peace, Nairobi Forward-looking Strategies for the Advancement of Women, 26 July 1985. Accessed on 19 October 2015: http://www.un-documents.net/nflsaw.htm; United Nations, Report of the World Conference of the United Nations Decade for Women: Equality, Development and Peace, *14–30 July 1980*. Accessed on 19 October 2015: http://www.un.org/womenwatch/daw/beijing/otherconferences/Copenhagen/Copenhagen%20Full%20Optimized.pdf; Oberstes Gericht der DDR, Sekretariat des Präsidenten, Leitungsberatungen, 1986–1987, DP/2/2037, BArch; Frank-Rainer Schurich, *Tödliche Lust. Sexualstraftaten in der DDR* (Berlin: Edition Ost, 1997).

[80] For a parallel example, see Anita Kurimay and Judit Takács, 'Emergence of the Hungarian Homosexual Movement in Late Refrigerator Socialism', *Sexualities*, Vol. 20, No. 5–6 (2017): pp. 585–603.

5

Feminism and Domestic Violence Activism in the GDR

In the autumn of 1987, the third East German *Frauenfest* (Women's Festival) was held at the Lutheran Church of Reconciliation in Dresden. Organised outside of the auspices of the state, the weekend-long event was run by the local lesbian *Arbeitskreis Homosexualität* (working-group on homosexuality) and supported by other dissident women's groups, including Women for Peace Dresden, Lesbian Group Jena and members of the Fennpfuhl women's group in Berlin. The festival was a women-only event aimed at engaging participants in a critical discussion of life and womanhood under socialism. Indeed, as the flyers for the festival made clear, it was a space for *all* women to come together, with an organising committee made up of 'lesbian and non-lesbian Christians and non-Christians'.[1] At the festival, the participants attended lectures, focus groups and feedback sessions where the organisers invited them to discuss and share their experiences of being women in East Germany. But it was also a social occasion, with communal meal breaks and a dance party on the Saturday night. There was even childcare so that mothers could attend.[2]

While this was one of several independent women's events in the GDR, what made this festival stand out was its focus on the theme of 'Power in Relationships'. For the organisers, it was important to 'recognise the forms and consequences of the exertion of power in personal relationships, at work and in society'.[3] In preparation for the festival, organisers even asked participants to consider their own experiences of coercion and power, where and how they exercised it and what consequences there had been. These reflections formed the basis of the festival's focus groups, which examined various issues of power, including the

---

[1] 'Einladung zum 3. Dresdener Frauenfest vom 2. bis 4. Oktober 1987', GZ/A1/2359, RHG.
[2] Ibid.; 'Programm zum 3. Dresdener Frauenfest „Macht in Beziehungen"', GZ/A1/2359, RHG; Samirah Kenawi, *Frauengruppen in der DDR der 80er Jahre. Eine Dokumentation* (Berlin: GrauZone, 1995).
[3] 'Einladung', GZ/A1/2359, RHG.

social pressures lesbians experience, dependence and subordination in intimate relationships and even violence in language.[4] Much like consciousness-raising groups in the West, this critical self-reflection served a political purpose: bringing women together through their shared experiences of power and oppression.

But it was the festival's keynote address that really caught the public's attention. On the evening of Friday, 2 October, Ines Walter gave a lecture on violence in the family.[5] The audience assembled at the church that night was mixed; although the festival was for women only, men were allowed to attend the keynote. In her talk, Walter tackled the kinds of common assumptions that shrouded domestic abuse. 'Many see the abuse of women as an individual problem', began Walter, 'it is important to counter this false view: *all* women experience powerlessness and vulnerability during their lifetime.'[6] More than this, Walter also took the SED and state institutions to task for failing to protect women. 'The fact that violence against women exists – and not as a "problem of a few sick men", but as a general social problem – is documented in the high divorce rates, in women's calls for help to the police, in the marriage and sexual counselling centres and in the child welfare system', she argued. Even worse for Walter was the fact that 'the workers of these institutions know the difficulties women face! But there isn't any (or hardly any) help.'[7]

The lecture ended with Walter and the head of the *Arbeitskreis Homosexualität*, Karin Dauenheimer, calling for the creation of a 'Place of Protection'. Much like a women's shelter, this would be a space where women experiencing domestic abuse would be taken seriously and supported to make their own decisions. They also envisioned it as a place where women could find information on their options and legal rights and where they would be 'encouraged to value their bodily autonomy more than prevailing – and mistaken – norms.'[8]

Such an engaged approach to domestic abuse contrasted starkly with the SED's official position. Rather than blame bourgeois capitalist gender norms or a failed socialist consciousness, the Dresden *Frauenfest* saw violence against women as a systemic problem that was reflective of broader issues of gender inequality present throughout East Germany. This clearly resonates with feminist work against gender-based violence; just as West German feminists sought to draw attention to the connection between gendered power imbalances and violence against women,

---

[4] Christiane Dietrich, 'Gewalt gegen Frauen: Berliner Haus der Caritas bietet Hilfesuchenden Schutz', *Glaube und Heimat*, 25 October 1987, A1/0300, RHG.

[5] At the time of writing, the background of Ines Walter remains unknown and the archive holding her estate does not have any information on her biography. However, from reviewing her files, it appears as though she worked within the Protestant Church as a youth or social worker.

[6] 'Kurzinformation zum Referat „Gewalt in der Familie" zum 3. Dresdner Frauenfest 2.-4.10.87', GZ/A1/2359, RHG.

[7] Ibid.

[8] Ibid.; Dietrich, 'Gewalt gegen Frauen', A1/0300, RHG.

so too did activists in the GDR. But in the context of state socialism, such an approach carried a very different weight. By questioning the official narrative of violence against women, the Dresden *Frauenfest* were doing more than just criticising the state's approach to domestic abuse. In a state built on claims of gender equality and support for women and the family, Walter's exposé challenged the very legitimacy of SED rule.

Historians have typically linked this kind of grassroots activism to the snowball of social and political shifts that culminated in the collapse of socialism and the end of the Cold War.[9] Similarly to *Alltagsfilme*, events like the Dresden *Frauenfest* were evidence of a growing disillusionment that was spreading across the GDR and the Communist Bloc more generally. Much of this dissent within Eastern Europe was driven by the worsening economic position of the socialist states, problems of material deprivation and popular frustration at the lack of social and political freedoms. In the GDR, Honecker's authoritarian-style leadership and refusal to adopt the key Soviet reforms of glasnost and perestroika only further heightened tensions. For many East Germans, the SED seemed increasingly anti-quated and out of touch with the changing times, especially following the start of reform efforts in Poland and Hungary.[10] Throughout the 1980s, what began as a small dissidence movement slowly grew into mass protest and, along with mounting international pressure and internal crises facing the SED, culminated in the fall of the Berlin Wall and German reunification.

But what would happen if we shifted our focus? What different kind of insights would there be if we saw women's activism not as a history of the Cold War, but rather as a history of feminism? This chapter examines this question and asks what East German activism against gender-based violence tells us about the development and practice of feminism in Germany. This means that instead of concentrating on how activists challenged and questioned the state, we ask how they thought and spoke about violence against women and how they sought to address it.

By approaching the topic this way, it is clear that East German activists drew from, translated and even developed 'western' feminist approaches to violence

---

[9] Mary Fulbrook, *The People's State. East German Society from Hitler to Honecker* (New Haven: Yale University Press, 2005); Ehrhart Neubert, *Geschichte der Opposition in der DDR 1949–1989* (Bonn: Bundeszentrale für politische Bildung, 1997); Ehrhart Neubert, *Unsere Revolution. Die Geschichte der Jahre 1989/90* (Munich: Piper, 2009); Tobias Hochscherf, Christoph Laucht and Andrew Plowman, eds, *Divided, but not Disconnected: German Experiences of the Cold War* (New York: Berghahn, 2010). Also see the critiques of Konrad H. Jarausch in 'Beyond the National Narrative: Implications of Reunification for Recent German history', *German History*, Vol. 28, No. 4 (2010): pp. 498–514.

[10] Jeffrey Kopstein, *The Politics of Economic Decline in East Germany, 1945–1989* (Chapel Hill: University of North Carolina Press, 1997); Esther von Richthofen, *Bringing Culture to the Masses. Control, Compromise and Participation in the GDR* (New York: Oxford University Press, 2009); Jonathan Zatlin, *The Currency of Socialism. Money and Political Culture in East Germany* (Cambridge: Cambridge University Press, 2007).

against women. They read from key western feminist texts, hosted influential West German female politicians and maintained contact with activists from across the Iron Curtain. While some historians have questioned whether feminism or a women's movement ever really existed under socialism, by examining activism against gender-based violence, this chapter clearly shows that it did. In many ways, the story of this activism, both in East Germany and later in the new federal states of a reunified Germany, is a testament to feminism's success.

Feminism gave GDR activists a language and a framework for thinking about violence against women at a time when critical discussion on the topic was strictly controlled. Moreover, feminism provided East German activists a platform to call for greater support for women's rights and protection for women living with violence. While there was little time for these activists to create change before the collapse of socialism in 1989, this work took on renewed importance after the fall of the Berlin Wall. At that time, the delegitimisation of the SED and the integration of the GDR into the Federal Republic paved new avenues for activists tackling violence against women. Indeed, domestic violence projects in eastern Germany quickly received financial and political support from the new authorities and women's shelters spread throughout the states of the former GDR. The years of work that West German feminists spent getting domestic violence on the liberal political agenda were paying off. The fact that activists in the new German states could move relatively seamlessly from grassroots organising under socialism to publicly funded service in a newly reunified state shows how feminism, and feminists, had successfully transformed Germany's political landscape.

However, this is not just a history of the success of West German feminism. Drawing primarily from grey literature (for example, activist materials and publications, non-state magazines and journals), as well as novels, women's writing and three oral history interviews, this chapter also explores the differences between East German approaches to violence against women and those developed in the West. In West Germany, feminism, the women's movement and activism to address domestic violence were intimately connected. Domestic abuse was a formative issue for women activists in the 1970s and it was out of this movement that the first shelters and services for women living with an abusive partner were developed. Feminism not only infused the very way in which domestic violence was understood in West Germany, but it also shaped how it was addressed.

This was not necessarily the case in East Germany, where activism against gender-based violence often emerged out of the dissidence movement. While there were feminists working to address gender-based violence within the women's movement in the GDR, there were also activists who did not take a feminist or even a gendered approach to violence against women. What united these different groups was their opposition to the state, which in turn infused the way they understood gender-based violence. For these activists, it was not just a gender issue.

Instead, they conceived of it more broadly: as one of a litany of social problems that the SED were failing to address. This approach was reflective of a broader shift happening within women's rights, as they slowly came to be considered human rights. As such, this chapter uses activism against gender-based violence in the GDR as a way of exploring the changing meaning and practice of feminism in the late 20th century.

Typically, discussions of feminism in East Germany begin with women's literature. From the mid-1970s to mid-1980s, an increasing number of women writers began to assert their voices and experiences of womanhood under socialism. Novels like *The Life and Adventures of Trobadora Beatriz as Chronicled by her Minstrel Laura* (1974) by Irmtraud Morgner, *Franziska Linkerhand* (1974) by Brigitte Reimann and *The Quest for Christa T.* (1968) by Christa Wolf were some of the first works written by women in the GDR that focused on women's lives. In contrast to other novels from the time, male characters took a backseat, with the narratives revolving around heterosexual women's experiences, including single motherhood, sexuality, marriage and advancement in the workplace.[11] Centring women – their lives, struggles, thoughts and feelings – not only marked an important expression of women's subjectivity, but was also a radical change from the idealised heroines of socialist realist literature.

But what has made these works such an important starting point for feminism is the way they asserted a deep longing for more out of life and questioned the very ability of socialism to fulfil women or even to allow for their self-realisation.[12] In different ways, each author gave voice to what they saw as a broadly felt sentiment of frustration and dissatisfaction among women in East Germany. They used their writing 'as a forum to probe the question of whether the emancipated socialist woman was in fact living a fully human life'.[13] Gerti Tetzner's 1974 novel *Karen W.*, for example, begins *in medias res* with the protagonist, Karen, lying awake thinking, while her partner, Peters, snores in the bed beside her. 'Before,

---

[11] Nancy Lukens and Dorothy Rosenberg, *Daughters of Eve. Women's Writing from the German Democratic Republic* (Lincoln: University of Nebraska Press, 1993).

[12] Silke von der Emde, 'Places of Wonder: Fantasy and Utopia in Irmtraud Morgner's Salman Trilogy', *New German Critique*, No. 82, East German Film (Winter, 2001): pp. 167–192; Sonja Hilzinger, '*Als ganzer Mensch zu leben...*' *Emanzipatorische Tendenzen in der neuen Frauen-Literatur der DDR* (Frankfurt am Main: Peter Lang, 1985); Susanne Rinner, *The German Student Movement and the Literary Imagination: Transnational Memories of Protest and Dissent* (New York: Berghahn, 2013). For an alternative reading, see John Griffith Urang, *Legal Tender. Love and Legitimacy in the East German Cultural Imagination* (Ithaca: Cornell University Press, 2010). Similar demands were also made by female film-makers. Especially in the 1980s, women directors increasingly portrayed the difficulties women faced as they sought to shape the direction of their own lives. See Andrea Rinke, *Images of Women in East German Cinema, 1972–1982: Socialist Models, Private Dreamers and Rebels* (Lewiston: Edwin Mellen Press, 2006).

[13] Lukens and Rosenberg, *Daughters of Eve*, p. 13.

I used to need him breathing beside me', she reflected, '... before all this brooding started.' No longer fulfilled by her life with Peters, Karen longed for something more: 'with every remaining day, I become more restless than the week before: my life is passing me by, strength and youth seep away unused and irretrievable.'[14] At this moment, and within the first few pages of the book, Karen decides to leave her life and moves back to her childhood village with her daughter. Four years later, in 1978, Christa Wolf similarly wrote that for women in the GDR 'what they have achieved and take for granted is no longer enough.' Instead, women's 'first concern is no longer what they have, but who they are.'[15] In what has been labelled Wolf's first discussion on feminism, she underscored that women under socialism were 'signalling a radical expectation: to be able to live as a whole person, to make use of all their senses and abilities.'[16]

Such expressions of unhappiness and dissatisfaction were commonplace among feminists and within the transnational women's movements of the 1960s.[17] Both Wolf and Tetzner's revelations of East German women's internal struggle closely echo those made by American feminist Betty Friedan 15 years earlier when, in the first paragraph of *The Feminine Mystique*, she asked 'is this all?'[18] West German feminist Helke Sander similarly wrote in 1968 that 'every thinking woman is emotionally fed up with this system, even if she can't articulate it. she's fed up because she senses that this system will never be ready to even slightly fulfil her desires.'[19]

In other historical contexts, these moments of feminist awakening are seen as the starting point for a women's movement borne out of identity politics and shared experiences of gendered oppression.[20] Yet this has not been the case in studies of women's activism in East Germany. For many scholars, feminism in the GDR was something that only ever existed in literature; it never translated into a fully fledged women's movement.[21] Instead, Wolf, alongside the other

---

[14] Gerti Tetzner, *Karen W.* (West Berlin: Luchterhand, 1976, 2nd ed.), pp. 5–6.

[15] Christa Wolf, 'Berührung', *Neue Deutsche Literatur* 2 (1978), quoted in Edith Altbach, Jeanette Clausen, Dagmar Schultz and Naomi Stephan, eds, *German Feminism: Readings in Politics and Literature* (Albany: State University of New York Press, 1984), p. 166.

[16] Ibid., p. 167.

[17] See discussion in Sara Ahmed, 'Happiness and Queer Politics', *World Picture* 3 (2009): pp. 1–20.

[18] Betty Friedan, *The Feminine Mystique* (New York: W.W. Norton, 2001, originally published 1963), p. 57.

[19] Helke Sander, '1. versuch. die richtigen fragen zu finden' (February 1968) in *Die Neue Frauenbewegung in Deutschland: Abschied vom kleinen Unterschied. Eine Quellensammlung*, edited by Ilse Lenz, 2nd ed. (Wiesbaden: VS Verlag für Sozialwissenschaften, 2010), p. 53. Lack of capitalisation in the original. On literature and the East German 1968, see Rinner, *The German Student Movement and the Literary Imagination.*

[20] See, for example, Lenz, *Die Neue Frauenbewegung.*

[21] Eva Maleck-Lewy and Bernhard Maleck, 'The Women's Movement in East and West Germany' in *1968. The World Transformed*, edited by Carole Fink, Philipp Gassert and Detlef Junker (Cambridge: Cambridge University Press, 1998): pp. 373–396; Lisa DiCaprio, 'East German Feminists. The Lila Manifesto', *Feminist Studies*, Vol. 16, No. 3 (Autumn, 1990), pp. 621–626; Christiane Lemke, *Die Ursachen des Umbruchs 1989. Politische Sozialisation in der ehemaligen DDR* (Opladen: Westdeutscher Verlag, 1991); Kenawi, *Frauengruppen in der DDR;*

writers, is presented as a feminist avant-garde without popular support. Going even further, Christiane Lemke has argued that one of the reasons women's literature was so popular was precisely because there was no women's movement in the GDR.[22] This is only thought to have changed in 1989, when political conditions enabled the mass mobilisation of women and the formation of a women's movement.[23]

Such an interpretation is particularly striking because, between 1982 and 1989, there were nearly 200 different non-state women's groups across East Germany. Although women's organisational life in the GDR had long been controlled by the SED, things were starting to change in the late 1970s. Since its founding in 1947, the official socialist women's group, the *Demokratischer Frauenbund Deutschlands* (Democratic Women's League of Germany or DFD), had monopolised women's organising. However, the 6 March 1978 agreement between representatives of the Protestant Church in East Germany and the SED awarded relative autonomy to the Church. From this point on, the Church, which had long been a safe haven for opposition voices in the GDR, took on the role of '*ersatz*-public sphere' as it gave shelter to an increasing number of non-state dissident groups.[24]

It was from this milieu that women's organising emerged. Focusing on issues as varied as feminist theology, sexuality and the environment and sheltered within the Church, they held meetings, hosted events like the Dresden *Frauenfest*, took part in dissident activities and worked to create networks between women, men and other activist groups. While some may only have attracted a handful of members, the largest non-state women's group, the Berlin-based *Frauen für den Frieden* (Women for Peace), had chapters throughout the country and acted as an important hub of women's activism.[25] Even though some groups, like *Frauen für den Frieden*, outwardly refused the label 'feminist', by holding political discussions in women-only spaces and challenging the SED state, their work 'furthered the

---

Anne Hampele, 'Ein Jahr Unabhängiger Frauenverband – Teil II: Frauenbewegung und UFV im letzten Jahr der DDR', *Berliner Arbeitshefte und Berichte zur sozialwissenschaftlichen Forschung* 48 (1990); Brigitte Young, *Triumph of the Fatherland: German Unification and the Marginalization of Women* (Ann Arbor: University of Michigan Press, 1999).

[22] Lemke, *Die Ursachen des Umbruchs 1989*.

[23] Maleck-Lewy and Maleck, 'The Women's Movement in East and West Germany'; DiCaprio, 'East German Feminists'. See also Ingrid Miethe's work on women in the GDR opposition movement. Although Miethe acknowledges the context of pre-1989 activism (especially women's involvement in the peace movement), she still frames her narrative around the collapse of socialism and the mass movements that developed during and after 1989/1990. Ingrid Miethe, *Frauen in der DDR-Opposition. Lebens- und kollektivgeschichtliche Verläufe in einer Frauenfriedensgruppe* (Opladen: Leske + Budrich, 1999).

[24] Neubert, *Geschichte der Opposition*. Of course this does not mean there was no surveillance of these groups or that the SED did not try to exert its influence over them. See Corey Ross, *The East German Dictatorship: Problems and Perspectives in the Interpretation of the GDR* (London: Arnold, 2002).

[25] On the development and evolution of *Frauen für den Frieden*, see Susanne Kranz, 'Frauen für den Frieden – Oppositional Group or Bored Troublemakers?', *Journal of International Women's Studies*, Vol. 16, No. 2 (2015): pp. 141–154.

potential for emancipation of GDR women as a whole in the 1980s'.[26] In addition, many of the women involved in these groups read and drew inspiration from East (and also West) German feminist writers. Given this activist work, why have scholars been so hesitant to acknowledge the existence of a women's movement in East Germany before 1989?

One key reason lies in the fact that many studies of women's activism and dissidence in the GDR are framed around the fall of the Berlin Wall and German reunification.[27] Scholars have sought to understand how socialism came to collapse and the role ordinary men and women played in ending the Cold War. Moreover, in light of reunification and the integration of East German states into the West German political system, there has been intense interest in citizens' political engagement under socialism and how this impacted democratic participation after 1990. Women and women's roles have played a particularly important part in this scholarship, as reunification and the collapse of socialism brought women's issues to the fore. Across the former Eastern Bloc, women were hit hard by unemployment and many of the new nationalist regimes implemented pronatalist and patriarchal reforms.[28] In Germany, abortion reform was a key issue in the reunification process, as East German women and West German feminists fought to have the liberal GDR abortion law enacted in the newly reunified state.

But in trying to link women's activism and protest with the broader political transformation of East Germany, the scholarship has often focused on questions of size, impact and public engagement. Given the limited public sphere and small size of women's groups in the GDR prior to 1989, this has inevitably led scholars to doubt the existence of a women's movement and to question the impact of dissidence on political developments. However, there are some significant shortcomings with this approach. Firstly, it diminishes the much longer history of protest and dissent in the GDR to a single moment of collapse.[29] Secondly, and most importantly, it also draws from interpretations of social activism based on experiences in western democracies, where social and political conditions enabled much larger protest movements to develop. In this way, much of the existing scholarship on feminism and women's activism in East Germany comes close to concretising a normative model based on the trajectories of western women's movements.

[26] Young, *Triumph of the Fatherland*, p. 73.
[27] A similar argument is also made by Anna von der Goltz in her study of 1968. See Anna von der Goltz, 'Attraction and Aversion in Germany's 1968: Encountering the Western Revolution in East Berlin', *Journal of Contemporary History* Vol. 50, No. 3 (2015): pp. 536–559.
[28] See Nanette Funk, Magda Müller, Robin Ostow, Michael Bodeman and Matthias Weiss, 'Dossier on Women in Eastern Europe', *Social Text*, No. 27 (1990): pp. 88–122; Susan Gal and Gail Kligman, *The Politics of Gender after Socialism* (Princeton: Princeton University Press, 2000).
[29] von der Goltz, 'Attraction and Aversion'; Neubert, *Geschichte der Opposition*; Rinner, *The German Student Movement and the Literary Imagination*; Stefan Wolle, *Der Traum von der Revolte: Die DDR 1968* (Berlin: Christoph Links Verlag, 2008).

In Eva Maleck-Lewy and Bernhard Maleck's chapter on the women's movement in divided Germany, for example, they argue that the East German women's movement did not develop until 1989, when political conditions finally enabled women to organise autonomously.[30] From this perspective, groups that had existed prior to 1989 are seen merely as precursors, whose significance is only made clear following the ousting of Erich Honecker as the SED leader in October 1989. Similarly, Christine Schenk and Christiane Schindler say that given the 'lack of democracy' in the GDR, only a rudimentary women's movement was able to develop.[31] In making these arguments, the authors implicitly underscore a way of thinking where women's emancipation has been exported to the wider world from the West and is only possible under the conditions of a capitalist, liberal democracy. This is something that has long been critiqued by postcolonial historians exploring feminism within the developing world. As Kumari Jayawardena has argued, this Eurocentric vision of feminism only reifies racial and colonial hierarchies.[32] It also misses the possibility that forms of feminism can originate and develop differently outside of the western, liberal context.

Certainly, there were key differences between women's rights activism in East and West Germany. The SED's work to address women's inequality meant that many of the rights that feminists in West Germany fought for were already implemented in the GDR. East German women had legal access to first trimester abortions from 1972 and contraception was covered by public health insurance. Although access to abortion in the first trimester of pregnancy was legislated in West Germany in 1974, the reform was declared invalid by the Federal Constitutional Court in 1975 and a more restrictive law introduced. The liberalisation of this law remained one of the women's movement's most active campaigns. Similarly, while male-breadwinner households remained the norm in the Federal Republic, female employment was much higher under socialism. Various SED social policies and extensive childcare provision also enabled mothers to work in paid employment. Although East German women worked predominantly in traditionally female sectors, such as the service industry and education, and remained responsible for the majority of housework and child rearing, the issues most fundamental to West German feminism simply did not preoccupy East German activists.

But this does not mean that there was no feminism or women's rights movement in the GDR. Following Jayawardena, in order to understand what East German activists against domestic violence achieved, we must examine their

---

[30] Maleck-Lewy and Maleck, 'The Women's Movement in East and West Germany'.
[31] Christine Schenk and Christiane Schindler, 'Frauenbewegung in Ostdeutschland – Innenansichten' in *Gefährtinnen der Macht. Politische Partizipation von Frauen im vereinigten Deutschland – eine Zwischenbilanz*, edited by Eva Maleck-Lewy and Virginia Penrose (Berlin: Edition Sigma, 1995), pp. 183–203 p. 185.
[32] Kumari Jayawardena, *Feminism and Nationalism in the Third World* (London: Zed, 1986).

work in the context of the GDR and not just as a precursor to 1989.[33] None of the people attending the Dresden *Frauenfest* in 1987 knew that in only two years' time socialism in East Germany was going to collapse, so why should that frame our historical analysis? Adopting this approach, it becomes apparent that much of what East German activists did to combat violence against women drew from and built on West German feminism. At the same time, their work also challenged it and moved feminism in different directions.

East German Activism against Domestic Violence in the 1980s

The most important group to address violence against women in the GDR was the Weimar *Frauenteestube* or Women's Tea Parlour. The group first formed in 1983 after two Weimar women attended the second annual Peace Workshop in Berlin. At the time, this was one of the most important events for dissidents and activists in East Germany and it inspired the Weimar women to form a local chapter of *Frauen für den Frieden*.[34] Although they may have started as a peace group, they soon turned to other issues. After receiving access to rooms at the Johanneskirche in Weimar in 1984, the group – now able to meet regularly and hold events – began to focus more on women's issues. They got involved in other women's activities throughout the GDR, meeting with activists in Berlin and hosting various talks on pedagogy, feminist theology and motherhood.

As the group continued, their work increasingly engaged with western feminism. According to founding Weimar activist Petra Streit, her 'A-Ha! moment' came after reading her first feminist book from the West. She describes it as a moment where 'suddenly the lights were switched on'. From this moment, Streit read widely on women's issues, saying that she knew 'more about the situation of women in Western Europe, America and Asia' than she did about women in the GDR.[35] But this interest in women's lives was also driven by a creeping awareness that her understanding of womanhood did not match the vision being sold by the SED. As she put it, 'I read in the newspaper (if they even bother to report on women) that we are equal, that everything is great for us, that everything is

---

[33] For other examples of studies that move away from Cold War frameworks, see the contributions found in Juliane Fürst and Josie McLellan, eds, *Dropping Out Of Socialism: The Creation of Alternative Spheres in the Soviet Bloc* (New York: Lexington Books, 2017) and Joachim Häberlen, Mark Keck-Szajbel and Kate Mahoney, eds, *Politics of Authenticity: Counter-Cultures and Radical Movements Across the Iron Curtain, 1968–1989* (New York: Berghahn, 2019), especially the chapter by Maria Bühner.

[34] Eberhard Kuhrt, Hannsjörg F. Buck and Gunter Holzweißig, eds, *Opposition in der DDR von den 70er Jahren bis zum Zusammenbruch der SED-Herrschaft* (Opladen: Leske and Opladen, 1999); Miethe, *Frauen in der DDR-Opposition*.

[35] 'Projekt: Wie leben Frauen in der DDR', GZ/PS/00, RHG. See also: Kenawi, *Frauengruppen in der DDR*, p. 300.

being done for us, etc. But the experiences of women and the GDR-women's literature say something different to those few newspaper articles. How is it really for women in the GDR?'[36]

This question proved decisive. Exploring women's lives and experiences was central to developing an independent approach to violence against women. The paucity of critical discussion in East Germany meant that one of the first tasks facing women's groups seeking to address gender violence was the creation of a language capable of expressing shared experiences of violence. Finding common ground between women was no easy task though; as one member of the Eisenach women's group remarked 'it is very difficult to create something like a formula or definition [for violence against women], since each one of us have experienced and evaluated their surroundings (workplace, family) differently.'[37]

This interest in the position of women in the GDR led Streit and the *Frauenteestube* to investigate violence against women more fully. Following meetings with notable Berlin activist Ulrike Poppe in 1986 and early 1987, the group began to focus their work on rape and sexual violence under socialism, a topic otherwise largely neglected by the SED. From this point, up to the summer of 1989, the group took on various projects aimed at increasing awareness of sexual violence and reforming the law of rape in the GDR. In their own words, they examined 'the contempt of women, concepts of male ownership of women's bodies, [and] male sexuality as a demonstration of power and aggression' in incidents of rape.[38]

From 1987 onwards, the group initiated numerous activities in their campaign against sexual violence. One of their major projects was a grassroots survey examining women's experiences of rape and sexual violence, but they also created a reform agenda to revise Paragraph 121, the Criminal Code provision on rape in East Germany and presented lectures on the subject of sexual violence to other women's groups across the GDR. It was at these lectures that the group distributed copies of the survey for the audience to complete, handing out some before and after the presentation. They also allowed women to take copies of the survey home to distribute among their circle of friends and acquaintances, with the explicit instruction that they should hand it out to women from different age groups to increase the diversity of respondents. Once completed, women could then mail their survey back to the *Frauenteestube* for collation.

The survey itself consisted of eight key questions and was designed to allow respondents to remain anonymous. The first questions focused on rape, asking the respondents whether they had been raped or had survived an attempted rape. The survey then broadened this focus, asking about experiences of other forms

[36] Ibid.
[37] Brief an Herrn Scholz, Betreff 'Gewalt gegen Frauen', A1/2524, RHG.
[38] 'Vergewaltigung', G2/A1/1232, RHG.

of sexual and gender-based violence, including sexual harassment, flashing and childhood sexual abuse. The final questions asked about the longer-term impact of abuse and violence – whether, for example, it had changed the respondent's relationships with men.[39]

Between 1987 and 1989, the group collected 151 completed surveys and the results clearly indicated that sexual violence was a widespread phenomenon in the GDR. Twenty-two per cent of respondents said they had been raped and of this 73 per cent said it happened once, 9 per cent twice and 3 per cent four times. A further 44 per cent said they had survived an attempted rape, the majority for whom it only happened once. Experiences of sexual harassment were very high, with 70 per cent of respondents reporting that they had been flashed and a further 66 per cent stating they had experienced another form of sexual harassment, including unwanted physical touching or verbal harassment. It is also clear that these experiences had a lasting impact on women: 51 per cent of respondents stated that they were either experiencing or had experienced mental health issues because of violence and harassment. For the vast majority this was anxiety, but women also listed feelings of insecurity, changes to their physical health and a change in their attitudes towards and relationships with men.[40]

Alongside these important findings, the survey clearly shows that the Weimar group drew inspiration from feminism. Not only did they use grassroots feminist methodologies that privileged women's voices and experiences, but the way they conceptualised violence also reflected contemporary feminist discussions. Like their counterparts in West Germany, the Weimar group understood violence against women as something that ran much deeper within the fabric of society than mere physical assault. Instead, it was bound up in myriad actions against women's personhood and was something that had a long-lasting impact on women's emotional and physical well-being and sense of self. For example, although the survey was ostensibly about rape, it also asked women about their experiences of sexual harassment, assault and even child abuse, thereby connecting violence to broader gendered oppression and inequality. Furthermore, by asking about the long-term impact of violence, the Weimar group acknowledged the way in which acts of violence can reverberate throughout a woman's life. It is also noteworthy that the survey asked about 'sexual harassment'. While rape and assault had legal definitions, sexual harassment was still a relatively new concept at this time; American feminist Catherine Mackinnon's groundbreaking work on the topic had only just come out in English in 1979 and was not available in German translation.

---

[39] For more on the survey, see GZ/PS/00, RHG and Kenawi, *Frauengruppen in der DDR*.
[40] Ute Schäfer, *Auswertung der Fragebögen der Weimarer Frauengruppe*, Köln, 21 February 1992, GZ/PS/00, RHG.

But while they drew from feminism, these activists did not simply replicate western feminist thought and practice. Whereas West Berlin activists seeking funding from the state and political legitimacy had to make violence against women legible, this simply was not the case in the GDR. The Weimar *Frauenteestube* did not have to create clearly defined distinctions between rape, assault, domestic violence and harassment because they were working outside of, and against, the state. This allowed them to develop a much more amorphous and holistic understanding of violence against women. Indeed, the survey enabled women to define their own experiences and often in ways that challenged feminist politics. In several survey responses, women listed non-consensual sex with an intimate partner as sexual harassment and not rape. In one case, a 25-year-old woman listed 'sex that I didn't want or didn't feel like having' with her boyfriend as a form of sexual harassment. Similarly, a 35-year-old woman, who, although she had not reported being raped, said that she had frequently been forced into sex during arguments with her husband. While we do not know what the Tea Parlour made of such assertions, in the context of a state where women were not encouraged to speak openly about abuse or sexual violence this survey gave women a voice and a language to define their experiences. It also gave weight to the activists' critiques of the SED's failure to address violence against women, as they had hard proof that it was more than just a few 'bad men' who abused women.

The other projects of the *Frauenteestube* also reflect an attempt to translate feminism for life and politics under socialism.[41] This is most clearly visible in the group's work to challenge the law of rape in the East German Criminal Code. Paragraph 121 defined rape as 'whoever forces a woman through violence or through threat of violence to life or health into extra-marital sex, or coerces a defenceless or mentally ill woman into extra-marital sex will be punished with a sentence of between one and five years.'[42] In their critique, the *Frauenteestube* took issue with three key aspects of this law: the restriction of rape to non-marital relationships; the standard of consent, in particular the requirement that the woman be threatened with violence; and lastly, the limitation of rape to women.

With respect to rape as limited to non-marital sex, the Weimar group's critique clearly echoed the ideas of 19th-century German socialist leader August Bebel, whose pioneering work *Woman and Socialism* linked women's oppression by men to the broader class struggle.[43] Specifically, the Weimar women argued that by excluding rape within marriage, the legal system was upholding bourgeois values,

---

[41] A similar argument is made by Zsófia Lóránd in her study of Yugoslav feminism. See Zsófia Lóránd, ' "A Politically Non-Dangerous Revolution is not a Revolution": Critical Readings of the Concept of Sexual Revolution by Yugoslav Feminists in the 1970s', *European Review of History*, Vol. 22, No. 1 (2014): pp. 120–137.

[42] Para. 121, Strafgesetzbuch, DDR (1968).

[43] August Bebel, *Woman Under Socialism*, trans. Daniel de Leon (New York: Schocken Books, 1971).

in particular 'the traditional view of rape as an injury to a man's property rights over women'.[44] Similarly, the restriction of rape to vaginal penetration, they argued, was based on an outdated and equally bourgeois view that criminalising rape is about preventing unwanted children and protecting the virginity of young women.

As their discussion continued, they drew increasingly from feminist critiques to challenge the standard of consent in East German rape law. In particular, the *Frauenteestube* criticised the way that according to the law a mere 'no' did not prove lack of consent, but rather that a woman had to show signs of having physically resisted her rapist. They further argued that this had the effect of disregarding women's right to sexual self-determination and also ignored the way society socialises women to be passive.[45] By maintaining these laws, they argued, the courts were protecting women only to safeguard their reproductive capabilities and not because women had a right to bodily and sexual integrity. In making this claim, the Weimar group was able to use both socialist and feminist frameworks to make a radical claim for women's rights.

What is most striking is the fact that the Weimar group's reform agenda on rape explicitly included men as capable of being raped.[46] Primarily, including men in their critique of Paragraph 121 was a way of highlighting just how unfair it was to confine the definition of rape to vaginal penetration. 'How can lawmakers think, for example, that oral or anal rape are any less dehumanising and brutal than vaginal rape for the victim, either female or male?', the group argued. The inclusion of men also had a broader resonance. On the one hand, including men may have been a way of appealing to the importance of gender equality in socialism. By showing how both women and men were affected by the law, the activists could make a larger claim for reform.

On the other hand, it also spoke to a solidarity between men and women dissidents in East Germany. Not only were they both victims of sexual violence, but, more importantly, they were victims of the regime. This is one of the most unique aspects of the development of feminist politics in East Germany.[47] While West German feminism emerged out of antagonism with male-dominated organisations like the SDS and the APO, in East Germany the relationships between male and female dissidents were not as contentious.[48] The Weimar *Frauenteestube* grew out of and in cooperation – not conflict – with the broader dissidence movement. As such, it was the state, not men, which was the target of their critiques.[49]

---

[44] 'Vortrag zum Thema Vergewaltigung', G2/A1/1227, RHG.

[45] Ibid.

[46] Verfassung Art. 20 Abs. 2, A1/1227, 1986–1989, RHG.

[47] Young, *Triumph of the Fatherland*, p. 73.

[48] On this topic, see Katharina Karcher, *Sisters in Arms. Militant Feminisms in the Federal Republic of German since 1968* (Oxford: Berghahn, 2017).

[49] A similar argument is made by Miethe in her examination of the women's peace movement. According to Miethe, although women in groups like Berlin's Women for Peace saw 'the woman

Questioning and challenging the state was fundamental to the work of women tackling gender-based violence. This is not only evident in their work to reform Paragraph 121, but also in the survey, which was positioned in direct contrast to the state's approach to gender-based violence. 'Over the course of our research into the topic of rape', the survey began, 'we have discovered that there are no available statistics in the GDR. According to the police, sexual crimes are very rare in comparison to other criminal acts. We want to create an overview for ourselves and ask for your support.'[50] Similar sentiments were echoed in the keynote address of the Dresden *Frauenfest*. According to speaker Ines Walter, 'it is striking that there are no statistics or research on woman abuse (both within and outside of the family) and that such a dangerous phenomenon has not been seen as worthy of study.'[51] This approach also meant that women's rights activism was more open to men. Not only did the reform agenda of the *Frauenteestube* include men as victims of rape, but the keynote lecture of the Dresden *Frauenfest* was open to both women and men. It also meant that responding to gender-based violence was not only thought of as a women's issue, enabling men to get involved in activism against domestic violence.

Indeed, one of the earliest responses to domestic violence emerged not out of a women's group or even out of a grassroots activist organisation. As early as 1981, Caritas, a Catholic welfare organisation, was attempting to open a crisis shelter in Berlin.[52] Initially opened in 1984, the shelter was set up in a former vicarage on the edge of Berlin, where counsellors and residents lived side-by-side. In 1986, it moved to Berlin's Hohenschönhausen neighbourhood. This new shelter, named *Caritas-Haus. Wohnen für Menschen in schwierigen Lebenssituationen* (Caritas House: Accommodation for People in Difficult Circumstances), started taking in clients in 1987 and consisted of a staff of male and female volunteers, social workers and a psychologist.

Significantly, this project was not planned exclusively as a women's shelter; rather, it was designed as a general crisis shelter to address the myriad issues of homelessness and drug and alcohol addiction that existed in the GDR. However, the broad mandate of 'difficult circumstances' meant that women escaping violence in the home soon arrived at the shelter looking for support. This came as a

---

question as important ... the oppression of the GDR system was foregrounded'. Miethe, *Frauen in der DDR-Opposition*, pp. 82–83.

[50] GZ/PS/00, RHG.

[51] 'Programm zum 3. Dresdener Frauenfest 'Macht in Beziehungen'', GZ/A1/2359, RHG.

[52] Although Caritas is a Catholic organisation, research has shown that the role of religion in the East German Caritas organisation was muted and instead allowed people to 'invoke Christian charity without speaking'. See Josef Pilvousek, 'Caritas in SBZ/DDR und Neuen Bundesländern' in *Religion und Kirchen in Ost (Mittel) Europa: Deutschland-Ost*, edited by Karl Gabriel, Josef Pilvousek and Miklos Tomka (Ostfildern: Schwabenverlag, 2003): pp. 50–62. See also Christoph Kösters, ed, *Caritas in der SMZ/DDR, 1945-1989* (Paderborn: Ferdinand Schöningh Verlag, 2001) and Esther Peperkamp and Małgorzata Rajtar, eds, *Religion and the Secular in Eastern Germany, 1945 to the Present* (Leiden: Brill, 2010).

'total surprise' for the Caritas workers, who had never considered domestic violence as an issue and yet were increasingly faced with women in need of help and
protection from their abusive partners.[53] To what extent then can we compare this
work to that of the Weimar *Frauenteestube*? Is it really feminist?

Whether planned as a domestic violence support service or not, the Caritas
shelter certainly represented an important intervention in protecting women's
rights and tackling gender inequality in the GDR. It enabled women to leave abusive relationships and gave them access to support services that were not invested
in the socialist mission of the state. In addition, the Caritas House had links to
the growing East German women's movement and was even taken up as a model
for future feminist action. The Hohenschönhausen house was actively promoted
among women's groups as a refuge from domestic violence. Following the 1987
Dresden *Frauenfest*, gay rights activist Marinka Körzendörfer advertised the new
project in the magazine *UNION*. Similarly, Christine Dietrich, one of the festival's
organisers, wrote an article on the subject of violence against women for the
Protestant magazine *Glaube+Heimat*. In this piece, Dietrich drew attention to the
Caritas project as 'the first place in the GDR where affected women could turn to
for help'.[54] She further called for the construction of other refuges and for readers
to 'search for other potential support services for abused women in municipal and
protestant bodies'.[55]

Moreover, the Caritas House was embedded within the same dissident
networks as women's feminist activism against gender-based violence. For
these activists, addressing domestic violence was about more than just helping
women: it was about challenging SED rule and compensating for the failing
regime. Much like grassroots feminist organising, Caritas' work originated from
the same desire for more out of socialism. They were keenly aware that significant
social problems were simply being swept under the carpet by the SED and, like the
various women's groups, they attempted to fill the gaps in the crumbling 'welfare
dictatorship'.[56] Indeed, for one former Caritas volunteer, creating a service outside
of the auspices of the state was about 'doing something different' from what the
system expected.[57]

Taken together then, the Weimar *Frauenteestube* and the Caritas shelter
reveal the diversity and unique nature of GDR feminism. Emerging as it did out

---

[53] Interview with 'Joachim', Berlin, 30 January 2014.
[54] Dietrich, 'Gewalt gegen Frauen', A1/ 0300, RHG; Marinka Körzendörfer, 'Zwanglos über Zwänge
reden', *UNION*, 24/25 October 1987, ZA/17, RHG.
[55] Ibid.
[56] Konrad H. Jarausch, ed, *Dictatorship as Experience: Towards a Socio-Cultural History of the GDR*
(New York: Berghahn Books, 1999); Thomas Kochan, *Blauer Würger: So trank die DDR* (Berlin: Aufbau
Verlag, 2011).
[57] Interview with 'Joachim', Berlin, 30 January 2014.

of the nexus of western feminist politics, 'real-existing socialism' and the dissident movement, women's rights activism in the GDR was not only more open to men and less separatist, but it was also much more invested in partnerships with welfare organisations and legal reform. In West Berlin, by comparison, Caritas only opened a shelter in 1983 – seven years after the first model shelter – and many activists remained reluctant to engage with the state up until German reunification. Although groups like the *Frauenteestube* took up West German feminist literature and approaches, they also pushed it in different directions, translating feminist politics to fit a dissident socialist context.

In this way, the history of domestic violence activism in the GDR is more than just a part of the history of feminism. It is also part of a history of dissidence. However, the historiography has highlighted one important limitation: for most of the 1980s, dissidence in the GDR was a small affair. Although the achievements of the groups examined here are significant, it was only after 1989, with the implosion of the SED and the fall of the Berlin Wall that a mass movement against domestic violence developed in the East. From this point on, activism against domestic violence changed radically. While both the Weimar *Frauenteestube* and the Caritas shelter continued their work beyond 1989, the impetus for addressing violence against women shifted to new projects that much more closely fit the western model of feminist activism. But this did not mean that the patterns and relationships established in GDR activism disappeared entirely.

East and West Come Face to Face: Domestic Violence Activism After 1989

In the months before and after the collapse of socialism in East Germany, there was an explosion of protest, as popular discontent became increasingly vocal across the GDR. Groups formed at this time like the *Unabhängiger Frauenverband* (UFV, or Independent Women's Association) and *Neues Forum* (New Forum) allowed women to come together as never before. Just like the independent women's groups under socialism, these new spaces allowed women to forge connections and engage in issues that mattered to them as women.[58] From this point on, a movement against domestic abuse and violence against women was able to grow in the East. Reunification saw the start of many projects aimed at assisting women

---

[58] For a brief overview of the founding of the UFV, see Anne Hampele, 'The Organized Women's Movement in the Collapse of the GDR: The Independent Women's Association (UFV)' in *Gender Politics and Post-Communism: Reflections from Eastern Europe and the Former Soviet Union*, edited by Nanette Funk and Magda Mueller (New York: Routledge, 1993): pp. 180–193; Daphne Hornig and Christine Steiner, *Auf der Suche nach der Bewegung. Zur Frauenbewegung in der DDR vor und nach der Wende* (Hamburg: Frauen-Anstiftung eV, 1992).

in violent living situations and throughout the early 1990s, shelters spread across the former GDR.[59]

However, unlike the struggles to get domestic abuse taken seriously in West Germany, shelters and projects were taken up with much less fuss in the former East.[60] On the one hand, this was due to the do-it-yourself grassroots approach that had dominated activism against gender-based violence in the GDR. Activists were used to compensating for the state's failings and this served them well after 1989. Indeed, when one activist asked UFV founder Ina Merkel whether there were any plans to open a women's shelter, she was told 'you have to do it yourselves.'[61] Encouraged by this attitude, this activist would go on to organise the first independent women's shelter in former East Berlin.

On the other hand, East German activism's success was also due to the work of feminists in the West. By the time of reunification, feminists had been working to address domestic violence for almost 15 years. By 1989, the women's shelter system was not only institutionalised in West Germany, but addressing violence against women was firmly integrated into West German political life. East German activists were certainly able to benefit from this: they could both draw on the experiences and strategies of other West German shelters and they could use these connections as support to legitimise domestic violence intervention as an important political issue.

The stories of two of the earliest shelters to open in the East – the *erstes autonomes Frauenhaus* (First Autonomous Women's Shelter) in Leipzig and the Hestia Women's Shelter in East Berlin – reflect the very different way in which domestic violence projects were taken up in the new federal states. Like the West German shelters, these were organised following feminist principles of self-help and empowerment and they closely followed the western definitions of violence against women and models of intervention. Interestingly though, both these shelters emerged as new projects beginning in 1989. They did not develop out of the women's or dissidents' movements, but rather out of the context of the collapse of the socialist regime.

One of the Leipzig shelter's founders, Jennifer, worked as a nurse in a women's ward in the GDR. During this time, she saw many young women who, seeing no other way out of their abusive relationships, had attempted suicide. Although she believed that the SED would never permit a women's shelter to be opened, after seeing East German media coverage of domestic violence projects in West Berlin,

---

[59] Kenawi, *Frauengruppen in der DDR*; Young, *Triumph of the Fatherland*; Hampele, 'Ein Jahr Unabhängiger Frauenverband'.

[60] See, for example, 12. Sitzung Stadtverornetenversammlung von Berlin, 19.9.1990, C Rep 100-01/241, LAB; Magistratsbeschluss, Nr. 49/90 vom 3. Juli 1990, C Rep 100-05/2218, LAB.

[61] Interview with 'Sophie', Berlin, 4 February 2014.

she started to make plans for a shelter in Leipzig. She even had friends in Cologne send her literature on domestic violence.[62] By 1989, political developments enabled her to start work on a refuge for women. In the months prior to the fall of the Berlin Wall, she was able to travel to Cologne and meet with shelter workers there. By the time the Wall fell in November 1989, Jennifer and three other women had already begun to map out a support project for women in crisis. The four women had all met at a women's meeting organised by the political group *Neues Forum* and, by early December 1989, they had submitted an application to the City Planning Commission demanding that an unoccupied house be made available for the construction of a women's shelter.[63]

Following a similar trajectory, Sophie, the founder of what would become the Hestia Shelter in Berlin, was a volunteer with Child and Youth Services under socialism and had encountered many young people and mothers who were experiencing violence in the home. In late 1989, she joined a group of 20 women, all from different social backgrounds, interested in helping women who were living with violence. In comparison to the professional team composing the West Berlin house at this time, none of this group were trained social workers, but they had either had voluntary experience working in the welfare sector, or had first-hand experiences of violence against women. In February 1990, the East Berlin women formed the Association for the Protection of Physically and Psychologically Threatened and Abused Women and their Children, later renamed Hestia. After this, they began contacting various political bodies, such as the town council of Berlin and the regional Round Tables (forums held between the citizens' movement and government bodies to enable reform), in hopes of being granted one of the many empty properties left behind following the overthrow of the SED.

Much like the West German activists in the mid-1970s, for both the Leipzig and Berlin groups the second stage of their activism was to break the taboo of domestic violence and create public awareness. The two groups forwarded copies of their shelter proposals to regional newspapers and published statistics and data on violence against women under socialism.[64] The Leipzig women's festival also promoted the group's work, bringing many new volunteers to the shelter project. Similarly, the newly installed City Commissioner for Equal Opportunity in East Berlin hosted a hearing on the issue of violence against women in September 1990, where the film *The Power of Men is the Forbearance of Women* (1978), based on stories of the Grunewald shelter in West Berlin, was screened.

More generally, the years 1989 and 1990 saw a media boom on the subject of violence against women as the cause of domestic abuse was quickly taken up. Newspaper articles and radio shows, both mainstream and feminist-oriented,

---

[62] Interview with 'Jennifer', Leipzig, 17 October 2013 and her private archives.
[63] Private archives of 'Jennifer'.
[64] 'Rede 20jähriges Jubiläum', private archive of 'Sophie'; private archives of 'Jennifer'.

revealed how under socialism domestic abuse had been a taboo that 'contradicted the official ideal of the intact family'.[65] They further focused on women's stories of abuse and the task of opening shelters, highlighting the SED's failure to protect women, repeating popular feminist critiques of domestic violence as a 'social problem' based in 'patriarchal structures and the real discrimination of women in the home and at work'.[66] At the same time, social researchers began to collect data on violence against women, with the first statistics on rape and domestic violence in the East German criminal justice system published in 1990.[67] While these stories led some observers to conclude that domestic violence did not exist as widely under socialism, they did not create the same widespread anxieties or questioning of shelter projects as was the case in the West in the 1970s.[68]

This popular support for domestic violence activism was certainly due to the years of groundwork laid by West German feminists. But it was also because activists capitalised on the growing delegitimisation of the SED and socialist rule. Just as the West Berlin shelter initiative legitimised their work by linking their project to the London Chiswick refuge, by emphasising how stigmatised domestic violence was under socialism, East German activists took full advantage of the changing political climate. The proposals of both the Leipzig shelter and the first autonomous shelter in East Berlin underscored that under socialism 'there were no social or legal regulations' addressing violence in the family.[69] Positioning their efforts in this manner allowed these projects to garner support by casting their work in opposition to the illegitimate SED regime. Indeed, the projects in Leipzig and East Berlin were quickly embraced by the new political organisations of the *Wende*, both receiving funding and property within a year of application. By early 1990, the Leipzig District Assembly concluded that a women's shelter was needed,

---

[65] 'Gewalt und Angst in den Familien darf keine private Angelegenheit mehr bleiben', *Berliner Zeitung*, 25 April 1990, p. 9; 'Wer gibt schon gern zu. Daß alles kaputt ist?', *Neue Zeit*, 1 June 1990, p. 3; '(K) eine Chance für längst notwendige Frauenprojekte?', *Berliner Zeitung*, 20 June 1990, p. 7; 'Männerfrage wird gestellt', *Berliner Zeitung*, 4 June 1990, p. 7; 'Irgendwo im Ostteil der Stadt – Frauenhaus "Bora"', *Neues Deutschland*, 6 September 1990, p. 7; '"Asyl" für mißhandelte Frauen', *Neue Zeit*, 6 September 1990, p. 7; 'Gewalt gegen Frauen', *Neue Zeit*, 17 September 1990, p. 9; 'Zufluchtswohnungen für Frauen in Berlin', *Die Tageszeitung*, 24 July 1990; 'Leipziger Frauenhaus öffnet seine Türen', *Neues Deutschland*, 8 October 1990.

[66] 'Gewalt und Angst in den Familien', p. 9.

[67] Marina Beyer, *Frauenreport '90. Im Auftrag der Beauftragten des Ministerrates für die Gleichstellung von Frauen und Männern* (Berlin: Verlag die Wissenschaft Berlin, 1990), pp. 197–198.

[68] Dinah Dodds and Pam Allen-Thompson, *The Wall in My Backyard. East German Women in Transition* (Amherst: University of Massachusetts Press, 1994); Monika Schröttle, *Politik und Gewalt im Geschlechterverhältnis: eine empirische Untersuchung über Ausmaß, Ursache und Hintergründe von Gewalt gegen Frauen in ostdeutschen Paarbeziehungen vor und nach der deutsch-deutschen Vereinigung* (Bielefeld: Kleine Verlag, 1999); Pressemitteilung zur Vorlage 49/90, Tagesordnungspunkt 11 der Magistratssitzung vom 3.7.1990, C Rep 100-05/2218, LAB.

[69] Private archive of 'Jennifer'. See also Wir fordern den Berliner Runden Tisch auf, den o.g. Verein beim Aufbau eines autonomen Frauenhauses zu unterstützen, A1/2836, RHG; Beschluss/Vorlage der Magistrat der Stadt Magdeburg beschliessst: Ausbau und die Einrichtung eines Frauenhauses für die Stadt Magdeburg, A1/1542, RHG.

after members of the Party of Democratic Socialism (PDS, the successor party of the SED) and the DFD introduced a draft resolution. In the summer of that same year, the District Administration gave the Leipzig group a former Stasi building.[70] Soon thereafter the group was given a start-up grant of 50,000DM from the last East German Ministry for Family, Youth and Sport after writing to its Minister, Christa Schmidt. The Leipzig shelter opened on 2 November 1990 and, with space for 24 women and children, was immediately full. By 1991, the shelter was funded through the city budget and in 1993 they were granted a larger house to help with overcrowding, which finally opened in 1994.

A similar process took place in East Berlin as the initiative group worked to establish a women's shelter. Much like the Leipzig shelter, it is clear they received significant political support. Before even receiving funding for the project, the Berlin group was granted a former residence of the National People's Army (NVA) through the petition of a citizens' initiative in early 1990.[71] Although possession of this building caused some difficulties, with the title only being passed on to the Municipal Authorities in East Berlin from the former Ministry for Disarmament and Defence in late September 1990, the official backing that the proposed shelter received from political authorities in both East and West meant that the shelter was fully funded. Only a few months after being given the residence, the initiative group met with the West Berlin Senator for Construction and Living, who promised 331,200DM for the renovation of the NVA building, with the money due to come from the 25 million DM fund for the reconstruction of East Berlin. In addition, following a proposal by Eva Kunz, the City Commissioner for Equal Opportunity, by 3 July, the East Berlin Municipal Authorities had agreed to provide 628,800DM over two years for the shelter's renovation and furnishing. By September 1990, the Federal Ministry for Women had provided enough money to pay the salaries of four shelter workers. Due to lengthy renovations, the Hestia shelter would not open until 19 May 1993, but in the meantime, the group was busy. They organised the Contact Office for Women in Crisis, where women in abusive relationships could find support and legal assistance; they leased 12 emergency apartments throughout Berlin and finally, on 1 January 1992, they took over a shelter in Marzahn, which had previously been supported through the local authorities, all before their proposed project had even opened.

While we might question whether the processes of opening these two shelters was so straightforward, or if it is simply a function of memory and the delegitimisation of the GDR, what is clear is that the shelters received overwhelming support in ways that shelters in West Berlin did not in the early years of domestic violence activism.[72] Whereas West Berlin activists had to struggle for legitimacy,

---

[70] Private archive of 'Jennifer'.
[71] 'Rede 20jähriges Jubiläum', private archive of 'Sophie'.
[72] For an in-depth examination of post-reunification feminist projects, see Katja M. Guenther, *Making Their Place: Feminism after Socialism in Eastern Germany* (Stanford: Stanford University Press, 2010).

by the time reunification came, political support for addressing domestic violence had become a part of political life, if not also a cornerstone of West German liberalism. Indeed, when Eva Kunz wrote to the Municipal Chambers in June 1990, urging them to sponsor the East Berlin shelter, she emphasised that 'we cannot politically afford to have this project die in administrative channels!'[73]

That domestic violence was a serious issue and that feminist approaches were a legitimate framework for tackling violence against women were simply not questioned in the same way. The relative ease with which many of the early East German shelter projects gained political traction highlights the success of the West German shelter movement in getting violence against women on the political agenda. Of course, this institutionalisation of feminist politics came at a cost. Shelter activism in the West was deradicalised, which, as the next chapter shows, would have important consequences for the ongoing discussion and development of women's rights over reunification.

Conclusion

In her book, *How We Survived Communism and Even Laughed*, Croatian writer Slavenka Drakulić recalled her first encounter with some of Western Europe's most well-known feminists. In 1978, at the first international feminist conference 'Comrade Women' held in Belgrade, Drakulić met Alice Schwarzer, together with the French and Italian activists Christine Delphy and Dacia Maraini. Although the conference inspired Drakulić to start a feminist group in Zagreb, the meeting also revealed some key differences between the experiences of women behind the Iron Curtain. 'We thought they were too radical when they told us that they were harassed by men on our streets ... Or when they talked about wearing high-heeled shoes as a sign of women's subordination. We didn't see it quite like that; we wore such shoes and even loved them', reflected Drakulić. Going even further, she remembered, 'how we gossiped about their greasy hair, no bra, no make-up'.[74]

Clearly then, what it meant to be a feminist woman in Yugoslavia was expressed and understood very differently to how it was in Western Europe.[75] Whereas clothing for Western European feminists was connected with the

---

[73] Brief von Eva Kunz an die Magistratskanzlei 22.6.90, C Rep 100-05/2218, LAB.
[74] Slavenka Drakulić, *How We Survived Communism and Even Laughed* (Hutchinson: London, 1992), p. 128. For more on Yugoslav feminism, see Lóránd, '"A Politically Non-Dangerous Revolution is not a Revolution"'; Zsófia Lóránd, 'New Feminism, Women's Subjectivity, and Feminist Politics: Conceptual Transfers and Activist Inspirations in Yugoslavia in the 1970s and 1980s' in Häberlen, Keck-Szajbel and Mahoney, *Politics of Authenticity*, pp. 110–130.
[75] On New Yugoslav Feminism, see Zsófia Lóránd, *The Feminist Challenge to the Socialist State in Yugoslavia* (London: Palgrave Macmillan, 2018).

dangers of consumerism and the objectification of women's bodies, in the context of a socialist economy, with limited options for shopping, owning well-fitting, fashionable clothing had a very different political meaning and significance for women. Ready-to-wear items were highly sought after and often required extensive tailoring, taking up much of women's spare time.[76] As such, clothing under socialism was as much an expression of a woman's individuality, as it was of women's labour and politics.

While this difference may seem trivial, for Drakulić it pointed to a much larger tension between feminists across the Cold War divide. There is a palpable sense of frustration throughout Drakulić's writing as she constantly pushes back against a western tide trying to dictate the experiences and narratives of women and feminism, under socialism. Similar tensions are also visible in the literature on feminism and the women's movement in the GDR. Feminism and activism against gender-based violence was practiced differently under socialism. But, significantly, this does not mean it was not feminist.

Writing in 2006, sociologist Myra Marx Ferree highlighted a problematic elision between the terms 'feminism' and 'women's movement'. She argued that while feminism was 'activism for the purpose of challenging and changing women's subordination to men', the women's movement was a constituency.[77] As the history of activism against gender-based violence in East Germany makes clear, this is an important distinction. In West Germany and in many other western countries, there is an intimate connection between feminism, the women's movement and domestic violence activism. It was women who first broached the issue and it was feminist politics that drove the way it was tackled.[78]

In East Germany, responding to violence against women was certainly a feminist issue. It involved challenging women's subordination and the patriarchal structures that underpinned and obscured gender-based violence. East German activists also drew from western feminist thought and practice. But, unlike West Germany, gender-based violence was not an issue that was confined to the women's movement. Indeed, the history of activism against gender-based violence in the GDR highlights the limitation of focusing on the women's movement as the locus of feminism. In the context of a weakening state and growing popular unrest, domestic violence activism tapped into a much broader movement. It was about more than just men abusing women, it was also about a state that had failed its

---

[76] Judd Stitziel, *Fashioning Socialism. Clothing, Politics and Consumer Culture in East Germany* (Oxford: Berg, 2005).

[77] Myra Marx Ferree, 'Globalization and Feminism. Opportunities and Obstacles for Activism in the Global Arena' in *Global Feminism. Transnational Women's Activism Organizing and Human Rights*, edited by Myra Marx Ferree and Aili Mari Tripp (New York: New York University Press, 2006): pp. 3–23, p. 6.

[78] For a history of the shelter movement in the US, see Elizabeth B.A. Miller, 'Moving to the Head of the River: The Early Years of the US Battered Women's Movement', (Ph.D. Diss., University of Kansas, 2010).

citizens. This meant that women and men alike could challenge violence against women, just as women and men could both experience gender-based violence. Moreover, as Ferree has highlighted, 'feminist mobilizations' can take place 'in a variety of organizational contexts, from women's movements to positions within governments', or, as in East Germany, within a Catholic welfare organisation.[79]

In many ways, the year 1989 brought an end to the unique form of feminism which developed under socialism in East Germany. In the new liberal-capitalist system, activists were required to adopt the definitions and categorisations used in West Germany. The broad definition of violence against women that had evolved in the GDR was replaced with labels of domestic violence, sexual violence, assault and rape. But the SED's collapse also enabled the growth and support of domestic violence initiatives. The decades of work by West German feminists and domestic violence activists meant that supporting shelters was political common sense in the newly expanded Federal Republic. Shelter proposals were relatively seamlessly picked up and funded in the former East and the western system of institutionalised women's shelters was implemented.

And yet, at the same time as highlighting the success of the West Berlin feminist movement, East German shelters were also spaces in which women and activists negotiated the gendered process of reunification and the new forms of citizenship brought with it. For East German women, reunification was often synonymous with the loss of rights. They faced higher levels of unemployment and poverty, as former state-owned companies were shut down and many of the rights afforded to women under socialism, such as abortion, were taken away.[80] In addition, as the *Wende* progressed, tensions between West German and East German feminists ran high. While West German feminists idealised the formal gender equality granted under socialism, they also saw women from the East as 'conformist, middle-brow mummies' who were less emancipated than women in the West. Meanwhile, East German feminists were frustrated by the heavy-handedness of the West, who allowed the repeal of the East German abortion law.[81]

---

[79] Ferree, 'Globalization and Feminism', p. 6.
[80] Nanette Funk, 'Abortion and German Unification' in Funk and Mueller, *Gender Politics and Post-Communism*, pp. 194–200; Barbara Łobodzińska, ed, *Family, Women, and Employment in Central-Eastern Europe* (Westport: Greenwood Press, 1995); Myra Marx Ferree, '"The Time of Chaos was the Best": Feminist Mobilization and Demobilization in East Germany', *Gender and Society*, Vol. 8, No. 4 (1994): pp. 597–623; Andrea Wuerth, 'National Politics/Local Identities: Abortion Rights Activism in Post-Wall Berlin', *Feminist Studies*, Vol. 25, No. 3 (1999): pp. 601–631.
[81] Ulrike Helwerth, 'Abschied vom feministischen Paradies', *WeibBlick* 2/92, pp. 18–20, p. 19. Also: Elizabeth Heineman, *What Difference Does a Husband Make?: Women and Marital Status in Nazi and Postwar Germany* (Berkeley: University of California Press, 1999); Monika Schröttle, 'West "beforscht" Ost. Politische, forschungstische und methodische Überlegungen zur Frage der Ost-West-Forschung aus feministischer Sicht' in *Veränderungen – Identitätsfindung im Prozeß. Frauenforschung im Jahre sieben nach der Wende*, edited by Ulrike Diedrich and Heidi Stecker (Bielefeld: Kleine Verlag, 1997), pp. 139–157.

These tensions were visible in the shelter system, as activists came to terms with the transition, often pushing back against what was felt to be the steamroller of the West. Although both Jennifer and Sophie recall feeling very supported by the West German shelter movement, for Sophie it was often more a question of needing time and space away from the western movement, so that they, as East Germans, could form their own concepts of shelter organising. Pushing back against the simple transposition of western models into the East, Sophie sought to develop feminist principles for the East German context, resulting in the creation of the *Ost-Arbeitsgemeinschaft Frauenhäuser* (Eastern Working Group of Women's Shelters or OAG) allowing shelter workers in the former East to separate from the western movement and discuss the peculiarities of their situation.[82] Over time, this group became increasingly enmeshed with the West German movement and by the end of the 1990s, the OAG was closed and East German shelters teamed up with the *Zentrale Informationsstelle autonomer Frauenhäuser* or Central Information Point for Autonomous Women's Shelters, established during the 1980s in West Germany.[83]

Despite benefiting from the successes of West German feminism, domestic violence activism in the former East Germany after 1990 did not simply replicate western practices. Much like the Weimar *Frauenteestube*, they adapted them and translated them to their political and social realities. Indeed, in many respects, the approach to domestic violence developed in the GDR would define the shape of activism against gender-based violence in reunified Germany.

---

[82] Interview with 'Sophie', Berlin, 4 February 2014.
[83] Ibid.; Zentrale Informationsstelle autonomer Frauenhäuser, 'Geschichte'. Accessed on 3 August 2022: https://autonome-frauenhaeuser-zif.de/autonome-frauenhaeuser/#geschichte.

6

The Possibilities of Feminism After Reunification

'Many still say that the best day of their life was 3 December 1989', wrote the journalists Ulrike Helwerth and Gislinde Schwarz in 1995.[1] On that day, a small group of women activists known as the *Initiativkomitee zur Gründung eines unabhängigen Frauenverbandes der DDR* (Initiative Committee to Found an Independent GDR Women's Association), organised a women's meeting and celebration at the East Berlin *Volksbühne*. Unsure how many women would attend this grassroots event, the group feared the space would be too large. Their worries quickly proved unfounded, as nearly 1,200 women arrived at the theatre; the fire brigade even sought to shut down the gathering over fears of over-crowding. Women came from all over East Germany, many already belonging to one of the women's activist groups formed in the late 1980s. There were even some 'curious' women from the West.[2] But what brought them all together was a desire to share their experiences, feelings and thoughts: about the GDR, the future of East Germany and socialism and simply about being a woman.

This meeting was both a response to and yet also enabled by the democratic awakening and rapid political transformation facing East Germany after the fall of the Berlin Wall on 9 November 1989. Within a month, SED-leader Egon Krenz was replaced by the moderate – and popular – socialist Hans Modrow, who promised major reform. The Central Round Table in Berlin brought members of the SED and other Socialist organisations together with representatives of the many citizen's initiatives in an effort to work collaboratively towards reform. However, despite these attempts to rework socialism in East Germany, the SED was unable to keep hold of the reins, reforming as the Party of Democratic Socialism in December 1989. At the same time, the vision of western prosperity offered to East Germans now able

---

[1] Ulrike Helwerth and Gislinde Schwarz, *Von Muttis und Emanzen. Feministinnen in Ost- und Westdeutschland* (Frankfurt am Main: Fischer Taschenbuch Verlag, 1995): p. 9.
[2] Ibid.

to cross the Cold War border, alongside Helmut Kohl's Ten-Point Plan and visit to Dresden in late 1989, only encouraged an intensifying drive towards reunification.

This deeply concerned the organisers of the women's meeting. 'In the current state of radical social upheaval', their flyer pronounced 'the interests of women have, till now, played a subordinate role.'[3] They feared both a 'further worsening of the social position of women' and a 'renewed exclusion of women from important political and economic decision making.'[4] In response, they called on women to take the initiative: 'Let's organise ourselves! We will represent our own interests!'[5] This is what the meeting was for: to bring East German women together so that their voices would be heard.

On a stage decorated with hanging laundry, women gave speeches, performed skits and sang together (see Figures 6.1 and 6.2). There was also a reading of Ina Merkel's manifesto 'Without Women there is no State!' – a call to arms for the women of East Germany to create a democratic women's movement. As Merkel argued, 'we must see that women's issues aren't peripheral social problems, but fundamental existential issues ... if we women want to ensure that our particular interests – developed as they have out of our specific life-situation and experiences – aren't just taken into consideration, we must develop our own strategy.'[6]

This is precisely what happened. The women at the *Volksbühne* that day formed an association, bringing together independent women's groups, initiatives, clubs and even the women's factions of the SED and its affiliated organisations from around East Germany. This new association was not aimed at replacing these groups, but was rather to act as an umbrella organisation, advancing and representing women's political interests at the state level. This is how the *Unabhängiger Frauenverband* (UFV or Independent Women's Association) was born.[7]

For all of these reasons, 3 December 1989 and the women's meeting in the *Volksbühne* is remembered as a pivotal moment for women and women's rights in the GDR. It represented a hope for change and the belief that together women could be heard and their concerns taken seriously after decades of SED rule. For

---

[3] Lila Offensive, 'Aufruf an all Frauen, 26.11.1989', *Frauen in die Offensive: Texte und Arbeitspapiere der Gruppe 'Lila Offensive'* (Berlin: Dietz, 1990): pp. 12–13.

[4] Ibid.

[5] Ibid.

[6] Ina Merkel, 'Ohne Frauen ist kein Staat zu Machen' in *Aufbruch! Frauenbewegung in der DDR: Dokumentation*, edited by Cordula Kahlau (Munich: Frauenoffensive, 1990), pp. 28–38, p. 29.

[7] For a brief overview of the founding of the UFV, see Anne Hampele, 'The Organized Women's Movement in the Collapse of the GDR: The Independent Women's Association (UFV)' in *Gender Politics and Post-Communism: Reflections from Eastern Europe and the Former Soviet Union*, edited by Nanette Funk and Magda Mueller (New York: Routledge, 1993): pp. 180–193; Daphne Hornig and Christine Steiner, *Auf der Suche nach der Bewegung. Zur Frauenbewegung in der DDR vor und nach der Wende* (Hamburg: Frauen-Anstiftung eV, 1992); Kahlau, *Aufbruch!*.

Figure 6.1 Founding UFV members sitting on stage at the Berlin *Volksbühne* on 3 December 1989. From left to right: Petra Wunderlich (foreground), Christina Schenk, Brigitta Kasse, Katrin Bastian, Gabi Zekina and Christiane Schindler.

Credit: Uwe Pelz. Robert Havemann Archive, Berlin (Fo GZ 2108).

UFV founding members Christina Schenk[8] and Christiane Schindler, it was 'a very euphoric time, in which many women activists thought that this "Wende" was – or rather could be – a revolution. That now there was a real possibility that feminist politics could be incorporated into the upcoming restructuring of the GDR society.'[9] Or, as Helwerth and Schwarz put it, the meeting was 'a high point, a hope for women in the East, but also in the West'.[10]

But almost immediately after the meeting, it became clear that the UFV's vision of a 'different, reformed GDR' was not going to be realised.[11] Instead, a rapid reunification with West Germany was becoming increasingly inevitable and would be confirmed in the *Volkskammer* election of March 1990 where the Alliance for Germany won over 48 per cent of the vote, campaigning on the promise of

---

[8] At the time of his activism with the UFV, politician Christian Schenk worked and published under the name Christina Schenk. As such, the text will refer to him using this name. It is not intended to erase or deny his identity as a man.

[9] Christina Schenk and Christiane Schindler, 'Frauenbewegung in Ostdeutschland – eine kleine Einführung', *Beiträge zur feministischen Theorie und Praxis: Feminis-muss*, No. 35 (1993): pp. 131–146, p. 134.

[10] Helwerth and Schwarz, *Von Muttis und Emanzen*, p. 9.

[11] Schenk and Schindler, 'Frauenbewegung in Ostdeutschland', p. 135.

Figure 6.2 Actress Walfriede Schmitt takes the Berlin *Volksbühne* stage at the formation of the UFV, 3 December 1989.

Credit: Uwe Pelz. Robert Havemann Archive, Berlin (Fo GZ 2111).

reunification. According to Schenk and Schindler, 'from one day to the next, a fundamental shift in the political self-understanding of the UFV was required' as they again found themselves in the political opposition, fighting to protect the few gains that had been made. Attempts to find common ground between feminists across the former Cold War divide were also a struggle, as they viewed each other with suspicion. This change in mood is perhaps best revealed by a cosmetologist in Mecklenburg-Vorpommern, who argued that 'this is not what we went to the street for, not for a capitalist society. No one took to the streets for that. We wanted more justice, more equality. We wanted an economic system that functioned reasonably well.'[12]

Reunification certainly has a complicated place in the histories of gender and feminism in Germany. At once a moment of hope and the possibility of feminist solidarity, it quickly became a time of intense concern and anxiety for the gains women had already won. And ultimately, it was a time of loss and confrontation with the divisions that remained between women from across the Iron Curtain. Indeed, much of the scholarship on reunification and the end of the Cold War frames it as a patriarchal and nationalistic process that curtailed women's rights and opportunities.[13] In this vein, scholars have typically labelled East German women as the 'losers' of reunification.[14] A bibliography on women in the GDR before and after reunification compiled by Centre for Transdisciplinary Gender Studies at the Humboldt University in Berlin even has an entire section on the 'Women as Losers Thesis', listing 32 different German texts written on the subject between 1989 and 2000.[15]

One of the key issues that scholars of gender and reunification point to is the failure to reform Paragraph 218 and ensure women's access to abortion in

---

[12] Ingrid Sandole-Staroste, *Women in Transition. Between Socialism and Capitalism* (London: Praeger, 2002): p. 175.

[13] Brigitte Young: *Triumph of the Fatherland: German Unification and the Marginalization of Women* (Ann Arbor: University of Michigan Press, 1999); Andrea Wuerth, 'National Politics/Local Identities: Abortion Rights Activism in Post-Wall Berlin', *Feminist Studies*, Vol. 25 No. 3 (1999): pp. 601–631; Funk and Mueller, *Gender Politics and Post-Communism*; Helwerth and Schwarz, *Von Muttis und Emanzen*; Myra Marx Ferree, *Varieties of Feminism: German Gender Politics in Global Perspective* (Stanford: Stanford University Press, 2012); Susan Gal and Gail Kligman, *The Politics of Gender after Socialism* (Princeton: Princeton University Press, 2000).

[14] Hanna Behrend, 'East German Women – Chief Losers in German Unification' in *Family, Women, and Employment in Central-Eastern Europe*, edited by Barbara Łobodzińska (Westport: Greenwood Press, 1995), pp. 113–122; 'Frauen befürchten historischen Rückschritt', *Die Tageszeitung*, 2 May 1990. See also the discussion of representations of East German women in Elizabeth Mittman, 'Gender, Citizenship, and the Public Sphere in Postunification Germany: Experiments in Feminist Journalism', *Signs*, Vol. 32, No. 3 (2007): pp. 759–791; Myra Marx Ferree, 'German Unification and Feminist Identity' in *Transitions, Environments, Translations. Feminisms in International Politics*, edited by Joan Scott, Cora Kaplan and Debra Keats (New York: Routledge, 1997): pp. 46–55.

[15] Karin Aleksander, *Frauen und Geschlechterverhältnisse in der DDR und in den neuen Bundesländern. Eine Bibliographie* (Berlin: Trafo, 2005).

the new German state. While free, on-demand abortion was available to women in the first trimester of pregnancy from 1972 in East Germany, in the West, the implementation of the *Indikationsmodell* in 1976 meant that abortion could only be performed in the first 12 weeks of pregnancy if a doctor certified that there was a valid reason for an abortion. This could include medical danger, social difficulties for the mother, eugenic concerns or if the pregnancy was the result of rape or incest.[16]

This discrepancy between a liberal socialist law and a much more restrictive West German Paragraph 218 led to abortion becoming a flashpoint for women's activism across reunification.[17] Whereas East German women fought to protect their reproductive rights, women in the West saw it as an opportunity to enact reform and revitalise the abortion campaign that had stagnated since the mid-1970s. Yet the two groups struggled to find common ground and craft a shared platform. As such, scholars have positioned abortion reform as a symbolic reflection of the transformation of women's rights over reunification: from the hope for change, to the inability of feminists to come together and the ultimate loss of rights, as the East German provision was replaced with a much more limited version of the West German law.

By focusing on the failed abortion campaign, other trajectories of women's activism after 1989 have been rendered invisible by a scholarship centred on the loss of women's rights and the failure of feminism. This chapter challenges that narrative. Specifically, it uses the post-reunification development of activism against gender-based violence as a counterweight to the centrality of abortion in the scholarship on gender and reunification. Although abortion reform failed, gender-based and domestic violence activism were revitalised after reunification. As the previous chapter showed, almost immediately after the fall of the Wall, activists in Leipzig and Berlin started work on opening domestic violence shelters and throughout the 1990s, a network of shelters and services opened throughout the former Democratic Republic. These activists were not only able to take advantage of the delegitimisation of socialism and the SED, but they could also capitalise on the extensive work that feminists in the West had done to place domestic violence on the political agenda.

---

[16] On abortion in divided Germany, see Kristina Schulz, *Der lange Atem der Provokation: Die Frauenbewegung in der Bundesrepublik und in Frankreich 1968–1976* (Frankfurt am Main: Campus, 2002); Dagmar Herzog, *Unlearning Eugenics: Sexuality, Reproduction and Disability in Post-Nazi Europe* (Madison: University of Wisconsin Press, 2018); Gabrielle Grafenhorst, ed, *Abtreibung. Erfahrungsberichte zu einem Tabu* (Munich: Deutscher Taschenbuch Verlag, 1992); Katja Krolzik-Matthei, 'Abtreibung in der DDR. Annäherung einen Diskurs', *diskus*, Vol. 218, No. 12 (2018): pp. 33–37; Katja Krolzik-Matthei, *§218. Feministische Perspektiven auf die Abtreibungsdebatte in Deutschland* (Münster: Unrast Verlag, 2015).

[17] Indeed, abortion and reproduction were central issues throughout the former Communist Bloc during the transition to democracy. See Gal and Kligman, *The Politics of Gender*.

Even more than this, some of the most significant developments in domestic violence activism to take place since the opening of the first shelter in 1976 came about following the fall of the Berlin Wall. Since reunification, responding to domestic violence has only become more and more entrenched in the German political landscape. In particular, the creation and ongoing support for the intervention project *Berliner Initiative gegen Gewalt an Frauen* (BIG e.V. or Berlin Initiative against Violence towards Women), the introduction of the *Gewaltschutzgesetz* in 2002 and the criminalisation of rape within marriage in 1997 have made Germany into a European leader in the protection of women's rights to freedom from violence. These developments not only reflect a renegotiation of some of the most fundamental tenets of feminist approaches to domestic violence, but they came about as a result of successful collaboration between activists from across the Cold War divide.

Comparing the experiences of abortion rights activists with those working to address domestic violence, this chapter asks what happened to the hopes of 1989 as a moment of reform and change for women's lives.[18] Its aims are twofold. Firstly, it complicates the typical characterisation of women as the 'losers' of reunification and narratives of the failure of (East German) women's activism. Although women may have struggled to work together to reform abortion, the same cannot be said for domestic violence. By decentring abortion from the history of women's activism in reunified Germany, this chapter reveals the legacies – if not successes – of East German approaches to feminism and domestic violence activism.

The second aim of this chapter is to ask why some women's issues, like domestic violence, found political traction, where others, in this case reproductive rights, did not. What was so special about domestic violence? Certainly, abortion reform was a very different struggle to domestic violence work. Alongside religious concerns and questions surrounding the rights of the foetus, feminists were also fighting to protect a right granted by what was increasingly seen as an illegitimate, if not totalitarian, state. Reforming Paragraph 218 was also much more time sensitive – it was only a matter of months between the *Volkskammer* elections and the eventual reunification of Germany in October 1990. More generally though, abortion reform clashed with the broader reinscription of patriarchal gender norms taking place during reunification. Ensuring women's sexual autonomy and reproductive choice simply did not fit with the Kohl government, which had been chipping away at abortion law in West Germany since the 1980s. In contrast, domestic violence activism – with its emphasis on women's

---

[18] On this question, see Paul Betts, '1989 at Thirty: A Recast Legacy', *Past and Present* No. 244, No. 1 (2019): pp. 271–305.

vulnerability and victimhood – resonated more fully with the new political land-scape of reunified Germany.

This distinction is telling. Ultimately, this chapter argues that only those rights that fit most closely with gendered ideals and norms, such as protecting women from domestic violence, have made inroads in the Federal Republic. This suggests that women are protected from male violence because they are women, not because they have a right to personal security or self-determination. Such a limited vision of women's rights was, in part, enabled by the institutionalisation and deradicalisation of feminist practices throughout the 1970s and 1980s.

The 1980s were a relatively quiet time for the women's movement in West Germany. After the flurry of activism in the late 1960s and early 1970s, by 1980 the women's movement was fragmented, often along political lines and divided into various issue-based groups and projects.[19] Sociologists Ilse Lenz and Myra Marx Ferree have gone the furthest in detailing the different periods of activism in the New Women's Movement in Germany. For both Lenz and Ferree, whereas the years up to 1975 were marked by a convergence around consciousness raising and the articulation of women's needs and issues, from 1976 onwards there was an increasing pluralisation of women's activism.[20]

What is particularly striking about this periodisation is that it reflects the divergent trajectories of reproductive rights activism and the work to address domestic violence. As the first chapter showed, reproductive rights were a crucial battleground for feminists in the early 1970s and the Paragraph 218 campaign brought women together as never before. Although feminists developed a mass movement, bringing women, men and the legal and medical communities together in protest against the criminalisation of abortion, their reform agenda was ultimately defeated. Despite a 1974 reform allowing unrestricted abortion in the first trimester, by February 1975 the Federal Constitutional Court had determined that this law was incompatible with the constitutional guarantee of the right to life. The reform was revoked in early 1976 and replaced with the *Indikationsmodell*, permitting abortion only when certain, strict, criteria were met. While protest against this law continued after 1976 – including the bombing of the Constitutional Court in Karlsruhe by militant feminists and underground trips to abortion clinics in the Netherlands organised by the Frankfurt Women's Centre – the court's decision more or less brought an end to mass abortion activism in West Germany until the late 1980s.

---

[19] Ilse Lenz, ed, *Die Neue Frauenbewegung in Deutschland: Abschied vom kleinen Unterschied. Eine Quellensammlung*, 2nd ed. (Wiesbaden: VS Verlag für Sozialwissenschaften, 2010); Ferree, *Varieties of Feminism*; Katharina Karcher, *Sisters in Arms. Militant Feminisms in the Federal Republic of Germany since 1968* (New York: Berghahn, 2017).
[20] Lenz, *Die Neue Frauenbewegung*; Ferree, *Varieties of Feminism*.

This was, of course, the precise time that domestic violence was starting to find political traction in West Germany. Indeed, the changes evident within the feminist movement from the 1970s to the 1980s echo the developments of reproductive rights and domestic violence activism. Speaking at a conference on 20 years of domestic violence work in Germany, psychologist Sabine Scheffler argued that the women's shelter movement emerged precisely in response to the disappointments of abortion activism. After the initial 'euphoria' of having reformed Paragraph 218, feminists turned away from legal change, instead wanting to find different ways of helping women.[21] This also reflects the periodisations of Lenz and Ferree, who both see the mid-1970s as a moment of transition for the New Women's Movement. From the initial articulation of women's concerns emerging out of 1968 and the flurry of protest and campaigning of the early 1970s, the mid-1970s and 1980s were, by contrast, a time of consolidation, professionalisation and institutionalisation.[22]

In Berlin, shelter activists' focus was on maintaining public financial support for domestic violence projects. This was a particularly important question because the model phase of the first shelter in Grunewald was coming to an end in 1980. As a model project, the Grunewald shelter was primarily financed by the federal government; only 20 per cent of its costs came from the Berlin Senate. In order to keep this shelter open, an additional 360,000DM needed to be sourced. At the same time, a new feminist initiative sought to open a second shelter, as reports on the constant overcrowding and poor living conditions of the first shelter circulated in the media.[23] Although the building's maximum capacity was only meant to be 70 people, an open-door policy meant that by autumn 1978, the Grunewald shelter was averaging 50 to 60 women and 50 to 60 children taken in per month. With only 15 bedrooms, this often meant there were up to 12 people sleeping in one room.[24] On 12 October 1978, at a meeting between the Senator for Family, Youth and Sport and the Governing Mayor of Berlin, it was agreed that the need for a second shelter was 'indisputable'. What

---

[21] 'Gespräch zwischen Margit Brückner, Carole Hagemann-White, Sabine Scheffler und Birgit Rommelspacher', in *Dokumentation Fachforum 2 – Frauenhaus in Bewegung, 20.-22.11.1996* (Berlin: Diakonisches Werk der Evangelischen Kirche in Deutschland, 1996), p. 22.

[22] Ferree, *Varieties of Feminism.*

[23] 'Kinder verlassen tagsüber das überfüllte Frauenhaus. Aber Trennung von Müttern wird abgelehnt – warum kein Mann im Hause arbeitet – dokumentation vorbereitet', *Der Tagesspiegel*, 7 February 1978; 'Im überfüllten Frauenhaus muss im Keller übernachtet werden', *Der Tagesspiegel*, 26 June 1979; 'Spandau: zweites Frauenhaus', *Spandauer Volksblatt*, 26 June 1979; Ursula von Bentheim, 'Senatorin Ilse Reichel will sich für ein zweites Frauenhaus stark machen', *Die Welt*, 26 June 1979.

[24] Bericht über den Modellversuch 'Hilfen für misshandelte Frauen' (Frauenhaus), B Rep 002/12504a, LAB; Carol Hagemann-White, Barbara Kavemann, Johanna Kootz, Ute Weinmann, Carola Christine Wildt, Roswitha Burgard and Ursula Scheu, *Hilfen für mißhandelte Frauen: Abschlussbericht der wissenschaftlichen Begleitung des Modellprojekts Frauenhaus Berlin* (Stuttgart: Verlag W. Kohlhammer, 1981); Report from the Senator for Youth, Family and Sport regarding arguments for and against the financing of women's shelters through Federal Social Welfare Act, 1.4.1979, B Rep 002/12504, LAB; Brief von Frauenselbsthilfe e.V. an den Petitionausschuss, B Rep 002/12504, LAB.

remained at issue was how to finance it alongside taking on the full financial support for the Grunewald shelter.[25]

The Senate Office for Family, Youth and Sport was strongly in support of using Paragraph 72 of the Federal Social Welfare Act to fund shelter work.[26] This paragraph maintained that individuals who 'face particular social difficulties preventing them from participating in society' are entitled to assistance to overcome these difficulties if they are unable to do so themselves.[27] According to the Senate Office, this financial support could then be channelled towards the shelter's running costs. However, from summer 1978, feminists in West Berlin and throughout the Federal Republic pushed back against proposals to use Paragraph 72 as a source of funding.[28] As Bernhard Gotto shows, feminists in West Germany saw the use of this provision as putting shelters into the position of the 'long-arm of the welfare state', as almost two-thirds of their work would be taken up by bureaucratic administration associated with Paragraph 72. Not only would shelter workers have to sign up women for welfare support, but they would have to distribute weekly cheques to residents, setting money aside from each resident to put towards the shelter. Alongside keeping meticulous records of these transactions, the shelters would also have to submit ledgers to the Welfare Office every three months.[29]

Certainly, as Gotto argues, this kind of bureaucratic work challenged the very foundations of the autonomous women's shelter movement to remain apart from the state and for women to help women. Much like the criticisms of volunteers at the mundane and often trivial realities of shelter work in Hamburg discussed in Chapter 3, as an article in *Sozialmagazin* highlighted, funding through Paragraph 72 represented the 'systematic destruction of the original concept of the women's shelter movement … Leaving an abusive husband becomes increasingly less an act of self-liberation and ever more an act of subjugation. But this time to the real-terms of bureaucracy.'[30]

What is striking though, is that a very different approach was taken by shelter activists in Berlin. The shelter movement in Berlin was already largely integrated into the bureaucracy of the state due to the oversight imposed on the model-shelter

---

[25] Gespräch mit dem Regierenden Bürgermeister von Berlin am 12.10.1978 über Einrichtung eines 2. Zentrums für misshandelte Frauen, B Rep 002/12504, LAB.

[26] Ibid.

[27] Bundessozialhilfegesetz 1961 (Germany, West) §72.

[28] On the Federal discussion of shelter funding, see Rundeschreiben an Bundesländer aufgrund Gespräch mit allen Gleichstellungsstellen zur Finanzierungsfrage Frauenhaus, B189-25421, BArch-K. See also Unterrichtung durch die Bundesregierung. Zweiter Bericht der Bundesregierung über die Lage der Frauenhäuser für misshandelte Frauen und Kinder, Drucksache 11/2848, 1 September 1988. See also Bernhard Gotto, *Enttäuschung in der Demokratie. Erfahrung und Deutung von politischem Engagement in der Bundesrepublik Deutschland während der 1970er und 1980er Jahre* (Berlin: De Gruyter, 2018).

[29] Gotto, *Enttäuschung in der Demokratie.*

[30] Quoted in ibid., p. 179.

project in Grunewald. As such, rather than reflect on feminist principles of autonomy and self-administration, Berlin activists instead emphasised women's vulnerability and victimhood.[31] For those activists associated with the proposed second shelter in Berlin, the use of this paragraph was tantamount to victim-blaming by suggesting that it was the women themselves, not the violent men, who were incapable of living in society. In newspaper articles, shelter residents spoke out about feeling 'branded as a fringe group' by the welfare provision, arguing that using the paragraph went against the core values of feminists, who had worked to get domestic violence understood as a widespread issue facing all women. Further still, shelter workers had serious concerns regarding women's privacy and whether courts would come to 'false conclusions' in divorce and custody cases, with respect to former residents' abilities as mothers.[32]

This tactic not only resonated within the media, but also politically.[33] From late 1978 into early 1979, members of the Berlin State Parliament raised numerous information requests, inquiring into the state of the second shelter and how it would be financed. Sitting FDP member Jürgen Wahl raised the general question of financing in October 1978, followed by a more pointed enquiry by SPD parliamentarian Gisela Fechner in March 1979, who asked whether the second shelter could be financed through the state budget.[34] At the same time, the Berlin FDP pledged their support for the shelter projects and called on state financing to be made available for the second shelter.[35] By April, the Berlin-branch of the German Trade Union Confederation was also calling for the immediate establishment and financing of a second shelter in Berlin.[36]

Although the Senate Office for Family, Youth and Sport maintained that the Federal Social Welfare Act was not discriminatory, the mounting pressure led them to make concessions.[37] In March and April 1979, they offered some funding for the second shelter's furnishing, on the basis that the rent and any additional costs be capped at 120,000DM per year. The living costs, meanwhile, would have

---

[31] Brief von Frauenselbsthilfe e.V. an den Petitionausschuss, 29.3.1979, B Rep 002/12504, LAB.

[32] 'Haben Berliner Beamte kein Verständnis für Frauen in Not? Die Mitarbeiterinnen im Frauenhaus klagen über Ignoranz und Vorurteile', *Spandauer Volksblatt*, 2 November 1978; 'Problem der Misshandlung in Familien bewusst gemacht', *Der Tagesspiegel*, 2 November 1978.

[33] In the media, see 'Das zweite Frauenhaus könnte schon im Januar seine Pforten öffnen', *Der Tagesspiegel*, 4 December 1978; 'Zweites Frauenhaus noch ohne finanzielle Hilfe', *Morgenpost*, 24 January 1979; 'Im überfüllten Frauenhaus muss im Keller übernachtet werden', *Der Tagesspiegel*, 26 June 1979.

[34] Kleine Anfrage Nr. 3694 from Abg. Gisela Fechner (SPD), 17.3.1979 and Mundliche Anfragen (wegen ablaufs der Fragestunde in der 95. Sitzung des Abg. am 26. Oktober 1978 nicht behandelt), B Rep 002/12504, LAB.

[35] FDP Pressemitteilung, Nachrichtenspiegel, 25 January 1979, B Rep 002/12504, LAB.

[36] Letter from the Deutscher Gewerkschaftsbund, Landesbezirk Berlin, 25. April 1979 and Antrag – angenommen auf dem 11. Ordentlichen DGB-Bundeskongress – Mai 1978, B Rep 002/12504, LAB.

[37] Argument für und gegen eine Finanzierung auf der Grundlage des BSHG, SenJug, 1. April, 1979. B Rep 002/12504, LAB; response to Gisela Fechner, SPD, kleine Anfrage from 17.3.1979, B Rep 002/12504, LAB.

to be covered by the shelter residents themselves. They even supported the potential reformulation of Paragraph 72 to address the concerns of shelter activists.[38] While the shelter group agreed to consider this alternative, the finance ministry maintained its reservations with respect to these suggestions, preferring instead to wait for the official results of the evaluation of the model shelter project to be published by the federal government.[39]

By summer 1979, however, the matter had reached crisis point. Not only did calls for the creation of a second shelter continue, but the ongoing capacity issues in the first shelter increased the urgency of finding a resolution to the financing question. The final nail in the coffin came after the German Association for Public and Private Welfare withdrew their support for using Paragraph 72, arguing that women escaping abuse did not meet the conditions of being unable to 'participate in society'.[40] In June, then, the shelter initiative was offered the use of a former clinic in Spandau and the budget for both the first and proposed second shelter were written in to the 1980 Berlin state budget.[41] Given the ongoing demand, by early July the Berlin Senate had promised a further 400,000DM for the furnishing and internal repairs of the building in Spandau, so that the second shelter could open as soon as possible. On 1 September 1979, the second shelter opened with space for 40 women and children. Further money for the shelter's extensive renovation was then made available in 1980 as the shelter's financing entered the state budget.[42]

For most of the 1980s, feminist domestic violence activists in West Berlin sought to maintain the concessions they had won and focused on developing and professionalising their work with women leaving abuse. It was only after the fall of the Wall in 1989 that two further autonomous women's shelters were opened in Berlin. By that time, domestic violence activism was in a very different position to abortion rights. Women's shelters were an established part of the West German welfare system. The shelter movement had spread throughout West Germany and the federal government launched a further pilot project, this time in Rendsburg, Schleswig-Holstein, evaluating how to address domestic violence in rural areas. Although domestic violence work was still firmly enmeshed in feminist politics, as we have seen in Chapter 3, it had gone through an extensive process of professionalisation. Shelters were staffed by social workers, medical professionals and lawyers trained to work with and help women living with violence. Increasingly specialised projects addressing issues of sexual violence or violence against

---

[38] Argument für und gegen eine Finanzierung auf der Grundlage des BSHG, Sen Jug, 1. April, 1979. B Rep 002/12504, LAB.

[39] Brief von Senatsverwaltung an den RBm, 26.3.1979, B Rep 002/12504, LAB.

[40] Finanzierung auf der grundlage des para 72 BSHG, 27.6.1979, B Rep 002/12504, LAB.

[41] Ibid.

[42] Minutes from discussion in Hauptausschuss about the second shelter (4.7.79), B Rep 002/12504, LAB.

children and girls opened throughout the 1980s. Even religious social welfare organisations were getting involved in combating violence against women, with organisations such as Caritas and Diakonie opening shelters in West Berlin in the 1980s.[43] While the FDP and SPD had long supported the cause in Berlin, by the early 1980s, the CDU was also on board and women's projects aimed at ongoing counselling for abuse survivors received cross-partisan and popular support.[44] The anxieties of the 1970s surrounding feminism had ebbed.

The question of abortion, however, returned in West Germany throughout the second half of the 1980s. At this time, under Helmut Kohl's conservative government, Christian Democrats, Catholic and religious officials and right-to-life advocates began work to undo the rights offered by Paragraph 218 at both a federal and state level. In 1982 alone – the year Kohl became Chancellor – Heiner Geißler, the CDU-Family Minister formed an Inter-Ministerial Working Group on the Protection of Unborn Life and the Catholic Bishop Conference began work on a 'Choose Life' programme. Mass right-to-life marches were held in Bonn in 1984 and 1986, and in summer 1984, the federal foundation 'Mother and Child. Protection for Unborn Life' was created to provide pregnant women with 'unbureaucratic financial advice to make the decision to continue pregnancy and for the life of the child easier'.[45]

Feminists immediately responded. During the 1983 election campaign, feminist magazine *EMMA* used its editorial to call on women to once against take up the 'fight for what should already be common sense'.[46] At the same time, the independent reproductive and sexual health counselling service Pro-Familia, developed a federal action plan to protect Paragraph 218 and feminist activists called for a national protest in Karlsruhe on 26 February 1983. This date marked the eight-year anniversary of the Constitutional Court decision that struck down first-trimester abortions in 1975.[47]

But efforts to limit women's access to abortion continued, culminating in the 1988/89 trial of gynaecologist Dr Horst Thiessen in Memmingen, Bavaria. Thiessen, who came to the attention of authorities after his records were investigated on suspicion of tax evasion, was charged with violating Paragraph 218

---

[43] Other smaller services opened during the 1980s include: Emergency housing through Brunhilde e.V., Zuffs Kreuzberg/Neukölln and Zuffs Tempelhof. See A Rep 400 Berlin 1.20-1.23 ohne 1.26.8b.6, FFBIZ; Linda Jent and Regula Wyss, *Selbstverteidigung für Frauen* (Basel: Mond Buch, 1984).

[44] Inhalts-Protokoll Ausschuss für Frauenfragen 13. Sitzung, 3.11.1982, 'Besprechung über Arbeit und Förderungsmöglichkeiten für die Arbeit der Frauenhäuser', B Rep 002/12505, LAB.

[45] See Bundesstiftung Mutter und Kind. Schutz des ungeborenen Leben. Accessed on 12 May 2022: https://www.bundesstiftung-mutter-und-kind.de/ueber-die-stiftung/; Sekretariat der Deutschen Bischofskonferenze, ed., *Wähle das Leben. Hirtenwort der am Grabe des heiligen Bonifatius versammelten deutschen Bischöffe*. 22. September 1982. See also: Herzog, *Unlearning Eugenics* and Lenz, *Die Neue Frauenbewegung*.

[46] '§218. Warum die CDU angst davor hat', *EMMA*, February 1983, p. 6.

[47] Ibid.

and performing illegal abortions. Over the course of the investigation, the records of all of Thiessen's patients who had received an abortion since 1980 were reviewed. The court then subsequently also brought proceedings against 279 women and 78 men, of whom 156 received fines for having either received or helped someone obtain an illegal abortion. The 'Memmingen Trial', as it became known, was subject to allegations of judicial prejudice and widespread criticism from women's groups, Social Democrats, the Greens and even the media, all of whom framed it as a 'witch-hunt'.[48] In particular, both the feminist and national press criticised Bavarian prosecutors for requiring witnesses to provide intimate and personal details of their sex lives and their decision to have an abortion, while others were 'dragged up before the court like criminals on a conveyor belt of punishment'.[49] In spite of this, on 5 May 1989, Thiessen was found guilty and sentenced to two-and-a-half-years in prison and a three-year suspension from practicing medicine. This was reduced to one-and-a-half-years' probation on appeal.

By the time the Wall fell, then, abortion was on the minds of West German feminists. Moreover, the experience of Memmingen had left women both mobilised and angry at these attempts to curtail their reproductive rights. In comparison, domestic violence initiatives were well embedded in the Federal Republic's social system. While abortion rights activists fought against long-standing gender norms and religious ideals, the work of domestic violence projects fit more closely with gendered images of women as vulnerable and as victims. This distinction would play out in the divergent trajectories of feminist collaboration across reunification.

A Feminist Failure? Abortion, Reunification and the Inability to Get Along

The early 1990s were a difficult time for women. Reunification, and the collapse of the Soviet Bloc more generally, brought social and political upheaval to Germany and Eastern Europe and had a major impact on women's lives. Unemployment soared with the disappearance of 3 million jobs, as the introduction of a free market economy forced unprofitable East German businesses to close.[50] Although both men and women faced unemployment in East Germany, women were the fastest growing unemployed population. By September 1990, 53.2 per cent of

---

[48] 'Grob geklotzt', *Der Spiegel*, 4 September 1988; '"Das sind politisch motivierte Prozesse"', *Der Spiegel*, 19 September 1988; 'Abtreibung. Bayrisches Landrecht', *Der Spiegel*, 11 September 1988; 'Hexenjagd in Bayern', Cover Issue of *Der Spiegel* from 38/1988. See also Alice Schwarzer, 'Politische Prozesse von Weimar bis Memmingen', *EMMA*, No. 4 (1989): pp. 4–6; 'Jagd auf Frauen', EMMA, No. 11 (1988), p. 9; 'Hexenjagd', *EMMA*, No. 9 (1988), p. 6.
[49] 'Grob geklotzt'.
[50] Łobodzińska *Family, Women, and Employment*, p. 102.

women in the former East were unemployed, a figure which had risen to 70 per cent by the end of 1993.[51] Women's employment was also affected by the withdrawal of the socialist support network that had facilitated so many women to combine paid employment with motherhood. Many women were required to take on increased childcare duties and either move to part-time employment or leave the workforce altogether, as socialist kindergartens and childcare centres closed and paid maternity leave was reduced.[52]

At the same time, the growing conservatism of western democracies, including the FRG, the US and the UK, during the late 1980s, combined with slowly creeping nationalism throughout Germany and the Eastern Bloc, also affected women, most devastatingly in the Yugoslav Wars.[53] There is also anecdotal evidence from the time that reunification brought with it an increase in domestic abuse.[54] Reflecting this, Annette Niemeyer, an East German activist from the UFV, argued that reunification took 'the direction of convincing women to accept exclusively the role of mother, homemaker and appendage to men'.[55]

Within this context, women's issues came to the fore, as East German activists attempted to create a space for women's voices and rights in the new state. The UFV, in particular, actively contested the gendered impact and process of reunification. From its founding on 3 December 1989 until its dissolution in 1998, the UFV represented (East) German women's political interests.[56] They were one of

---

[51] Nanette Funk, Magda Müller, Robin Ostow, Michael Bodeman and Matthias Weiss. 'Dossier on Women in Eastern Europe', *Social Text*, No. 27 (1990): p. 91; Stefan Brockmann, 'Introduction: The Reunification Debate', *New German Critique*, No. 52 (1991): pp. 3–30.

[52] 'Frauen befürchten historischen Rückschritt'.

[53] Herzog, *Unlearning Eugenics*; Zsófia Lóránd, *The Feminist Challenge to the Socialist State in Yugoslavia* (London: Palgrave Macmillan, 2018); Funk and Mueller, *Gender Politics and Post-Communism*; Sabrina Ramet, ed, *Gender Politics in the Western Balkans: Women and Society in Yugoslavia and the Yugoslav Successor States* (University Park: Pennsylvania State University Press, 1999); Kristi S. Long, *We All Fought for Freedom: Women in Poland's Solidarity Movement* (Boulder: Westview Press, 1996); Malgorzata Fidelis, *Women, Communism, and Industrialization in Postwar Poland* (Cambridge: Cambridge University Press, 2010); Joanna Goven, 'The Gendered Foundations of Hungarian Socialism: State, Society, and the Anti-Politics of Anti-Feminism, 1948–1990', (Ph.D. diss., University of California at Berkeley, 1993).

[54] Dinah Dodds and Pam Allen-Thompson, eds, *The Wall in My Backyard: East German Women in Transition.* (Amherst: University of Massachusetts Press, 1994). While anecdotal, this reflects other findings on the links between social and economic upheaval and family violence. See, for example, Daniel Schneider, Kristen Harknett and Sara McLanahan, 'Intimate Partner Violence in the Great Recession', *Demography*, Vol. 53, No. 2 (2016): pp. 471–505, or the vast amount of media reporting on the rise of domestic violence during the Covid-19 pandemic, including 'Häusliche Gewalt und Corona. Eine doppelte Bedrohung', *Taz*, 17 May 2020. On the global situation, see Amanda Taub and Jane Bradley, 'As Domestic Abuse Rises, UK Failings Leave Victims in Peril', *New York Times*, 2 July 2020.

[55] Quoted in Staroste, *Women in Transition*, p. 44.

[56] The UFV were particularly associated with the East Berlin women's movement. Regions, like Leipzig, that already had strong women's networks were less involved in the UFV's work. See Young, *Triumph of the Fatherland* and Hornig and Steiner, *Auf der Suche nach der Bewegung*.

the most public and outwardly visible feminist organisations in the GDR, and were the major representative of women's rights over the course of reunification. According to their programme, they sought to 'liberate the word feminism from prejudice' and 'abolish gendered hierarchies and power relations'.[57] As an umbrella organisation for women's groups in the GDR, the UFV represented and supported women's issues and activism at a local and national level. Much of their early work, however, focused on attaining political representation for women and women's rights. The UFV were a key voice for women on the Central Round Table in Berlin; in this role, they secured women's rights through the creation of a social charter in early March 1990.[58] This charter was designed to guide the East German government's position in its negotiations with its counterparts in the West.[59]

By upholding principles of welfare, equality and fairness, as well as including strong provisions on women's rights, the social charter sought to protect the welfare and social rights of East Germans during the transition. Similarly, the UFV ensured the protection of women's rights in the draft East German constitution of April 1990, including women's right to equality at work, public life and education and to 'self-determined pregnancy'.[60] They also pushed for women's political involvement and representation, most notably in their document the *Essential Features of Equality between the Sexes*. This included calls on the Berlin Round Table to appoint a Councillor for Gender Equality to the East Berlin *Magistrat* and more broadly for the creation of women's equality representation at all levels of government, including the creation of a Ministry for Equality and equal opportunity legislation.[61] They even fielded candidates as the sole women-only party in the first democratic elections in East Germany in March 1990, where they ran in an electoral alliance with the Green Party and Bündnis 90.

---

[57] 'Programm des Unabhängige Frauenverbandes', in Kahlau, *Aufbruch!*, pp. 67–77, p. 68.

[58] 'Forderung einer Sozialcharta durch den Unabhängiger Frauenverband, UFV - Gründungskongress 17.2.90', and Grundlinien und Standpunkte für eine Sozialcharta (Beschluss der Volkskammer vom 2. März 1990). Accessed on 12 May 2022: https://www.ddr89.de/ufv/UFV6.html. For a detailed discussion of the UFV's inclusion on the Central Round Table and their work on the Social Charter, see Young: *Triumph of the Fatherland*.

[59] Helmut Herles and Ewald Rose, eds, *Vom Runden Tisch zum Parlament* (Bonn: Verlag Bouvier, 1990): pp. 169 and 238.

[60] Entwurf Verfassung der Deutschen Demokratischen Republik. Arbeitsgruppe 'Neue Verfassung der DDR' des Runden Tisches, Berlin, April 1990. Artikel 3 (2) und 4 (3).

[61] Antrag from the UFV an den berliner Runden Tisch am 4.1.1990, A/0012, RHG; Tatiana Böhm, 'The Women's Question as a Democratic Question: In Search of Civil Society', in Funk and Mueller, *Gender Politics and Post-Communism*: pp. 151–159; 'Forderung einer Sozialcharta durch den Unabhängiger Frauenverband, UFV - Gründungskongress 17.2.90.' and Grundlinien und Standpunkte für eine Sozialcharta (Beschluss der Volkskammer vom 2. März 1990. Accessed on 12 May 2022: https://www.ddr89.de/ufv/UFV6.html. Young also says that the UFV vacillated between calling for the creation of a Ministry of Gender Equality and the creation of a State Secretary for Gender Equality. For more details, see Young, *Triumph of the Fatherland*.

The results of this election, however, sent a clear message to the UFV: reforming the GDR was no longer an option, as reunification with the Federal Republic loomed. The UFV quickly set aside their visions of the future and the promises of the social charter and draft constitution, and instead turned their attention to developing gender policy. In particular, they took up the key women's issues of female unemployment, childcare, violence against women and abortion. They called for former Stasi buildings to be made available for women's shelters, criticised employment offices for pushing women out of the workforce and, in Berlin, they successfully used their representative in the city council, Gabi Zekina, to press for support for the development of women's projects.[62]

This was also a time when the UFV sought to broaden their platform by working with West German feminists.[63] As founding UFV member and Minister without Portfolio in the Modrow government, Tatjana Böhm argued,

> The chances and possibilities to start on the road to civil society, which would have incorporated the democratic order of the FRG, the experiences of the fall revolution of the GDR, and the experiences of the [East German] women's movement could not be used. But the questions of legal fundamental rights of women opened up a new discussion in the women's movement in East and West Germany. It provided the possibility for a joint East-West German women's discussion.[64]

Coming less than a year since the Memmingen decision, abortion was one of the primary issues that brought this coalition together. However, the expectation of a mutual collaboration of women from East and West – suggested by Böhm – would not quite come to fruition.

From the very beginning, the UFV and abortion rights activists faced an uphill battle. One of the biggest difficulties was the speed of political developments. The UFV was only officially constituted as a political association on 17 February 1990, giving them less than a month to prepare for the March elections.[65] Furthermore, the decision to unify through Article 23 of the Basic Law, a provision that allowed for the incorporation of German territory into the Federal Republic without needing a referendum or a renegotiation of the Constitution, meant that the whole process moved incredibly quickly.[66] Indeed, the first step towards official

---

[62] Kleine Anfrage to the Stadträtin für Gleichstellung (Eva Kunz) from 20.6.1990; Bericht über geleistete Arbeit der AG "Gleichstellung" und des UFV und DFD am Runden Tisch Berlin in der Zeit von Dez. 1989 bis Mai 1990, A/0012, RHG.

[63] See also discussion in: Wuerth, 'National Politics/Local Identities'.

[64] Böhm, 'The Women's Question', p. 157.

[65] These elections had originally been scheduled for May. See Konrad H. Jarausch, *The Rush to German Unity* (New York: Oxford University Press, 1994).

[66] Although the use of Article 23 was strongly contested by East Germans and feminists from both sides of Germany, who instead advocated for the use of Article 146, which would have required the creation of a new constitution, Article 23 was fervently supported by the governing CDU, especially the Minister for the Interior and lead West German reunification negotiator, Wolfgang Schäuble. See Jarausch, *The Rush to German Unity*; Michael G. Huelshoff, Andrei S. Markovits and Simon Reich, eds,

reunification – the First State Treaty – was finalised within a month after the March elections and it was only five months later that the two German states, divided for 40 years, would be united as one.[67]

The speed of transformation meant that political discussions were largely focused on major economic, security and electoral questions. Women's issues and women's rights were marginalised from this process.[68] There was only one mention of women in the First State Treaty and this was in the context of providing vocational education and retraining, where the 'interests of women and the disabled' should be taken into account.[69] This was particularly shocking for East German feminists, including the UFV, for whom the 'view "over there"', as Christina Schenk and Christiane Schindler put it, was increasingly taking on new meaning. If they were to forge a platform for women's rights across reunification, not only would women from both Germanies have to work together, but East German activists would have to learn more about the way politics operated in the West.[70]

After not being included in the First State Treaty, feminists set their sights on the negotiation of the Unification Treaty, where abortion would become a key issue. Already in late April 1990, women from across the Berlin Wall had formed an *Ost-West-Frauenkongress* (East-West Women's Congress). This Congress, constituted by the UFV, the West Berlin women's network Goldrausch and autonomous feminists from Munich, was vocal in criticising the social market economy as a system that inherently relies on women's unpaid labour and had submitted demands for the inclusion of women and women's issues in the negotiation process to all governments in East and West Germany.[71] Women associated with the UFV also formed a *Frauenpolitischer Runde Tisch* (Women's Political Round Table) in Berlin. Like the other round tables and citizen's groups established during 1990, this was intended as a forum to give women a platform to address their concerns about reunification. Alongside a working group on the consequences of economic

---

From Bundesrepublik to Deutschland: German Politics after Reunification (Ann Arbor: University of Michigan Press, 1993).

[67] The speed with which reunification took place has also shaped historical narratives, with Konrad H. Jarausch's detailed history of reunification aptly titled *The Rush to German Unity* and even Myra Marx Ferree calling it a 'time of chaos'. See Jarausch, *The Rush to German Unity*; Myra Marx Ferree, '"The Time of Chaos was Best." Feminist Mobilization and Demobilization in East Germany', *Gender and Society*, Vol. 8, No. 4 (1994): pp. 597–623.

[68] For a detailed history of the UFV's work to get women's issues included in the reunification process, see Young, *Triumph of the Fatherland*.

[69] Article 19, Vertrag über die Schaffung einer Währungs-, Wirtschafts- und Sozialunion zwischen der Bundesrepublik Deutschland und der DDR (18.5.1990). See also Young, *Triumph of the Fatherland*; Schenk and Schindler, 'Frauenbewegung in Ostdeutschland'.

[70] Schenk and Schindler, 'Frauenbewegung in Ostdeutschland', p. 135.

[71] Ost-West Kongress 27–29.4.1990, Resolution of East-West Women Congress, 27–29 April 1990. A/0076, RHG; 'Aus der Resolution an die Regierungen und Parlamente beider deutscher Staaten', *Für Dich*, No. 20 (1990).

and monetary unification, the *Frauenpolitischer Runde Tisch* had a working group on 'self-determined pregnancy', which proved particularly important for creating a coalition to address abortion. This working group was formed out of representatives from various women's groups, political parties and citizen's initiatives from both East and West, including the West Berlin Feminist Women's Health Centre, the DFD, *Neues Forum*, the SPD, Green Party and even a representative of the GDR Women's Minister, Christa Schmidt (CDU).[72]

The proliferation of these groups led to widespread action on abortion throughout the summer of 1990. On 16 June 1990, women's groups from both East and West organised mass demonstrations in Berlin and Bonn, respectively. In Berlin, UFV activists even blocked the former East–West border strip between the Brandenburg Gate and Potsdamer Platz in symbolic protest against the imposition of Paragraph 218 on the former GDR.[73] The UFV also gathered 50,000 signatures from people in favour of retaining women's access to first-trimester abortion. The working group on self-determined pregnancy similarly ran letter-writing campaigns, teach-ins and demonstrations.[74] On 29 September – the week prior to official reunification on 3 October – they also organised a mass protest under the banner of 'Against the Take-Over of the GDR. For a Self-Determined Life'.[75] As the announcement in the Berlin daily, *Die Tageszeitung* made clear, 'For months now, Herr "Reunifiers" have been tearing a woman's most personal decision to shreds. Paragraph 218, introduced at the founding of the German Empire in 1871, shall once against be slipped over the heads of women in the GDR.'[76]

However, even at this peak of protest against Paragraph 218, there were tensions between women from the East and West. In a report on the *Ost-West-Frauenkongress*, Ulrike Helwerth called the 'low' level of participation (some 500 participants) 'disappointing'. Moreover, the event showed that 'the sisters are still somewhat alien to one another. The rapid merging of the [feminist] family did not work as well as it did with political parties.'[77] While the two sides found common ground on the topics of pornography and violence against women, abortion proved especially divisive. The very different experiences of women from East and West and the impact this had on their activism shaped how they envisioned reproductive rights reform. In particular, the presentation on abortion from Leipzig activist Karin Raab symbolised the chasm between

---

[72] 'Runder Tisch für Frauen', *Die Tageszeitung*, 6 August 1990. See also: Young, *Triumph of the Fatherland* and Wuerth, 'National Politics/Local Identities'.

[73] Lenz, *Die Neue Frauenbewegung*, p. 871.

[74] Wuerth, 'National Politics/Local Identities'.

[75] 'Gegen Einverleibung der DDR. Für selbstbestimmtes Leben', *Die Tageszeitung*, 4 September 1990. See also: Wuerth, 'National Politics/Local Identities'.

[76] Ibid.

[77] Ulrike Helwerth, '"Für uns steht jetzt alles auf dem Spiel"', *Die Tageszeitung*, 30 April 1990. Also see discussion in Schenk and Schindler, 'Frauenbewegung in Ostdeutschland'.

East and West German feminists. Raab, who favoured keeping the East German abortion law, advocated mandatory counselling for women prior to receiving an abortion. For Raab, this was a response to the 'cold' and clinical way abortions had been carried out in the GDR.[78] Although many East German attendees were not convinced by Raab's plan, the West German participants were 'horrified'. For women from the West, Raab's presentation raised the spectre of pro-life counselling and the efforts made in Bavaria and Baden-Württemberg to restrict women's access to abortion. What had started as an attempt to develop a common strategy and platform for women's rights over reunification ended as a 'malicious dispute' between feminists.[79]

Nevertheless, this activism echoed in political circles. For many in the West German CDU, reunification was not only a chance to solidify pro-life politics in West German law, but also to extend them to the East. For the SPD and the Greens, however, it was a renewed opportunity for liberalisation. Even the FDP, the CDU's coalition partner, wavered in their support of the CDU.[80] Political parties in the former GDR, meanwhile, overwhelmingly supported protecting East German women's right to first-term abortions. Christa Schmidt, the CDU (East) Minister for Women and the Family, organised a postcard action with the UFV. In August 1990, the East German Parliament received 26,500 postcards, the vast majority of which supported carrying over East German abortion laws. Indeed, abortion was an issue that proved to be so contentious that it threatened to derail the entire process of reunification, with the popular German magazine *Der Spiegel* arguing that 'the fight over abortion is dividing the nation just before its unification.'[81] While CDU politicians debated the meaning of abortion – whether it was a woman's right or legislated murder – the overall trend was to back away from a clear decision on the matter.[82] Due to this ongoing conflict, the Unification Treaty provided for a transition period, where separate abortion laws

---

[78] For an overview of women's experiences of abortion in the GDR, see Grafenhorst, *Abtreibung*. Also, Krolzik-Matthei, 'Abtreibung in der DDR'.

[79] Helwerth and Schwarz, *Von Muttis und Emanzen*, p. 10.

[80] A particular sticking point was whether to apply the locality principle ('*Wohnortprinzip*') or the crime-scene principle ('*Tatortprinzip*') to the transition period where East/West had different abortion laws. According to the locality principle, a woman from West Germany could not simply go and get an abortion in the former East Germany, as she would be bound by the laws of Paragraph 218. According to the crime-scene principle, however, it was only where the abortion was performed that was factored into which law would be applied. While the CDU favoured the locality principle, the FDP swapped sides and instead advocated for the crime-scene principle. In response, the CDU dropped the locality principle. However, as Young notes, 'The question of women's rights never even figured in this bizarre legal wrangling. This debate was the ultimate triumph of male values of process over the more female-oriented values of content.' See Young, *Triumph of the Fatherland*, p. 173; Jarausch, *Rush To German Unity*. Also: 'Zug gegen die Wand', *Der Spiegel*, 27 August 1990.

[81] 'Die sind tierisch hinterm Mond', *Der Spiegel*, 14 May 1990, p. 70.

[82] Ibid.

would continue for East and West, with a final decision on the matter to be made by the end of 1992.[83]

Although this delay gave activists more time to rally support, as time wore on, the collaboration between East and West German activists dwindled, as did the strength of the UFV. While East German feminists and the UFV continued to advocate for women's right to first-term abortions, many West German feminists backed away from this demand, instead looking to settle for a compromise to protect the rights they already had.[84] The tensions apparent at the *Ost-West-Frauenkongress* only deepened furthered. At the 1991 conference on abortion organised by the *Frauenpolitischer Runde Tisch*, one UFV representative complained that the conference was 'too West-heavy' and there was little representation of East German women.[85] As a result of these difficulties between the two groups, the monthly working group meetings were mainly attended by UFV women and other East German activists.

At the same time, as Birgit Sauer notes, the political debate on abortion was dominated by a discourse of life and the protection of life.[86] Christian Democratic parliamentarian Claus Jäger even argued that, should the West German law be reformed, abortions would reach 'Holocaust numbers, which, in the face of German history, would weigh heavily on the conscience of politicians if we did not stop this avalanche of death'.[87] In this context, by evoking the spectre of the industrialised mass murder of millions by the Nazi government, even those politicians seeking to decriminalise abortion had to frame their platforms in the terms of protecting life.

Finally, after a marathon 16-hour debate, the German Federal Parliament passed the new abortion law on 26 June 1992. In this Compromise Agreement, abortion was decriminalised and permitted within the first trimester on the basis that the woman receive counselling and go through a three-day waiting period prior to the procedure. A late-term abortion could also be performed if the woman's physical or mental health was endangered.[88] Importantly, Christina Schenk of the UFV and Petra Bläss of the Party of Democratic Socialism – the

---

[83] Article 31 (4), Vertrag zwischen der undesrepublik Deutschland und der Deutschen Demokratischen Republik über die Herstellung der Einheit Deutschlands (31.8.1990).

[84] Wuerth, 'National Politics/Local Identities', p. 613.

[85] Ibid., p. 615.

[86] On the longer trajectory of the discourse, see Myra Marx Ferree, William Anthony Gamson, Jürgen Gerhards and Dieter Rucht, *Shaping Abortion Discourse: Democracy and the Public Sphere in Germany and the United States* (Cambridge: Cambridge University Press, 2002).

[87] Claus Jäger, Deutscher Bundestag. Stenographischer Bericht, 99. Sitzung. Bonn, Thursday 25 June 1992, p. 8283. Also: Birgit Sauer, ' "Doing Gender". Das Parlament als Ort der Geschlechterkonstruktion. Eine Analyse der Bundestagdebatte um die Neuregelung des Schwangerschaftsabbruches' in *Sprache des Parlaments und Semiotik der Demokratie. Studien zur politischen Kommunikation in der Moderne*, edited by Andreas Dörner and Ludgera Vogt (Berlin: De Gruyter, 1995): pp. 172–199.

[88] Strafgesetzbuch 1871 (Germany) §218.

only two parliamentarians to vote against the new law on the grounds that the law did not respect women's right to self-determination and that the pro-life counselling was designed to influence women's decision – were from East Germany.[89] Much like the 1974 reform, however, this law was subject to a legal challenge and the Constitutional Court again determined that it went against the constitutional guarantee of the protection of human life.[90] In 1995, an amended law was introduced. While similar to the Compromise Agreement, under this new law abortion was recriminalised and the pre-abortion counselling requirement was to be explicitly pro-life.[91]

As early as February 1990, UFV member and representative on the Central Round Table Uta Röth succinctly captured the journey of women's activism over reunification: 'Women's awakening – that's how we started. Then came the upheaval. And then the collapse.'[92] The hopes of protecting East German women's reproductive rights and liberalising West German law never came to fruition, as feminists across the East–West divide struggled both to have their voices heard and to work together effectively. Certainly, the systems present in each state shaped expectations and visions of feminism and emancipated womanhood. A particular sticking point in collaboration was the question of autonomy and working with the state. East German feminists sought out political participation and wanted to change 'the state'.[93] While they supported women's projects, they were wary of retreating into 'niches'. They also worked alongside men. As an article in the formerly official socialist women's magazine *Für Dich* so succinctly captured, 'Feminism, in our understanding, does not mean the total exclusion of men. If equality is to be actually viable, actually effective, then male self-understandings must develop in parallel with female self-understandings.'[94] Much of this flew in the face of West German feminist practice, based as it was on autonomy, separatism and project work. Although these differences were decisive in hampering cooperation on abortion, they may explain why domestic violence work, particularly in reunified Berlin, fared better.

---

[89] Wuerth, 'National Politics/Local Identities', p. 606.

[90] BVerfG, Order of the Second Senate of 28 May 1993 – 2 BvF 2/90 –, paras. 1–434.

[91] Eva Maleck-Lewy and Myra Marx Ferree, 'Talking about Women and Wombs: The Discourse of Abortion and Reproductive Rights in the GDR during and after the Wende', in Gal and Kligman, *The Politics of Gender*: pp. 92–117; Elizabeth Clements, 'The Abortion Debate in Unified Germany', in *Women and the Wende. Social Effects and Cultural Reflections of the German Unification Process*, edited by Elizabeth Boa and Janet Wharton (Amsterdam: Rodopi, 1994): pp. 38–52.

[92] Röth, quoted in Gislinde Schwarz, 'Kein einig Frauenland: Die Frauenbewegung in den neuen Bundesländern' in *Die Bürgerbewegungen in der DDR und in den ostdeutschen Bundesländern*, edited by Gerda Haufe and Karl Bruckmeier (Opladen: Westdeutsche Verlag, 1993): pp. 219–239, p. 235.

[93] Christina Schenk, quoted in Young, *Triumph of the Fatherland*, p. 93.

[94] Bärbel Klässner, 'Feminismus-Geschichte eines Wortes', *Für Dich*, No. 6 (1990), pp. 18–19, p. 19.

A Feminist Success? The Revitalisation of Domestic Violence Activism after 1990

The years following reunification saw the beginnings of one of the most significant domestic violence projects in Germany: the *Berliner Initiative gegen Gewalt an Frauen* (BIG e.V.). One of the largest domestic violence projects in Germany, this initiative represented the successful collaboration of activists and anti-violence workers from East and West. Drawing from international examples of domestic violence intervention, alongside the work of the West German shelter movement and East German approaches to reform, BIG brought about legislative action against violence in the home. While abortion rights activism may not have succeeded, the work of BIG e.V. highlights the successes of post-*Wende* women's rights activism.

The *Berliner Initiative gegen Gewalt an Frauen* began life as a working group of men and women from both West and East Berlin. Comprised of members of the women's movement, shelter and crisis centre workers, counsellors and activists from anti-violence projects, this group's focus was to create a different strategy for assisting those living with abuse; one that did more than just provide services for women and that actually tackled the root causes of violence itself.[95] Examining anti-violence work and best practices for addressing domestic abuse within Germany and abroad, the initiative concluded that 'effective protection for women and children who are being abused can only be achieved when domestic violence is firmly condemned by society, which includes the criminal justice system.'[96]

According to the group, the best way to achieve this kind of societal change was to follow the example of the Domestic Abuse Intervention Project pioneered in Duluth, Minnesota. What was particularly important for the working group was both the Duluth model's overall success and its stress on the importance of collaboration between projects, social services and state institutions.[97] If the working group wanted the criminal justice system to take domestic violence seriously, they knew they would need the help and cooperation of the police and the courts. Further still, they believed that any reform could not just offer increased services to women and children, but also needed to address the perpetrator and hold them accountable for their actions.[98] Supported by the Berlin Senate Office

---

[95] BIG e.V., *Berliner Interventionsprojekt gegen häusliche Gewalt. Alte Ziele auf neuen Wegen. Ein neuartiges Projekt gegen Männergewalt an Frauen stellt sich vor* (Berlin: BIG e.V., 1996).

[96] Ibid., p. 5.

[97] According to BIG e.V., the 'most decisive' factor leading them to use the Duluth model was the fact that 80 per cent of women who had used the services of the Project stated they had not experienced further abuse. See BIG e.V., *Berliner Interventionsprojekt gegen häusliche Gewalt*. For more details on the Duluth model, see Domestic Abuse Intervention Programs, Home of the Duluth Model. Accessed on 28 October 2015: https://www.theduluthmodel.org/.

[98] BIG e.V., *Berliner Interventionsprojekt gegen häusliche Gewalt*.

for Employment, Education and Women and the Federal Ministry for Family, Seniors, Women and Youth, the group began working with the police, the legal system, the Foreigner's Office and youth and social services to create a broad and long-lasting alliance against domestic violence. In 1994, this working group formally became the *Berliner Initiative gegen Gewalt an Frauen* and, starting in 1995, they received four years of federal and Berlin state funding as a model project for domestic violence intervention.[99]

The project proceeded in two phases: planning and organising. The planning phase, from 1995 to 1996, focused on building connections between institutions and projects. During this time, round tables and working groups were formed by BIG e.V., not only to bring the various organisations and bodies together, but also to discuss the major issues they faced when addressing domestic violence.[100] As a result, seven key areas were identified where improved work and cooperation was needed. These included: police intervention, criminal law, civil law, support services for women, migrant women, training/education for abusers and children and youth. These issues then became the focus for work during the three-year organisation phase, as the approximately 150 people involved divided into working groups to draft plans for the creation of practical steps for improving the way these concerns were addressed in domestic violence intervention.[101]

At the end of the organisation phase, the working groups had made significant achievements that were garnering attention throughout Germany. Not only had they drafted a manual for police intervention in instances of domestic violence and a proposed law for improving women's protection in civil law – which in turn created the impetus for the *Gewaltschutzgesetz* – but they also developed the first set of guidelines for supporting female migrants who were living with an abusive partner, the first Germany-wide domestic violence hotline and the first video on the situation of children experiencing or witnessing domestic abuse. Finally, they also developed an educational programme for the perpetrators of domestic violence. Labelled by the Federal Minister for Family, Seniors, Women and Youth as one of the most significant pilot projects supported by the federal government, the model of cooperation and intervention established by BIG e.V. has since spread throughout Germany and resulted in both federal legal reform and improved police responses to domestic disturbances.[102]

The work undertaken by BIG e.V. to address domestic violence clearly highlights the success of East/West collaborations to ensure women's rights in the wake of reunification. But, it also shows the way women's activism against domestic violence had

---

[99] Ibid.

[100] Patricia Schneider, Ulrike Kreyssig, Dorothea Hecht and Monika Trieselmann, *Von 1995 bis 2005. 10 Jahre BIG, Berliner Interventionszentrale bei häuslicher Gewalt* (Berlin: BIG e.V., 2005).

[101] Ibid.; BIG e.V., *Berliner Interventionsprojekt gegen häusliche Gewalt*.

[102] Dr Ursula von der Leyen, Federal Minister for Family, Seniors, Women and Youth, quoted in Schneider, Kreyssig, Hecht and Trieselmann, *Von 1995 bis 2005*, p. 9.

developed and changed since the opening of the first shelter in 1976. There are certainly several parallels to the initial shelter project: both were model projects that received Berlin state and federal funding and were evaluated by an external research team, and, indeed, many of the researchers involved in examining BIG e.V. had also contributed to the report on the Berlin model shelter. In both cases, the people involved in the shelters were professionals who had first-hand experience supporting those living with domestic violence. Further still, and similar to the connections between the shelter movement and Chiswick Women's Aid, BIG e.V. drew legitimacy for their work from an established international approach to domestic violence.

However, there are also significant differences between BIG e.V. and the Grunewald model shelter, which suggest an East German influence on contemporary activism. One of the biggest distinctions between women's activism in the East and the West was the involvement of men: whereas the West German women's movement was intensely separatist, East German women were open to the inclusion of men in their work.[103] In a similar vein, by addressing the perpetrators of violence and seeking to rehabilitate and educate them, BIG e.V. has grown away from the women-centred approach of early activism.[104] By including men in their work, whether as activists or as clients, BIG e.V. has deviated from the traditional approaches of West German feminist activism, and, in doing so, acknowledged the limitations of expecting women to bear the prime responsibility for dealing with domestic violence. In addition, the push for legal reform also suggests an eastern influence. As the example of the Weimar *Frauenteestube* shows, East German groups were far more open to pushing for legal reform, whereas the West German movement was firmly determined to work outside of the auspices of the state.

Indeed, the work of BIG e.V. to bring about greater legal protection for women reflected a broader trend of legislative reform in the late 1990s that sought to address issues of familial violence, pointing to a much more active role of the German state in combating violence against women. Not only was rape in marriage criminalised in 1997, but in 1999 the four-year residency requirement for migrant women living in Germany under a family visa was reduced to two and migrant women living with an abusive husband could use the 'hardship clause' to separate from their husband while maintaining residency. Significantly, both these reforms had long been actively fought for by activists and politicians: while much of the work to amend the residency legislation began in the 1980s, the first call to amend West German rape law came in 1972 when the Social Democrats proposed an amendment to the Criminal Code, a call which would be repeated throughout the 1980s by both the

---

[103] Ferree, *Varieties of Feminism*; Young, *Triumph of the Fatherland*.
[104] Barbara Kavemann, Beate Leopold, Gesa Schirrmacher and Carol Hagemann-White, *Modelle der Kooperation gegen häusliche Gewalt: "Wir sind ein Kooperationsmodell, kein Konfrontationsmodell"; Ergebnisse der wissenschaftlichen Begleitung des Berliner Interventionsprojekts gegen häusliche Gewalt (BIG)* (Stuttgart: Kohlhammer, 2001).

Social Democrats and the Greens.[105] In stark comparison to the 25 years of activism calling for the criminalisation of rape in marriage, the legislation drafted by BIG e.V. during its model period from 1995 to 1999, quickly found political traction, with the *Gewaltschutzgesetz* enacted in 2001 and implemented in 2002.

BIG's proposal was aimed at ending the contemporary system that required women and children to flee while their abuser remained at home. This meant improving both the law and legal process. For example, prior to the *Gewaltschutzgesetz*, there were no grounds for the allocation of an apartment in instances of violence within de facto/common-law couples. In cases of married couples, the person seeking the apartment on the basis of abuse had to meet a high threshold of '*schwere Härte*' (extreme hardship).[106] As a result, the BIG proposal recommended that a basis of claim for abuse be established in the Civil Code, which provided a foundation for claims to the allocation of shared living spaces and for the application of a restraining order. Furthermore, they called for the burden of proof to be placed on the abuser in instances of repeated abuse.

In May 1999, this proposal was presented at a conference organised by the Federal Ministry of Family, Seniors, Women and Youth on the possibilities of improving protective measures for women living with abuse available in civil law. The first action plan on combating violence against women arose from this conference and was closely followed by a draft proposal for a 'Law for the Improvement of Civil Law Protection in Instances of Violence, as well as the Simplification of the Allocation of Marital Homes'.[107] Although this proposal took up many of the issues presented within the BIG reform agenda, it called instead for the creation of a specific law, rather than an amendment to the Civil Code.[108] This proposal was then passed through the Bundestag in 2001, with the *Gewaltschutzgesetz* coming into force in 2002. As a result, when police now intervene in domestic disputes in Germany, they are able to take the keys away from the abuser and order them to leave for a certain period of time.[109]

---

[105] 'Endlich: Vergewaltigung in der Ehe gilt künftig als Verbrechen', *Die Zeit*, 16 May 1997; 'German Law Criminalizes Marital Rape', *Ms. Magazine*. Accessed on 29 October 2015: http://www.msm agazine.com/news/uswirestory.asp?id=4131. On other legislative attempts at criminalising rape in marriage, see Gerhard Schröder, 'SPD strebt besseren Schutz für Opfer von Sexualdelikten an', *SPD informiert*, 17 February 1984; *Gesetzesantrag Fraktion der Grünen zum §177 StGB*, A Rep 400 BRD 22.5 (2) 1980–2005, FFBIZ; Deutsche Bundestag, 40. Sitzung, 1 December 1983; *Gesetzentwurf, der Fraktion Die Grünen. Entwurf eines Strafrechtsänderungsgesetzes (StrÄndG)*, Deutscher Bundestag, 10. Wahlperiode, 2 November 1983.
[106] BIG Koordinierung, *10 Jahre Gewaltschutzgesetz* (Berlin: BIG e.V, 2012).
[107] Ibid. See also: *Aktionsplan der Bundesregierung zur Bekämpfung von Gewalt gegen Frauen*.
[108] BIG Koordinierung, *10 Jahre*; Bundesministerium für Justiz, Entwurf eines Gesetzes zur Verbesserung des zivilgerichtlichen Schutzes bei Gewalttaten und Nachstellungen sowie zur Erleichterung der Überlassung der Ehewohnung bei Trennung (Stand 13.12.2000).
[109] Bundesministerium für Familie, Senioren, Frauen und Jugend and Bundesministerium für Justiz und für Verbraucherschutz. *Mehr Schutz bei häuslicher Gewalt: Informationen zum Gewaltschutzgesetz* (Berlin: Bundesministerium für Familie, Senioren, Frauen und Jugend, 2003).

Of course, there are several reasons why the *Gewaltschutzgesetz* was so swiftly taken up. Not only was it initially proposed by a project sponsored in part by the federal government, but the 1990s witnessed an international acknowledgement that violence against women was an issue of human rights.[110] In 1994, the United Nations General Assembly adopted a Declaration on the Elimination of Violence against Women, which had been on the agenda since the 1985 Nairobi World Conference to Review and Appraise the Achievements of the United Nations Decade for Women. In this declaration, the Assembly affirmed that 'violence against women constitutes a violation of the rights and fundamental freedoms of women.'[111] Two years later, the Commission on Human Rights issued a report on domestic violence, which clearly labelled it as a human rights violation.[112] At the European level, the late 1990s also saw several important steps to address violence against women in Europe: in 1996, the first EU policy regarding human trafficking was enacted with the Incentive and Exchange Programme for Persons Responsible for Combating Trade in Human Beings and the Sexual Exploitation of Children and in 1997 an EU resolution called for the creation of a 'zero tolerance of violence against women' campaign.[113] Also significant for the German case was the introduction of the Federal Law on the Protection of the Family against Violence in Austria in 1997, which provided a working example for legal reform in the Federal Republic.[114] Within this context, it is no surprise that Germany became much more active in creating legislative reform to address gender violence. But this still does not explain why the trajectory of domestic violence activism fared so differently to abortion rights.

As Ilse Lenz argues, the 1990s were marked by a 'transformation of the women's movement', developed out of an engagement with the approaches of East German feminism and international debates.[115] This is certainly evident in domestic violence activism. Unlike the fight for reproductive rights, domestic

---

[110] Celia Donert, 'Whose Utopia? Gender, Ideology, and Human Rights at the 1975 World Congress of Women in East Berlin' in *The Breakthrough: Human Rights in the 1970s*, edited by Jan Eckel and Samuel Moyn (Philadelphia: University of Pennsylvania Press, 2014): pp. 68–87; Celia Donert, 'Women's Rights in Cold War Europe: Disentangling Feminist Histories', *Past and Present*, Supplement 8 (2013): pp. 178–202.

[111] United Nations, General Assembly Resolution 48/104, *Declaration on the Elimination of Violence against Women*, A/Res/48/104 (23 February 1994).

[112] United Nations, Economic and Social Council, *Report of the Special Rapporteur on violence against women, its causes and consequences, Ms. Radhika Coomaraswamy, submitted in accordance with Commission on Human Rights resolution 1995/85, E/CN.4/1996/53* (5 February 1996). Accessed on 29 October 2015: http://www.awf.or.jp/pdf/h0003.pdf.

[113] Incentive and Exchange Programme for Persons Responsible for Combating Trade in Human Beings and the Sexual Exploitation of Children (STOP) [1996] OJ L 322; Sophie Jacquot, *Transformations in EU Gender Equality. From Emergence to Dismantling* (New York: Palgrave Macmillan, 2015).

[114] Bundesgesetz zum Schutz vor Gewalt in der Familie 1996 (Austria). The Austrian law also played a large role in the initial reform platform proposed by BIG e.V. See BIG Koordinierung, *10 Jahre*.

[115] Lenz, *Die Neue Frauenbewegung*, p. 867.

violence intervention and prevention were already a firm part of the West German liberal agenda by the time of reunification. Whereas abortion activists were attempting to protect a right that existed in what was increasingly seen as an illegitimate and inhumane state, domestic violence activism was about building up a system of established and professionalised social service practices in the East. Moreover, the SED's growing delegitimisation served to support activists working against domestic violence, who could capitalise on the socialist state's failure to assist women living with a violent partner. Abortion rights activists, however, had to contend with accusations of the immorality of socialism, in particular its exploitation of women's (re)productive labour. Abortion rights were also complicated by religion and ideas about the rights of the foetus that had been increasingly politicised in West Germany since the 1980s. It is also no coincidence that this new domestic violence initiative took off in Berlin. Domestic violence activists in West Berlin had been working with the government since the mid-1970s, which fit closely with the way East German activists envisioned women's politics and projects.

The growth of domestic violence support services highlights the successes of one facet of women's rights activism post-1990. It shows how – on some issues – feminist activists from across the Berlin Wall were able to work together to protect women's rights. In contrast to much of the scholarship, women were not simply the 'losers' of reunification. But, in the context of the failed abortion reform, we might also ask what the different trajectories of feminist activism might tell us about the ways in which women's rights are negotiated and protected in reunified Germany.

Conclusion

On the 20th anniversary of the reunification of Germany, the *New York Times* published an article profiling the differences between women of the former East and West Germanies. Despite two decades of living under one state, the piece highlights that division still separates the lives of women in Germany. While the fall of the Berlin Wall had a disproportionate impact on women from the former East, it is these same women who are now better off than their western sisters. Women from the east of Germany, the article argues, 'are more self-confident, better-educated and more mobile ... They have children earlier and are more likely to work full time. More of them are happy with their looks and their sexuality and fewer of them diet.'[116] Further still, although wages are lower in the East,

---

[116] Katrin Bennhold, '20 Years After Fall of Wall, Women of Former East Germany Thrive', *New York Times*, 2 October 2010. Accessed on 20 October 2015: http://www.nytimes.com/2010/10/06/world/eur ope/06iht-letter.html?_r=0.

the pay gap between men and women is only 6 per cent, as opposed to 24 per cent in the West. Citing examples like now-former Chancellor Angela Merkel and then-Deputy SPD leader Manuela Schwesig – both of whom grew up in the former GDR – the article shows that while 'West German women wobble … Eastern women have no fear.'[117]

Given these differences, we might rightfully question the designation of women as the 'losers' of reunification. Indeed, it now appears as if East German men are some of the most significantly affected by the long-term transformations shaping Germany after reunification. In the former East German states, male unemployment exceeds female (7.4 per cent as compared to 6 per cent) and there is a smaller gap between male and female education attainment.[118] Men in East Germany are also more likely to identify with far-right politics; one-third of male voters in Saxony in 2017 voted for the populist Alternative for Germany (AfD) party. As Petra Köpping, the former State Minister for Integration and Equality and current State Minister for Social Affairs and Cohesion in Saxony, argues, 'We have a crisis of masculinity in the East and it is feeding the far right.'[119] How then should we judge the gendered impacts of reunification?

On the one hand, the failure to gain abortion rights, and the gendered processes of reunification more generally, reveal a reinscription of patriarchal gender norms. As scholars have argued, there are clear parallels between the regulation of gender and family roles in the post-1945 period and across the *Wende*. East German women returned to the family; they lost their jobs, their access to social services and their reproductive rights.[120] On the other hand, the success of domestic violence activism challenges this narrative of division and failure. Instead, it reveals a success story of feminist activism and a further cementing of women's rights and their protection from violence. This is typified by the *Gewaltschutzgesetz*. Writing in 2012 to celebrate the 10-year anniversary of the introduction of the Act, BIG e.V. argued that 'the achievement of a law,

---

[117] Ibid. Of course, what remains undiscussed in the article is the issue of increasing male unemployment in the former East, which has surpassed female unemployment. See Anne Goedicke, 'A "Ready-Made State": The Mode of Institutional Transition in East Germany After 1989' in *After the Fall of the Wall: Life Courses in the Transformation of East Germany*, edited by Martin Diewald, Anne Goedicke and Karl Ulrich Mayer (Stanford: Stanford University Press, 2006): pp. 44–64.

[118] Andreas Ammermüller and Andrea Maria Weber, 'Educational Attainment and Returns to Education in Germany – An Analysis by Subject of Degree, Gender and Region', *Discussion Paper No. 05–17* (Mannheim: Zentrum für Europäische Wirtschaftsforschung GmBH, 2005).

[119] 'One Legacy of Merkel? Angry East German Men Fueling the Far Right', *New York Times*, 5 November 2018. Accessed 12 May 2022: https://www.nytimes.com/2018/11/05/world/europe/merkel-east-germany-nationalists-populism.html. See also: Petra Köpping, *Integriert doch erst mal uns! Eine Streitschrift für den Osten* (Berlin: Christoph Links Verlag, 2018)

[120] Elizabeth Heineman, *What Difference Does a Husband Make?: Women and Marital Status in Nazi and Postwar Germany* (Berkeley: University of California Press, 1999); Robert G. Moeller, *Protecting Motherhood: Women and the Family in the Politics of Postwar West Germany* (Berkeley: University of California Press, 1993); Wuerth, 'National Politics/Local Identities'.

which makes it clear that the abuser must go, was long overdue. It has not only led to better protection for women and children confronted with domestic violence, but also to a change in social perceptions.'[121]

But, what exactly are the 'social perceptions' that have changed? And what values is this law protecting? Despite the significance of this legal reform for providing protection for women and children living with violence and for taking a political stance against domestic abuse, it is also important to interrogate the values and principles that underpin the legislation. Namely, we must ask what is 'wrong' with domestic violence. What is the harm being done and what is the law protecting?[122] One answer might be that domestic violence represents a violation of women's rights as human beings to bodily integrity and physical autonomy, and that by enacting the *Gewaltschutzgesetz* and supporting women's shelters, the German government has enshrined these principles in law. However, if this were the case, why are women's reproductive choices limited?

The failure of the *Wende* abortion reform movement suggests firstly that the recognition of women's rights to physical autonomy in Germany is limited, and secondly that the legislative action on domestic violence is about more than just providing women with bodily security. The delegitimisation of East Germany was not only about denouncing the control and violence of organisations like the Stasi, but, as the abortion debate made clear, it was also about condemning the vision of womanhood promoted under socialism and replacing it with long-standing heteropatriarchal ideals of stay-at-home mothers.[123] Projects that sought to address domestic violence fit more snugly with this model – not only did they speak to the illegitimacy of socialism, but they also reflected images of women as vulnerable and in need of protection that were not present in reproductive rights activism. It would seem then that the cost of the institutionalisation of feminist practices represented in the official adoption of domestic violence activism has been the entrenchment of a limited vision of women's rights, one that acknowledges a right to bodily integrity only so far as to protect women from male violence, but not one that grants women a right to self-determination.

---

[121] BIG Koordinierung, *10 Jahre*, p. 6.
[122] In asking this question, I follow an established tradition of feminist legal scholarship. See Dorothy E. Roberts, 'Rape, Violence, and Women's Autonomy', *Chicago-Kent Law Review*, Vol. 69 (1993): pp. 359–388.
[123] Wuerth, 'National Politics/Local Identities'.

Conclusion

I want to return to the stories of two women already discussed: Frau A. from Leipzig and Monika from West Berlin. Both women lived with violent partners and turned to the official channels available in each state in an attempt to end the violence. When Frau A. first reported her husband to the police for assault in 1986, she 'had the feeling, that at least as far as the two police officers were concerned, whatever took place within a marriage, so long as it didn't disturb the peace in the building or anything, wasn't such a big deal'.[1] When she attempted to divorce her husband, she was told she would need a doctor's certificate, which her doctor refused to give her on the basis that her injuries could have been sustained by falling down the stairs. At the divorce hearing, her application was denied and she was required to attend two reconciliation sessions with her husband. Following reunification, Frau A. was one of the first residents at the women's shelter in Leipzig.

Monika from West Berlin had similar experiences. After informing child services about her violent husband in the early 1970s, she was accompanied home by a social worker.[2] Once there, the social worker spoke to the husband, who 'hammed it up, saying that he has to work very hard and do overtime' and further blamed his 'sick and unstable' wife for the abuse he perpetrated.[3] According to Monika, 'suddenly everything changed. She [the social worker] advised me to get some medication prescribed by the doctor and told my husband that he shouldn't hit me or the children, which he promised to do'.[4] Before she left, the social worker told Monika that if she were older, she would have thought she was going through menopause, dismissing her stories of abuse as hormonal. It was only after the first shelter opened in West Berlin that Monika could find the support she needed.

---

[1] Gabriela Eßbach and Vera Fünfstück, *Frauen mit Gewalterfahrung in der ehemaligen DDR: Wahrnehmungszugänge und Bewältigungsstratigen. Eine Untersuchung aus dem Blickwinkel autonomer Frauenhausarbeit in Sachsen* (Diplomarbeit, Evangelischen Fachhochschule für Sozialarbeit Dresden, 1997), p. III.

[2] Carol Hagemann-White, Barbara Kavemann, Johanna Kootz, Ute Weinmann, Carola Christine Wildt, Roswitha Burgard and Ursula Scheu, *Hilfen für mißhandelte Frauen: Abschlussbericht der wissenschaftlichen Begleitung des Modellprojekts Frauenhaus Berlin* (Stuttgart: Verlag W. Kohlhammer, 1981).

[3] Ibid., p. 109.

[4] Ibid.

Juxtaposing these experiences highlights significant similarities in the lives of women experiencing domestic abuse in divided Germany. But it also reveals key differences in access to, and opportunities for, support. As a way of concluding, I want to use the stories of Frau A. and Monika to reflect on what domestic violence can tell us about the histories of Germany and feminism.

A History of Germany

On both sides of the Berlin Wall, women's stories of abuse were ignored. Whether in East or West, women like Monika and Frau A. were dismissed and disbelieved by police and social services, neighbours, family and friends. As so many examples in this book have shown, women could not simply leave an abusive relationship. Not only did women's own emotional and familial ties stop them from leaving, but prevailing patriarchal attitudes, legal stumbling blocks, associated issues of drug and alcohol addiction and access to resources all contributed to making women stay with their abuser.[5]

Such experiences blur a seemingly clear separation between the two Germanies. Despite very different ideological and political positions on gender, these similarities point to the continued existence of shared patriarchal structures that have been a constitutive part of German state-making since the 19th century. These structures not only survived the ruptures in German politics, culture and society across the first half of the 20th century, but persevered beyond the establishment of the divided states in 1949. Although the two Germanies may have used markedly different rhetoric on women's roles – as historians have highlighted – they often adopted similar approaches in practice. Both the Federal Republic and German Democratic Republic were concerned with reconstruction and stabilising their economies and populations in the aftermath of the Second World War, and both saw the family and the roles of men and women in it as an important site for this reconstruction.

In many respects, the responses to domestic abuse reveal the afterlives of these post-war attempts to (re-)establish stability in Germany via the home and family.[6] Domestic violence disrupted and challenged these post-war ideals and both states

---

[5] Jane Freeland, 'Domestic Abuse, Women's Lives and Citizenship: East and West Policies during the 1960s and 1970s' in *Gendering Post-1945 German History: Entanglements*, edited by Friederike Brühöfener, Karen Hagemann and Donna Harsch (New York: Berghahn, 2019): pp. 253–273.

[6] Robert G. Moeller, *Protecting Motherhood: Women and the Family in the Politics of Postwar West Germany* (Berkeley: University of California Press, 1993); Annette Timm, *The Politics of Fertility in Twentieth-Century Berlin* (New York: Cambridge University Press, 2010); Jennifer V. Evans 'The Moral State: Men, Mining and Masculinity in the early GDR', *German History*, Vol. 23, No.3 (2005): pp. 355–370; Elizabeth Heineman, *What Difference Does a Husband Make?: Women and Marital Status in Nazi and Postwar Germany* (Berkeley: University of California Press, 1999); Dagmar Herzog, *Sex After Fascism: Memory and Morality in Twentieth-Century Germany* (Princeton: Princeton University Press, 2005); Uta G. Poiger, 'Krise der Männlichkeit. Remaskulinisierung in beiden deutschen Nachkriegsgesellschaften' in *Nachkrieg in Deutschland*, edited by Klaus Naumann (Hamburg: Hamburg Institut für Sozialforschung, 2001): pp. 227–266.

sought responses that served to balance the maintenance of the status quo with legal guarantees and women's own claims of equality. This was certainly the case in the GDR, where official valuations of equality between men and women defined public discussions of domestic abuse. Violence in the home was antithetical to socialism and was consistently framed as either an export or holdover from capitalism. As the many divorce cases discussed in this book show, legal determinations prioritised the legitimisation and perpetuation of socialism by ensuring families stayed together. Women's safety in the home was simply not a priority.

In the Federal Republic, the struggle to get domestic violence on the political agenda and the eventual co-optation of feminist politics similarly exposes the long shadow cast by post-war reconstruction. Indeed, the struggle for women's rights, discussed in Robert Moeller's analysis of the debates on gender equality and the status of the family from the 1950s, continued well into the 1970s and 1980s.[7] The construction of women's shelters spoke to these very issues, as the public and politicians negotiated the role of the state in the private sphere, weighing up feminist calls for women's rights to personal safety against the constitutional guarantee of the family as a 'protected institution'.

The similar responses to domestic violence also shed light on the processes of social change shaping Germany in the 1970s. In the histories of both East and West Germany, the long 1970s are closely linked with the liberalisation of norms and mores, social change and an increased focus on quality of life and values such as self-fulfilment, expression, autonomy and democratic participation, all associated with a shift towards post-materialism.[8] These developments certainly impacted women's lives and can be found in feminist practices. Across the Berlin Wall, women gathered in groups to engage in self-discovery and find fulfilment as women. The sexual revolution and liberalising legal reform also brought changes to women's intimate lives, as the normalisation of birth control and divorce provided more space for women's sexual expression, pleasure and personal happiness.

Unsurprisingly then, changes to the family, sexuality and the spread of social movements like feminism, have been held up by historians as examples of the successes of liberalisation in divided Germany.[9] What is less clear, though, are the

---

[7] Moeller, *Protecting Motherhood*.

[8] The 'long 1970s' refers to the period from the late 1960s to the early 1980s. See: Poul Villaume, Rasmus Mariager and Helle Porsdam, eds, *The 'Long 1970s': Human Rights, East-West Détente and Transnational Relations* (Oxford: Routledge, 2016); Timothy Brown, *West Germany and the Global Sixties: The Anti-Authoritarian Revolt, 1962–1978* (London: Cambridge University Press, 2013); Joachim C. Häberlen, 'Feeling like a Child: Dreams and Practices of Sexuality in the West German Alternative Left during the Long 1970s', *Journal of the History of Sexuality*, Vol. 25, No. 2 (2016): pp. 219–245; Simon Hall, 'Protest Movements in the 1970s: The Long 1960s', *Journal of Contemporary History*, Vol. 43, No. 4 (2008): pp. 655–672.

[9] Konrad H. Jarausch, *After Hitler: Recivilizing Germans, 1945–1995* (Oxford: Oxford University Press, 2006); Ulrich Herbert, ed, *Wandlungsprozesse in Westdeutschland: Belastung, Integration, Liberalisierung, 1945–1980* (Göttingen: Wallstein, 2002); Christina von Hodenberg, 'Writing Women's Agency into the History of the Federal Republic: "1968," Historians, and Gender', *Central European History*, Vol. 52, No.1 (2019): pp. 87–106.

agents that made these developments possible. Historians have variously looked at the media, at consumer practices and the marketplace, at everyday life and at ideals and political change as sites for the spread and growth of value change, democratisation and liberalisation.[10] However, if we centre women's enduring inequality in these histories, not only does a less precipitous story of social change emerge, but the importance of women's activism to driving change forward is made clear.

Examining feminist activism against domestic violence reveals social change as a gendered process. Despite different sites for the discussion of domestic violence, the net effect was often the same: women were responsible for addressing violence in the home and it was their (mostly unpaid) labour that enabled change. In the West, it was feminists who first politicised violence against women, created shelters and services to support women and put domestic violence on the political agenda.[11] This work was further developed by working-class women and women of colour who fundamentally shaped liberalisation by making feminism more attentive to intersectionality. Although women's equality was a very different political terrain under socialism, it was still predominantly women who advanced and nuanced discussions of women's rights, as well as sought to create change for women experiencing abuse following the fall of the Berlin Wall.

In the West, the gendered cleavages of social change only deepened as the state and the media took up domestic violence activism. Although the co-optation of feminist activism may have helped to drive liberalisation and the popular support for (certain) women's rights, it was also a process that relied on the concomitant reinscription of gender norms and the deradicalisation and depoliticisation of feminism. As domestic violence work gained political traction, the radical critiques of patriarchy and gender inequality inherent to feminist activism were muted by politicians, the media and even feminists themselves. Indeed, the media appears as an important interlocutor for negotiating this balance of change and stasis. By obscuring the feminist origins of domestic violence activism and instead relying on gendered images of victimised women, the media was able to promote liberalisation, while at the same time reinscribing patriarchal norms.

---

[10] Axel Schildt, 'Das Jahrhundert der Massenmedien. Ansichten zu einer künftigen Geschichte der Öffentlichkeit', *Geschichte und Gesellschaft*, Vol. 27, No. 2 (2001); pp. 177–206; Christina von Hodenberg, *Television's Moment: Sitcom Audiences and the Sixties Cultural Revolution* (New York: Berghahn, 2015); Elizabeth Heineman, *Before Porn Was Legal: The Erotica Empire of Beate Uhse* (Chicago: University of Chicago Press, 2013); Christopher Neumaier, *Familie im 20. Jahrhundert: Konflikte um Ideale, Politiken und Praktiken* (Berlin: De Gruyter, 2019).

[11] This was similarly the case for anti-racism initiatives, which have historically been driven by the work of people of colour and migrants. See, for example, Jennifer Miller, 'Her Fight is Your Fight: "Guest Worker" Labor Activism in the Early 1970s West Germany', *International Labor and Working-Class History*, 84 (2013), pp. 226–247. On the intersections of race and feminism, see Neval Gültekin, Brigitte Schulz and Brigitte Sellach, eds, *Ausländische und deutsche Frauen im Gespräch. Sind wir uns denn so fremd?*, 2nd ed. (Berlin: Sub-Rosa-Frauenverlag, 1985).

Against this backdrop, it is clear that support for domestic violence activism and social change was built on both gendered rhetoric and largely unacknowledged and unpaid women's labour. In a 1989 study on family allowances, Robert Moeller argued that 'measures intended to "protect" women are often responses to genuine social needs, but once in place, they may limit the ways certain problems are perceived and the areas where solutions are sought and obscure alternative perceptions and other potential solutions.'[12] In the case of domestic violence activism, the political, media and popular support for shelter projects also served to maintain a gendered and racialised patriarchal system that relied on women's work and for a long time limited alternative intervention strategies. It was not until after German reunification that the large-scale domestic violence project, Berlin Initiative against Violence towards Women, would transform responses to domestic violence, including spearheading the introduction of the *Gewaltschutzgesetz* in 2002.

This is not to discount the important role of East Germans in driving domestic violence activism and social change. As I have argued, East Germans had markedly different approaches to activism and addressing violence against women; they were less separatist, worked towards creating legal change and adopted a broader understanding of gender-based violence. Although East German shelter projects benefited from the trailblazing work of West German feminists, they also left their traces in the work of groups like BIG e.V.

Thinking about the successes of domestic violence activism in the former GDR also sheds light on the enduring legacies of socialism. While the failure to protect the East German abortion law was certainly a blow to the collaboration of women activists from the East and West, the same cannot be said for the support of initiatives addressing violence against women. Calling women the 'losers' of reunification also seems particularly short-sighted given that, in the 30 years since the fall of the Berlin Wall, women from the former East Germany have thrived. They have higher rates of education attainment and employment in comparison to men and are less likely to vote for the far-right populist party, Alternative for Germany.[13] East German women also appear to still be contributing to value change and women's equality in reunified Germany. Recent economic research has shown how egalitarian gender norms developed under socialism have not only continued to shape women's lives in the former East, but have also impacted women from the former West. Women from the former GDR typically return to work following childbirth after a year of leave, echoing the *Babyjahr* policy

[12] Robert G. Moeller, 'Reconstructing the Family in Reconstruction Germany: Women and Social Policy in the Federal Republic, 1949–1955' *Feminist Studies*, Vol. 15, No. 1 (1989): pp. 137–169, p. 139.
[13] Andreas Ammermüller and Andrea Maria Weber, 'Educational Attainment and Returns to Education in Germany– An Analysis by Subject of Degree, Gender and Region', *Discussion Paper No. 05–17* (Mannheim: Zentrum für Europäische Wirtschaftsforschung GmBH, 2005).

introduced under Erich Honecker. In comparison, women from the old FRG only return after three years of leave and typically at reduced hours. However, women from the former West who either work in the East or with East German women also adopt the practices of the former socialist regime and return to work at similar rates as East German women.[14]

But, as this book has argued, these successes must be thought of in conjunction with those rights that have not found such support. While domestic violence activism fits snugly with patriarchal gender norms and paternalistic ideas of protecting women, other issues of women's autonomy have proven more challenging to assert. Abortion, long connected with issues of national vitality, became a flashpoint for the confrontation of resurgent nationalism in (Eastern) Europe in the early 1990s and communist efforts to uphold gender equality. Women's rights – as a lynchpin of both liberalism and communism – stood at the heart of reunification.

This did not end with the transition from communism. As the rise in anti-gender rhetoric, protest and policies across much of Central and Eastern Europe – including the recent abortion ban in Poland – shows, the negotiation of communist legacies and conservative, nationalistic visions of women's roles is still shaping debates about women's rights to this very day. While some commentators see the recent resurgence of populism, antifeminism, racism and transphobia as examples of a 'backlash' against the spirit and meaning of 1989, Paul Betts has argued that 'the unrest of 1989 carried within it the seeds of illiberalism.'[15]

Indeed, the tension between responses to domestic violence and reproductive rights activism reflects the very ambiguities of 1989. Backing shelter projects in the former GDR while delaying, and then denying, reproductive rights allowed for the simultaneous support of women's rights with the delegitimisation of socialism and the weakening of the feminist activism that had hampered reunification. This process was enabled by the very institutionalisation and deradicalisation of feminist domestic violence activism that had been taking place in the West since 1976.

By looking at the different trajectories of domestic violence and reproductive rights activism, the contours of the feminist transformation of Germany before, during and after reunification are laid bare. But it was not only feminism that changed Germany. Through feminist engagement with the state, media and politicians, Germany also changed feminism.

---

[14] Barbara Boelmann, Anna Raute and Uta Schönberg, 'Wind of Change? Cultural Determinants of Maternal Labor Supply', *Working Paper No. 914* (London: Queen Mary University London, School of Economics and Finance, 2020).

[15] Paul Betts, '1989 at Thirty. A Recast Legacy', *Past and Present*, Vol. 244, No. 1 (2019): pp. 271–305, p. 272.

A History of Feminism

Feminism tangibly shaped the lives of women in divided Germany. After 1976 in West Berlin, the Grunewald shelter gave women like Monika the ability to find safety away from their violent partner. Women in the East had no such official opportunities. Their only options were to attempt divorce proceedings, either legally or illegally find alternative accommodation, or work through the criminal or social court systems. It was only in 1986, following the opening of the Caritas shelter in Berlin-Hohenschönhausen, that women in East Germany could access emergency housing. Services specifically aimed at supporting women with domestic violence only opened in 1990 – by then the former GDR.

As I have argued, responding to domestic violence is one of the great successes of feminism. In East and West Germany, it was feminism that changed the way violence against women was understood and addressed. Feminists in West Berlin not only opened the first women's shelter in either German state in 1976, but they also placed domestic abuse onto the political agenda. They worked with the media and politicians from across the political spectrum to bring attention to women's stories of male abuse and to challenge popular myths about violence against women. This work led to a network of services and shelters throughout West Berlin and paved the way to the rapid support for domestic violence projects in the reunified city. By giving women like Monika and Frau A. access to support and, most importantly, to accommodation away from their abusers, feminists fundamentally changed the lives of women.

Even in East Germany, a nascent movement to address violence against women brought change to the lives of women under socialism in the final years of division. Groups like the Weimar *Frauenteestube*, events such as the Dresden *Frauenfest* and even films including *Until Death Do Us Part*, gave women and men a forum in which to talk about their experiences of violence in ways that were simply not possible in official channels. The Caritas shelter further provided women with an option for leaving a violent spouse. The proximity of East German developments to the fall of the Berlin Wall and reunification means that we will never know what would have become of the growing women's movement under socialism. However, the role of East German activists in post-reunification domestic violence work and their willingness to work with the state, suggests that East German feminist approaches have continued to play a part in shaping the direction of feminism in Germany.

Yet, in spite of these successes, this book has also shone a light on some uncomfortable histories of feminist activism. Although race and class were key issues in the formative early years of women's activism in the student movement, this did not immediately translate into intersectional feminism. In their work to get domestic violence on the political agenda, activists often relied on racialised and racist images of violent, backward foreign masculinities. Despite advocating for the rights of migrant women, white feminists also spoke for – and even over – them at a time when the lives of certain migrants to West Germany were highly politicised, surveilled and precarious. Activists more generally struggled to confront their own privileges with respect to class and the desires of shelter residents for practical support over feminist consciousness raising.

The tensions between feminists from the two Germanies during reunification are also frustrating. Why were they unable to work together to advocate for reproductive rights? And why could they not set aside their differences to advance the rights of all women? Even though West German, American and other European feminisms had shaped East German feminist politics, the two groups of women were plagued by disunity. Years of separation and living under different political and gender regimes had fundamentally shaped feminism on both sides of the Wall in ways that made solidarity difficult, if not at times impossible.

But these were also productive confrontations. Feminism transformed in response to the criticisms of women of colour and migrants. Shelter work improved its service provision in response to the needs of residents. And since reunification, feminism and women's equality in Germany have been shaped by the experiences of women from the former East. Feminism in 2022 is not what it was in 1968, 1976, or 1989. It has grown, evolved and developed over time. As this book has shown, this trajectory has not always been linear, but, like a kaleidoscope, has been refracted, inflected and pluralised.

One major question still remains: to what extent did feminists participate in the co-optation of their politics? Certainly, the West Berlin shelter group wanted public funds for their project. They sought to work with politicians and the government and they shaped their project to speak to them. Stories of innocent, victimised women and violent (foreign) men made domestic violence legible to a political structure built on racialised, heteropatriarchal gender norms. It was these stories that were then picked up by the mass media, who depoliticised them and removed the feminist political scaffolding. There are even cases when activists decontextualised their own work from its feminist origins – all in order to ensure support for their project.

But why does co-optation matter? Is it really important that supporting shelter work was less about empowering women and challenging inequality and more about protecting vulnerable and powerless women? This may seem like a reasonable trade-off, given the significance of shelter work to helping women experiencing abuse. However, as criminological research has shown, patterns and preferences in policing and arresting practices are deeply interwoven with gender norms. Women who act in stereotypically 'unfeminine' ways in front of police (for example, shouting, swearing, fighting) are more likely to face arrest or reprimand, or simply not be helped by law enforcement.[16] By embedding ideas about how abused women should act or look and about why women should be protected from violence, feminist mainstreaming has had a tangible impact on women's rights. As the comparison with reproductive rights makes clear: women have equal rights on the basis of being women, not necessarily out of an allegiance to women's fundamental rights to physical and personal autonomy and self-determination.

A foundational premise of this book is that the stories we tell matter. How we narrate the history of feminism is just as important as the stories we tell to advocate for women's rights. As Clare Hemmings argues, histories of feminism's failures validate and feed into other narratives that label feminism as outdated, ineffectual and unnecessary. They perpetuate the idea that women's rights have been secured and that feminism is 'over'.[17] At a time when feminism is under renewed attack, such narratives must be challenged and resisted. That is precisely what this book has sought to do. In telling the history of feminist activism against domestic violence, this book has analysed the mixed legacies of a movement, its successes, failures, divisions, solidarities and the extent of its transformations over time.

In doing so, it has revealed the ways in which feminists both contested and complied with normative structures of power, and has shown the preconditions and boundaries of the fight for gender equality. But advocating for the rights of women to live free from violence on the basis of gendered and racialised images only limited the horizons of women's rights. It tied gender equality to a particular vision of femininity, in a way that has impacted the extension of women's reproductive rights and to this day feeds into transphobic 'feminisms' that seek to protect only cis-gendered women.

It also underscored racist messages about the incompatibility of foreign masculinities with liberal German society in ways that continue to echo to this day. In the first few days of 2016, reports emerged of widespread attacks – sexual assaults, muggings, rapes – on women during the New Year's Eve celebrations in Cologne. According to the media, responsibility for the attacks lay squarely on the shoulders of non-German, refugee and migrant men from North Africa and the Middle East and their failure to assimilate. Feminism, and support for (German) women's rights, became entwined with racist pronouncements about the failure of multiculturalism and the incompatibility of Islam with liberal values in much of the commentary on the incidents.[18] Alice Schwarzer even endorsed such renderings when she blamed the attacks on 'predominantly Algerian, Moroccan,

---

[16] Eve Buzawa and Carl Buzawa, *Domestic Violence: The Criminal Justice Response* (3rd ed.) (Thousand Oaks: Sage Publications, 2003).

[17] Clare Hemmings, *Why Stories Matter: The Political Grammar of Feminist Theory* (Durham: Duke University Press, 2011).

[18] Sabine Hark and Paula-Irene Villa, *The Future of Difference. Beyond the Toxic Entanglement of Racism, Sexism and Feminism* (trans. Sophie Lewis) (London: Verso Books, 2020).

North African men', who were not accustomed to 'European' norms and were 'in the majority undocumented'.[19]

The attacks in Cologne and the subsequent media discussion reveal the cost of feminist mainstreaming. As this book has shown, at the heart of support for domestic and gender-based violence initiatives was a reinscription of heteropatriarchal, racialised and class-based norms – the very power hierarchies that enable, silence and conceal violence against women and perpetuate a system in which some lives are valued more than others. This is why the stories told about feminism, and also the stories feminism tells, matter. Because feminism should not be a weapon used against racialised men, the trans community, or migrants.

But this story is far from over. While writing this book, the introduction of Covid-19 lockdown measures put intimate and familial relationships under intense strain and contributed to a massive increase in the numbers of women murdered by their husbands, rising calls to domestic violence hotlines and overburdened women's shelters across Europe and the United States. At such a time, it is clear that the legacies of feminist transformations, from the *Tomatenwurf* to Cologne, have never been more pressing.

---

[19] Alice Schwarzer, *Düsseldorfer Reden*, 2019. Accessed on 12 May 2022: https://vimeo.com/333390 553. See also discussion of Schwarzer in Hark and Villa, *The Future of Difference*.

Bibliography

Archives

Archiv des Liberalismus, Gummersbach (AdL)
Bundesarchiv Berlin (BArch)
Bundesarchiv Koblenz (BArch-K)
Bundesfilmarchiv, Berlin (BArch-Film)
Bundesbeauftragte für die Unterlagen des Staatssicherheitsdienstes der ehemaligen
  Deutschen Demokratischen Republik, Berlin (BStU)
Frauenforschungs-, -bildungs- und -informationszentrum, Berlin (FFBIZ)
Grünes Gedächtnis Archiv, Berlin (GG)
Landesarchiv Berlin (LAB)
Papiertiger, Berlin
Robert Havemann Archiv, Berlin (RHG)
Spinnboden Archiv, Berlin
United Nations Archive, New York (UN-Arch)

Interviews

All interviewees have been fully anonymised.
'Jennifer', social worker, Leipzig, 17 October 2013
'Sophie', social worker, Berlin, 4 February 2014
'Dagmar', sociologist, Osnabrück, 5 August 2013
'Joachim', social worker, Berlin, 30 January 2014

Published Sources

Primary

'Aber scheiden lassen will er sich nicht'. *Schwäbische Zeitung*, 10 May 1977.
'Abhängig von der Gunst des Mannes. Initiative für Ausländerinnen'. *Die Tageszeitung*, 18 January 1983.

'Abtreibung: Aufstand der Schwestern'. *Der Spiegel*, 11 March 1974.

'Abtreibung. Bayrisches Landrecht'. *Der Spiegel*, 11 September 1988.

' "Asyl" für mißhandelte Frauen'. *Neue Zeit*, 6 September 1990, p. 7.

'Aus der Resolution an die Regierungen und Parlamente beider deutscher Staaten'. *Für Dich*, No. 20 (1990).

Bebel, August. *Woman Under Socialism*, trans. Daniel de Leon (New York: Schocken Books, 1971).

von Behr, Sophie. 'Darum haben Männer im Frauenhaus nichts zu suchen', *EMMA*, No. 6 (1978), pp. 32–36.

Benard, Cheryl and Edit Schlaffer. *Die ganz gewöhnliche Gewalt in der Ehe. Texte zu einer Soziologie von Macht und Liebe* (Hamburg: Rowohlt Taschenbuch Verlag, 1978).

Bennhold, Katrin. '20 Years After Fall of Wall, Women of Former East Germany Thrive', *New York Times*, 5 October 2010. Accessed on 20 October 2015: http://www.nytimes.com/2010/10/06/world/europe/06iht-letter.html?_r=0

Benser, Günter and Gerhard Naumann, eds. *Dokumente zur Geschichte der SED, 1971–1986*, 3rd ed. (Berlin: Dietz Verlag, 1986).

von Bentheim, Ursula. 'Senatorin Ilse Reichel will sich für ein zweites Frauenhaus stark machen', *Die Welt*, 26 June 1979.

Beyer, Marina. *Frauenreport '90. Im Auftrag der Beauftragten des Ministerrates für die Gleichstellung von Frauen und Männern* (Berlin: Verlag die Wissenschaft Berlin, 1990).

BIG e.V. *Berliner Interventionsprojekt gegen häusliche Gewalt. Alte Ziele auf neuen Wegen. Ein neuartiges Projekt gegen Männergewalt an Frauen stellt sich vor* (Berlin: BIG e.V., 1996).

BIG Koordinierung. *10 Jahre Gewaltschutzgesetz* (Berlin: BIG e.V, 2012).

Bodamer, Joachim. *Schule der Ehe* (Freiburg: Herder-Bücherei, 1960).

Bovenschen, Sylvia, Sigrid Damm-Rüger and Sybille Plogstedt. 'Antiautoritärer Anspruch und Frauenemanzipation - Die Revolte in der Revolte'. 1 June 1988. Accessed on 10 November 2020: http://www.infopartisan.net/archive/1968/index.html

Bovet, Theodor. *Die Ehe – ihre Krise und Neuwerdung* (Tübingen: Katzmann Verlag, 1951).

Brot und Rosen. *Frauenhandbuch Nr. 1. Abtreibung und Verhütungsmittel* (Berlin: Brot und Rosen Selbstverlag, 1972).

Brot und Rosen. ' "Einladung" (1974)', *FrauenMediaTurm*. Accessed on 10 November 2020: https://frauenmediaturm.de/wp-content/uploads/2018/04/74_0a_EinlBrotRosen.jpg.

Buhmann, Inga. *Ich habe mir eine Geschichte geschrieben* (Frankfurt am Main: Zweitausendeins, 1983).

Bundesministerium für Familie, Senioren, Frauen und Jugend. *Aktionsplan der Bundesregierung zur Bekämpfung von Gewalt gegen Frauen. December 1999* (Berlin: Bundesministerium für Familie, Senioren, Frauen und Jugend, 1999).

Bundesministerium für Familie, Senioren, Frauen und Jugend and Bundesministerium der Justiz und für Verbraucherschutz. *Mehr Schutz bei häuslicher Gewalt: Informationen zum Gewaltschutzgesetz* (Berlin: Bundesministerium für Familie, Senioren, Frauen und Jugend, 2003).

Bundesministerium für Familie, Senioren, Frauen und Jugend. *Bericht der Bundesregierung zur Situation der Frauenhäuser, Fachberatungsstellen und anderer Unterstützungsangebote für gewaltbetroffene Frauen und deren Kinder* (Berlin: Bundesministerium für Familie, Senioren, Frauen und Jugend, 2013).

Bundesministerium für Familie, Senioren, Frauen und Jugend. Formen der Gewalt erkennen, 22 December 2021. Accessed on 3 August 2022: https://www.bmfsfj.de/bmfsfj/themen/gleichstellung/frauen-vor-gewalt-schuetzen/haeusliche-gewalt/formen-der-gewalt-erkennen-80642

BVerfG, Order of the Second Senate of 28 May 1993 – 2 BvF 2/90 –, paras. 1–434.

'Das sind politisch motivierte Prozesse'. *Der Spiegel*, 19 September 1988.

'Das zweite Frauenhaus könnte schon im Januar seine Pforten öffnen'. *Der Tagesspiegel*, 4 December1978.

Deutscher Bundestag. Stenographischer Bericht, 99. Sitzung. Bonn, 25 June 1992.

'Die rose Zeiten sind vorbei'. *Der Spiegel*, 25 November 1968.

'Die sind tierisch hinterm Mond'. *Der Spiegel*, 14 May 1990, p. 70.

Dobash, Emerson and Russell Dobash. *Violence Against Wives: A Case Against the Patriarchy* (New York: Free Press, 1979).

Drakulić, Slavenka. *How We Survived Communism and Even Laughed* (Hutchinson: London, 1992).

Dutschke, Gretchen. *Wir hatten ein barbarisches, schönes Leben. Rudi Dutschke: Eine Biographie* (Cologne: Kiepenheuer and Witsch, 1996).

Ehrhardt, Justus. *Strassen ohne Ende* (Berlin: Agis Verlag, 1931).

'Endlich: Vergewaltigung in der Ehe gilt künftig als Verbrechen'. *Die Zeit*, 16 May 1997.

Eßbach, Gabriela and Vera Fünfstück. *Frauen mit Gewalterfahrung in der ehemaligen DDR: Wahrnehmungszugänge und Bewältigungsstratigen. Eine Untersuchung aus dem Blickwinkel autonomer Frauenhausarbeit in Sachsen* (Diplomarbeit, Evangelischen Fachhochschule für Sozialarbeit Dresden, 1997).

European Union Agency for Fundamental Rights. *Violence Against Women: An EU-Wide Survey* (Luxembourg: Publications Office of the European Union, 2014).

'Frauen befürchten historischen Rückschritt'. *Die Tageszeitung*, 2 May 1990.

' "Frauen gemeinsam sind stark", Flugblatt, 1973'. *FrauenMediaTurm*. Accessed on 10 November 2020: https://frauenmediaturm.de/wp-content/uploads/2018/04/73_D6_Rundbrief_gr.jpg.

Frauen gegen Männergewalt. Berliner Frauenhaus für misshandelte Frauen. Erster Erfahrungsbericht (Berlin: Frauenselbstverlag Berlin-West, 1978).

Frauengruppe am Institut für Publizistik. 'Frauen starren stumpfsinnig vor sich hin', *Courage*, No. 2 (1977): p. 35.

Frauen in die Offensive: Texte und Arbeitspapiere der Gruppe 'Lila Offensive' (Berlin: Dietz, 1990).

Frauenjahrbuch '75 (Frankfurt am Main: Verlag Roter Stern, 1975).

Frauenjahrbuch '76 (Munich: Verlag Frauenoffensive, 1976).

'Frauenmißhandlung in der Bundesrepublik. Schrei, wenn du kannst!'. *Das da*, February, 1977.

'Frau lebte wie Sklavin'. *Bonner Rundschau*, 24 April 1975.

Friedan, Betty. *The Feminine Mystique* (New York: W.W. Norton, 2001; originally published 1963).

Gayford, J.J. 'Wife Battering: A Preliminary Survey of 100 Cases', *British Medical Journal*, No. 1 (January 1975): pp. 194–197.

'Gegen Einverleibung der DDR. Für selbstbestimmtes Leben'. *Die Tageszeitung*, 4 September 1990.

Gelles, Richard J. 'Child Abuse as Psychopathology: A Sociological Critique and Reformulation', *American Journal of Orthopsychiatry*, No. 43 (July 1973): pp. 611–621.

Gelles, Richard J. 'Violence in the Family: A Review of Research in the Seventies', *Journal of Marriage and Family*, Vol. 42, No. 4 (1980), pp. 873–885.

'German Law Criminalizes Marital Rape'. *Ms. Magazine*. Accessed on October 29 2015: http://www.msmagazine.com/news/uswirestory.asp?id=4131.

'Gespräch zwischen Margit Brückner, Carole Hagemann-White, Sabine Scheffler und Birgit Rommelspacher', in *Dokumentation Fachforum 2 – Frauenhaus in Bewegung, 20.-22.11.1996* (Berlin: Diakonisches Werk der Evangelischen Kirche in Deutschland, 1996), p. 22.

'Gewalt gegen Frauen'. *Neue Zeit*, 17 September 1990, p. 9.

'Gewalt und Angst in den Familien darf keine private Angelegenheit mehr bleiben'. *Berliner Zeitung*, 25 April 1990, p. 9.

Glowacz, Horst. 'Neue Formen der gerichtlichen Tätigkeit in Zivil- und Familiensachen,' *Neue Justiz*, No. 15 (1960): pp. 493–495.

Grafenhorst, Gabrielle, ed. *Abtreibung. Erfahrungsberichte zu einem Tabu* (Munich: Deutscher Taschenbuch Verlag, 1992).

'Grob geklotzt'. *Der Spiegel*, 4 September 1988.

Gültekin, Neval, Brigitte Schulz and Brigitte Sellach, eds. *Ausländische und deutsche Frauen im Gespräch. Sind wir uns denn so fremd?* 2nd ed. (Berlin: Sub-Rosa-Frauenverlag, 1985).

Gysi, Jutta, Jürgen Dorbritz and Ursula Hespel. *Protokolle und Informationen. Informationen über Ehescheidungen in der DDR, 1/89* (Berlin: Wissenschaftlicher Rat für Sozialpolitik und Demografie, 1989).

'Haben Berliner Beamte kein Verständnis für Frauen in Not? Die Mitarbeiterinnen im Frauenhaus klagen über Ignoranz und Vorurteile'. *Spandauer Volksblatt*, 2 November 1978.

Haffner, Sarah. 'Gewalt in der Ehe: was können Frauen dagegen tun?—eine Dokumentation', *Der Tagesspiegel*, 14 November 1976.

Haffner, Sarah, ed. *Gewalt in der Ehe und was Frauen dagegen tun* (Berlin: Wagenbach, 1981).

Hagemann-White, Carol, Barbara Kavemann, Johanna Kootz, Ute Weinmann, Carola Christine Wildt, Roswitha Burgard and Ursula Scheu. *Hilfen für mißhandelte Frauen: Abschlussbericht der wissenschaftlichen Begleitung des Modellprojekts Frauenhaus Berlin* (Stuttgart: Kohlhamer, 1981).

Hagemann-White, Carol. 'Die Frauenhausbewegung' in *Der große Unterschied. Die neue Frauenbewegung und die siebziger Jahre*, edited by Kristine von Soden (Berlin (West): Elefanten Press, 1988), pp. 48–52.

'Häusliche Gewalt und Corona. Eine doppelte Bedrohung'. *Taz*, 17 May 2020.

Haug, Frigga. 'The Women's Movement in West Germany', *New Left Review*, Vol. 155, No.1 (1986): pp. 50–74.

Heinze, Gerhard. *Die Tätigkeit der Konfliktkommissionen im VEB Transformatorenwerk 'Karl Liebknecht' Berlin-Oberschöneweide bei der Erziehung aller Werktätigen des Betriebes zur Unterstützung des Produktionsaufgebotes im Kampf um eine hohe Qualität der Arbeit* (Diplomarbeit, Hochschule der Deutschen Gewerkschaften 'Fritz Heckert', 1962).

Held, Ginger. 'Gustav, der Knüppel und die Folgen', *Frankfurter Rundschau*, 13 November 1976.

Held, Monika. 'Warum schlagen eigentlich so viele Männer ihre Frauen? Von kleinauf heißt's: Du bist nichts und er ist alles', *Metall*, 14 December 1976.

Helwerth, Ulrike. 'Für uns steht jetzt alles auf dem Spiel', *Die Tageszeitung*, 30 April 1990.

Helwerth, Ulrike. 'Abschied vom feministischen Paradies', *WeibBlick*, No. 2 (1992): pp. 18–20.

Helwerth, Ulrike and Gislinde Schwarz. *Von Muttis und Emanzen. Feministinnen in Ost- und Westdeutschland* (Frankfurt am Main: Fischer Taschenbuch Verlag, 1995).

'Hexenjagd'. *EMMA*, No. 9 (1988), p. 6.

Hirsch, Rudolf. *Eros and Ehe vor Gericht: Gerichtsberichte* (Berlin: Verlag das Neue Berlin, 1980).

Huter, Carl Heinrich. *Wie Ehen glücklich werden* (Stuttgart: Annelies Huter Verlag, 1953).

'Im überfüllten Frauenhaus muss im Keller übernachtet werden'. *Tagesspiegel*, 26 June 1979.

Initiativgruppe 218 Letzte Versuch, 'Rundbrief. 20 February 1974', *FrauenMedia Turm*. Accessed on 10 November 2020: https://frauenmediaturm.de/wp-cont ent/uploads/2018/06/Rundbrief_Aktion_letzter_Versuch_1974.jpg.

'Irgendwo im Ostteil der Stadt —Frauenhaus "Bora"'. *Neues Deutschland*, 6 September 1990, p. 7.

'Jagd auf Frauen'. *EMMA*, No. 11 (1988), p. 9.

Janßen, Karl-Hein. 'Keine Abtreibung auf dem Bildschirm? Warum und wie eine Panorama-Sendung verhindert wurde', *Die Zeit*, 15 March 1974.

Jent, Linda and Regula Wyss. *Selbstverteidigung für Frauen* (Basel: Mond Buch, 1984).

Jones, Kelsie Brynn. 'Trans-Exclusionary Radical Feminism: What exactly is it and why does it hurt?', *The Huffington Post Blog*, 2 February 2016. Accessed on 6 March 2016: http://www.huffingtonpost.com/kelsie-brynn-jones/transexclusionary-radical-terf_b_5632332.html

Judt, Matthias, ed. *DDR-Geschichte in Dokumenten. Beschlüsse, Berichte, interne Materialien und Alltagszeugnisse* (Berlin: Christoph Links Verlag, 1997).

Kahlau, Cordula, ed. *Aufbruch! Frauenbewegung in der DDR: Dokumentation* (Munich: Frauenoffensive, 1990).

Kaltenbach, Karin. 'Karin Kaltenbach über die Mentorin des Frauenhauses Barbara von Renthe-Fink', *Feministische Projekte in Berlin, 1974–78*. Accessed on 10 November 2020: https://feministberlin.de/gewalt/frauenhaus/

Kätzel, Ute. *Die 68erinnen. Porträt einer rebellischen Frauengeneration* (Berlin: Rowohlt, 2002).

Kavemann, Barbara, Beate Leopold, Gesa Schirrmacher and Carol Hagemann-White. *Modelle der Kooperation gegen häusliche Gewalt: "Wir sind ein Kooperationsmodell, kein Konfrontationsmodell"; Ergebnisse der wissenschaftlichen Begleitung des Berliner Interventionsprojekts gegen häusliche Gewalt (BIG)* (Stuttgart: Kohlhammer, 2001).

'(K)eine Chance für längst notwendige Frauenprojekte?'. *Berliner Zeitung*, 20 June 1990, p. 7.

Kenawi, Samirah. *Frauengruppen in der DDR der 80er Jahre. Eine Dokumentation* (Berlin: GrauZone, 1995).

'Kinder verlassen tagsüber das überfüllte Frauenhaus. Aber Trennung von Müttern wird abgelehnt – warum kein Mann im Hause arbeitet – dokumentation vorbereitet'. *Tagesspiegel*, 7 February 1978.

Klässner, Bärbel. 'Feminismus-Geschichte eines Wortes', *Für Dich*, No. 6 (1990), pp. 18–19.

Knietzsch, Horst. 'Aufgefordert, über den anderen nachzudenken „Bis dass der Tod euch scheidet", ein DEFA-Film', *Neues Deutschland*, 29 May 1979.

Langer, Sabine, Felix Posorski and Rudolph Winkler, *Die Konfliktkommission hat eingeladen…Über die Tätigkeit der Konflikt- und Schiedskommissionen* (Berlin: Staatsverlag der Deutschen Demokratischen Republik, 1984).

Lehmann, Nadja. 'Projektvorstellung 'Interkulturelles Frauenhaus'', *Berlin Forum Gewaltprävention, BFG*, No. 1 (2002): pp. 116–123.

'Leipziger Frauenhaus öffnet seine Türen.' *Neues Deutschland*, 8 October 1990.

Leonhardt, Rudolf Walter. 'Die Frauen als Opfer der Männer', *Die Zeit*, 27 February 1976.

Lenz, Ilse, ed. *Die Neue Frauenbewegung in Deutschland: Abschied vom kleinen Unterschied. Eine Quellensammlung*, 2nd ed. (Wiesbaden: VS Verlag für Sozialwissenschaften, 2010).

Louis, Chantal. 'Ein Blick ins Frauenhaus', *EMMA*, No. 1 (2010): pp. 125–129.

'Männerfrage wird gestellt'. *Berliner Zeitung*, 4 June 1990, p. 7.

Mansfeld, Cornelia. 'Ausländerinnen im Frauenhaus', *Courage*, No. 4 (1978): p. 18.

Meinhof, Ulrike. 'Die Frauen im SDS', *Konkret*, 7 October 1968.

Menschik, Jutta. 'Schrei Leise. Gewalt gegen Frauen. Erst zögernd beginnen die Betroffenen darueber zu sprechen', *Deutsche Volkszeitung*, 23 September 1976.

Ministerium der Justiz und Bundesvorstand des FDGB, eds. *Gesellschaftliche Gerichte: Konfliktkommission, Schiedskommission* (Berlin: Verlag Tribüne, 1989).

'NDR sendet Abtreibungsfilm allein'. *Frankfurter Neue Presse*, 13 March 1974.

'One Legacy of Merkel? Angry East German Men Fueling the Far Right'. *New York Times*, 5 November 2018. Accessed on 10 November 2020: https://www.nytimes.com/2018/11/05/world/europe/merkel-east-germany-nationalists-populism.html.

von Paczensky, Susanne. *Gemischte Gefühle: Von Frauen, die ungewollt schwanger sind* (Munich: C.H. Beck, 1987).

Perincioli, Cristina. *Berlin wird feministisch! Das Beste, was von der 68er Bewegung blieb* (Berlin: Querverlag, 2015).

Pfeil, Ulrike. 'In der Festung des Mannes. Von den Schwierigkeiten, ein "privates" Problem öffentlich anzugehen', *Stuttgarter Zeitung*, 22 May 1978.

Pizzey, Erin. *Scream Quietly or the Neighbours will Hear* (Harmondsworth: Penguin Books, 1974).

'Problem der Misshandlung in Familien bewusst gemacht'. *Der Tagesspiegel*, 2 November 1978.

'Protokoll zum Plenum des Bundesfrauenkongresses am 12. März 1972 in Frankfurt/M', *FrauenMediaTurm*. Accessed on 10 November 2020: https://frauenmediaturm.de/neue-frauenbewegung/protokoll-plenum-bundesfrauenkongress/

Quast, Günter. 'Eine Meldung der NDR-Pressestelle', 11 March 1974.

Rapp, Tobias and Claudia Voigt. 'Kinder sind die Falle', *Der Spiegel*, 10 January 2011.

Rebetsky, Ursula and Arthur Boeck. 'Wer seine Frau schlägt, schlägt die Genossenschaft. Mittelalter und Neuzeit in Damsdorf. Nur eine Familienangelegenheit?', *Neues Deutschland*, 9 February 1962.

'Rechtsprechung. Familienrecht'. *Neue Justiz*, No. 21 (1963): p. 697.

Reichel, Ilse. 'Vorbemerkung' in *Gewalt in Familien: Erfahrungen mit Krisenzentren für mißhandelte Frauen in England*, edited by Ilse Haase-Schur (Berlin: Landespressedienst, 9 July 1976).

Riemann, Tord. *Recht und Gesetz im Sozialismus. Eine Information über die Rechtspflege in der Deutschen Demokratischen Republik* (Berlin: Panorama DDR, 1976).

'Runder Tisch für Frauen'. *Die Tageszeitung*, 6 August 1990.

Russell, Diana E.H. 'Report on the International Trial on Crimes Against Women,' *Frontiers: A Journal of Women's Studies*, Vol. 2, No. 1 (1977): pp. 1–6.

Sander, Helke. 'Der Seele ist das Gemeinsame eigen, das sich mehrt,' in *Wie weit flog die Tomate?: Eine 68erinnen-Gala der Reflexion* (Berlin: Heinrich Böll Stiftung, 1999): pp. 43–56.

Sandole-Staroste, Ingrid. *Women in Transition. Between Socialism and Capitalism* (London: Praeger, 2002).

Sanger, Margaret. *An Autobiography* (London: Victor Gollancz, 1939).

Schenk, Christina and Christiane Schindler. 'Frauenbewegung in Ostdeutschland – eine kleine Einführung,' *Beiträge zur feministischen Theorie und Praxis: Feminis-muss*, No. 35 (1993): pp. 131–146.

Schenk, Christine and Christiane Schindler. 'Frauenbewegung in Ostdeutschland – Innenansichten,' in *Gefährtinnen der Macht. Politische Partizipation von Frauen im vereinigten Deutschland – eine Zwischenbilanz*, edited by Eva Maleck-Lewy and Virginia Penrose (Berlin: Edition Sigma, 1995): pp. 183–203.

Schippke, Ulrich. 'Mein Mann hat mich vergewaltigt,' *Stern* No. 17 (1976): pp. 68–73.

Schlußbericht der Enquete-Kommission 'Überwindung der Folgen der SED-Diktatur im Prozeß der deutschn Einheit'. Deutscher Bundestag, 13. Wahlperiode. Drucksache 13/11000, 10 June 1998.

Schneider, Patricia, Ulrike Kreyssig, Dorothea Hecht and Monika Trieselmann. *Von 1995 bis 2005. 10 Jahre BIG, Berliner Interventionszentrale bei häuslicher Gewalt* (Berlin: BIG e.V., 2005).

Schrader-Klebert, Karin. 'Die kulturelle Revolution der Frau', *Kursbuch*, No. 17 (June 1969): pp. 1–46.

'Schreien nützt nichts. Brutalität in der Ehe—Bericht von Sarah Haffner'. *Frankfurter Rundschau*, 27 April 1976.

'Schrei leise'. *Der Spiegel*, 18 January 1976, pp. 112–15.

'Schrei leise'. *Hessische Allgemein*, 25 September 1976.

Schröder, Gerhard. 'SPD strebt besseren Schutz für Opfer von Sexualdelikten an', *SPD informiert*, 17 February 1984.

Schultz, Leroy G. 'The Wife Assaulter', *Journal of Social Therapy*, Vol. 6, No. 2 (1960): pp. 103–111.

Schwarz, Gislinde. 'Kein einig Frauenland: Die Frauenbewegung in den neuen Bundesländern,' in *Die Bürgerbewegungen in der DDR und in den ostdeutschen Bundesländern*, edited by Gerda Haufe and Karl Bruckmeier (Opladen: Westdeutsche Verlag, 1993): pp. 219–239.

Schwarzer, Alice. 'Ein Tag im Haus für geschlagene Frauen', *EMMA*, March 1977, p. 9.

Schwarzer, Alice. 'Nach 100 Jahren wieder Frauenklinik', *EMMA*, May 1977, p. 9.

Schwarzer, Alice. *So fing es an! 10 Jahre Frauenbewegung* (Cologne: Emma-Frauenverlags GmbH, 1981).

Schwarzer, Alice. 'Politische Prozesse von Weimar bis Memmingen', *EMMA*, No. 4 (1989): pp. 4–6.

Schwarzer, Alice. *Lebenslauf* (Cologne: Kiepenheuer and Witsch, 2011).

Schwarzer, Alice. *Düsseldorfer Reden*, 2019. Accessed on 12 May 2022: https://vimeo.com/333390553.

Sekretariat der Deutschen Bischofskonferenze, ed. *Wähle das Leben. Hirtenwort der am Grabe des heiligen Bonifatius versammelten deutschen Bischöffe*, 22 September 1982.

Snell, John, Richard J. Rosenwald and Ames Robey. 'The Wifebeater's Wife: A Study of Family Interaction', *Archives of General Psychiatry*, Vol. 11, No. 2 (1964): pp. 107–112.

'Soziale Hilfe für geprügelte Frauen'. *Die demokratische Gemeinde*, July 1976: pp. 579–580.

'Spandau: zweites Frauenhaus'. *Spandauer Volksblatt*, 26 June 1979.

Spinetta, John J. and David Rigler. 'The Child Abusing Parent: A Psychological Review', *Psychological Bulletin* 77 (April 1972): pp. 296–304.

'Sprengsatz für die Moral'. *Der Spiegel*, 18 March 1974.

Statkowa, Susanne. 'Zuflucht ohne Recht', *Berliner Zeitung*, 5 August 1978.

'Statt Blumen'. *Der Spiegel*, 25 November 1974, pp. 160–162.

Steinert, Erika and Ute Straub. *Interaktionsort Frauenhaus. Möglichkeiten und Grenzen einen feministischen Projektes* (Heidelberg: Verlag des Wunderhorn, 1988).

Straub, Ute. *Interaktionsort Frauenhaus. Institutionalisierung und Professionalisierung des Frauenhausprojekts* (Ph.D. dissertation, Ruprecht-Karls University, 1987).

'Tabuthema wird nun endlich öffentlich diskutiert'. *Metall*, 14 December 1976.

Taub, Amanda and Jane Bradley. 'As Domestic Abuse Rises, UK Failings Leave Victims in Peril', *New York Times*, 2 July 2020.

Tekin, Ayse. 'Unterschiede wahren, Zusammenarbeit möglich machen' in *Beiträge zur feministischen Theorie und Praxis*, No. 17 (1994), pp. 103–110.

Tetzner, Gerti. *Karen W.*, 2nd ed. (West Berlin: Luchterhand, 1976).

'Über uns'. *Papatya: anonyme Kriseneinrichtung für Mädchen und junge Frauen mit Migrationshintergrund*. Accessed on 30 August 2015: http://www.papatya.org/ueber-uns.html.

United Nations. *Report of the World Conference of the United Nations Decade for Women: Equality, Development and Peace*, 14–30 July 1980. Accessed on 19 October 2015: http://www.un.org/womenwatch/daw/beijing/otherconferences/Copenhagen/Copenhagen%20Full%20Optimized.pdf.

United Nations, World Conference to review and appraise the achievements of the United Nations Decade for Women: Equality, Development and Peace. *Nairobi Forward-looking Strategies for the Advancement of Women*, 26 July 1985. Accessed 19 October 2015: http://www.un-documents.net/nflsaw.htm.

United Nations. General Assembly Resolution 48/104, *Declaration on the Elimination of Violence against Women*, A/Res/48/104, 23 February 1994.

United Nations, Economic and Social Council. *Report of the Special Rapporteur on violence against women, its causes and consequences, Ms. Radhika Coomaraswamy, submitted in accordance with Commission on Human Rights resolution 1995/85*, E/CN.4/1996/53, 5 February 1996. Accessed on 29 October 2015: http://www.awf.or.jp/pdf/h0003.pdf.

'Unter dem Mantel des Helfenwollens: Fünf Szenen aus dem Frauenhausalltag'. *Courage*, No. 11 (1981): p. 16.

'Von hinten gegriffen'. *Der Spiegel*, 24 February 1975.

Voss, Peter. 'Meine Meinung: Schläge und Prügel-das haben unsere Frauen nicht verdient', *Neue Welt*, 17 June 1976, p. 2.

Walter, Birgit. 'Lebensweise im Kapitalismus: Frauenhäuser als letzte Zuflucht. Zunehmende Brutalität im Ehealltag in westeuropäischen Ländern', *Berliner Zeitung*, 21 November 1981, p. 4.

Weiss, Ilja. 'Warum Männer Frauen schlagen: Strafe häufigstes Motiv – Kaum Folgen für die Täter', *Darmstädter Echo*, 18 December 1976.

'Wer gibt schon gern zu. Daß alles kaputt ist?'. *Neue Zeit*, 1 June 1990, p. 3.

'Wer glaubt noch an die Revolution?'. *Die Tageszeitung*, 10 February 1981.

White, Penny. 'Why I No Longer Hate TERFs', *The Feminist Current*. Accessed on 2 February 2016: https://www.feministcurrent.com/2015/11/10/why-i-no-longer-hate-terfs/.

'Wir haben abgetrieben!'. *Stern*, 6 June 1971.

'Wir machen das Haus zu'. *Courage*, No. 1 (1981): pp. 4–5.

Wolfram, Margarete. 'Die Grundung von Ehe und Familie erfordert hohe gesellschaftliche Verantwortung', *Der Schöffe*, No. 22 (1975): pp. ix–xiv.

World Health Organization, on behalf of the United Nations Inter-Agency Working Group on Violence Against Women Estimation and Data (VAW-IAWGED). *Violence Against Women Prevalence Estimates, 2018: Global, Regional and National Prevalence Estimates for Intimate Partner Violence Against Women and Global and Regional Prevalence Estimates for Non-Partner Sexual Violence Against Women* (Geneva: World Health Organization, 2021).

Zentrale Informationsstelle autonomer Frauenhäuser. 'Geschichte'. Accessed on 3 August 2022: https://autonome-frauenhaeuser-zif.de/autonome-frauenhaeuser/#geschichte.

'Zuflucht für misshandelte Frauen'. *Der Abend*, 1 November 1976.

'Zufluchtswohnungen für Frauen in Berlin'. *Die Tageszeitung*, 24 July 1990.

'Zug gegen die Wand'. *Der Spiegel*, 26 August 1990.

'Zweites Frauenhaus noch ohne finanzielle Hilfe'. *Morgenpost*, 24 January 1979.

'329 Mediziner bezichtigen sich des Verstoßes gegen Paragraph 218 "Hiermit erkläre ich …"'. *Der Spiegel*, 11 March 1974, p. 30.

'§218. Warum die CDU angst davor hat'. *EMMA*, No. 2 (1983): p. 6.

Secondary

Abrams, Lynn. 'Martyrs or Matriarchs? Working-Class Women's Experience of Marriage in Germany before the First World War', *Women's History Review*, Vol. 1, No.3 (1992): pp. 357–376.

Abrams, Lynn. 'Concubinage, Cohabitation and the Law: Class and Gender Relations in Nineteenth Century Germany', Vol. 5, No. 1 (1993): pp. 81–100.

Abrams, Lynn and Elizabeth Harvey, eds. *Gender Relations in German History: Power, Agency and Experience from the Sixteenth to the Twentieth Century* (Durham: Duke University Press, 1996).

Ahmed, Sara. 'Happiness and Queer Politics', *World Picture* No. 3 (2009): pp. 1–20.

Aleksander, Karin. *Frauen und Geschlechterverhältnisse in der DDR und in den neuen Bundesländern. Eine Bibliographie* (Berlin: Trafo, 2005).

Allen, Ann Taylor. 'Mothers of the New Generation: Adele Schreiber, Helene Stöcker and the Evolution of a German Idea of Motherhood, 1900–1914', *Signs*, Vol. 10, No. 3 (1985): pp. 418–438.

Allen, Ann Taylor. *Feminism and Motherhood in Germany, 1800–1914* (New Brunswick: Rutgers University Press, 1991).

Allen, Ann Taylor. 'Feminism and Eugenics in Germany and Britain, 1900–1940. A Comparative Perspective', *German Studies Review*, Vol. 23, No. 3 (2000): pp. 477–505.

Allen, Ann Taylor. *Women in Twentieth-Century Europe* (Basingstoke and New York: Palgrave Macmillan, 2007).

Alemdaroğlu, Ayça. 'Politics of the Body and Eugenic Discourse in Early Republican Turkey', *Body and Society*, Vol. 11, No. 3 (2005): pp. 61–76.

Altbach, Edith, Jeanette Clausen, Dagmar Schultz and Naomi Stephan, eds. *German Feminism: Readings in Politics and Literature* (Albany: State University of New York Press, 1984).

Ammermüller, Andreas and Andrea Maria Weber. 'Educational Attainment and Returns to Education in Germany– An Analysis by Subject of Degree, Gender and Region', *Discussion Paper No. 05-17* (Mannheim: Zentrum für Europäische Wirtschaftsforschung GmBH, 2005).

Arias, Ileana and Steven R.H. Beach. 'Validity of Self-Reports of Marital Violence', *Journal of Family Violence*, Vol. 2, No. 2 (1987): pp. 139–149.

Attwood, Lynne. *Gender and Housing in Soviet Russia: Private Life in a Public Space* (Manchester: Manchester University Press, 2010).

Bayly, C.A., Sven Beckert, Matthew Connelly, Isabel Hofmeyr, Wendy Kozol and Patricia Seed. 'AHR Conversation: On Transnational History', *American Historical Review*, Vol. 111, No. 5 (2006): pp. 1441–1464.

Beck, Birgit. 'The Military Trials of Sexual Crimes Committed by Soldiers in the Wehrmacht, 1939–1944' in *Homefront: The Military, War and Gender in Twentieth-Century Germany*, edited by Karen Hagemann and Stefanie Schüler-Springorum (New York: Berg, 2002): pp. 255–274.

von Behren, Dirk. 'Kurze Geschichte des Paragrafen 218 Strafgesetzbuch', *Aus Politik und Zeitgeschichte*, Vol. 20 (2019): pp. 12–19.

Behrend, Hanna. 'East German Women – Chief Losers in German Unification' in *Family, Women, and Employment in Central-Eastern Europe*, edited by Barbara Łobodzińska (Westport: Greenwood Press, 1995): pp. 113–122.

Bergen, Raquel Kennedy, Jeffrey L. Edleson and Claire M. Renzetti. *Violence Against Women: Classic Papers* (Boston: Pearson, 2005).

Betts, Paul. *Within Walls: Private Life in the German Democratic Republic* (New York: Oxford University Press, 2010).

Betts, Paul. '1989 at Thirty. A Recast Legacy', *Past and Present*, Vol. 244, No. 1 (2019): pp. 271–305.

Bielby, Clare. *Violent Women in Print: Representations in the West German Print Media of the 1960s and 1970s* (Rochester: Camden House, 2012).

Biess, Frank. *Homecomings: Returning POWs and the Legacies of Defeat in Postwar Germany* (Princeton: Princeton University Press, 2006).

Biess, Frank and Astrid M. Eckert. 'Why Do We Need New Narratives for the History of the Federal Republic', *Central European History*, Vol. 52, No. 1 (2019): pp. 1–18.

Bingham, Adrian. *Gender, Modernity, and the Popular Press in Inter-war Britain* (Oxford: Oxford University Press, 2004).

Boak, Helen. *Women in the Weimar Republic* (Manchester: Manchester University Press, 2013).

Bock, Gisela. 'Racism and Sexism in Nazi Germany' in *When Biology Became Destiny: Women in Weimar and Nazi Germany*, edited by Renate Bridenthal, Atina Grossmann and Marion Kaplan (New York: Monthly Review Press, 1984): pp. 271–296.

Bock, Gisela. 'Die Frauen und der Nationalsozialismus: Bemerkungen zu einem Buch von Claudia Koonz', *Geschichte und Gesellschaft*, Vol. 15, No. 4 (1989): pp. 563–579.

Bock, Jessica. *Frauenbewegung in Ostdeutschland. Aufbruch, Revolte und Transformation in Leipzig 1980-2000* (Halle: Mitteldeutscher Verlag, 2020).

Boelmann, Barbara, Anna Raute and Uta Schönberg. 'Wind of Change? Cultural Determinants of Maternal Labor Supply', *Working Paper No. 914* (London: Queen Mary University London, School of Economics and Finance, 2020).

Böhm, Tatiana. 'The Women's Question as a Democratic Question: In Search of Civil Society' in *Gender Politics and Post-Communism: Reflections from Eastern Europe and the Former Soviet Union*, edited by Nanette Funk and Magda Mueller (New York: Routledge, 1993): pp. 151–159.

Bonfiglioli, Chiara. 'Communisms, Generations and Waves. The Cases of Italy, Yugoslavia and Cuba' in *Gender, Generations and Communism in Central and Eastern Europe and Beyond*, edited by Anna Artwińska and Agnieszka Mrozik (New York: Routledge, 2020): pp. 66–81.

Bösch, Frank, ed. *Geteilte Geschichte: Ost- und Westdeutschland 1970–2000* (Göttingen: Vandenhoek and Ruprecht, 2015).

Bourke, Joanna. *Rape: A History from 1860 to the Present Day* (London: Virago, 2007).

Boxer, Marilyn J. and Jean H. Quataert, eds. *Socialist Women. European Socialist Feminism in the Nineteenth and Early Twentieth Centuries* (New York: Elsevier, 1978).

Bracke, Maud Anne. 'Inventing Reproductive Rights: Sex, Population, and Feminism in Europe, 1945–1990'. Podcasts of the German Historical Institute London, 15 July 2020.

Breines, Winifred. *The Trouble Between Us: An Uneasy History of White and Black Women in the Feminist Movement* (Oxford: Oxford University Press, 2006).

Bridenthal, Renate, Atina Grossmann and Marion Kaplan, eds. *When Biology Became Destiny: Women in Weimar and Nazi Germany* (New York: Monthly Review Press, 1984).

Brockmann, Stefan. 'Introduction: The Reunification Debate', *New German Critique*, No. 52 (1991): pp. 3–30.

Brodie, Janet Farrell. *Contraception and Abortion in Nineteenth-Century America* (Ithaca: Cornell University Press, 1994).

Brown, Timothy. *West Germany and the Global Sixties: The Anti-Authoritarian Revolt, 1962–1978* (London: Cambridge University Press, 2013).

Brown, Wendy. *States of Injury: Power and Freedom in Late Modernity* (Princeton: Princeton University Press, 1995).

Brücker, Eva. ' "Und ich bin heil da rausgekommen": Gewalt und Sexualität in einer Berliner Arbeiternachbarschaft zwischen 1916/17 und 1958' in *Physische Gewalt: Studien zur Geschichte der Neuzeit*, edited by Thomas Lindenberger and Alf Lüdtke (Frankfurt am Main: Suhrkamp Verlag, 1995): pp. 337–365.

Brückweh, Kerstin Clemens Villinger and Kathrin Zöller, eds. *Die lange Geschichte der 'Wende': Geschichtswissenschaft im Dialog* (Berlin: Christoph Links Verlag, 2020).

Brückweh, Kerstin and Mirjam Brusius. 'Home Sweet Home: A "Schriftgespräch" on Doing the Long History of 1989', *German Historical Institute London Bulletin*, Vol. XLIII, No. 1 (2021): pp. 66–86.

Brühöfener, Friederike, Karen Hagemann and Donna Harsch, eds. *Gendering Post-1945 German History: Entanglements* (New York: Berghahn, 2019).

Bühner, Maria. 'The Rise of a New Consciousness: Lesbian Activism in East Germany in the 1980s' in *The Politics of Authenticity: Counter-Culture and Radical Movements Across the Iron Curtain, 1968–1989*, edited by Joachim Häberlen, Mark Keck-Szajbel and Kate Mahoney (New York: Berghahn, 2019): pp. 151–173.

Bumiller, Kristin. *In An Abusive State: How Neoliberalism Appropriated the Feminist Movement Against Sexual Violence* (Durham: Duke University Press, 2008).

Burton, Antoinette. 'Thinking Beyond the Boundaries: Empire, Feminism and the Domain of History', *Social History*, Vol. 26, No. 1 (2001): pp. 60–71.

Butler, Judith. *Gender Trouble: Feminism and the Subversion of Identity* (London: Routledge, 1990).

Buzawa, Eve and Carl Buzawa. *Domestic Violence: The Criminal Justice Response*, 3rd ed. (Thousand Oaks: Sage Publications, 2003).

Cahill, Ann. *Rethinking Rape* (Ithaca: Cornell University Press, 2001).

Canning, Kathleen. *History in Practice: Historical Perspectives on Bodies, Class and Citizenship* (Ithaca: Cornell University Press, 2006).

Castillo, Greg. *Cold War on the Home Front: The Soft Power of Mid Century Design* (Minneapolis: University of Minnesota Press, 2010).

Clements, Elizabeth. 'The Abortion Debate in Unified Germany' in *Women and the Wende. Social Effects and Cultural Reflections of the German Unification Process*, edited by Elizabeth Boa and Janet Wharton (Amsterdam: Rodopi, 1994): pp. 38–52.

Conrad, Sebastian and Shalini Randeria, eds. *Jenseits des Eurozentrismus: Postkoloniale Perspektiven in den Geschichts- und Kulturwissenschaften* (Frankfurt am Main: Campus, 2002).

Cooper, Frederick and Ann Laura Stoler, eds. *Tensions in Empire: Colonial Cultures in a Bourgeois World* (Berkeley: University of California Press, 1997).

Cornils, Ingo. *Writing the Revolution. The Construction of '1968' in Germany* (Rochester: Camden House, 2016).

Czarnowski, Gabriella. 'The Value of Marriage for the Volksgemeinschaft: Policies towards Women and Marriage under National Socialism' in *Fascist Italy and Nazi Germany: Comparisons and Contrasts*, edited by Richard Bessel (Cambridge: Cambridge University Press, 1996): pp. 94–112.

Daniel, Ute. *Arbeiterfrauen in der Kriegsgesellschaft. Beruf, Familien und Politik im Ersten Welt Krieg* (Göttingen: Vandenhoeck and Ruprecht, 1989).

Davin, Anna. 'Imperialism and Motherhood', *History Workshop*, No. 5 (1978): pp. 9–65.

Davis, Belinda J. *Home Fires Burning: Food, Politics, and Everyday Life in World War I Berlin* (Chapel Hill: University of North Carolina Press, 2000).

Davis, Belinda. 'The Personal is Political: Gender, Politics, and Political Activism in Modern German History' in *Gendering Modern German History. Rewriting Historiography*, edited by Karen Hagemann and Jean H. Quataert (New York: Berghahn, 2007): pp. 107–127.

Dehnavi, Morvarid. *Das politisierte Geschlecht. Biographische Wege zum Studentinnenprotest von '1968' und zur Neuen Frauenbewegung* (Bielefeld: Transcript Verlag, 2013).

Delap, Lucy. *Feminisms: A Global History* (London: Penguin Books, 2020).

DiCaprio, Lisa. 'East German Feminists. The Lila Manifesto', *Feminist Studies*, Vol. 16, No. 3 (Autumn 1990): pp. 621–626.

Dobash, Russell P., R. Emerson Dobash, Margo Wilson and Martin Daly. 'The Myth of Sexual Symmetry in Marital Violence', *Social Problems*, Vol. 39, No. 1 (1992): pp. 71–91.

Dodds, Dinah and Pam Allen-Thompson. *The Wall in My Backyard. East German Women in Transition* (Amherst: University of Massachusetts Press, 1994).

Dollard, Catherine L. *The Surplus Woman: Unmarried in Imperial Germany, 1871–1918* (New York: Berghahn, 2009).

Donert, Celia. 'Women's Rights in Cold War Europe: Disentangling Feminist Histories', *Past and Present*, Supplement 8 (2013): pp. 178–202.

Donert, Celia. 'Whose Utopia? Gender, Ideology, and Human Rights at the 1975 World Congress of Women in East Berlin' in *The Breakthrough: Human Rights in the 1970s*, edited by Jan Eckel and Samuel Moyn (Philadelphia: University of Pennsylvania Press, 2014): pp. 68–87.

Drayton, Richard and David Motadel. 'Discussion: The Futures of Global History', *Journal of Global History*, Vol. 13, No. 1 (2018): pp. 1–21.

Ellis, John. *Seeing Things: Television in the Age of Uncertainty* (London: I.B. Tauris, 2000).

von der Emde, Silke. 'Places of Wonder: Fantasy and Utopia in Irmtraud Morgner's Salman Trilogy', *New German Critique*, No. 82 (Winter, 2001): pp. 167–192.

Enke, Anne. 'Smuggling Sex through the Gates: Race, Sexuality, and the Politics of Space in Second Wave Feminism', *American Quarterly*, Vol. 55, No. 4 (2003): pp. 635–667.

Evans, Jennifer V. 'Constructing Borders: Image and Identity in "Die Frau von Heute," 1945–1949' in *Conquering Women: Women and War in the German Cultural Imagination*, edited by Hilary Collier Sy-Quia and Susanne Baackmann (Berkeley: University of California, 2000): pp. 40–60.

Evans, Jennifer V. 'The Moral State: Men, Mining and Masculinity in the early GDR', *German History*, Vol. 23, No.3 (2005): pp. 355–370.

Evans, Jennifer V. *Life among the Ruins: Cityscape and Sexuality in Cold War Berlin* (New York: Palgrave, 2011).

Evans, Richard J. *The Feminist Movement in Germany, 1894–1933* (London: Sage Publications, 1976).

Fahlenbrach, Kathrin, Erling Siversten and Rolf Weremskjold, eds. *Media and Revolt: Strategies and Performances from the 1960s to the Present* (New York: Berghahn, 2014).

Fehrenbach, Heide. *Cinema in Democratizing Germany: Reconstructing National Identity after Hitler* (Chapel Hill: University of North Carolina Press, 1995).

Feinstein, Joshua. *The Triumph of the Ordinary: Depictions of Daily Life in the East German Cinema, 1949–1989* (Chapel Hill: University of North Carolina Press, 2002).

Ferree, Myra Marx. 'Equality and Autonomy: Feminist Politics in the United States and West Germany' in *The Women's Movements of the United States and Western Europe. Consciousness, Political Opportunity, and Public Policy*, edited by Mary Fainsod Katzenstein and Carol McClurg Mueller (Philadelphia: Temple University Press, 1987): pp. 172–195.

Ferree, Myra Marx. ' "The Time of Chaos was the Best": Feminist Mobilization and Demobilization in East Germany', *Gender and Society*, Vol. 8, No. 4 (1994): pp. 597–623.

Ferree, Myra Marx. 'German Unification and Feminist Identity' in *Transitions, Environments, Translations. Feminisms in International Politics*, edited by Joan Scott, Cora Kaplan and Debra Keats (New York: Routledge, 1997): pp. 46–55.

Ferree, Myra Marx, William Anthony Gamson, Jürgen Gerhards and Dieter Rucht. *Shaping Abortion Discourse: Democracy and the Public Sphere in Germany and the United States* (Cambridge: Cambridge University Press, 2002).

Ferree, Myra Marx. 'Globalization and Feminism. Opportunities and Obstacles for Activism in the Global Arena' in *Global Feminism. Transnational Women's Activism Organizing and Human Rights*, edited by Myra Marx Ferree and Aili Mari Tripp (New York: New York University Press, 2006): pp. 3–23.

Ferree, Myra Marx and Aili Mari Tripp, eds. *Global Feminism. Transnational Women's Activism Organizing and Human Rights* (New York: New York University Press, 2006).

Ferree, Myra Marx. *Varieties of Feminism: German Gender Politics in Global Perspective* (Stanford: Stanford University Press, 2012).

Fichter, Tilman and Siegward Lönnendonker. *Kleine Geschichte des SDS. Der Sozialistische Deutsche Studentenbund von 1946 bis zur Selbstauflösung* (Berlin: Rotbuch Verlag, 1977).

Fidelis, Malgorzata. *Women, Communism, and Industrialization in Postwar Poland* (Cambridge: Cambridge University Press, 2010).

Field, Deborah A. 'Irreconcilable Differences: Divorce and Conceptions of Private Life in the Khrushchev Era', *Russian Review*, Vol. 57, No. 4 (1998): pp. 599–613.

Fink, Carole, Philipp Gassert and Detlef Junker, eds. *1968. The World Transformed* (Cambridge: Cambridge University Press, 1998).

Fisher, Kate and Simon Szreter. ' "They Prefer Withdrawal": The Choice of Birth Control in Britain, 1918–1950', *The Journal of Interdisciplinary History*, Vol. 34, No. 2 (2003): pp. 263–291.

Florvil, Tiffany N. *Mobilizing Black Germany: Afro-German Women and the Making of a Transnational Movement* (Champaign: University of Illinois Press, 2020).

Freeland, Jane. 'Creating Good Socialist Women: Continuities, Desire and Degeneration in Slatan Dudow's "The Destinies of Women" ', *Journal of Women's History*, Vol. 29, No. 1 (2017): pp. 87–110.

Freeland, Jane. 'Domestic Abuse, Women's Lives and Citizenship: East and West Policies during the 1960s and 1970s' in *Gendering Post-1945 German History: Entanglements*, edited by Friederike Brühöfener, Karen Hagemann and Donna Harsch (New York: Berghahn, 2019): pp. 253–273.

Freeland, Jane. 'Gendering Value Change: Domestic Violence and Feminism in 1970s West Berlin', *German History*, Vol. 38, No. 4 (2020): pp. 638–655.

Frevert, Ute. *Frauen-Geschichte. Zwischen Bürgerlicher Verbesserung und Neuer Weiblichkeit* (Frankfurt am Main: Suhrkamp Verlag, 1986).

Fulbrook, Mary. *The People's State: East German Society from Hitler to Honecker* (New Haven: Yale University Press, 2005).

Fulbrook, Mary, ed. *Power and Society in the GDR, 1961–1979* (New York: Berghahn, 2009).

Funk, Nanette. 'Abortion and German Unification' in *Gender Politics and Post-Communism: Reflections from Eastern Europe and the Former Soviet Union*, edited by Nanette Funk and Magda Mueller (New York: Routledge, 1993): pp. 194–200.

Funk, Nanette, Magda Müller, Robin Ostow, Michael Bodeman and Matthias Weiss. 'Dossier on Women in Eastern Europe', *Social Text*, No. 27 (1990): pp. 88–122.

Funk, Nanette and Magda Mueller, eds. *Gender Politics and Post-Communism: Reflections from Eastern Europe and the Former Soviet Union* (New York: Routledge, 1993).

Fürst, Juliane and Josie McLellan, eds. *Dropping Out of Socialism: The Creation of Alternative Spheres in the Soviet Bloc* (Lanham: Lexington Books, 2017).

Gal, Susan and Gail Kligman, eds. *The Politics of Gender after Socialism* (Princeton: Princeton University Press, 2000).

Ganeva, Mila. 'Fashion Amidst the Ruins: Revisiting the Early Rubble Films "And the Heavens Above" (1947) and "The Murderers Are Among Us" (1946)', *German Studies Review*, Vol. 37, No. 1 (2014): pp. 61–85.

Gehmacher, Johanna. 'The Productions of Historical Feminisms: Archival Practices and Political Activism'. Paper presented at the conference 'Archiving, Recording and Representing Feminism: The Global History of Women's Emancipation in the 20th Century'. German Historical Institute London, 10–12 December 2020.

Gembries, Ann-Katrin, Theresia Theuke and Isabel Heineman, eds. *Children by Choice? Changing Values, Reproduction and Family Planning in the 20th Century* (Berlin: De Gruyter, 2018).

Gerhard, Ute. *Verhältnisse und Verhinderungen: Frauenarbeit, Familie und Rechte der Frauen im 19. Jahrhundert mit Dokumenten* (Frankfurt am Main: Suhrkamp Verlag, 1978).

Ghodsee, Kristen. 'Revisiting the United Nations Decade for Women: Brief Reflections on Feminism, Capitalism and Cold War Politics in the Early Years of the International Women's Movement', *Women's Studies International Forum*, Vol. 33, No. 1 (2010): pp. 3–12.

Gill, Rosalind. *Gender and the Media* (Cambridge: Polity, 2007).

Goltermann, Svenja. *The War in their Minds: German Soldiers and their Violent Pasts in West Germany* (Ann Arbor: University of Michigan Press, 2017).

Goedicke, Anne. 'A "Ready-Made State": The Mode of Institutional Transition in East Germany After 1989' in *After the Fall of the Wall: Life Courses in the Transformation of East Germany*, edited by Martin Diewald, Anne Goedicke and Karl Ulrich Mayer (Stanford: Stanford University Press, 2006): pp. 44–64.

von der Goltz, Anna. 'Attraction and Aversion in Germany's 1968: Encountering the Western Revolution in East Berlin', *Journal of Contemporary History*, Vol. 50, No. 3 (2015): pp. 536–559.

Gordon, Linda. *Woman's Body, Woman's Right: A Social History of Birth Control in America* (New York: Viking, 1976).

Gotto, Bernhard. *Enttäuschung in der Demokratie. Erfahrung und Deutung von politischem Engagement in der Bundesrepublik Deutschland während der 1970er und 1980er Jahre* (Berlin: De Gruyter, 2018).

Goven, Joanna. 'The Gendered Foundations of Hungarian Socialism: State, Society, and the Anti-Politics of Anti-Feminism, 1948–1990' (Ph.D. dissertation, University of California at Berkeley, 1993).

Grafenhorst, Gabrielle, ed. *Abtreibung. Erfahrungsberichte zu einem Tabu* (Munich: Deutscher Taschenbuch Verlag, 1992).

Greven-Aschoff, Barbara. *Die bürgerliche Frauenbewegung in Deutschland, 1894– 1933* (Göttingen: Vandenhoek and Ruprecht, 1981).

Grewal, Inderpal and Caren Kaplan. *Scattered Hegemonies: Postmodernity and Transnational Feminist Practices* (Minneapolis: University of Minnesota Press, 1994).

Grossmann, Atina. 'Feminist Debates about Women and National Socialism', *Gender and History*, Vol. 3, No. 3 (1991): pp. 350–358.

Grossmann, Atina. 'A Question of Silence. The Rape of German Women by Occupation Soldiers', *October*, Vol. 72 (1995): pp. 42–63;

Grossmann, Atina. *Reforming Sex: The German Movement for Birth Control and Abortion Reform, 1920–1950* (New York: Oxford University Press, 1995).

Grossmann, Atina. *Jews, Germans and Allies: Close Encounters in Occupied Germany* (Princeton: Princeton University Press, 2007).

Grosz, Elizabeth. 'Histories of a Feminist Future', *Signs*, Vol. 25, No. 4 (2000): pp. 1017–1021.

Guenther, Katja M. *Making Their Place: Feminism after Socialism in Eastern Germany* (Stanford: Stanford University Press, 2010).

de Haan, Francisca, Margaret Allen, June Purvis and Krassimira Daskalova, eds. *Women's Activism. Global Perspectives from the 1890s to the Present* (New York: Routledge, 2013).

Häberlen, Joachim C. 'Feeling like a Child: Dreams and Practices of Sexuality in the West German Alternative Left during the Long 1970s', *Journal of the History of Sexuality*, Vol. 25, No. 2 (2016): pp. 219–245.

Häberlen, Joachim, Mark Keck-Szajbel and Kate Mahoney, eds. *The Politics of Authentic Subjectivity: Countercultures and Radical Movements across the Iron Curtain, 1968–1989* (New York: Berghahn, 2018).

Hájková, Anna. 'Sexual Barter in Times of Genocide: Negotiating the Sexual Economy of the Theresienstadt Ghetto', *Signs*, Vol. 38, No. 3 (2013): pp. 503–533.

Hájková, Anna, Elissa Mailänder, Atina Grossmann, Doris Bergen and Patrick Farges. 'Holocaust and the History of Gender and Sexuality', *German History*, Vol. 36, No. 1 (2018): pp. 78–100.

Hall, Simon. 'Protest Movements in the 1970s: The Long 1960s', *Journal of Contemporary History*, Vol. 43, No. 4 (2008): pp. 655–672.

Hampele, Anne. 'Ein Jahr Unabhängiger Frauenverband – Teil II: Frauenbewegung und UFV im letzten Jahr der DDR', *Berliner Arbeitshefte und Berichte zur sozialwissenschaftlichen Forschung*, 48 (1990).

Hampele, Anne. 'The Organized Women's Movement in the Collapse of the GDR: The Independent Women's Association (UFV)' in *Gender Politics and Post-Communism: Reflections from Eastern Europe and the Former Soviet Union*, edited by Nanette Funk and Magda Mueller (New York: Routledge, 1993): pp. 180–193.

Hanshew, Karrin. *Terror and Democracy in West Germany* (Cambridge: Cambridge University Press, 2012).

Hark, Sabine and Paula-Irene Villa. *The Future of Difference. Beyond the Toxic Entanglement of Racism, Sexism and Feminism*, trans. Sophie Lewis (London: Verso Books, 2020).

Harris, Steven E. *Communism on Tomorrow Street: Mass Housing and Everyday Life after Stalin* (Baltimore: Johns Hopkins University Press, 2013).

Harsch, Donna. 'Society, the State and Abortion in East Germany, 1950–1972', *American Historical Review*, Vol. 102, No. 1 (1997): pp. 53–84.

Harsch, Donna. *Revenge of the Domestic: Women, the Family, and Communism in the German Democratic Republic* (Princeton: Princeton University Press, 2007).

Harvey, Elizabeth. 'The Failure of Feminism? Young Women and the Bourgeois Feminist Movement in Weimar Germany 1918–1933', *Central European History*, Vol. 28, No. 1 (1995): pp. 1–28.

Harvey, Elizabeth. *Women and the Nazi East: Agents and Witnesses of Germanization* (New Haven: Yale University Press, 2003).

Heineman, Elizabeth. 'Complete Families, Half Families, No Families at All: Female-Headed Households and the Reconstruction of the Family in the Early Federal Republic', *Central European History*, Vol. 29, No. 1 (1996): pp. 19–60.

Heineman, Elizabeth. 'The Hour of the Woman: Memories of Germany's "Crisis Years" and West German National Identity', *American Historical Review*, Vol. 101, No. 2 (1996): pp. 354–395.

Heineman, Elizabeth. *What Difference Does a Husband Make? Women and Marital Status in Nazi and Postwar Germany* (Berkeley: University of California Press, 1999).

Heineman, Elizabeth. *Before Porn Was Legal: The Erotica Empire of Beate Uhse* (Chicago: University of Chicago Press, 2013).

Hemmings, Clare. *Why Stories Matter: The Political Grammar of Feminist Theory* (Durham: Duke University Press, 2011).

Herbert, Ulrich, ed. *Wandlungsprozesse in Westdeutschland: Belastung, Integration, Liberalisierung, 1945–1980* (Göttingen: Wallstein, 2002).

Herbert, Ulrich. *Geschichte Deutschlands im 20. Jahrhundert* (Munich: C.H. Beck, 2014).

Herles, Helmut and Ewald Rose, eds. *Vom Runden Tisch zum Parlament* (Bonn: Verlag Bouvier, 1990).

Herwig, Malte. *Die Flakhelfer: Wie aus Hitlers jüngsten Parteimitgliedern Deutschland führende Demokraten wurden* (Munich: Deutsche Verlags-Anstallt, 2003).

Herzog, Dagmar. *Sex After Fascism: Memory and Morality in Twentieth-Century Germany* (Princeton: Princeton University Press, 2005).

Herzog, Dagmar. *Unlearning Eugenics: Sexuality, Reproduction, and Disability in Post-Nazi Europe* (Madison: University of Wisconsin, 2018).

Hewitt, Nancy, ed. *No Permanent Waves: Recasting Histories of U.S. Feminism* (New Brunswick: Rutgers University Press, 2010).

Hilzinger, Sonja. *'Als ganzer Mensch zu leben … ' Emanzipatorische Tendenzen in der neuen Frauen-Literatur der DDR* (Frankfurt am Main: Peter Lang, 1985).

Hochscherf, Tobias, Christoph Laucht and Andrew Plowman, eds. *Divided, but not Disconnected: German Experiences of the Cold War* (New York: Berghahn, 2010).

von Hodenberg, Christina. 'Mass Media and the Generation of Conflict: West Germany's Long-Sixties and the Formation of a Critical Public Sphere', *Contemporary European History*, Vol. 15, No. 3 (2006): pp. 367–395.

von Hodenberg, Christina. 'Der Kampf um die Redaktionen. «1968» und der Wandel der westdeutschen Massenmedien' in *Wo '1968' liegt: Reform und Revolte in der Geschichte der Bundesrepublik*, edited by Christina von Hodenberg and Detlef Siegfried (Göttingen: Vandenhoeck and Ruprecht, 2006): pp. 139–163.

von Hodenberg, Christina. *Television's Moment: Sitcom Audiences and the Sixties Cultural Revolution* (New York: Berghahn, 2015).

von Hodenberg, Christina. 'Square-Eyed Farmers and Gloomy Ethnographers: The Advent of Television in the West German Village', *Journal of Contemporary History*, Vol. 51 (2016): pp. 839–865.

von Hodenberg, Christina. *Das andere Achtundsechzig: Gesellschaftsgeschichte eine Revolte* (Munich: C.H. Beck, 2018).

von Hodenberg, Christina. 'Writing Women's Agency into the History of the Federal Republic: "1968", Historians, and Gender', *Central European History*, Vol. 52, No.1 (2019): pp. 87–106.

Höhn, Maria. *GIs and Fräuleins: The German-American Encounter in 1950s West Germany* (Chapel Hill: University of North Carolina Press, 2002).

Honeycutt, Karen. 'Socialism and Feminism in Imperial Germany', *Signs*, Vol. 5, No. 1 (1979): pp. 30–41.

Hornig, Daphne and Christine Steiner. *Auf der Suche nach der Bewegung. Zur Frauenbewegung in der DDR vor und nach der Wende* (Hamburg: Frauen-Anstiftung eV, 1992).

Huelshoff, Michael G., Andrei S. Markovits and Simon Reich, eds. *From Bundesrepublik to Deutschland: German Politics after Reunification* (Ann Arbor: University of Michigan Press, 1993).

Inglehart, Ronald. *The Silent Revolution. Changing Values and Political Styles among Western Publics* (Princeton: Princeton University Press, 1977).

Institute for Alcohol Studies, *Alcohol, Domestic Abuse and Sexual Assault* (London: Institute for Alcohol Studies, 2014).

Jacquot, Sophie. *Transformations in EU Gender Equality. From Emergence to Dismantling* (New York: Palgrave Macmillan, 2015).

Jarausch, Konrad H. *The Rush to German Unity* (New York: Oxford University Press, 1994).

Jarausch, Konrad H., ed. *Dictatorship as Experience: Towards a Socio-Cultural History of the GDR* (New York: Berghahn Books, 1999).

Jarausch, Konrad H. *After Hitler: Recivilizing Germans, 1945–1995* (Oxford: Oxford University Press, 2006).

Jarausch, Konrad H. 'Beyond the National Narrative: Implications of Reunification for Recent German History', *German History*, Vol. 28, No. 4 (2010): pp. 498–514.

Jayawardena, Kumari. *Feminism and Nationalism in the Third World* (London: Zed, 1986).

Jeffords, Susan. 'The "Remasculinization" of Germany in the 1950s: Discussion' *Signs*, Vol. 24, No. 1 (1998): pp. 163–169.

Jerouschek, Günter. 'Die juristische Konstruktion des Abtreibungsverbots' in *Frauen in der Geschichte des Rechts: von der frühen Neuzeit bis zur Gegenwart*, edited by Ute Gerhard (Munich: C.H. Beck, 1997): pp. 248–264.

Johnson, Janet Elise. *Gender Violence in Russia: The Politics of Feminist Intervention* (Bloomington: Indiana University Press, 2009).

Jolly, Margaretta. *Sisterhood and After: An Oral History of the UK Women's Liberation Movement, 1968–Present* (Oxford: Oxford University Press, 2019).

Joshi, Vandana. 'The "Private" became "Public": Wives as Denouncers in the Third Reich', *Journal of Contemporary History*, Vol. 37, No. 3 (2002): pp. 419–435.

Jung, Nora. 'Eastern European Women with Western Eyes' in *Stirring It: Challenges for Feminism*, edited by Gabriele Griffin, Marianne Hester and Shrin Rai (London: Taylor and Francis, 1994): pp. 195–211.

Kapczynski, Jennifer. *The German Patient: Crisis and Recovery in Postwar Culture* (Ann Arbor: University of Michigan Press, 2008).

Kapczynski, Jennifer. 'Postwar Ghosts: "Heimatfilm" and the Specter of Male Violence', *German Studies Review*, Vol. 33, No. 2 (2010): pp. 305–330.

Kaplan, Marion. *Beyond Dignity and Despair: Jewish Life in Nazi Germany* (Oxford: Oxford University Press, 1996).

Karcher, Katharina. *Sisters in Arms. Militant Feminisms in the Federal Republic of Germany since 1968* (Oxford: Berghahn, 2017).

Kašić, Biljana. 'Feminist Cross-Mainstreaming within "East-West" Mapping', *European Journal of Women's Studies*, Vol. 11, No. 4 (2004): pp. 473–485.

Klausen, Susanne. *Abortion under Apartheid: Nationalism, Sexuality, and Women's Reproductive Rights in South Africa* (New York: Oxford University Press, 2015).

Klausen, Susanne and Alison Bashford. 'Eugenics, Feminism and Fertility Control' in *The Oxford Handbook of the History of Eugenics* (Oxford: Oxford University Press, August 2010): pp. 98–115.

Klimke, Martin and Joachim Scharloth, eds. *1968 in Europe. A History of Protest and Activism, 1956–1977* (New York: Palgrave Macmillan, 2008).

Klumbyte, Neringa and Gulnaz Sharafutdinova, eds. *Soviet Society in the Era of Late Socialism, 1964–1985* (Lanham: Lexington Books, 2013).

Kochan, Thomas. *Blauer Würger: So trank die DDR* (Berlin: Aufbau Verlag, 2011).

Koonz, Claudia. *Mothers in the Fatherland: Women, the Family and Nazi Politics* (New York: St Martin's Press, 1987).

Köpping, Petra. *Integriert doch erst mal uns! Eine Streitschrift für den Osten* (Berlin: Christoph Links Verlag, 2018).

Kopstein, Jeffrey. *The Politics of Economic Decline in East Germany, 1945–1989* (Chapel Hill: University of North Carolina Press, 1997).

Kösters, Christoph, ed. *Caritas in der SMZ/DDR, 1945–1989* (Paderborn: Ferdinand Schöningh Verlag, 2001).

Kramer, Nicole. *Volksgenossinnen an der Heimatfront. Mobilisierung, Verhalten, Erinnerung* (Göttingen: Vandenhoek and Ruprecht, 2011).

Kranz, Susanne. 'Frauen für den Frieden – Oppositional Group or Bored Troublemakers?', *Journal of International Women's Studies*, Vol. 16, No. 2 (2015): pp. 141–154.

Kriszio, Marianne. 'Frauen im Studium' in *Handbuch zur Frauenbildung*, edited by Wiltrud Gieseke (Opladen: Leske und Budrich, 2001): pp. 293–302.

Krolzik-Matthei, Katja. 'Abtreibung in der DDR. Annäherung einen Diskurs', *diskus*, Vol. 218, No. 12 (2018): pp. 33–37.

Krolzik-Matthei, Katja. *§218. Feministische Perspektiven auf die Abtreibungsdebatte in Deutschland* (Münster: Unrast Verlag, 2015).

Kuhrt, Eberhard, Hannsjörg F. Buck and Gunter Holzweißig, eds. *Opposition in der DDR von den 70er Jahren bis zum Zusammenbruch der SED-Herrschaft* (Opladen: Leske and Opladen, 1999).

Kurimay, Anita and Judit Takács, 'Emergence of the Hungarian Homosexual Movement in Late Refrigerator Socialism', *Sexualities*, Vol. 20, No. 5–6 (2017): pp. 585–603.

Leask, Phil, Sara Ann Sewell and Heléna Tóth. 'Families' in *Ruptures in the Everyday. Views of Modern Germany from the Ground*, edited by Andrew Stuart Bergerson and Leonard Schmieding (New York: Berghahn Books, 2017).

Leask, Phil. *Friendship Without Borders: Women's Stories of Power, Politics, and Everyday Life Across East and West Germany* (New York: Berghahn Books, 2020).

Lebow, Katherine. *Unfinished Utopia: Nowa Huta, Stalinism and Polish Society, 1949–56* (Ithaca: Cornell University Press, 2013).

Lemke, Christiane. *Die Ursachen des Umbruchs 1989. Politische Sozialisation in der ehemaligen DDR* (Opladen: Westdeutscher Verlag, 1991).

Lenz, Ilse. 'Wer sich wo und wie erinnern wollte? Die Neuen Frauenbewegungen und soziale Ungleichheit nach Klasse, "Rasse" und Migration' in *Erinnern, vergessen, umdeuten? Europäische Frauenbewegungen im 19. und 20. Jahrhundert*, edited by Angelika Schaser, Sylvia Schraut and Petra Steymans-Kurs (Frankfurt am Main: Campus, 2019): pp. 255–284.

Lewis, Margaret Brannan. *Infanticide and Abortion in Early Modern Germany* (London: Routledge, 2016).

Lindenberger, Thomas and Alf Lüdtke, eds. *Physische Gewalt: Studien zur Geschichte der Neuzeit* (Frankfurt am Main: Suhrkamp Verlag, 1995).

Łobodzińska, Barbara, ed. *Family, Women, and Employment in Central-Eastern Europe* (Westport: Greenwood Press, 1995).

Long, Kristi S. *We All Fought for Freedom: Women in Poland's Solidarity Movement* (Boulder: Westview Press, 1996).

Lönnendonker, Siegward, ed. *Linksintellektueller Aufbruch zwischen 'Kulturrevolution' und 'kultureller Zerstörung': Der Sozialistische Deutsche Studentenbund (SDS) in der Nachkriegsgeschichte 1946–1969* (Wiesbaden: VS Verlag, 1998).

Lóránd, Zsófia. ' "A Politically Non-Dangerous Revolution is not a Revolution": Critical Readings of the Concept of Sexual Revolution by Yugoslav Feminists in the 1970s" ', *European Review of History*, Vol. 22, No. 1 (2014): pp. 120–137.

Lóránd, Zsófia. *The Feminist Challenge to the Socialist State in Yugoslavia* (London: Palgrave Macmillan, 2018).

Lóránd, Zsófia. 'Feminism and Violence against Women in Yugoslavia during State Socialism' in *Women, Global Protest Movement and Political Agency: Rethinking the Legacy of 1968*, edited by Sarah Colvin and Katharina Karcher (London: Routledge, 2019): pp. 84–97.

Lóránd, Zsófia. 'New Feminism, Women's Subjectivity, and Feminist Politics: Conceptual Transfers and Activist Inspirations in Yugoslavia in the 1970s and 1980s' in *Politics of Authenticity: Counter-Cultures and Radical Movements Across the Iron Curtain, 1968–1989*, edited by Joachim Häberlen, Mark Keck-Szajbel and Kate Mahoney (New York: Berghahn, 2019): pp. 110–130.

Lower, Wendy. *Hitler's Furies: Women in the Nazi Killing Fields* (London: Chatto and Windus, 2013).

Lukens, Nancy and Dorothy Rosenberg. *Daughters of Eve. Women's Writing from the German Democratic Republic* (Lincoln: University of Nebraska Press, 1993).

Madarasz, Jeannette. *Conflict and Compromise in East Germany, 1971–1989* (New York: Palgrave MacMillan, 2003).

Mailänder, Elissa. *Gewalt im Dienstalltag: Die SS-Aufseherinnen des Konzentrations- und Vernichtungslagers Majdanek 1942–1944* (Hamburg: Hamburger Edition, 2009).

Maleck-Lewy, Eva and Myra Marx Ferree. 'Talking about Women and Wombs: The Discourse of Abortion and Reproductive Rights in the GDR during and after the Wende' in *Reproducing Gender. Politics, Publics, and Everyday Life after Socialism*, edited by Susan Gal and Gail Kligman (Princeton: Princeton University Press, 2000): pp. 92–117.

Maleck-Lewy, Eva and Bernhard Maleck. 'The Women's Movement in East and West Germany' in *1968. The World Transformed*, edited by Carole Fink, Philipp Gassert and Detlef Junker (Cambridge: Cambridge University Press, 1998): pp. 373–396.

Marwick, Arthur. *The Sixties: Cultural Revolution in Britain, France, Italy and the United States* (New York: A & C Black, 1999).

Marzell, Pia. 'Sind wir uns denn so fremd? Aufbrüche in der Rassismusdebatte der Frauenbewegung', *History|Sexuality|Law*, 8 March 2021. Accessed on 10 June 2021: https://hsl.hypotheses.org/1608.

McLellan, Josie. 'State Socialist Bodies: East German Nudism from Ban to Boom', *Journal of Modern History*, Vol. 79, No. 1 (2007): pp. 48–79.

McLellan, Josie. *Love in the Time of Communism: Intimacy and Sexuality in the GDR* (Cambridge: Cambridge University Press, 2011).

McRobbie, Angela. *Feminism and Youth Culture* (Basingstoke: Macmillan, 2000).

McRobbie, Angela. 'Top Girls? Young Women and the Post-Feminist Sexual Contract', *Cultural Studies*, Vol. 21, Nos. 4–5 (2007): pp. 718–737.

McRobbie, Angela. *The Aftermath of Feminism: Gender, Culture and Social Change* (London: Sage, 2008).

Melzer, Patricia. *Death in the Shape of a Young Girl: Women's Political Violence in the Red Army Faction* (New York: New York University Press, 2015).

Merridale, Catherine. *Ivan's War: Life and Death in the Red Army, 1939–1945* (New York: Henry Holt and Company, 2006).

Mertens, Lothar. *Wider die sozialistische Familiennorm. Ehescheidung in der DDR 1950–1989* (Opladen: Westdeutscher Verlag, 1998).

Mertens, Lothar, ed. *Soziale Ungleichheit in der DDR. Zu einem tabuisierten Strukturmerkmal der SED-Diktatur* (Berlin: Duncker und Humblot, 2002).

Miethe, Ingrid. *Frauen in der DDR-Opposition. Lebens- und kollektivgeschichtliche Verläufe in einer Frauenfriedensgruppe* (Opladen: Leske + Budrich, 1999).

Millar, Erica. '"Too Many": Anxious White Nationalism and the Biopolitics of Abortion', *Australian Feminist Studies,* Vol. 30, No. 83 (2015): pp. 82–98.

Miller, Elizabeth B.A. 'Moving to the Head of the River: The Early Years of the U.S. Battered Women's Movement' (Ph.D. dissertation, University of Kansas, 2010).

Miller, Jennifer. 'Her Fight is Your Fight: "Guest Worker" Labor Activism in the Early 1970s West Germany', *International Labor and Working-Class History,* Vol. 84 (2013): pp. 226–247.

Millington, Richard. '"Crime has no chance": The Discourse of Everyday Criminality in the East German Press, 1961–1989', *Central European History,* Vol. 50, No. 1 (2017): pp. 59–85.

Mittman, Elizabeth. 'Gender, Citizenship, and the Public Sphere in Postunification Germany: Experiments in Feminist Journalism', *Signs,* Vol. 32, No. 3 (2007): pp. 759–791.

Moeller, Robert G. 'Reconstructing the Family in Reconstruction Germany: Women and Social Policy in the Federal Republic, 1949–1955', *Feminist Studies,* Vol. 15, No. 1 (1989): pp. 137–169.

Moeller, Robert G. *Protecting Motherhood: Women and the Family in the Politics of Postwar West Germany* (Berkeley: University of California Press, 1993).

Moeller, Robert G. 'The "Remasculinization" of Germany in the 1950s: Introduction', *Signs,* Vol. 24, No. 1 (1998): pp. 101–106.

Moeller, Robert G. *War Stories: The Search for a Usable Past in the Federal Republic of Germany* (Berkeley: University of California Press, 2001).

Mohanty, Chandra. '"Under Western Eyes" Revisited: Feminist Solidarity through Anticapitalist Struggles', *Signs,* Vol. 28, No. 2 (2002): pp. 499–535.

Mohanty, Chandra. *Feminism without Borders: Decolonizing Theory, Practicing Solidarity* (Durham: Duke University Press, 2003).

Molnar, Virag. *Building the State: Architecture, Politics and State Formation in Postwar Central Europe* (New York: Routledge, 2013).

Mühlhäuser, Regina. 'Vergewaltigung in Deutschland 1945: Nationaler Opferdiskurs und individuelles Erinnern betroffener Frauen' in *Nachkrieg in Deutschland,* edited by Klaus Naumann (Hamburg: Hamburg Institut für Sozialforschung, 2001): pp. 384–408.

Mühlhäuser, Regina. *Eroberungen. Sexuelle Gewalttaten und intime Beziehungen deutscher Soldaten in der Sowjetunion, 1941–1945* (Hamburg: Hamburger Edition, 2010).

Murdolo, Adele. 'Safe Homes for Immigrant and Refugee Women: Narrating Alternative Histories of the Women's Refuge Movement in Australia', *Frontiers: A Journal of Women's Studies,* Vol. 35, No. 3 (2014): pp. 126–153.

Naimark, Norman. *The Russians in Germany: A History of the Soviet Zone of Occupation, 1945–1949* (Cambridge: Belknap Press, 1995).

Narayan, Uma. *Dislocating Cultures: Identities, Traditions and Third-World Feminism* (New York: Routledge, 1997).

Neubert, Ehrhart. *Geschichte der Opposition in der DDR 1949–1989* (Bonn: Bundeszentrale für politische Bildung, 1997).

Neubert, Ehrhart. *Unsere Revolution. Die Geschichte der Jahre 1989/90* (Munich: Piper, 2009).

Neumaier, Christopher. *Familie im 20. Jahrhundert: Konflikte um Ideale, Politiken und Praktiken* (Berlin: De Gruyter, 2019).

von Oertzen, Christina. *Pleasures of a Surplus Income: Part-Time Work, Gender Politics and Social Change in West Germany, 1955–1969* (Oxford: Berghahn, 2007).

Ousmanova, Almira. 'On the Ruins of Orthodox Marxism: Gender and Cultural Studies in Eastern Europe', *Studies in Eastern European Thought*, Vol. 55, No. 1 (2003): pp. 37–50.

Pence, Katherine and Paul Betts, eds. *Socialist Modern: East German Everyday Culture and Politics* (Ann Arbor: University of Michigan Press, 2008).

Peperkamp, Esther and Małgorzata Rajtar, eds. *Religion and the Secular in Eastern Germany, 1945 to the Present* (Leiden: Brill, 2010).

Pilvousek, Josef. 'Caritas in SBZ/DDR und Neuen Bundesländern' in *Religion und Kirchen in Ost (Mittel) Europa: Deutschland-Ost*, edited by Karl Gabriel, Josef Pilvousek and Miklos Tomka (Ostfildern: Schwabenverlag, 2003): pp. 50–62.

Piper, Alana and Ana Stevenson, eds. *Gender Violence in Australia: Historical Perspectives* (Melbourne: Monash University Press, 2019).

Poiger, Uta G. *Jazz, Rock and Rebels: Cold War Politics and American Culture in a Divided Germany* (Berkeley: University of California Press, 2000).

Poiger, Uta G. 'Krise der Männlichkeit. Remaskulinisierung in beiden deutschen Nachkriegsgesellschaften' in *Nachkrieg in Deutschland*, edited by Klaus Naumann (Hamburg: Hamburg Institut für Sozialforschung, 2001): pp. 227–266.

Poiger, Uta G. 'Das Schöne und das Hässliche. Kosmetik, Feminismus und Punk in den siebziger und achtziger Jahren' in *Das Alternative Milieu. Antibürgerlicher Lebensstil und linke Politik in der Bundesrepublik Deutschland und Europa, 1968–1983* , edited by Sven Reichardt and Detlef Siegfried (Göttingen: Wallstein, 2010): pp. 222–243.

della Porta, Donatella. *Social Movements, Political Violence, and the State. A Comparative Analysis of Italy and Germany* (Cambridge: Cambridge University Press, 1995).

Port, Andrew. 'Love, Lust and Lies under Communism: Family Values and Adulterous Liaisons in Early East Germany', *Central European History*, Vol. 44 No. 3 (2011): pp. 474–505.

Poutrus, Kirsten. 'Von den Massenvergewaltigungen zum Mutterschutzgesetz: Abtreibungspolitik und Abtreibungspraxis in Ostdeutschland, 1945–1950' in *Die Grenzen der Diktatur. Staat und Gesellschaft in der DDR*, edited by Richard Bessel and Ralph Jessen (Göttingen: Vandenhoeck & Ruprecht, 1996): pp. 170–198.

Puar, Jasbir. *Terrorist Assemblages: Homonationalism in Queer Times* (Durham: Duke University Press, 2007).

Quataert, Jean H. 'Unequal Partners in an Uneasy Alliance: Women and the Working Class in Imperial Germany' in *Socialist Women. European Socialist Feminism in the Nineteenth and Early Twentieth Centuries*, edited by Marilyn J. Boxer and Jean H. Quataert (New York: Elsevier, 1978): pp. 112–145.

Quataert, Jean H. *Reluctant Feminists in German Social Democracy, 1885–1917* (Princeton: Princeton University Press, 1979).

Raithel, Thomas, Andreas Roedder and Andreas Wirsching. *Auf dem Weg in eine neue Moderne?: Die Bundesrepublik Deutschland in den siebziger und achtziger Jahren* (Munich: Oldenbourg, 2009).

Ramet, Sabrina, ed. *Gender Politics in the Western Balkans: Women and Society in Yugoslavia and the Yugoslav Successor States* (University Park: Pennsylvania State University Press, 1999).

Reichardt, Sven. *Authentizität und Gemeinschaft. Linksalternatives Leben in den siebziger und frühen achtziger Jahren* (Berlin: Suhrkamp Verlag, 2014).

Reid, Susan E. and David Crowley, eds. *Style and Socialism: Modernity and Material Culture in Post-War Eastern Europe* (Oxford: Berg, 2000).

Reid, Susan E. 'Cold War in the Kitchen: Gender and the De-Stalinization of Consumer Taste in the Soviet Union under Khrushchev', *Slavic Review*, Vol. 61, No. 2 (2002): pp. 211–252.

Reuther, Thomas. 'In Hitler's Shadow' in *The United States and Germany in the Era of the Cold War, 1945–1990: A Handbook*, edited by Detlef Junker, Phillipp Gassert, Wilfried Mausbach and David M. Morris (Cambridge: Cambridge University Press, 2004): pp. 601–607.

Richardson-Little, Ned. *The Human Rights Dictatorship: Socialism, Global Solidarity and Revolution in East Germany* (Cambridge: Cambridge University Press, 2020).

von Richthofen, Esther. *Bringing Culture to the Masses. Control, Compromise and Participation in the GDR* (New York: Oxford University Press, 2009).

Rinke, Andrea. *Images of Women in East German Cinema, 1972–1982: Socialist Models, Private Dreamers and Rebels* (Lewiston: Edwin Mellen Press, 2006).

Rinner, Susanne. *The German Student Movement and the Literary Imagination: Transnational Memories of Protest and Dissent* (New York: Berghahn, 2013).

Roberts, Dorothy E. 'Rape, Violence, and Women's Autonomy', *Chicago-Kent Law Review*, Vol. 69 (1993): pp. 359–388.

Roberts, Mary Louise. *What Soldiers Do: Sex and the American GI in World War II France* (Chicago: University of Chicago Press, 2013).

Rödder, Andreas and Wolfgang Elz. *Alte Werte – Neue Werte: Schlaglichter des Wertewandels* (Göttingen: Vandenhoeck & Ruprecht, 2008).

Roesch, Claudia. *Wunschkinder: Eine transnationale Geschichte der Familienplanung in der Bundesrepublik Deutschland* (Göttingen: Vandenhoeck & Ruprecht, 2021).

Roos, Julia. *Weimar through the Lens of Gender. Prostitution Reform, Woman's Emancipation, and German Democracy, 1919–33* (Ann Arbor: University of Michigan Press, 2010).

Ross, Corey. *The East German Dictatorship: Problems and Perspectives in the Interpretation of the GDR* (London: Arnold, 2002).

Rubin, Eli. *Synthetic Socialism. Plastics and Dictatorship in the German Democratic Republic* (Chapel Hill: University of North Carolina Press, 2008).

Rubin, Eli. *Amnesiopolis. Modernity, Space and Memory in East Germany* (New York: Oxford University Press, 2016).

Ryan, Barbara. 'Ideological Purity and Feminism: The US Women's Movement from 1966–1975', *Gender and Society*, Vol. 3, No. 2 (1989), pp. 239–257.

Sandoval, Chela. *Methodology of the Oppressed* (Minneapolis: University of Minnesota Press, 2000).

Sauer, Birgit. ' "Doing Gender". Das Parlament als Ort der Geschlechterkonstruktion. Eine Analyse der Bundestagdebatte um die Neuregelung des Schwangerschaftsabbruches' in *Sprache des Parlaments und Semiotik der Demokratie. Studien zur politischen Kommunikation in der Moderne*, edited by Andreas Dörner and Ludgera Vogt (Berlin: De Gruyter, 1995): pp. 172–199.

Schäffler, Eva. *Paarbeziehungen in Ostdeutschland. Auf dem Weg vom Real- zum Postsozialismus* (Wiesbaden: Harrassowitz Verlag, 2017).

Schaser, Angelika, Sylvia Schraut and Petra Steymans-Kurs, eds. *Erinnern, vergessen, umdeuten? Europäische Frauenbewegungen im 19. und 20. Jahrhundert* (Frankfurt am Main: Campus, 2019).

Schaser, Angelika. 'Helene Lange und Gertrud Bäumer als Historiographinnen der Frauenbewegung' in *Erinnern, vergessen, umdeuten? Europäische Frauenbewegungen im 19. und 20. Jahrhundert*, edited by Angelika Schaser, Sylvia Schraut and Petra Steymans-Kurs (Frankfurt am Main: Campus, 2019), pp. 170–197.

Scheffer, Edith. *Burned Bridge: How East and West Germans Made the Iron Curtain* (Oxford: Oxford University Press, 2011).

Schildt, Axel. 'Das Jahrhundert der Massenmedien. Ansichten zu einer künftigen Geschichte der Öffentlichkeit', *Geschichte und Gesellschaft*, Vol. 27, No. 2 (2001): pp. 177–206.

Schmacks, Yanara. ' "Motherhood is beautiful": Conceptions of Maternalism in the West German New Women's Movement between Eroticization and Ecological Protest', *Central European History*, Vol. 53, No. 4 (2020): pp. 811–834.

Schneider, Daniel, Kristen Harknett and Sara McLanahan. 'Intimate Partner Violence in the Great Recession', *Demography*, Vol. 53, No. 2 (2016): pp. 471–505.

Schröter, Anja. *Ostdeutsche Ehen vor Gericht. Scheidungspraxis im Umbruch 1980–2000* (Berlin: Christoph Links Verlag, 2018).

Schröttle, Monika. 'West "beforscht" Ost. Politische, forschungstische und methodische Überlegungen zur Frage der Ost-West-Forschung aus feministischer Sicht' in *Veränderungen – Identitätsfindung im Prozeß. Frauenforschung im Jahre sieben nach der Wende*, edited by Ulrike Diedrich and Heidi Stecker (Bielefeld: Kleine Verlag, 1997): pp. 139–157.

Schröttle, Monika. *Politik und Gewalt im Geschlechterverhältnis: eine empirische Untersuchung über Ausmaß, Ursache und Hintergründe von Gewalt gegen Frauen in ostdeutschen Paarbeziehungen vor und nach der deutsch-deutschen Vereinigung* (Bielefeld: Kleine Verlag, 1999).

Schulz, Kristina. *Der lange Atem der Provokation: Die Frauenbewegung in der Bundesrepublik und in Frankreich 1968–1976* (Frankfurt am Main: Campus, 2002).

Schulz, Kristina. 'Remembering 1968: Feminist Perspectives' in *Women, Global Protest Movements, and Political Agency. Rethinking the Legacy of 1968*, edited by Sarah Colvin and Katharina Karcher (Abingdon: Routledge, 2019): pp. 19–32.

Schulz, Kristina. 'Ohne Frauen keine Revolution', *Bundeszentrale für politische Bildung*, 6 March 2008. Accessed on 10 November 2020: https://www.bpb.de/geschichte/deutsche-geschichte/68er-bewegung/51859/frauen-und-68?p=all.

Schurich, Frank-Rainer. *Tödliche Lust. Sexualstraftaten in der DDR* (Berlin: Edition Ost, 1997).

Scott, Joan W. *The Fantasy of Feminist History* (Durham: Duke University Press, 2011).

Silies, Eva-Marie. *Liebe, Lust und Last. Die Pille als weibliche Generationserfahrung in der Bundesrepublik 1960–1980* (Göttingen: Wallstein Verlag, 2010).

Smith, Mark. *Property of Communists: The Urban Housing Program from Stalin to Khruschev* (DeKalb: Northern Illinois University Press, 2010).

Soder, Martin. *Hausarbeit und Stammtischsozialismus: Arbeiterfamilie und Alltag im Deutschen Kaiserreich* (Giessen: Focus Verlag, 1980).

Sperlich, Peter W. *The East German Social Courts: Law and Justice in a Marxist-Leninist Society* (Westport: Praeger, 2007).

Spohr, Julia. ' "Ein bißchen Gewalt dürfen Sie schon anwenden." Zum Umgang mit Gewalt in Paarbeziehungen in deutschen Ehe- und Partnerschaftsratgebern (1950er – 1990er Jahre)'. Paper presented at the conference Revolution der Paarbeziehungen? Der Wandel des Beziehungslebens in Bundesrepublik und DDR, Centre for Contemporary History, Potsdam [online], 12 March 2020.

Steinbacher, Sybille. *Wie der Sex nach Deutschland kam. Der Kampf um Sittlichkeit und Anstand in der frühen Bundesrepublik* (Munich: Siedler, 2011).

Stitziel, Judd. *Fashioning Socialism. Clothing, Politics and Consumer Culture in East Germany* (New York: Berg, 2005).

Stokes, Lauren. '"An Invasion of Guest Worker Children": Welfare Reform and the Stigmatisation of Family Migration', *Contemporary European History*, Vol. 28, No. 3 (2019), pp. 1–19.

Stokes, Lauren. 'The Permanent Refugee Crisis in the Federal Republic, 1949–', *Central European History*, Vol. 52, No. 1 (2019), pp. 19–44.

Thomas, Lynn M. *Politics of the Womb: Women, Reproduction, and the State in Kenya* (Berkeley: University of California Press, 2003).

Thomlinson, Natalie. *Race, Ethnicity and the Women's Movement in England, 1968–1993* (Basingstoke: Palgrave Macmillan, 2006).

Thompson, Becky. 'Multiracial Feminisms: Recasting the Chronology of Second-Wave Feminism', *Feminist Studies*, Vol 28, No. 2 (2002): pp. 336–360.

Timm, Annette. *The Politics of Fertility in Twentieth-Century Berlin* (New York: Cambridge University Press, 2010).

Timm, Annette. 'Mothers, Whores or Sentimental Dupes? Emotion and Race in Historiographical Debates about Women in the Third Reich' in *Beyond the Racial State: Rethinking Nazi Germany*, edited by Devin O. Pendas, Mark Roseman and Richard F. Wetzell (Cambridge: Cambridge University Press, 2017): pp. 335–361.

Treber, Leonie. *Mythos Trümmerfrauen: Von der Trümmerbeseitigung in der Kriegs- und Nachkriegszeit und der Entstehung eines deutschen Erinnerungsortes* (Essen: Klartext Verlag, 2014).

Urang, John Griffith. *Legal Tender. Love and Legitimacy in the East German Cultural Imagination* (Ithaca: Cornell University Press, 2010).

Usborne, Cornelie. *Cultures of Abortion in Weimar Germany* (Oxford: Berghahn, 2007).

Vaquas, Rida. 'Radical Books: August Bebel's Women and Socialism', *History Workshop Journal Online*, 14 August 2019. Accessed on 2 May 2022: https://www.historyworkshop.org.uk/radical-books-august-bebels-women-and-socialism/

Varga-Harris, Christine. 'Homemaking and the Aesthetic and Moral Perimeters of the Soviet Home during the Khrushchev Era', *Journal of Social History*, Vol. 41, No. 3 (2008): pp. 561–589.

Villaume, Poul, Rasmus Mariager and Helle Porsdam, eds. *The 'Long 1970s': Human Rights, East-West Détente and Transnational Relations* (Oxford: Routledge, 2016).

Waxman, Zoë. *Women in the Holocaust: A Feminist History* (Oxford: Oxford University Press, 2017).

Wehler, Hans-Ulrich. *Deutsche Gesellschaftsgeschichte, Bd. 5: Bundesrepublik und DDR, 1949–1990* (Munich: C.H. Beck, 2008).

Wekker, Gloria. 'Still Crazy after All These Years … Feminism for the New Millenium', *European Journal of Women's Studies*, Vol. 11, No. 4 (2004): pp. 487–500.

Werner, Michael and Bénédicte Zimmermann. 'Beyond Comparison: Histoire Croisée and the Challenge of Reflexivity', *History and Theory*, Vol. 45 (2006): pp. 30–50.

Wildenthal, Lora. *German Women for Empire, 1884–1945* (Durham: Duke University Press, 2001).

Wilson, Tikka Jan. 'Feminism and Institutionalized Racism: Inclusion and Exclusion at an Australian Feminist Refuge', *Feminist Review*, Vol. 52, No. 1 (1996):pp. 1–26.

Winkler, Heinrich August. *Der lange Weg nach Westen, Bd. 2: Deutsche Geschichte vom Dritten Reich bis zur Wiedervereinigung* (Munich: C. H. Beck, 2000).

Wolle, Stefan. *Der Traum von der Revolte: Die DDR 1968* (Berlin: Christoph Links Verlag, 2008).

Wuerth, Andrea. 'National Politics/Local Identities: Abortion Rights Activism in Post-Wall Berlin,' *Feminist Studies*, Vol. 25, No. 3 (1999): pp. 601–631.

Young, Brigitte. *Triumph of the Fatherland: German Unification and the Marginalization of Women* (Ann Arbor: University of Michigan Press, 1999).

Zahra, Tara. *The Lost Children: Reconstructing Europe's Families after World War II* (Cambridge: Harvard University Press, 2011).

Zarecor, Kimberly Elman. *Manufacturing a Socialist Modernity: Housing in Czechoslovakia, 1945–1960* (Pittsburgh: University of Pittsburgh Press, 2011).

Zatlin, Jonathan. *The Currency of Socialism. Money and Political Culture in East Germany* (Cambridge: Cambridge University Press, 2007).

Index

1968 *see* Student Movement
1989 143, 145, 146, 154, 155, 160, 168, 197;
    see also Cold War; German
    Reunification

Abortion
    and eugenics and population control
      41–43
    and German reunification 144, 167, 168,
      178–183, 189
      Collaboration between East and West
        German feminists 167, 178, 179,
        180, 181, 182, 183, 196
    and right to life 48, 169, 174, 181,
      182, 189
    Feminist campaign to decriminalise 24,
      40–41, 43–47, 54, 145, 167, 168,
      169, 174, 175
      Catalyst for domestic violence activism
        49, 170
      Impact on feminist practice and politics
        48–51, 55, 59
      see also We Had Abortions; *Panorama-
      Scandal*
    Fristenmodell 46, 48
    History of Paragraph 218 activism before
      1971 43
    Illegal 43, 44, 45, 47, 65
      Memmingen Trial 174–175, 178
    in reunified Germany 26
    in the GDR 13, 145, 160, 167, 181
    Indikationsmodell 46, 48, 167, 169
    Kohl government approach to 168, 174
    Legal development of Paragraph 218 42–43,
      169, 182
    Manifestes des 343 45, 46
    Self-determination and 8, 42, 43, 183
    Weimar reform movement 8, 43
Adenauer, Konrad 11
Aktionsrat zur Befreiung der Frauen (Action
      Council for the Liberation of
      Women) 27, 33–35, 36, 38, 40,
      44, 49, 54

Kinderläden 35, 38, 44
    see also Sander, Helke

Bebel, August 4–5, 38, 149
Berlin Wall
    Fall of 139, 144, 162
Berliner Initiative gegen Gewalt an Frauen (BIG
    e.V. or Berlin Initiative against
    Violence towards Women) 168,
    184–187, 190, 196
Betts, Paul 114, 125, 127, 131, 197
Bovenschen, Silvia 31, 36, 39, 49
Brandt, Willy 31, 38
Brot und Rosen (Bread and Roses) 40, 44, 46; *see
    also* Sander, Helke
Buhmann, Inga 32
Bund Deutscher Frauenvereine (Federation
    of German Women's
    Organisations) 5, 7, 8–9, 43
Bund für Mutterschutz (League for the
    Protection of Mothers) 7, 8, 43

Child Abuse 59, 65, 96, 148, 192
Chiswick Women's Aid 70, 71, 73, 74, 75, 79, 80,
    81, 83, 156, 186
    as model for West Berlin shelter 70, 71, 80,
      81, 99
    see also Pizzey, Erin; *Scream Quietly or the
      Neighbours Will Hear*
Church
    Catholic 4, 48, 50, 55, 57, 58, 79, 160, 174
      Caritas 151, 153, 174
    Protestant 4, 57, 58, 79
      and opposition movement in the GDR
        137, 138, 143, 146
Cold War 114, 163
    and division among feminists 23, 159, 166,
      168
    End of 139, 144
      as gendered process 166
    Family and gender in 11, 12, 117
    Role in the historiography 139, 144, 146
Communist Bloc

Disillusionment with 139
Impact of collapse on women 144

de Beauvoir, Simone 45, 71, 72
Delap, Lucy 22–23
Demokratischer Frauenbund Deutschlands
        (DFD or Democratic Women's
        League of Germany) 143, 157,
        180
Dissident Movement (GDR) 131, 139, 144, 150
    Link with activism against gender-based
        violence 140, 152, 159
    Link with feminism 143, 150, 153
Divorce 26, 62, 63, 67, 68, 88, 96, 114, 115, 116,
        118, 119, 120, 127, 128, 129, 130,
        135, 136, 172, 192, 194
    as response to domestic violence 61–62, 198
    Cases (GDR) 121–126, 194
    Fault-based system 61, 63, 65
    Law reform (FRG) 63, 64, 65
    Law reform (GDR) 120, 121, 126, 131, 135
    Rates (GDR) 111, 114, 120, 124, 127, 128,
        136, 138
Domestic Violence
    and class 58, 60, 62, 73, 81, 88, 98
    and constructing socialism 114, 115, 119,
        120, 131, 135, 194
        Prioritisation of men/masculinity 26, 114,
            118, 122, 123, 130, 131, 135
    and drug/alcohol addiction 64, 65, 66,
        96, 193
    and protection of children 63–64, 185
    as bourgeois/capitalist 110, 138, 194
    as issue of women's equality 52, 66, 67, 83, 86,
        156, 199
    as taboo 2, 25, 58, 59, 66, 111, 155, 156
    Critical discussion of (GDR) 111, 114, 131,
        133, 134, 138, 139, 198
    History of before 1945 60–62
    Official East German discussion of 110–111,
        114, 136, 151, 194
    Official recognition of (GDR) 111, 112, 119,
        136
    Perpetration and alcohol 60, 77, 126,
        127–128, 129
    Research into 98, 111, 151, 156
    Statistics (GDR) 111–112, 126, 151, 156
    Stumbling blocks to leaving 61, 64, 66, 67, 68,
        79, 88, 95, 126, 129, 193
    Women's experiences of 21, 64–66, 68, 88, 89,
        101–102, 114, 115, 118, 121–122,
        124, 126–127, 128, 129, 134–135,
        192, 193
Domestic Violence Activism *see also* Women's
        Shelters
    and legal reform 26, 153, 184, 185, 186, 187,
        188, 191, 196

Feminist
    and reassertion of patriarchal norms 20,
        85, 87, 109, 191, 196, 197, 199
    Deradicalisation of 60, 80–85, 87, 107,
        158, 195, 197
    Emergence of 29, 51–53, 195
    Legitimisation of 59, 70, 74, 75, 81, 82,
        87, 154
    Link with women's movement 159
    Principles and politics of 55, 68
    Transformation of 19, 20, 24, 25, 29, 55,
        59, 60, 80, 95–100, 101–107, 108,
        109, 154, 168, 196
    Use of racialised narratives 101, 102, 103,
        109, 200
    in reunified Germany 140, 154, 158, 167, 168,
        169, 184, 190, 195, 196, 198
        Collaboration between East and West
            German feminists 168, 184, 185,
            189, 196
        Impact of East German feminism in 22,
            24, 136, 153, 161, 168, 186, 188,
            196, 198, 199
    in the GDR 26, 151, 153
        Connections with West German activism
            154, 155
        Transformation of 153
    Institutionalisation of 29, 76, 100, 108, 109,
        154, 160, 173, 191, 197
    Political support for 55, 59, 86, 155,
        157, 167, 168, 170, 175, 189,
        194, 195, 196
    Popular support for 59, 86, 156, 196

Engels, Friedrich 5
European Union (EU)
    Action on violence against women 188
    Statistics on violence against women 3

Family
    and Adenauer government policies 11, 34,
        119
    and constructing socialism 26, 115, 116, 118,
        123, 124, 131
    and feminism 6, 7, 29
    and gender roles (GDR) 13, 116, 117, 118,
        119
    and patriarchal authority 4, 11, 28, 34, 53,
        57, 58, 59
    and post-war reconstruction 11, 193, 194
    in socialist thought 5
    in the Civil Code 4
    Maintenance of 84, 118, 124, 125, 126, 128,
        135, 194
    Significance under socialism 117–118, 121,
        124
    Socialist ideals of 122

Family Law Code (GDR) 13
  and divorce 121, 124
  and domestic violence 121, 124
  and liberalisation 121
  and SED visions of the family 121
Federal Republic of Germany (FRG)
  as 'success story' 15, 60, 86
  Federal Ministry for Youth, Family and
            Health 17, 77, 78, 80, 81, 82, 83,
            84, 91; *see also* Focke, Katharina
  Liberalisation 20, 29, 38, 59, 85, 86, 194, 195
  Migration to 65, 101, 104, 105
  Social change 196
    Role of women in 1, 19, 195, 196
  Value change 20, 59, 86, 194, 195
    as gendered 195
Feminism
  and liberalisation of Germany 15, 20, 24
  Anxieties about 17, 25, 28, 29, 47, 50, 54,
            56–58, 59, 78, 156, 174
  as identity in the GDR 23, 143
  Bourgeois 5–6, 7; *see also Bund für
            Mutterschutz* (League for
            the Protection of Mothers);
            Bund Deutscher Frauenvereine
            (Federation of German Women's
            Organisations)
  Co-optation of 16–17, 18, 60, 86, 90, 194,
            195, 199, 201
  Critiques of 16, 22, 23, 24, 145, 159
  Definition of 22, 159
  Deradicalisation of 16, 17, 20, 55, 80, 90, 109,
            169, 195
  Emergence of (FRG) 13, 36, 39–40
  Histories of 14, 21, 139, 200
  in the GDR 20, 21, 22, 23, 26, 140, 142, 144,
            145, 148, 149, 150, 152, 159, 160,
            161, 177, 183, 196
    as language and platform 140, 147, 149
  Institutionalisation of 16, 19, 90, 158, 169,
            170
  Meaning of (FRG) 49
  Meaning of across divided Germany 23, 179,
            183, 199
  Meaning of across Iron Curtain 158
  Narratives of 15–16, 200
  Periodisations of 23–24, 50, 51, 169, 170
  Postcolonial 15, 24
  Socialist 4–6
  Successes of 2, 3, 14, 16, 17, 20, 26, 47, 48, 51,
            67, 80, 83, 86, 87, 105, 140, 154,
            158, 160, 161, 168, 184, 189, 190,
            196, 197, 198, 200
  Tensions between East and West German 23,
            160, 178, 180, 181, 182, 183, 199
  Transformation of 16, 141, 188, 197, 199,
            200, 201

Translation across the Berlin Wall 22, 23, 24,
            140, 144, 146, 149, 150, 153, 159,
            161, 199
Feminist
  Confrontational protest 39, 46, 50, 54, 169
  Provokation of the media 29, 39, 45
  Solidarity
    Limitations of 23, 90, 95, 97, 108
Ferree, Myra Marx 22, 24, 39, 74, 159, 160, 169,
            170
First Conference of German and Foreign
            Women 66, 106
First World War 8
  Women during 7
Focke, Katharina 78, 79, 80, 84, 85
Frauen für den Frieden (Women for Peace) 143,
            146
Frauenteestube (Women's Tea Parlour) 146–151,
            152, 153, 161, 186, 198
  Survey on rape 147–149, 151
Friedan, Betty 34, 142

Gender Roles
  and post-war reconstruction 11, 34, 190,
            193, 194
  in the FRG 11, 13, 28, 53, 145, 191
  in the GDR 13, 123, 145
  Sexual-moral order 4, 6, 11, 28, 53, 193
German Democratic Republic (GDR)
  and the history of feminism in Germany 24
  Citizenship 117, 123, 125, 135
  Collapse of 139, 140
    Mass protest 153
  Comparison to Federal Republic 20–21
    Asymmetries and entanglements 20, 21
  Gender equality in 12, 23, 111, 119, 120, 121,
            150, 194
  Historiography 112–114, 135
  Legal system 115, 124
    Family matters 118
  Liberalisation 26, 114, 120, 121, 131,
            135, 194
  Material conditions 114, 139
    Housing shortage 124, 129, 131, 135, 136
  Political transition 162–163
    Women's activism during 20, 163, 166,
            176, 177, 179, 183
  Private sphere within 112, 113, 114
  Social problems in 151, 152
  Socialist ideal versus reality 132, 136
  Womanhood in 137, 141, 146, 159, 162, 191
German Reunification 112, 139, 144, 163, 164,
            178, 179
  and women's rights 158, 177, 179, 197
  as gendered process 190
  Feminist activism during 24, 140, 167,
            175, 178

Impact on women 26, 87, 160, 166, 167, 168, 175–176, 189
in historiography of women and gender in Germany 166–168
Women as losers of 166, 168, 189, 190, 196
Gewaltschutzgesetz (Protection from Violence Act) 1, 26, 168, 185, 187–188, 190–191, 196
Global History
and critiques of universalised categories 20
Methods 21

Haffner, Sarah 78, 79, 82
Hemmings, Clare 15, 200
Honecker, Erich 13, 113, 114, 120, 131, 132, 134, 139, 145, 197

International Tribunal on Crimes Against Women 52, 71–72, 73, 74, 75; *see also Violence against Women in Marriage, Psychiatry, Gynaecology, Rape, Film, Work and What Women Can Do about It*

Karcher, Katharina 38, 50, 73
Kohl, Helmut 163, 168, 174

Lenz, Ilse 24, 44, 101, 169, 170, 188

Marx, Karl 5
McLellan, Josie 21, 127
Media
and deradicalisation of feminism 19, 82–84, 87, 108, 195, 199
Feminist counter-media 18, 19, 40, 44
Courage 18, 40, 95, 99, 100
EMMA 18, 40, 55, 78, 88, 174
in the GDR
Alltagsfilme 131–132, 139
Portrayals of women and critique of state socialism 132
Representation of violence against women 132
and critique of state socialism 132, 133
Until Death Do Us Part 132–134, 198
Discussions of domestic violence 25, 119, 130–131
Liberalisation of 131
Women's Literature 141–142, 143, 147
and feminism 142
as expression of women's subjectivity 141
Mass media
and value change 18–19, 195
Objectification of women within 33, 50, 54, 55

Feminist critique of 72
Portrayals of battered women 54, 60, 83, 84, 87, 95, 195, 199
Portrayals of women activists 29, 32–33, 39, 54, 59
Television
Panorama-Scandal 47–48, 54, 55
Screaming is Useless Brutality in Marriage 78, 80, 81
Mass media publications
Berliner Zeitung 110
Bild 18, 53, 76
Der Spiegel 18, 33, 47, 50, 54, 72, 83, 84, 181
Neues Deutschland 119, 133
Stern 18, 46, 47, 50, 54, 55, 76, 77
Stern-Trial 55
We Had Abortions 46, 47, 48, 54, 55
Support for domestic violence activism 17, 18, 19, 25, 53, 75, 76–77, 78–80, 87, 155, 172, 195, 196
Support for Paragraph 218 campaign 45–48, 54, 175
Transformation after 1945 18
Men
and domestic violence activism 84, 151, 160, 186
and German reunification 190
and women's rights activism 138, 151, 153
as perpetrators of violence 17, 52, 73, 88, 133, 184, 185
as victims of feminism 58
as victims of gender-based violence 150, 151, 160
Racialised depictions as violent 17, 101, 103, 199, 200–201
Remasculinisation after 1945 11, 63
Merkel, Ina 154, 163; *see also Unabhängiger Frauenverband* (UFV or Independent Women's Association)
Moeller, Robert 11, 194, 196
Motherhood
and feminism 13, 14, 44, 54
as feminist catalyst 33–34
Feminism and natural motherhood 6, 8
in the GDR 141

National Socialism (Nazism) 9, 11
Domestic violence under 62
Feminism and 9
Historiography 10
Reproductive rights under 42
Women and 9–10, 62
Women's sexuality 123
Neue Justiz 115, 116, 118
New Left 27, 31, 98

Pizzey, Erin 70, 81, 83, 84
Police
  Response to Paragraph 218 campaign (FRG)
      47
  Responses to domestic violence 61, 199
  Responses to domestic violence (FRG) 67, 79,
      88, 89, 193
  Responses to domestic violence (GDR) 114,
      116, 126, 127, 128, 129, 131, 136,
      192, 193
  Responses to domestic violence (Reunified
      Germany) 184, 185, 187
  Responses to feminism 50, 72
Political Parties
  Alternative for Germany (AfD) 190, 196
  Christian Democratic Union (CDU) 11, 29,
      30, 46, 48, 50, 55, 104, 174, 180,
      181, 182
  Christian Social Union (CSU) 48
  Communist Party of Germany (KPD) 8, 9,
      13, 30
  Free Democratic Party (FDP) 30, 38, 46, 77,
      85, 172, 174, 181
  Grand Coalition (1966) 30, 31, 38
  Green Party 175, 177, 180, 181, 187
  Party of Democratic Socialism (PDS) 157,
      162, 182
  Social Democratic Party (SPD) 5, 7, 8, 25,
      30, 31, 38, 46, 55, 78, 96, 99, 104,
      172, 174, 175, 180, 181, 186,
      187, 190; *see also Sozialistischer
      Deutscher Studentenbund*
      (German Socialist Student
      Association, SDS)
  Socialist Unity Party (SED)
    and political transition 162, 163
    Approach to domestic violence 114, 138
    Attempts to shape the family 116, 117,
        124, 125
    Attitudes towards feminism 23
    Authority of 112, 114
    Collapse of 139, 153, 160, 162
    Constructing socialism 115, 116, 124
    Delegitimisation of 136, 139, 140, 143,
        156, 157, 167, 189, 191, 197
    Development under Honecker 113, 120,
        131
    Disillusionment with 139, 152
    Failure to protect women 119, 128, 135,
        138, 147, 149, 152, 156, 160, 189
    Family policy 117, 120
    Gender norms and 12, 13, 119
    Gender policies 13, 145, 197
    Legitimisation of socialist rule 12, 118,
        139
    Promise of equality 25, 132, 136, 145, 146
    Real-existing socialism 113, 132, 153

Women and 12, 117, 143
Postcolonialism 20, 145
Power
  and womanhood 87, 138
  Imbalances and hierarchies 52, 138, 177, 201
  Male 32, 50, 76, 101, 102, 103, 147
  of women 36
  Relationships 137
    Among feminists 106
  Structures 28, 54, 57, 72, 86, 104, 106, 109

Rape 76, 89, 102, 103, 129, 132, 147, 148, 149,
      160, 167, 200
  and German occupation 10–11, 12, 63
  Feminist understanding of 76
  in marriage 44, 65, 76, 77, 102, 129, 149, 168,
      186, 187
  Law (FRG) 186
  Law (GDR) 147, 149–150, 151
  Statistics (GDR) 148, 151, 156
Reproductive Rights 13, 17, 24, 26, 29, 40–41,
      43, 44, 48, 51, 54, 71, 72, 167,
      169, 170, 175, 180, 183, 188, 190,
      191, 194, 197, 199, 200
  Comparison to domestic violence
      protections 168–169, 188, 191, 197, 200
  see also Abortion
Responses to domestic violence
  by social services (FRG) 64, 77, 78, 192, 193
  by social services (GDR) 193
  by social services (reunified Germany) 185
  in the legal system (FRG) 67, 88, 119
  in the legal system (GDR) 25, 26, 114, 115,
      118–119, 120, 121–124, 125–
      126, 127, 128, 129–130, 131, 135,
      192, 194, 198
    communal jurisprudence 115–116, 198
  in the legal system (reunified Germany) 184,
      185
  Medical (FRG) 67, 96
  Medical (GDR) 126, 127, 192
Rüger, Sigrid 28, 36

Sander, Helke 27–28, 33, 34–35, 36, 40, 44, 142
Schwarzer, Alice 45–46, 47, 48, 49, 55, 78, 88,
      89, 158, 200; *see also EMMA*;
      We Had Abortions; *Stern*-Trial;
      Panorama-Scandal
Scream Quietly or the Neighbours Will Hear
      70, 83, 84; *see also* Pizzey, Erin;
      Chiswick Women's Aid
Second World War
  Women during 10
Sexual Harassment 132, 148, 149
Sexual Revolution 194
  in the FRG 32
  in the GDR 120

Sexuality
Women's 123–124
Stasi (East German secret police) 134, 135, 191
Student Movement 1, 24, 27, 29, 30–32, 34, 35,
36, 38–39, 49, 170, 198
Außerparlamentarische Opposition (APO
or Extra-Parliamentary
Opposition) 31, 36, 150
Sozialistischer Deutscher Studentenbund (SDS
or German Socialist Student
Association) 30–32, 33, 35–36,
38, 150
Treatment of women within 24, 27–28,
31–32, 33, 34, 35–36
Treatment of women within 13, 31–32
Women's activism within 36–38; *see also*
Aktionsrat zur Befreiung der
Frauen (Action Council for
the Liberation of Women);
Weiberräte

Ulbricht, Walter 13, 113
Unabhängiger Frauenverband (UFV or
Independent Women's
Association) 153, 154, 162–166,
176–183
United Nations
Decade for Women 70, 136, 188
Declaration on the Elimination of Violence
against Women 188
International Women's Year 70, 71, 72

Victimhood
Women's 70, 89, 175, 199
as strategy for support 17, 18, 25, 60, 68,
70, 83, 87, 169, 172, 195
Violence against Women
and domestic violence 14
and feminism (FRG) 13, 54
and the women's movement 14
as issue of women's equality 138, 148
as shared experience 72, 74, 75, 88–89, 91, 97,
103, 147
Feminist understanding of 72, 73, 74, 75,
89, 99
in the GDR
Activist approaches to 139, 140, 147, 151,
154, 159, 198
Feminist understandings of 139, 141, 148,
149, 159
Objectification as form of 55, 72
Rates and statistics of 2–3
Sexual violence 59, 108, 128, 147, 148, 160
Violence against Women in Marriage, Psychiatry,
Gynaecology, Rape, Film, Work
and What Women Can Do about
It 72, 73, 74
von Hodenberg, Christina 19, 32, 87

Walpurgis Night 73
Weiberräte 36–38, 44, 49, 54
West Berlin
as a hub of feminist activism 21, 40, 46, 189
Senate 17, 25, 52, 57, 59, 60, 66, 77, 78, 80, 82,
91, 104, 105, 170, 173
Office for Family, Youth and Sport
56, 77, 80, 82, 83, 91, 99, 170,
171, 172
Women's Centre 40, 50, 51, 59, 66, 71, 72, 73
Wirtschaftswunder (Economic Miracle), 18, 29,
105
Wolf, Christa 141, 142
Women
and Honecker government policies 13
as vulnerable 2, 18, 34, 52, 64, 86, 98, 135,
169, 172, 175, 191, 199
Battered women 19, 51, 53, 58, 88, 89, 90, 94,
95, 97, 98, 100, 109
in reunified Germany 161, 168, 189, 196
Migrant 19, 24, 71, 94, 100, 101, 102, 104,
106, 107, 108, 185, 186
Activism 101, 106, 108, 109, 199
Appropriation of 101, 102, 106, 109, 199
Difficulties in leaving abuse 65–66,
101–102, 103, 105, 107
Turkish guest-workers 101
Objectification of in Student Movement 13,
32
Political participation of 4, 6, 7
in the GDR 12, 144
Post-war reconstruction efforts and 10
Working-class 19, 24, 97
Women-helping-women 60, 74, 171
as therapeutic practice 74, 89
Women's Emancipation 7, 29, 38, 39, 49, 50,
54, 55, 74, 78, 84, 85, 94, 97,
144, 145
Women's Empowerment 60, 68, 74, 85, 87, 95, 99
and women's shelters 89, 92, 95, 100, 154, 199
in the media 75, 84
Women's Movement
Activism of women of colour 101, 109,
195, 199
Global movement against domestic violence
58, 66, 70, 71, 75, 86, 99
Imperial and Wilhelmine 5, 6, 39; *see*
also Feminism (Bourgeois);
Feminism (Socialist)
in the FRG 21, 36
Emergence of 39–40
see also New Women's Movement
in the GDR 13, 21, 26, 134, 137–139, 140,
142, 143–146, 152, 153, 159,
195, 198
New Women's Movement 1, 24, 38, 40, 51, 54,
73, 75, 170
Critique of racialised narratives 106

Emergence of 13, 24, 28, 29, 38, 120
Principles of 50, 87, 172
   Autonomy 49, 81, 171, 172, 183
   Separatism 49, 153, 183, 186
   Racial and class privileges within 90, 97,
     108, 109, 199
   Socialist origins of 28, 36–38
Tomatenwurf 27–28, 33, 35–36, 54, 201; *see
    also* Sander, Helke
Transnational 41, 54, 142, 158
Weimar Republic 8
Women's shelter movement 17, 19, 29, 55, 73,
   170, 171
Women's Rights
and gender norms 200
and post-communism 197
and post-war reconstruction 11, 12
as human rights 141, 188
Autonomy 18, 43, 44, 74, 138, 168, 191, 197,
   200
Civil rights 8, 23
Constitutional equality with men (FRG) 11,
   53, 102, 194
Constitutional equality with men (GDR)
   12, 194
Constitutional equality with men
   (Weimar) 8
Domestic violence as issue of 52, 58, 140,
   191, 194
Feminist understandings of 71
in historiography of modern Germany 3–14,
   15, 86
in reunified Germany 169, 189, 191
in the GDR 136, 145, 163
Political support for 16, 85
Popular support for 47, 195
Self-determination 23, 44, 74, 169, 191, 200
   in pregnancy 43, 177, 180, 183
   Sexual 7, 150
Suffrage 5, 7, 23
Women's self-help 60, 74, 87
as therapeutic practice 75, 81, 92, 94, 95, 96,
   97, 100, 107, 109, 154
in the media 75, 84
Political support for 84, 85
Women's Shelters
and normative power structures 109, 199,
   200, 201
and racialised power structures 104–105,
   109, 199
as alternative to social services 51, 52, 81, 91,
   95, 100, 171

Class differences within 19, 97, 100, 109
Critique of West German migration law
   103–104, 105
in reunified Germany 140, 154, 160, 161,
   167, 173
   Funding 140, 156, 157, 160
in the GDR 138
   Caritas House 151–152, 153, 198
   Erstes autonomes Frauenhaus (First
     Autonomous Women's Shelter),
     Leipzig 154–155, 156, 157,
     167, 192
   Hestia Women's Shelter, Berlin 154, 155,
     156, 157, 167
in West Berlin
   as pilot project 17, 25, 59, 77, 80, 86, 91,
     92, 170, 172, 173
   as political project 52, 89, 90, 91–92,
     94–96, 99, 102
   as women-only space 91
   Children at 57, 96
   Complaints about 56–58
   East German discussions of 110, 154
   Feminist campaign to open 17, 25, 66–76,
     77–80, 81–82, 86, 91–92, 198
     Second shelter 170, 172, 173
   Frauenhaus-Frauen helfen Frauen 91, 99
   Funding 17, 25, 55, 59, 76, 80, 81, 86, 87,
     91, 92, 100, 104, 106, 107, 108,
     149, 199
   Use of Federal Social Welfare Act
     170–173
     Feminist campaign against 171–172
   Kicked, Beaten, Humiliated 66, 67, 68, 70,
     73, 74, 75
   Projekt Frauenhaus (Project Women's
     Shelter) 51, 53, 55, 59, 70
Interactions and life within 90, 92, 93–98
Interkulturelle Initiative 107
Overcrowding within 93, 157, 170, 173
Political support for 17, 55, 157, 172, 174,
   191, 198, 199
Professionalisation of 100, 107, 109, 173
Residents of 20, 25, 56, 64, 65, 70, 75, 81, 82,
   88, 90, 91, 92, 93, 94, 95, 96, 97,
   98, 99, 100, 101, 104, 107, 109,
   151, 171, 172, 173, 192, 199
Statistics 2, 92–93, 94, 95, 96, 101
Transformation of 20, 25, 95–100, 186

Zetkin, Clara 5, 6, 38